D1527199

McGraw-Hill
Dictionary of
Wall Street
Acronyms, Initials,
and Abbreviations

Other McGraw-Hill Books by Jerry M. Rosenberg

McGraw-Hill Dictionary of Business Acronyms, Initials, and Abbreviations

McGraw-Hill Dictionary of Information Technology and Computer Acronyms, Initials, and Abbreviations

McGraw-Hill Dictionary of Wall Street Acronyms, Initials, and Abbreviations

Jerry M. Rosenberg, Ph.D.

Professor
Graduate School of Management
Department of Business Administration
Faculty of Arts and Sciences
Rutgers University

McGraw-Hill, Inc.

New York St. Louis San Francisco Auckland Bogotá
Caracas Lisbon London Madrid Mexico Milan
Montreal New Delhi Paris San Juan São Paulo
Singapore Sydney Tokyo Toronto

Library of Congress Cataloging-in-Publication Data

Rosenberg, Jerry Martin.
    McGraw-Hill dictionary of Wall Street acronyms, initials, and
    abbreviations / Jerry M. Rosenberg.
          p.   cm.
      ISBN 0-07-053934-0 (cloth) :   —ISBN 0-07-053736-4 (paper) :
      1. Investments—Acronyms. 2. Securities—Acronyms. 3. Stock
    -exchange—Acronyms. I. Title. II. Title: Dictionary of Wall
    Street acronyms, initials, and abbreviations.
    HG4513.R68   1991   91-24841
    332.6′32′03—dc20   CIP

1 2 3 4 5 6 7 8 9 0   DOC/DOC   9 7 6 5 4 3 2 1

ISBN   0-07-053934-0   {HC}
ISBN   0-07-053736-4   {PBK}

*The sponsoring editor for this book was Betsy Brown, the
editing supervisor was Alfred Bernardi, and the production
supervisor was Suzanne W. Babeuf. It was set in Century
Schoolbook by McGraw-Hill's Professional Book Group
composition unit.*

Printed and bound by R. R. Donnelley & Sons Company.

*This dictionary
is affectionately dedicated
to Elizabeth.
She warms my heart and delights the soul.*

Preface

Fifteen years after I had published the first in a series of five business-oriented dictionaries, I began to see the need for yet another type of dictionary. This time, the proposed book would be a lexicon containing business acronyms, initials, and abbreviations. What had I noticed in my day-to-day life as a business consultant and educator to convince me of the compelling need for such a book?

First of all, everyone knows that in today's business world we are all confronted daily with a variety of common (and not so common) abbreviated terms. Whether these terms are communicated in written or verbal form, confusion can arise, since most of them frequently convey several different meanings. For example, IBM is a three-letter word that is quickly identified throughout the world as initials for International Business Machines. However, these same three letters also stand for the Institute for Burn Medicine, Industrias Biologicas Mexicana (Mexican Biological Industries), intercontinental ballistic missile, and the International Brotherhood of Magicians. And the two-letter words, IB or IM, have a list of several dozen possible spelled-out forms.

An anecdote taken from my own professional life might serve to further highlight the potential trouble that can come about when one of these terms is misinterpreted. As a young college professor, I once had occasion to take a plane trip to Boston in order to attend a professional conference. Seated next to me on the plane was a relentless name-dropper who, during the course of his career as a reporter, claimed to have interviewed JFK (President John F. Kennedy), LBJ (President Lyndon B. Johnson), and so on and so forth! After he had exhausted this line of conversation, the reporter turned to me and asked if I did consulting work. Seeing that my opportunity to speak (and to shine) had at last arrived, I answered by saying that yes, indeed, I did consulting in Boston for ADL. The reporter was quite impressed to hear that I worked for Arthur D. Little, a first-rate consulting firm. His enthusiasm waned, however, when I corrected his error and informed him that I was a consultant to the Anti-Defamation League!

The story is amusing, but it nicely summarizes the reason I have written this book. Clarity and precision are necessary components of business communications. They will be improved only when we are aware of the many different meanings that have been applied to each acronym, initial, abbreviation, or symbol by the general business community at large. Thus, I have tried to include in this volume as many of the commonly used designations from Wall Street and the stock market and investment world as is possible. When this book is used in conjunction with a related dictionary, the user should be amply equipped to comprehend clearly and communicate effectively.

Lastly, there are a few decisions made in the preparation of this book that the reader should be aware of as he or she begins to use it:

1. Conventional symbols have been used without specific identification, for instance: - (hyphen); / (diagonal); & (ampersand); = (equal sign); * (asterisk).

2. The use of capital, lowercase, or a combination of both capital and lowercase letters for the spelled-out versions of abbreviations or acronyms has never been universally agreed upon. In most cases in this book, I have used the preferred or most commonly used form. When an abbreviation involves the use of proper names, then capital letters are the correct choice. Otherwise, the form of capitalization that is adopted is more a matter of style than of correctness.

3. Special attention has been given to the most recent newspaper and trade symbols used for publicly held corporations. The forms used in this book are those used by the New York Stock Exchange (NYSE), the American Stock Exchange (ASE), entries of NYSE and ASE as used by newspapers, and trading symbols of the National Association of Security Dealers—National Market System (NASNAM).

Acknowledgments

My library contains hundreds of sources of information that were used to prepare my five earlier dictionaries. These volumes have also been put to use in creating this book. In addition, both American and foreign agencies have been helpful in providing relevant information. I also received a good deal of assistance from trade associations (who, along with government departments, appear to be in the habit of creating new terms on a daily basis).

To the best of my knowledge, I have not quoted from any other copyrighted source. However, I have acquired much indirect assistance from the authors of numerous books, journal articles, and reference materials. Any attempt to list them here would be impossible.

Betsy Brown and Bill Sabin, my editors at McGraw-Hill, have been enlightened professional supporters of this dictionary. My wife, Ellen, my daughters, Elizabeth and Lauren, and my son-in-law, Robert, continue to be my inspiration. Time away from them, whether it is spent researching an article or struggling with a complex set of acronyms, initials, and abbreviations, is more than compensated for by their affection.

Finally, I acknowledge my reader—the ultimate judge. I continue to seek your critical comments and urge you to bring any errors or suggestions to my attention.

Jerry M. Rosenberg

About the Author

JERRY M. ROSENBERG, Ph.D., is professor at the Graduate School of Management and Department of Business Administration at Rutgers University. He is the author of the *McGraw-Hill Dictionary of Business Acronyms, Initials, and Abbreviations* and the *McGraw-Hill Dictionary of Information Technology and Computer Acronyms, Initials, and Abbreviations*—both just published by McGraw-Hill. Dr. Rosenberg's previous reference works include the *Dictionary of Business and Management*, the *Dictionary of Banking and Financial Services*, the *Dictionary of Computers and Information Processing*, and the *Dictionary of Artificial Intelligence and Robotics*. In addition, Dr. Rosenberg serves as a consultant to the *Oxford English Dictionary* and the *Random House Dictionary*. He is acclaimed "America's foremost business and technical lexicographer."

McGraw-Hill
Dictionary of
Wall Street
Acronyms, Initials,
and Abbreviations

a: accepte (accepted) (French)
account
action (share) (French)
argent
assented
audit
auditor

A: America
American
American Medical Buildings Inc. (ASE)
American Oil Company
Anchor Line
Class "A" or Series "A" (securities)
Total Average dollar inventory

A-1: First Class
First Rate
Highest class rating

Aa: High (Moody's bond rating)

A&A: Arcade and Attica (railroad)

AA: Active Account
Active Assets
Activity Account
After Arrival
Aluminum Company of America (NYSE)
Always Afloat
American Airlines
Ann Arbor (railroad)
Ansett Airways
Arithmetic Average
Assets Accounting
Audit Agency
High (Standard & Poor's bond rating)

Aaa: Best (Moody's bond rating)

AAA: American S&L Association of Florida (NYSE)
Standard & Poor's highest quality bond rating

AAC: Anacomp Inc. (NYSE)
Average Annual Cost

AACA: American Association of Certified Appraisers

AACT: American Association of Commodity Traders

AAD: Appropriation Account Data
At A Discount

AAHA: Awaiting Action of Higher Authority

AAHS: Alco Health Services Corp. (NAS NMS)

AAICA: Albany International Corp. (NAS NMS)

AAII: American Association of Individual Investors

AAL: Alexander & Alexander Services Inc. (NYSE)
American Airlines

AAlska: Arctic Alaska Fisheries Corp. (newspaper)

AAME: Atlantic American Corp. (NAS NMS)

AAPL: Apple Computer Inc. (NAS NMS)

AAR: AAR Corp. (newspaper)
Against All Risks

AARC: Ann Arbor Railroad Company

AARR: Ann Arbor Railroad

AASE: Australian Associated Stock Exchanges

AATI: Analysis & Technology Inc. (NAS NMS)

AAV: Assessed Annual Value

Ab: Aktiebolag (joint stock company) (Finland)

AB: ABI American Businessphones Inc. (ASE)

1

Adjustment Bond

Assembly Bill

Keystone Commuter (airline)

A/B: Aktiebolaget (joint stock company) (Swedish)

ABA: American Bankers Association

American Bankers Association Number

American Bar Association

Annual Budget Authorization

ABB: Akron & Barberton Belt (railroad)

ABBB: Association of Better Business Bureaus

ABBK: Abington Bancorp Inc. (Massachusetts) (NAS NMS)

AB&C: Atlanta, Birmingham and Coast (railroad)

ABC: American Broadcasting Company

Audit Bureau of Circulation

ABCV: Affiliated Banc Corp. (Massachusetts) (NAS NMS)

ABD: ABIOMED Inc. (ASE)

ABEX: American Brake Shoe Company

ABF: Airborne Freight Corp. (NYSE)

ABG: American Ship Building Co., The (NYSE)

ABGA: Allied Bankshares Inc. (Georgia) (NAS NMS)

ABI: ABI American Businessphones Inc. (newspaper)

AmBrit Inc. (ASE)

ABIG: American Bankers Insurance Group Inc. (NAS NMS)

Abimd: ABIOMED Inc. (newspaper)

ABIO: Applied Biosystems Inc. (NAS NMS)

Abitibi: Abitibi-Price Inc. (newspaper)

ABK: Alliance Bancorporation (ASE)

ABKR: Anchor Savings Bank FSB (New York) (NAS NMS)

ABktCT: American Bank of Connecticut (newspaper)

ABL: Alameda Belt Line (railroad)

American Biltrite Inc. (ASE)

ABldM: American Building Maintenance Industries (newspaper)

ABM: Advanced Bill of Materials

American Building Maintenance Industries (NYSE)

ABM G: ABM Gold Corp. (newspaper)

ABNCO: American Bank Note Company

ABNI: Available But Not Installed

ABP: Accounting Principles Board

American Business Products Inc. (NYSE)

ABQC: ABQ Corp. (NAS NMS)

ABrck: American Barrick Resources Corp. (newspaper)

ABRI: Abrams Industries Inc. (NAS NMS)

ABS: Albertson's Inc. (NYSE)

American Bureau of Shipping

Automated Bond System

ABSB: Alex. Brown Inc. (NAS NMS)

ABSI: ABS Industries Inc. (NAS NMS)

ABT: Abbott Laboratories (NYSE)

American Board of Trade

AbtLab: Abbott Laboratories (newspaper)

ABusPr: American Business Products Inc. (newspaper)

ABW: Advise By Wire

Armada Corp. (NYSE)

ABX: American Barrick Resources Corp. (NYSE)

ABY: Abitibi-Price Inc. (NYSE)

ABZ: Arkansas Best Corp. (NYSE)

a/c: account

AC: Account Current
Active Capital
Actual Cost
Air Canada (airline)
Algoma Central (railroad)
Alliance Capital Management
LP (NYSE)
Ante Christum (before Christ)
ACA: American Capital Management & Research Inc. (NYSE)
ACAD: Autodesk Inc. (NAS NMS)
AcapBd: American Capital Bond Fund Inc. (newspaper)
ACapCv: American Capital Convertible Securities Inc. (newspaper)
ACapIn: American Capital Income Trust (newspaper)
ACB: Advertising Checking Bureau
American Capital Bond Fund Inc. (NYSE)
Associated Credit Bureaus of America
Association of Customers' Brokers
ACB of A: Associated Credit Bureaus of America
ACBs: Associated Credit Bureaus
acc: accept
acceptance
accepted
account
accumulate
ACC: American Capital Corp. (ASE)
Annual Capital Charge
ACCA: Accelerated Capital Cost Allowance
Association of Certified and Corporate Accountants
ACCC: ACC Corp. (NAS NMS)
acce: acceptance
ACCM: Associated Communications Corp. (NAS NMS)

ACCOB: Adolp Coors Co. (NAS NMS)
accpt: accept
acceptance
ACCR: Annual Cost of Capital Recovery
Accrd Int: Accrued Interest
accred: accredited
acct: account
accountant
accounting
ACD: American Capital Income Trust (NYSE)
ACE: Acme Electric Corp. (NYSE)
Amex Commodities Exchange
Audit, Control and Evaluation
Automated Cost Estimates
One-Dollar Bill (slang)
ACEF: Association of Commodity Exchange Firms
ACentC: American Century Corp. (newspaper)
ACET: Aceto Corp. (NAS NMS)
ACF: American Car and Foundry Company
ACG: ACM Government Income Fund Inc. (NYSE)
Air Cargo Express (symbol)
ACGI: American Capacity Group Inc. (NAS NMS)
ACH: Automated Clearing House
AC&HBR: Algoma Central and Hudson Bay Railroad
ACHV: Archive Corp. (NAS NMS)
ACI: Actual Cost Incurred
Air Cargo Incorporated
Ashland Coal Inc. (NYSE)
ACIG: Academy Insurance Group Inc. (NAS NMS)
ACIP: Active Certificate Information Program
ACIX: American Carriers Inc. (NAS NMS)
ACK: Armstrong World Industries Inc. (NYSE)

ACL: Atlantic Coast Line (railroad)
Atlantic Container Line
(steamship)

ACLE: Accel International Corp.
(NAS NMS)

ACLV: Autoclave Engineers Inc.
(NAS NMS)

ACM: ACM Government Opportu-
nity Fund (newspaper)
Associative Communications
Multiplexer
Atlas Consolidated Mining &
Development Corp. (ASE)

ACME: Acme Steel Co. (NAS NMS)

AcmeC: Acme-Cleveland Corp.
(newspaper)

AcmeE: Acme Electric Corp. (newspaper)

AcmeU: Acme United Corp. (newspaper)

ACMIn: ACM Government Income
Fund Inc. (newspaper)

ACMR: American Capital Management & Research Inc.
(newspaper)

ACMS: CMS Enhancements Inc.
(NAS NMS)

ACMSc: ACM Government Securities
Fund Inc. (newspaper)

ACMSp: ACM Government Spectrum Fund (newspaper)

ACMT: ACMAT Corp. (NAS NMS)

ACOL: American Colloid Co. (NAS
NMS)

ACOM: Astrocom Corp. (NAS NMS)

ACP: American Real Estate Partners LP (NYSE)

A/CPay: Accounts Payable

ACPI: American Consumer Products Inc. (NAS NMS)

acpt: accept
acceptance

ACPT: Acceptance Insurance Holdings Inc. (NAS NMS)

Acq: Exchange Acquisition

acqt: acquit (paid in full) (French)

acquis: acquisition(s)

AC&R: American Cable and Radio
Corporation

ACR: Accelerated Cost Recovery
Angell Real Estate Company
Inc. (NYSE)

ACRA: Association of Company
Registration Agents

acrd: accrued

A/C Rec: Accounts Receivable

ACRL: American Cruise Line Inc.
(NYSE)

ACRS: Accelerated Capital Recov-
ery System
Accelerated Cost Recovery
System

AC&S: Atlantic City and Shore
(railroad)

ACS: American Capital Convertible
Securities Inc. (NYSE)
American Coal Shipping
(steamship)
American Crystal Sugar
Company

ACSN: Acuson Corp. (NAS NMS)

A/CS Pay: Accounts Payable

A/CS Rec: Accounts Receivable

ACT: American Century Corp.
(NYSE)
Analogical Circuit Technique

a cta: A Cuenta (On Account)
(Spanish)

ACTA: Action Auto Stores Inc.
(NAS NMS)

Action: Action Industries Inc.
(newspaper)

ACTM: Actmedia Inc. (NAS NMS)

actnt: accountant

Acton: Acton Corp. (newspaper)

ACTP: Advanced Computer Tech-
niques Corp. (NAS NMS)

Act Val: Actual Value

ACU: Acme United Corp. (ASE)

ACUs: Asian Currency Units

ACV: Actual Cash Value
Alberto-Culver Co. (NYSE)

ACWF: Actual Cost of Work Flow
ACWP: Actual Cost for Work Performed
ACX: Action Industries Inc. (ASE)
ACXM: Acxion Corp. (NAS NMS)
AC&Y: Akron, Canton & Youngstown (railroad)
ACY: American Cyanamid Co. (NYSE)
ACyan: American Cyanamid Co. (newspaper)
ad: advertisement
advertising
A&D: Accounting and Disbursing Assets and Depreciation
AD: Accrued Dividend
Aden Airways
Admission Directive (London Stock Exchange) (UK)
Advanced-Decline Line
After Date
Anno Domini (in the year of our Lord)
Ante Diem (before the day)
Assistant Director
Associate Director
Atlantic & Danville (railroad)
Availability Date
A-D: Advance-Decline ratio
ADAC: ADAC Laboratories (NAS NMS)
AdaEx: Adams Express Co., The (newspaper)
AdamMl: Adams-Millis Corp. (newspaper)
ADB: Adjusted Debit Balance
Adobe Resources Corp. (NYSE)
ADBE: Adobe Systems Inc. (NAS NMS)
ADC: American Dock Company
ADCC: Applied Data Communications Inc. (NAS NMS)
ADCO: Advantage Companies Inc. (NAS NMS)

American Dredging Company
ADCT: ADC Telecommunications Inc. (NAS NMS)
ADD: Ames Department Stores Inc. (NYSE)
ADDR: Addington Resources Inc. (NAS NMS)
ADI: Analog Devices Inc. (NYSE)
ADIA: Adia Services Inc. (NAS NMS)
ADIBOR: Abu Dhabi Interbank Offered Rate
ADIE: Autodie Corp. (NAS NMS)
adj: adjustment
ADL: Andal Corp. (ASE)
ADM: Archer-Daniels-Midland Co. (NYSE)
ADMG: Advanced Magnetics Inc. (NAS NMS)
admin: administration
administrative
administrator
admn: administration
admr: administrator
AdmRs: Adams Resources & Energy Inc. (newspaper)
ADMS: Advanced Marketing Services Inc. (NAS NMS)
AD&N: Ashley, Drew and Northern (railroad)
ADNOC: Abu Dhabi National Oil Company
ADO: Audiotronics Corp. (ASE)
Adobe: Adobe Resources Corp. (newspaper)
ADP: Allied Products Corp. (NYSE)
Automatic Data Processing
ADPC: Abu Dhabi Petroleum Company
Automatic Data Processing Center
ADPT: Adaptec Inc. (NAS NMS)
ADR: Asset Depreciation Range
American Depository Receipts
Asset Depreciation Range

Automatic Dividend Rein-
vestment

ADRS: Asset Depreciation Range
System

adv: advice
advise

ADV: Ad Valorem (in proportion to
the value)
Advest Group Inc., The
(NYSE)

Ad Val: Ad Valorem

ADVC: Advanced Circuits Inc.
(NAS NMS)

Adv Chgs: Advance Charges

Advest: Advest Group Inc., The
(newspaper)

Adv Frt: Advance Freight

ADVN: ADVANTA Corp. (NAS
NMS)

ADVO: Advo System Inc. (NAS
NMS)

Adv Pmt: Advance Payment

advt: advertise
advertisement
advertiser
advertising

ADX: Adams Express Co., The
(NYSE)

AE: Accommodation Endorsement
Account Executive
Accrued Expenditure
Adams Resources & Energy
Inc. (ASE)
Audit Entry

AEA: American Export Airlines

AEAGF: Agnico-Eagle Mines Ltd.
(NAS NMS)

A&EC: Atlantic and East Carolina
(railroad)

AEC: Atlantic & East Carolina
(railroad)

AEE: Aileen Inc. (NYSE)

AEFR: Aurora, Elgin & Fox River
(railroad)

AEGNY: AEGON N.V. (NAS
NMS)

AEIL: American Export-Isbrandtsen
Lines

AEL: Anglo Energy Inc. (ASE)
Audit Error List

AELN: AEL Industries Inc. (NAS
NMS)

AEIPw: American Electric Power
Company Inc. (newspa-
per)

AEN: Advance Evaluation Note
AMC Entertainment Inc.
(ASE)

AEP: Accrued Expenditure Paid
Aggregate Exercise Price
American Electric Power
Company Inc. (NYSE)

AEPC: Appalachian Electric Power
Company

AEPI: AEP Industries Inc. (NAS
NMS)

AEPP: Amend Existing Orders Per-
taining to

AERO: Aero Services International
Inc. (NAS NMS)

AET: Aetna Life & Casualty Co.
(NYSE)

AetnLf: Aetna Life & Casualty Co.
(newspaper)

AEU: Accrued Expenditure Unpaid

AEX: Air Express International
Corp. (ASE)

AExp: American Express Co. (newspaper)

A&F: Accounting and Finance
August and February (securities)

AFaml: American Family Corp.
(newspaper)

AFBD: Association of Futures Brokers and Dealers

AFC: American Fructose Corp.
(ASE)
Average Fixed Cost

AFCO: American First Corp. (NAS
NMS)

AFED: Atlantic Federal Savings Bank (Maryland) (NAS NMS)
affil: affiliated
AFFN: Australian Financial Futures Market
afft: affidavit
AFG: AFG Industries Inc. (NYSE) (newspaper)
AFGI: Ambassador Financial Group Inc. (NAS NMS)
AFH: Acceptance For Honor
AFIDA: Agricultural Foreign Investment Disclosure Act
AFIL: American Filtrona Corp. (NAS NMS)
afirm: affirmative
AFL: American Family Corp. (NYSE)
AFN: Alfin Inc. (ASE)
AFRA: Average Freight Rate Assessment
AFruc: American Fructose Corp. (newspaper)
AFS: New American Shoe Corp. (NYSE)
AFSL: AmFed Financial Corp. (NAS NMS)
AFT: Automatic Fund Transfers
AG: Advisory Group
Aggressive Growth
Aktiengesellschaft (joint stock company) (Austrian)
Allegheny International Inc. (NYSE)
Attorney General
silver (from argentum)
AGA: Airgas Inc. (NYSE)
agcy: agency
AGE: A.G. Edwards Inc. (NYSE)
AGF: American Government Income Fund (NYSE)
agg: aggregate
aggr: aggregate
AGH: Atlantis Group Inc. (ASE)
AGI: Adjusted Gross Income
Alpine Group Inc., The (ASE)

AGII: Argonaut Group Inc. (NAS NMS)
AGL: Angelica Corp. (NYSE)
AGM: Annual General Meeting
AGNC: Agency Rent-A-Car Inc. (NAS NMS)
AGnCp: American General Corp. (newspaper)
AGO: ABM Gold Corp. (ASE)
Adjutant General's Office
AGRE: American Greeting Corp. (NAS NMS)
AGS: AGS Computers Inc. (NYSE) (newspaper)
Alabama Great Southern (railroad)
AGSI: Advanced Genetic Sciences Inc. (NAS NMS)
agt: agent
agreement
agy: agency
A&H: Arm & Hammer (trademark)
AH: Allis-Chalmers Corp. (NYSE)
AHA: Alpha Industries Inc. (ASE)
AHB: Great Eastern Line (steamship)
AHC: Amerada Hess Corp. (NYSE)
AHE: American Health Properties Inc. (NYSE)
AHerit: American Heritage Life Investment Corp. (newspaper)
AHH: AmeriHealth Inc. (ASE)
AHI: American Healthcare Management Inc. (ASE)
AHL: American Heritage Life Investment Corp. (NYSE)
AHlthM: American Healthcare Management Inc. (newspaper)
AHltSv: American Health Services Corp. (newspaper)
AHM: H.F. Ahmanson & Co. (NYSE)

Ahmans: H.F. Ahmanson & Co. (newspaper)

AHO: American Hoist & Derrick Co. (NYSE)

AHoist: American Hoist & Derrick Co. (newspaper)

AHome: American Home Products Corp. (newspaper)

AHP: American Home Products Corp. (NYSE)

AHR: American Hotels & Realty Corp. (NYSE)

AHSC: American Home Shield Corp. (NAS NMS)

AHST: Associated Hosts Inc. (NAS NMS)

AHT: AIRCOA Hotel Partners LP (ASE)

AI: Accrued Interest
Accumulated Interest
Arrow Automotive Industries Inc. (ASE)

AIB: American Institute of Banking Association of Investment Brokers

AIBD: Association of International Bond Dealers

AIBDQ: Association of International Bond Dealers Quotation

AICPA: American Institute of Certified Public Accountants

AIF: AIFS Inc. (ASE)

AIFC: American Indemnity Financial Corp. (NAS NMS)

AIFS: AIFS Inc. (newspaper)

AIFTA: American Institute for Foreign Trade

AIG: American International Group Inc. (NYSE)

AII: Altex Industries Inc. (ASE)

AIIC: American Integrity Corp. (NAS NMS)

AIK: Assistance In Kind

AIL: AMCA International Ltd. (NYSE)

Aileen: Aileen Inc. (newspaper)

AILP: Automated Language Processing Systems Inc. (NAS NMS)

AIMA: As Interest May Appear

AIMB: American Institute of Mortgage Brokers

AIMG: Alliance Imaging Inc. (NAS NMS)

AIMT: AIM Telephones Inc. (NAS NMS)

AINC: American Income Life Insurance Co. (NAS NMS)

AIND: Arnold Industries Inc. (NAS NMS)

AIntGr: American International Group Inc. (newspaper)

AIP: American Israeli Paper Mills Ltd. (ASE)

AIR: AAR Corp. (NYSE)

AirbFrt: Airborne Freight Corp. (newspaper)

AIRC: AIRCOA Hospitality Services Inc. (NAS NMS)

AIRCAL: Air California

AIR CAN: Air Canada

Aircoa: AIRCOA Hotel Partners LP (newspaper)

AirExp: Air Express International Corp. (newspaper)

Airgas: Airgas Inc. (newspaper)

Airlease: Airlease Ltd. (newspaper)

AIRSY: Airshop Industries Ltd. (NAS NMS)

AIS: Ampal-American Israel Corp. (ASE)
Answer In Sentence

AIsrael: American Israeli Paper Mills Ltd. (newspaper)

AIT: American Information Technologies Corp. (NYSE)

AITX: Automatix Inc. (NAS NMS)

AIX: Amcast Industrial Corp. (NYSE)

aj: adjustment

AJ: Associated with Jobbers (London Stock Exchange) (UK)

AJE: Adjusting Journal Entry
AJG: Arthur J. Gallagher & Co.
(NYSE)
AJOJ: April, July, October, January (securities)
AK: Alaska Coastal-Ellis (airline)
AKA: Also Known As
Akusuhrkredit GMBH
AKV: Auslandskassenverein
AL: Accrued Liabilities
Alamanor (railroad)
Alcan Aluminum Ltd. (NYSE)
Alamco: Alamco Inc. (newspaper)
ALARA: As Low As Reasonably Achievable
ALASKA: Alaska Airlines
AlbaW: Alba-Waldensian Inc.
(newspaper)
Alberto: Alberto-Culver Co. (newspaper)
ALBM: Alpha 1 Biomedicals Inc.
(NAS NMS)
Albtsn: Albertson's Inc. (newspaper)
Alcan: Alcan Aluminum Ltd.
(newspaper)
ALCC: ALC Communications Corp.
(NAS NMS)
ALCI: AllCity Insurance Co. (NAS NMS)
ALCO: Alico Inc. (NAS NMS)
ALCOA: Alcoa Steamship Company
Aluminum Company of America (newspaper)
AlcoS: Alco Standard Corp. (newspaper)
ALD: Allied-Signal Inc. (NYSE)
At a Later Date
ALDC: Aldus Corp. (NAS NMS)
ALET: Aloette Cosmetics Inc. (NAS NMS)
ALEX: Alexander & Baldwin Inc.
(NAS NMS)
AlexAlx: Alexander & Alexander Services Inc. (newspaper)

Alexdr: Alexander's Inc. (newspaper)
ALFA: Alfa Corp. (NAS NMS)
ALFB: Abraham Lincoln Federal Savings Bank (Pennsylvania) (NAS NMS)
ALFD: Alabama Federal S&L Assn.
(NAS NMS)
ALFI: American League of Financial Institutions
Alfin: Alfin Inc. (newspaper)
ALFL: Alliance Financial Corp.
(NAS NMS)
ALG: Arkla Inc. (NYSE)
ALGH: Allegheny & Western Energy Corp. (NAS NMS)
ALGI: American Locker Group Inc.
(NAS NMS)
AlgInt: Allegheny International Inc.
(newspaper)
AlgLud: Allegheny Ludlum Corp.
(newspaper)
ALGO: Algorex Corp. (NAS NMS)
ALGR: ALLIED Group Inc. (NAS NMS)
ALK: Alaska Air Group Inc.
(NYSE)
ALL: Adams-Millis Corp. (NYSE)
Anchor Line Limited (steamship)
AL Lab: A.L. Laboratories Inc.
(newspaper)
ALLC: Allied Capital Corp. (NAS NMS)
AlldPd: Allied Products Corp.
(newspaper)
AllegCp: Allegheny Corp. (newspaper)
AllenG: Allen Group Inc. (newspaper)
AllgPw: Allegheny Power System Inc. (newspaper)
AlliBc: Alliance Bancorporation (newspaper)
AllisC: Allis-Chalmers Corp. (newspaper)

Allstr: Allstar Inns LP (newspaper)
ALLTL: ALLTEL Corp. (newspaper)
A&LM: Arkansas and Louisiana Missouri (railroad)
ALM: Allstate Municipal Income Trust (NYSE)
ALMI: Alpha Microsystems (NAS NMS)
ALN: Albany and Northern (railroad)
Allen Group, The (NYSE)
AlnCap: Alliance Capital Management LP (newspaper)
ALNT: Alliant Computer Systems Corp. (NAS NMS)
AlnTre: Alliance Tire & Rubber Company Ltd. (newspaper)
aloc: allocation
ALOG: Analogic Corp. (NAS NMS)
ALOHA: Aloha Airlines
alot: allotment
ALOT: Astro-Med Inc. (NAS NMS)
ALOY: Alloy Computer Products Inc. (NAS NMS)
AlphaIn: Alpha Industries Inc. (newspaper)
AlpinGr: Alpine Group Inc., The (newspaper)
ALQS: Aliquippa and Southern (railroad)
ALRN: Altron Inc. (NAS NMS)
ALS: Allegheny Ludlum Corp. (NYSE)
Alton & Southern (railroad)
AlskAir: Alaska Air Group Inc. (newspaper)
AlsMI: Allstate Municipal Income Trust II (newspaper)
AlstMu: Allstate Municipal Income Trust (newspaper)
ALT: Allstate Municipal Income Trust II (NYSE)
Altex: Altex Industries Inc. (newspaper)
ALTI: Altai Inc. (NAS NMS)

ALTO: Altos Computer Systems (NAS NMS)
ALTR: Altera Corp. (NAS NMS)
ALTS: Altus Bank, A Federal Savings Bank (Alabama) (NAS NMS)
ALWC: A. L. Williams Corp., The (NAS NMS)
ALWS: Allwaste Inc. (NAS NMS)
ALX: Alexander's Inc. (NYSE)
Alza: ALZA Corp. (newspaper)
am: amortissement (redemption of stock) (French)
AM: Active Market
After Market
Air Mail
AM International Inc. (NYSE)
Anno Mundi (in the year of the world)
Ante Meridiem (before noon)
AMA: Amfact Inc. (NYSE)
Asset Management Account
AMAT: Applied Materials Inc. (NAS NMS)
Amax: AMAX Inc. (newspaper)
AMB: Adjusted Monetary Base
American Brands (NYSE)
AMBAC: American Municipal Bond Assurance Corporation
AmBilt: American Biltrite Inc. (newspaper)
AMBJ: American City Business Journals Inc. (NAS NMS)
AMBld: American Medical Buildings Inc. (newspaper)
AmBrit: AmBrit Inc. (newspaper)
AmBrnd: American Brands Inc. (newspaper)
AMC: Amador Central (railroad)
AMC Entertainment Inc. (newspaper)
AMCA: AMCA International Ltd. (newspaper)
AmCap: American Capital Corp. (newspaper)

Amcast: Amcast Industrial Corp. (newspaper)

AMCC: American Continental Corp. (NAS NMS)

AMD: Advanced Micro Devices Inc. (NYSE) (newspaper)

Amdahl: Amdahl Corp. (newspaper)

AME: AMETEK Inc. (NYSE)

AMEA: A. M. E. Inc. (NAS NMS)

AMERICAN: American Airlines

Ameron: Ameron Inc. (newspaper)

AmesDp: Ames Department Stores Inc. (newspaper)

Ametk: AMETEK Inc. (newspaper)

AmevSc: AMEV Securities Inc. (newspaper)

AMEX: American Stock Exchange

Amexco: American Express Company

Amfac: Amfac Inc. (newspaper)

AmFGr: American First Guaranteed Income Fund (newspaper)

AMFI: AMCORE Financial Inc. (NAS NMS)

AMGN: Amgen Inc. (NAS NMS)

AmGvI: American Government Income Fund (newspaper)

AMH: Amdahl Corp. (ASE)

AmHes: Amerada Hess Corp. (newspaper)

Amhlth: AmeriHealth Inc. (newspaper)

AmHotl: Americana Hotels & Realty Corp. (newspaper)

AMI: Alternative Mortgage Instrument

AM Intl: AM International Inc. (newspaper)

AmIPrp: American Income Properties LP (newspaper)

AMJX: American Federal Savings Bank of Duval County (Florida) (NAS NMS)

AMK: American Technical Ceramics Corp. (ASE)

AMKG: Amoskeag Bank Shares Inc. (NAS NMS)

AML. American Mail Line (steamship)

AMLE: Amcole Energy Corp. (NAS NMS)

AmList: American List Corp. (newspaper)

AmLnd: American Land Cruisers Inc. (newspaper)

AMM: AMRE Inc. (NYSE)

AMMG: American Magnetics Corp. (NAS NMS)

AMN: Ameron Inc. (NYSE)

AMOCO: American Oil Company
American Oil Company (steamship)
Amoco Corp. (newspaper)

AmOil: American Oil & Gas Corp. (newspaper)

amort: amortissable (redeemable) (French)

AMOS: Amex Options Switching System
Amoskeag Co. (NAS NMS)

AMP: AMP Inc. (NYSE) (newspaper)

Ampal: Ampal-American Israel Corp. (newspaper)

Ampco: Ampco-Pittsburgh Corp. (newspaper)

AmPetf: American Petrofina Inc. (newspaper)

AMPH: American Physicians Service Group Inc. (NAS NMS)

AMPI: Amplicon Inc. (NAS NMS)

AMPS: Auction-Market Preferred Stock

AMR: American Airlines Corporation
AMR Corp. (NYSE) (newspaper)
Arcata and Mad River (railroad)

Amre: AMRE Inc. (newspaper)

Amrep: AMREP Corp. (newspaper)

AMRI: AmeriFirst Bank FSB (Florida) (NAS NMS)

AmRlty: American Realty Trust (newspaper)

Amrtc: American Information Technologies Corp. (newspaper)

AMS: American Shared Hospital Services (ASE)

AMSB: American Savings Financial Corp. (Washington) (NAS NMS)

AmShrd: American Shared Hospital Services (newspaper)

AMSR: Amserv Inc. (NAS NMS)

AmSth: AmSouth Bancorporation (newspaper)

AmStor: American Stores Co. (newspaper)

AMSW: American Software Inc. (NAS NMS)

AMSY: Amity Bancorp Inc. (NAS NMS)

amt: amount

AMT: Acme-Cleveland Corp. (NYSE)
Alternative Minimum Tax

AMTRAK (AMTRAC): American Railroad Tracks

AMV: AMEV Securities Inc. (NYSE)

AMW: Amwest Insurance Group Inc. (ASE)
Average Monthly Wage

AMWD: American Woodmark Corp. (NAS NMS)

Amwest: Amwest Insurance Group Inc. (newspaper)

AMWI: Air Midwest Inc. (NAS NMS)

AmWtr: American Water Works Company Inc. (newspaper)

AMX: AMAX Inc. (NYSE)

AmxG: Amax Gold Inc. (newspaper)

AMZ: American List Corp. (ASE)

AMze: American Maize-Products Co. (newspaper)

A&N: Albany and Northern (railroad)

AN: Account Number
Amoco Corp. (NYSE)
Apalachicola Northern (railroad)

Anacmp: Anacomp Inc. (newspaper)

Anadrk: Anadarko Petroleum Corp. (newspaper)

Analog: Analog Devices Inc. (newspaper)

ANAT: American National Insurance Co. (NAS NMS)

ANB&TC: American National Bank & Trust Company

AND: Andrea Radio Corp. (ASE)

Andal: Andal Corp. (newspaper)

ANDB: Andover Bancorp Inc. (Massachusetts) (NAS NMS)

ANDO: Andover Controls Corp. (NAS NMS)

ANDR: Andersen Group Inc. (NAS NMS)

Andrea: Andrea Radio Corp. (newspaper)

ANDW: Andrew Corp. (NAS NMS)

ANDY: Andros Analyzers Inc. (NAS NMS)

ANEN: Anaren Microwave Inc. (NAS NMS)

ANF: Angeles Finance Partners (ASE)

ANFM: August, November, February, May (securities)

ANG: Angeles Corp. (ASE)

AngE: Anglo Energy Inc. (newspaper)

Angeles: Angeles Corp. (newspaper)

Angelic: Angelica Corp. (newspaper)

AnglFn: Angeles Finance Partners (newspaper)

AngIRI: Angell Real Estate Company Inc. (newspaper)

AngMtg: Angeles Mortgage Partners Ltd. (newspaper)

Anheus: Anheuser-Busch Companies Inc. (newspaper)

ANLY: Analysts International Corp. (NAS NMS)

ANM: Angeles Mortgage Partners Ltd. (ASE)

ann: annual
annuity

ANN ARBOR: Detroit, Toledo and Ironton Railroad

ANN REPT: Annual Report

ANR: Angelina and Neches River (railroad)

ANSL: Anchor S&L Assn. (New Jersey) (NAS NMS)

ANSY: American Nursery Products Inc. (NAS NMS)

ANT: Anthony Industries Inc. (NYSE)

Anthm: Anthem Electronics Inc. (newspaper)

Anthony: Anthony Industries Inc. (newspaper)

ANUC: American Nuclear Corp. (NAS NMS)

A&O: April and October (securities)

AO: Account Of
Announcement of Opportunity

AOB: At Or Below

AOC: Aon Corp. (NYSE)

AOE: Auditing Order Error

AOF: ACM Government Opportunity Fund (NYSE)

AOG: American Oil & Gas Corp. (ASE)

AOI: AOI Coal Co. (ASE) (newspaper)

AON: All Or None order

Aon Cp: Aon Corp. (newspaper)

AORG: Allen Organ Co. (NAS NMS)

AOSM: Annual Ordinary Shareholders' Meeting

A&P: Great Atlantic & Pacific Tea Company

AP: Account Paid (or Payable)
Additional Premium
American Pioneer Lines (steamship)
Ampco-Pittsburgh Corp. (NYSE)
Apache Airlines
Associated Person
Authority to Pay (or Purchase)

APA: Apache Corp. (NYSE)
Apache Railway Company

Apache: Apache Corp. (newspaper)

APAS: American Passage Marketing Corp. (NAS NMS)

APB: Accounting Principles Board
Asia Pacific Fund Inc., The (NYSE)

APBI: Applied Bioscience International Inc. (NAS NMS)

APC: Anadarko Petroleum Corp. (NYSE)
Auditing Practices Committee
Attitude and Pointing Control System

APCI: Apollo Computer Inc. (NAS NMS)

APD: Air Products & Chemicals Inc. (NYSE)
Albany Port District (railroad)
Automated Payment and Deposit

APER: Atlantic Permanent Savings Bank FSB (Virginia) (NAS NMS)

ApexM: Apex Municipal Fund (newspaper)

APFC: American Pacific Corp. (NAS NMS)

APGI: A. P. Green Industries Inc. (NAS NMS)

API: American Petrofina Inc. (ASE)
Appreciation of Capital, Protection, Income

APIO: American Pioneer Savings Bank (Florida) (NAS NMS)

APL: American President Lines (steamship)

APM: Applied Magnetics Corp. (NYSE)

APOG: Apogee Enterprises Inc. (NAS NMS)

APOS: Advanced Polymer Systems Inc. (NAS NMS)

ApplBk: Apple Bank for Savings (New York) (newspaper)

ApplM: Applied Magnetics Corp. (newspaper)

APR: American Precision Industries Inc. (ASE)
Annual Percentage Rate
Annual Progress Reports

APrec: American Precision Industries Inc. (newspaper)

APresd: American President Companies Inc. (newspaper)

aprx: approximately

APS: American President Companies Ltd. (NYSE)
Assembly Programming System

APT: Automated Pit Trading (UK)

APWR: Applied Power Inc. (NAS NMS)

AQM: QMS Inc. (NYSE)

AQTN: Aequitron Medical Inc. (NAS NMS)

A&R: Aberdeen and Rockfish (railroad)
Account and Risk

AR: Account Receivable
Advisory Report
All Risks
Annual Report
Annual Return
ASARCO Inc. (NYSE)

ARA: Arcade and Attica Railroad

ARAI: Allied Research Associates Inc. (NAS NMS)

arb: arbitrager
arbitrary

ARB: American Realty Trust (NYSE)

ARBL: Assets Repriced Before Liabilities

ARBR: Arbor Drugs Inc. (NAS NMS)

ARC: Alexander Railroad (Southern)
ARC International Corp. (newspaper)
Atlantic Richfield Co. (NYSE)

ARCE: Air Cargo Equipment Corp. (NAS NMS)

ArchDn: Archer-Daniels-Midland Co. (newspaper)

ArcoCh: ARCO Chemical Co. (newspaper)

ARCS: Automated Revenue Collection System

ARDN: Arden Group Inc. (NAS NMS)

AREL: Alpharel Inc. (NAS NMS)

AREst: American Real Estate Partners LP (newspaper)

ARestr: American Restaurant Partners LP (newspaper)

ARIB: Aspen Ribbons Inc. (NAS NMS)

ARID: Aridtech Inc. (NAS NMS)

ARIG: American Reliance Group Inc. (NAS NMS)

Aristec: Aristech Chemical Corp. (newspaper)

ArizCm: Arizona Commerce Bank (newspaper)

ARK: Apple Bank for Savings (New York) (NYSE)

ArkBst: Arkansas Best Corp. (newspaper)

Arkla: Arkla Inc. (newspaper)

ArkRst: Ark Restaurants Corp. (newspaper)

ARM: Adjustable-Rate Mortgage
Armtek Corp. (NYSE)

Armada: Armada Corp. (newspaper)

Armco: Armco Inc. (newspaper)

ARMP: Average Revenue/Marginal
Physical Product

ARMR: Armor All Products Corp.
(NAS NMS)

Armtek: Armtek Corp. (newspaper)

Armtrn: Armatron International
Inc. (newspaper)

ArmWl: Armstrong World Industries Inc. (newspaper)

ARO: After Receipt of Order

ARON: Aaron Rents Inc. (NAS NMS)

AROS: Advance Ross Corp. (NAS
NMS)

AROW: Arrow Bank Corp. (NAS
NMS)

ArowE: Arrow Electronics Inc.
(newspaper)

ARPS: Adjustable-Rate Preferred
Stock

ARR: Alaska Railroad

ArrowA: Arrow Automotive Industries Inc. (newspaper)

ARS: Aristech Chemical Corp.
(NYSE)

ARSD: Arabian Shield Development Co. (NAS NMS)

ART: American Refrigerator Tran-
sit (railroad)
Armatron International Inc.
(ASE)

ARTEMIS: Administrative Real
Time Express Mort-
gage and Investment
System

Artra: ARTRA GROUP Inc. (newspaper)

ARTW: Art's-Way Manufacturing
Company Inc. (NAS NMS)

ARU: American Railway Union

ARV: Arvin Industries Inc. (NYSE)

Arvin: Arvin Industries Inc. (newspaper)

ARW: Arkansas Western (railway)
Arrow Electronics Inc.
(NYSE)

ARWS: Air Wisconsin Services Inc.
(NAS NMS)

ARX: ARX Inc. (NYSE) (newspaper)

ArzLd: Arizona Land Income Corp.
(ASE)

A/S: Aktjeselskap (joint stock company) (Norwegian)
Aktieselskab (joint stock company) (Danish)

A&S: Alton & Southern (railroad)

AS: Abilene & Southern (railroad)
Accumulated Surplus
Active Securities
Alaska Airlines
Armco Inc. (NYSE)
Assented Securities
Assessable Stock

ASA: Aluminum Stockholders
Association
American Society of Apprais-
ers
ASA Ltd. (NYSE) (newspa-
per)

A&SAB: Atlanta and St. Andrews
Bay (railroad)

ASAI: Atlantic Southeast Airlines
Inc. (NAS NMS)

ASAL: BankAtlantic: A Federal
Savings Bank (NAS NMS)

ASAP: As Soon As Possible

Asarco: ASARCO Inc. (newspaper)

ASBC: Associated Banc-Corp (NAS
NMS)

ASBI: Ameriana Savings Bank FSB
(Indiana) (NAS NMS)

ASBS: Asbestec Industries Inc.
(NAS NMS)

ASC: Adelaide Steamship Company
Alaska Steamship Company
American Stores Co. (NYSE)

ASCI: Associated Companies Inc.
(NAS NMS)

AsciE: American Science & Engineering Inc. (newspaper)
asd: assented (NYSE)
ASDA: Asbestos and Danville (railroad)
ASDE: Asbestos and Danville (railroad)
ASE: American Science & Engineering Inc. (ASE)
American Stock Exchange
ASEF: Association of Stock Exchange Firms
ASFS: Alaska State Ferry System
ASH: Ashland Oil Inc. (NYSE)
AshCoal: Ashland Coal Inc. (newspaper)
AShip: American Ship Building Co., The (newspaper)
AshOil: Ashland Oil Inc. (newspaper)
ASI: Astrex Inc. (ASE)
AsiaPc: Asia, Pacific Fund Inc., The (newspaper)
ASII: Automated Systems Inc. (NAS NMS)
ASKI: ASK Computer Systems Inc. (NAS NMS)
ASLFla: American S&L Assn. of Florida (newspaper)
ASM: Asamera Inc. (ASE)
ASMIF: Advanced Semiconductor Materials International N.V. (NAS NMS)
Asmr: Asamera Inc. (newspaper)
ASN: Alco Standard Corp. (NYSE)
Atlantic Steam Navigation (steamship)
ASO: AmSouth Bancorporation (NYSE)
ASP: American Selling Price
ASR: Accounting Series Release (SEC)
American Southwest Mortgage Investments Corp. (ASE)
assn: association
asst: assented

ASTA: AST Research Inc. (NAS NMS)
ASTE: Astec Industries Inc. (NAS NMS)
ASTHE: Average Straight Time Hourly Earnings
ASTR: Astrosystems Inc. (NAS NMS)
Astrex: Astrex Inc. (newspaper)
ASwM: American Southwest Mortgage Investment Corp. (newspaper)
ASX: Australian Stock Exchange
AT: ALLTEL Corp. (NYSE)
ATA: ARTRA GROUP Inc. (NYSE)
AtalSos: Atalanta/Sosnoff Capital Corp. (newspaper)
Atari: Atari Corp. (newspaper)
ATB: Across The Board
Atari Corp. (ASE)
Average Total Cost
ATBC: Atlantic Bancorporation (New Jersey) (NAS NMS)
ATCC: Airtran Corp. (NAS NMS)
ATCM: American Television & Communications Corp. (NAS NMS)
AT&E: A.T.& E. Corp. (newspaper)
ATE: Atlantic Energy Inc. (NYSE)
ATechC: American Technical Ceramics Corp. (newspaper)
ATEKF: Amertek Inc. (NAS NMS)
ATEL: Advanced Telecommunications Corp. (NAS NMS)
ATF: AT&T Stock Fund (ASE)
ATFC: Atico FInancial Corp. (NAS NMS)
ATG: Atlanta Gas Light Co. (NYSE)
ATH: Athlone Industries Inc. (NYSE)
Athlone: Athlone Industries Inc. (newspaper)
ATI: ATI Medical Inc. (ASE) (newspaper)

ATKM: Atek Metals Center Inc. (NAS NMS)

ATKN: Guy F. Atkinson Company of California (NAS NMS)

ATL: Atalanta/Sosnoff Capital Corp. (NYSE)

ATLANTIC: Atlantic Refining Company

Atlants: Atlantis Group Inc. (newspaper)

AtlasCp: Atlas Corp. (newspaper)

AtlEnrg: Atlantic Energy Inc. (newspaper)

ATLF: Atlantic Financial Federal (NAS NMS)

AtlGas: Atlanta Gas Light Co. (newspaper)

AtlRich: Atlantic Richfield Co. (newspaper)

AtlsCM: Atlas Consolidated Mining & Development Corp. (newspaper)

ATM: Anthem Electronics Inc. (NYSE)
At The Market
Automated Teller Machine
Automatic Teller Machine

AT&N: Alabama, Tennessee and Northern (railroad)

ATN: Acton Corp. (ASE)

ATNG: AlaTenn Resources Inc. (NAS NMS)

ATNN: American Telmedia Network Inc. (NAS NMS)

ATO: At The Opening

ATOC: Average Total Operating Cost

ATOG: Andover Togs Inc. (NAS NMS)

ATP: Authority To Purchase

ATPC: Athey Products Corp. (NAS NMS)

ATR: Alliance Tire & Rubber Company Ltd. (ASE)

ATRIMA: As Their Respective Interests May Appear

ATRO: Astronics Corp. (NAS NMS)

ATSF: Atchison, Topeka and Santa Fe (railroad)

AT&T: American Telephone and Telegraph Co. (newspaper)

ATTC: Auto-trol Technology Corp. (NAS NMS)

ATT Fd: AT&T Stock Fund (also known as Equity Income Fund) (newspaper)

atty: attorney

ATV: ARC International Corp. (ASE)

ATVC: American Travellers Corp. (NAS NMS)

ATW: A.T.& E. Corp. (ASE)
Atlantic and Western (railroad)

ATWD: Attwood Oceanics Inc. (NAS NMS)

ATX: A.T. Cross Co. (ASE)

AU: Amax Gold Inc. (NYSE)
gold (from aurum)

aud: audit
auditor

AUD: Automatic Data Processing Inc. (NYSE)

Audiotr: Audiotronics Corp. (newspaper)

AudVd: Audio/Video Affiliates Inc. (newspaper)

Audvx: Audiovox Corp. (newspaper)

AUG: Augat Inc. (NYSE)
Augusta (railroad)

Augat: Augat Inc. (newspaper)

AUS: Augusta and Summerville (railroad)
Ausimont Compo N.V. (NYSE)

Ausimt: Ausimont Compo N.V. (newspaper)

AUT: American Union Transport (steamship)

auth: authority

AUTO: AutoInfo Inc. (NAS NMS)
AutoDt: Automatic Data Processing Inc. (newspaper)
AUTR: Autotrol Corp. (NAS NMS)
av: average
AV: Actual Value
  Ad Valorem (in proportion to the value)
AVA: Audio/Video Affiliates Inc. (NYSE)
AVAK: Avantek Inc. (NAS NMS)
Avalon: Avalon Corp. (newspaper)
AVC: Average Variable Cost
AVCO: Average Cost
AVDL: Avondale Industries Inc. (NAS NMS)
AVE: AVEMCO Corp (NYSE)
Avery: Avery International Corp. (newspaper)
AVFC: AmVestors Financial Corp. (NAS NMS)
avg: average
AVGA: Avant-Garde Computing Inc. (NAS NMS)
AVL: Aroostook Valley (railroad)
  Avalon Corp. (NYSE)
AVMC: AVEMCO Corp. (newspaper)
Avnet: Avnet Inc. (newspaper)
Avon: Avon Products Inc. (newspaper)
AVP: Avon Products Inc. (NYSE)
AVRY: Avery Inc. (NAS NMS)
AVT: Ad Valorem Taxes
  Avnet Inc. (NYSE)
  Value-Added Tax
AVTR: Avatar Holdings Inc. (NAS NMS)
AVX: AVX Corp. (NYSE) (newspaper)
AVY: Avery International Corp. (NYSE)
A&W: Ahnapee and Western (railroad)
  Atlantic and Western (railroad)

AW: Arkansas Western (railroad)
AWAL: America West Airlines Inc. (NAS NMS)
AWCS: AW Computer Systems Inc. (NAS NMS)
AWK: American Water Works Company Inc. (NYSE)
A&WP: Atlanta and West Point (railroad)
AWS: Alba-Waldensian Inc. (ASE)
AWSJ: Asian Wall Street Journal
AWST: American Western Corp. (NAS NMS)
AWW: Algers, Winslow and Western (railway)
awy: airway
AXO: Alamco Inc. (ASE)
AXP: American Express Co. (NYSE)
AXR: AMREP Corp. (NYSE)
AXXN: Action Auto Rentals Inc. (NAS NMS)
AXXX: Artel Communications Corp. (NAS NMS)
A&Y: Atlantic and Yadkin (railroad)
AY: Allegheny and Western (railway)
  Annual Yield
AYD: Aydin Corp. (NYSE)
Aydin: Aydin Corp. (newspaper)
AYP: Allegheny Power System Inc. (NYSE)
AYSS: Allegheny and South Side (railroad)
AZ: Atlas Corp. (NYSE)
AZA: ALZA Corp. (ASE)
AZB: Arizona Commerce Bank (ASE)
AZE: American Maize-Products Co. (ASE)
AZL: Arizona Land Income Corp. (ASE)
AZTC: Aztec Manufacturing Co. (NAS NMS)

b: bani (currency of Romania)
 belga (currency of Belgium)
 benefit (profit) (French)
 bid
 billet (bill) (French)
 bills
 bolivar (currency of Venezuela)
 boliviano (currency of Bolivia)
 bond
 brief (currency) (German)
 speculative (Standard & Poor's bond rating)
B: Balanced Fund
 Barnes Group Inc. (NYSE)
 Base (money)
 Boston Stock Exchange
 Class "B" Preferred or Common Stock
 Series "B" Bonds or Debentures
B/A: Billed At
Ba: Speculative Elements (Moody's bond rating)
B&A: Baltimore and Annapolis (railroad)
 Bangor and Aroostook (railroad)
 Bid and Asked
 Boston and Albany (railroad)
BA: Bank Acceptance
 Boeing Co., The (NYSE)
 Budget Authority
 Bureau of Accounts
BAB: British Airways Plc. (NYSE)
BAC: BankAmerica Corp. (NYSE)
 Bendix Aviation Company
 Boeing Airplane Company
 Budget At Completion
back: backwardation
BACS: Bankers Automated Clearing Services

BACV: Budget at Completion Variance
BAD: Bank Account Debits Tax
Badger: Badger Meter Inc. (newspaper)
BA & F: Budget, Accounting, and Finance
BAFO: Best and Final Offer
BAI: Bank Administration Institute
Bairnco: Bairnco Corp. (newspaper)
Baker: Michael Baker Corp. (newspaper)
BakrHu: Baker Hughes Inc. (newspaper)
bal: balance
BAL: Baldwin Securities Corp. (ASE)
 Bonanza Airlines
balce: balance
Baldor: Baldor Electric Co. (newspaper)
BaldsS: Baldwin Securities Corp. (newspaper)
Baldwin: Baldwin Technology Company Inc. (newspaper)
Ball: Ball Corp. (newspaper)
BallyMf: Bally Manufacturing Corp. (newspaper)
BALPA: Balance of Payments
bals: Balboas (currency unit of Panama)
BaltBcp: Baltimore Bancorp (Maryland) (newspaper)
BaltGE: Baltimore Gas & Electric Co. (newspaper)
BambP: Bamberger Polymers Inc. (newspaper)
BAMI: Basic American Medical Inc. (NAS NMS)

BAN: Banister Continental Ltd.
(ASE)
Bank Anticipation Note
Bandag: Bandag Inc. (newspaper)
BanFd: Bancroft Convertible Fund
Inc. (newspaper)
BANG: Bangor Hydro-Electric Co.
(NAS NMS)
BANK: International Bank for Re-
construction and Develop-
ment
Bank Clgs: Bank Clearings
bankcy: bankruptcy
BankTr: Bankers Trust New York
Corp. (newspaper)
Banner: Banner Industries Inc.
(newspaper)
banq: banque (bank) (French)
BANQ: Burritt InterFinancial
Bancorporation (NAS
NMS)
BANs: Bond Anticipation Notes
Banstr: Banister Continental Ltd.
(newspaper)
BanTx: BancTEXAS Group Inc.
(newspaper)
BANTSA: Bank of American Na-
tional Trust and Sav-
ings Association
BA&P: Butte, Anaconda & Pacific
(railroad)
BAP: Billet à Payer (Bill Payable)
(French)
BAR: Bangor and Aroostook Rail-
road
Barry Wright Corp. (NYSE)
Billet à Recevoir (Bill Receiv-
able) (French)
BARC: Baltimore and Annapolis
Railroad Company
Barrett Resources Corp.
(NAS NMS)
Barclay: Barclays PLC (newspaper)
Bard: C.R. Bard Inc. (newspaper)
BARD: Barden Corp. (NAS NMS)
barg: bargain

Barister: Barrister Information Sys-
tems Corp. (newspaper)
Barnet: Barnett Banks of Florida
Inc. (newspaper)
BarnGP: Barnes Group Inc. (news-
paper)
Barnwl: Barnwell Industries Inc.
(newspaper)
B&ARR: Boston and Albany Rail-
road
BarrLb: Barr Laboratories Inc.
(newspaper)
Baruch: Baruch-Foster Corp. (news-
paper)
BARY: Barry's Jeweler's Inc. (NAS
NMS)
BaryWr: Barry Wright Corp. (news-
paper)
BAS: BASIX Corp. (NYSE)
Budget Allocation Summary
BASE: BankAmericard Service Ex-
change
Base Ten Systems Inc. (NAS
NMS)
Brokerage Accounting Sys-
tem Elements
BASIC: Banking And Securities
Industry Committee
BASIS: Bank Automated Service
Information System
BASIX: BASIX Corp. (newspaper)
BAT: B.A.T. Industries PLC (news-
paper)
BatlMt: Battle Mountain Gold Co.
(newspaper)
BAU: Business As Usual
Bausch: Bausch & Lomb Inc.
(newspaper)
BAW: Blue Arrow PLC (NYSE)
BAX: Baxter International Inc.
(NYSE)
Baxter: Baxter International Inc.
(newspaper)
BAY: Bay Financial Corp. (NYSE)
BayFin: Bay Financial Corp. (news-
paper)

BAYL: Bayly Corp. (NAS NMS)
Bayou: Bayou Steel Corporation of La Place (newspaper)
BayStG: Bay State Gas Co. (newspaper)
BB: Baby Bond
Banco de Bilbao (bank of Spain)
Bank Building & Equipment Corporation of America (ASE)
Bearer Bond
Big Board
Birmingham Belt (railroad)
Bureau of the Budget
Buy Back
BBA: Banque Belge d'Afrique (Bank of Spain)
BBAHF: Basic Resources International Ltd. (NAS NMS)
BBB: Baltimore Bancorp (Maryland) (NYSE)
Banker's Blanket Bond
Better Business Bureau
Buy Back
Medium (Standard & Poor's bond rating)
Quality rating for a municipal or corporate bond
BBC: Bergen Brunswig Corp. (ASE)
BBE: Belden & Blake Energy Co. (ASE)
BBEC: Blockbuster Entertainment Corp. (NAS NMS)
BBF: Barnett Banks of Florida Inc. (NYSE)
BBGS: Babbage's Inc. (NAS NMS)
BBIF: BB & T Financial Corp. (NAS NMS)
BBN: Bolt Beranek & Newman Inc. (NYSE)
BBNK: BayBanks Inc. (NAS NMS)
BBO: Billion Barrels of Oil
BBPI: Barry Blau & Partners Inc. (NAS NMS)
BBR: B-B Real Estate Investment Corp. (ASE)

BBRC: Burr-Brown Corp. (NAS NMS)
BB REI: B-B Real Estate Investment Corp. (newspaper)
BBY: Best Buy Company Inc. (NYSE)
B&C: Barre and Chelsea (railroad)
Bennettsville and Cheraw (railroad)
BC: Bad Check
Before Christ
Bellefonte Central (railroad)
Bills for Collection
Blue Chip
Bogus Check
Brunswick Corp. (NYSE)
BCC: Boise Cascade Corp. (NYSE)
BCE: BCE Inc. (NYSE) (newspaper)
Before Common Era
BCelts: Boston Celtics LP (newspaper)
BCF: Burlington Coat Factory Warehouse Corp. (NYSE)
BCKY: Buckeye Financial Corp. (NAS NMS)
BCL: Biocraft Laboratories Inc. (NYSE)
Bristol City Line (steamship)
BCM: Banco Central S.A. (NYSE)
BCO: Blessings Corp. (ASE)
BCP: Borden Chemicals & Plastics LP (NYSE)
Budget Change Proposal
BCR: Bank Cash Ratio
Bank Cash Reserve
C.R. Bard Inc. (NYSE)
BCRR: Boyne City Railroad
BCS: Barclays PLC (NYSE)
BCV: Bancroft Convertible Fund Inc. (ASE)
B&D: Black & Decker
bd: board
bond
BD: Back Deliveries
Bad Delivery
Bank Dividends

Bank Draft
Bills Discounted
Bloedel-Donovan (railroad)
Brought Down
B/D: Broker-Dealer
BDC: Beneficiary Developing Country
BDEL: Bank of Delaware Corp. (NAS NMS)
BDEP: BanPonce Corp. (NAS NMS)
B/DFT: Bank Draft
BDG: Bandag Inc. (NYSE)
BDGT: Budget Rent a Car Corp. (NAS NMS)
BDK: Black & Decker Corp., The (NYSE)
BDM: BDM International Inc. (ASE) (newspaper)
BDO: Bottom Dropped Out
B/DOE: Barrels per Day Oil Equivalent
BDR: Bearer Depositary Receipt
Bd Rts: Bond Rights
BDS: Broker's Daily Statement
BDSC: Black Diamond Steamship Corporation
BDX: Becton Dickinson & Co. (NYSE)
B&E: Baltimore and Eastern (railroad)
B of E: Bank of England (UK)
BE: Baltimore and Eastern (railroad)
Bank of England (UK)
Benguet Corp. (NYSE)
Bill of Entry
Bill of Exchange
Break Even Point
B/E: Bill of Exchange
BEA: Break Even Analysis
BEAM: Bidders Early Alert Message
Beard: Beard Co., The (newspaper)
Bearing: Bearings Inc. (newspaper)
BearSt: The Bear Stearns Companies Inc. (newspaper)
BEB: British Export Board (UK)

BEBA: Beeba's Creations Inc. (NAS NMS)
BEC: Beard Co., The (ASE)
BECO: Boston Edison Company
BECR: Bercor Inc. (NAS NMS)
BectDk: Becton, Dickinson & Co. (newspaper)
BEDT: Brooklyn Eastern District Terminal (railroad)
BEEM: Beech Mountain (railroad)
BEIH: BEI Holdings Ltd. (NAS NMS)
Beker: Beker Industries Corp. (newspaper)
BEL: Bell Atlantic Corp. (NYSE)
BeldBlk: Belden & Blake Energy Co. (newspaper)
BELF: Bel Fuse Inc. (NAS NMS)
Bel Fcs: Belgian Francs
BelIn: Bell Industries Inc. (newspaper)
Bell: Bell System (American Telephone and Telegraph)
BellAtl: Bell Atlantic Corp. (newspaper)
BellSo: BellSouth Corp. (newspaper)
BeloAH: A.H. Belco Corp. (newspaper)
Belvdre: Belvedere Corp. (newspaper)
BEM: Beaufort and Morehead (railroad)
Bemis: Bemis Company Inc. (newspaper)
BEN: Franklin Resources Inc. (NYSE)
benef: beneficiary
BenfCp: Beneficial Corp. (newspaper)
BengtB: Benguet Corp. (newspaper)
BENH: BankEast Corp. (NAS NMS)
BENJ: Benjamin Franklin S&L Assn. (Oregon) (NAS NSM)
BEP: BET Public Limited Co. (NYSE)
BER: Bearings Inc. (NYSE)
BergBr: Bergen Brunswig Corp. (newspaper)

BERK: Berkline Corp., The (NAS NMS)
Berkey: Berkey Inc. (newspaper)
BermSt: Bermuda Star Lines Inc. (newspaper)
BES: Best Products Company Inc. (NYSE)
BestBy: Best Buy Company Inc. (newspaper)
BestPd: Best Products Company Inc. (newspaper)
BET: Bethlehem Corp., The (ASE) BET Public Limited Co. (newspaper)
BethCo: Bethlehem Corp., The (newspaper)
BethStl: Bethlehem Steel Corp. (newspaper)
BETZ: Betz Laboratories Inc. (NAS NMS)
BEV: Beverly Enterprises Inc. (NYSE)
BevIP: Beverly Investment Properties Inc. (newspaper)
Bevrly: Beverly Enterprises Inc. (newspaper)
BEZ: Baldor Electric Co. (NYSE)
BEZRY: C. H. Beazer Holdings PLC (NAS NMS)
BF: Backdoor Financing
Balanced Fund
Banque de France (Bank of France)
Belgian franc
BFBS: Brookfield Bancshares Corp. (Illinois) (NAS NMS)
BFC: BankAtlantic Financial Corp. (ASE)
Bellefonte Central (railroad)
Budget and Forecast Calendarization
BFCP: Broadway Financial Corp. (NAS NMS)
BFCS: Boston Five Bancorp Inc. (NAS NMS)
bfcy: beneficiary
BFD: Brown-Forman Corp. (ASE)

BFI: Browning-Ferris Industries Inc. (NYSE)
BFO: Baruch-Foster Corp. (ASE)
BFP: Bona Fide Purchaser
BFPV: Bona Fide Purchaser for Value
BFS: B.F. Saul Real Estate Investment Trust (NYSE)
BFX: Buffton Corp. (ASE)
BFY: Budget Fiscal Year
BG: Brown Group Inc. (NYSE)
BGAS: Berkshire Gas Co., The (NAS NMS)
BGBR: Big Bear Inc. (NAS NMS)
BGC: Bay State Gas Co. (NYSE)
BGD: Billion Gallons per Day
BG&E: Baltimore Gas and Electric
BGE: Baltimore Gas & Electric Co. (NYSE)
BGENF: Biogen N. V. (NAS NMS)
BGG: Briggs & Stratton Corp. (NYSE)
BGSS: BGS Systems Inc. (NAS NMS)
bgt: bought
BH: Bank Holiday
Bath and Hammondsport (railroad)
B&H: B&H Ocean Carriers Ltd. (newspaper)
Bell & Howell Corporation
BHA: Biscayne Holdings Inc. (ASE)
BHAG: BHA Group Inc. (NAS NMS)
BHAMY: Becham Group PLC (NAS NMS)
BHC: Bank Holding Company
Brock Hotel Corp. (NYSE)
BHI: Baker Hughes Inc. (NYSE)
BHL: Bunker Hill Income Securities Inc. (NYSE)
BHNC: Bank of New Hampshire Corp. (NAS NMS)
BHO: B&H Ocean Carriers Ltd. (ASE)
BHP: Broken Hill Proprietary, The (steamship)

Broken Hill Proprietary Company Ltd., The (NYSE) (newspaper)

B&HS: Bonhomie & Hattiesburg Southern (railroad)

BHY: Belding Heminway Company Inc. (NYSE)

B&I: Bankruptcy and Insolvency

BI: Bell Industries Inc. (NYSE) Braniff International (airline)

BIBOR: Bahrain Inter-Bank Offered Rate

BIC: BIC Corp. (ASE)

BicCp: BIC Corp. (newspaper)

BID: Bid for (NYSE) Sotheby's Holdings Inc. (ASE)

BIDCO: Business and Industrial Development Corporation

BIF: Bank Insurance Fund

BIFFEX: Baltic International Freight Futures Exchange

BIG: Bond International Gold Inc. (NYSE)

BIGB: Big B Inc. (NAS NMS)

BILT: Microbilt Corp. (NAS NMS)

BIM: ICN Biomedicals Inc. (ASE)

BIN: Binks Manufacturing Co. (ASE)

BINC: Biospherics Inc. (NAS NMS)

BIND: Bindley Western Industries Inc. (NAS NMS)

BING: Binghamton Savings Bank (NAS NMS)

BinkMF: Binks Manufacturing Co. (newspaper)

BIO: Bio-Rad Laboratories Inc. (ASE)

Biocft: Biocraft Laboratories Inc. (newspaper)

BIOP: Bioplasty Inc. (NAS NMS)

Biophm: Biopharmaceuticals Inc. (newspaper)

BioR: Bio-Rad Laboratories Inc. (newspaper)

BIOT: BioTechnica International Inc. (NAS NMS)

Biother: Biotherapeutics Inc. (newspaper)

BIOW: Banks of Iowa Inc. (NAS NMS)

BIP: Beverly Investment Properties Inc. (NYSE)

BIR: Birmingham Steel Corp. (NYSE)

BIRD: Bird Inc. (NAS NMS)

BirmStl: Birmingham Steel Corp. (newspaper)

BIRT: Birtcher Corp., The (NAS NMS)

BIS: Barrister Information Systems Corp. (ASE)

BiscH: Biscayne Holdings Inc. (newspaper)

BISH: Bishop Inc. (NAS NMS)

biz: business

B of J: Bank of Japan

BJIC: Ben & Jerry's Homemade Inc. (NAS NMS)

bk: backwardation bank

BK: Bank of New York Company Inc., The (NYSE)

BkatlFn: BankAtlantic Financial Corp. (newspaper)

BKB: Bank of Boston Corp. (NYSE)

BkBost: Bank of Boston Corp. (newspaper)

BKC: American Bank of Connecticut (ASE)

bkcy: bankruptcy

BKFR: Baker Fentress & Co. (NAS NMS)

bkg: banking bookkeeping

BKH: Black Hills Corp. (NYSE)

BKHT: Berkshire Hathaway Inc. (NAS NMS)

BKI: Beker Industries Corp. (NYSE)

BKInv: Burger King Investors Master LP (newspaper)

BKLY: W. R. Berkley Corp. (NAS NMS)

BklyUG: Brooklyn Union Gas Co., The (newspaper)

BkNE: Bank of New England Corp. (newspaper)

BKNG: Banknorth Group Inc. (NAS NMS)

BKNT: Banker's Note Inc. (NAS NMS)

BkNY: Bank of New York Company Inc., The (newspaper)

BKP: Burger King Investors Master LP (NYSE)

bkpg: bookkeeping

bkpr: bookkeeper

bkpt: bankrupt

bkr: broker

BKR: Michael Baker Corp. (ASE)

bkrupt: bankrupt

bks: books

BkSFr: Bank of San Francisco Holding Co. (newspaper)

BKSO: Bank South Corp. (NAS NMS)

BKST: Bank of Stamford (California) (NAS NMS)

BKT: Blackstone Income Trust Inc. (NYSE)

bktcy: bankruptcy

Bk Town: Banking Town

BKVT: BankVermont Corp. (NAS NMS)

bky: bankruptcy

BKY: Berkey Inc. (NYSE)

B/L: Basic Letter
Bill of Lading

B & L: Bausch & Lomb
Building and Loan (association or bank)
Burns and Laird Line (steamship)

BL: Bank Larceny
Bibby Line (steamship)
Bill of Lading
Booth Line (steamship)
Brothers Air Service (airline)

BLA: Baltimore and Annapolis (railroad)

British Land of America Inc. (NYSE)

BlackD: Black & Decker Corp., The (newspaper)

BLAK: Black Industries Inc. (NAS NMS)

BLAS: Blasius Industries Inc. (NAS NMS)

B/L Atchd: Bill of Lading Attached

BLC: A.H. Belo Corp. (NYSE)

BLCC: Balchem Corp. (NAS NMS)

BLD: Baldwin Technology Company Inc. (ASE)

B&LE: Bessemer and Lake Erie (railroad)

Blessg: Blessings Corp. (newspaper)

BLI: Businessland Inc. (NYSE)

BLII: Britton Lee Inc. (NAS NMS)

BlkHC: Black Hills Corp. (newspaper)

BlkHR: H & R Block Inc. (newspaper)

Blkstn: Blackstone Income Trust Inc. (newspaper)

BLL: Ball Corp. (NYSE)

BLLW: W. Bell & Company Inc. (NAS NMS)

BLOC: Block Drug Co. (NAS NMS)

Blount: Blount Inc. (newspaper)

BLR: Bolar Pharmaceutical Company Inc. (ASE)

BlrPh: Bolar Pharmaceutical Company Inc. (newspaper)

BLS: BellSouth Corp. (NYSE)
Ben Line Steamers
Bureau of Labor Statistics

BLSC: Bio-Logic Systems Corp. (NAS NMS)

BLT: Blount Inc. (ASE)

BLU: Blue Chip Value Fund Inc. (NYSE)

BluChp: Blue Chip Value Fund Inc. (newspaper)

BLUD: Immucor Inc. (NAS NMS)

BlueAr: Blue Arrow PLC (newspaper)

BLV: Belvedere Corp. (ASE)
BLVD: Boulevard Bancorp Inc.
(NAS NMS)
BLY: Bally Manufacturing Corp.
(NYSE)
BLYVY: Blyvooruitzicht Gold Min-
ing Company Ltd. (NAS
NMS)
B&M: Boston and Maine (railroad)
BM: Bear Market
Beaver, Meade and Englewood
(railroad)
Bill of Material
Bond Maturity
Boston and Maine (railroad)
Business Machine
Buyer's Market
B of M: Bank of Montreal
BMAC: BMA Corp. (NAS NMS)
BMC: BMC Industries Inc. (NYSE)
(newspaper)
BMCC: Bando McGlocklin Capital
Corp. (NAS NMS)
BMD: A. L. Laboratories Inc. (ASE)
BMDS: Bio-Medicus Inc. (NAS
NMS)
BM&E: Beaver, Meade and Engle-
wood (railroad)
BMED: Ballard Medical Products
Inc. (NAS NMS)
BMET: Biomet Inc. (NAS NMS)
BMG: Battle Mountain Gold Co.
(NYSE)
BMI: Badger Meter Inc. (ASE)
BMJF: BMJ Financial Corp. (NAS
NMS)
B&ML: Belfast & Moosehead Lake
(railroad)
BMP: Burnham American Proper-
ties Inc. (ASE)
BMPR: Bimonthly Progress Report
BMRA: Biomerica Inc. (NAS NMS)
BMRG: BMR Financial Group Inc.
(NAS NMS)
B&MRR: Beaufort and Morehead
Railroad

BMRR: Beech Mountain Railroad
BMS: Bemis Company Inc. (NYSE)
BMTCD: Bryn Mawr Bank Corp.
(Pennsylvania) (NAS
NMS)
BMW: Bayerische Motoren Werke
(Bavarian Motor Works)
BMY: Bristol-Myers Squibb Co.
(NYSE)
B&N: Bauxite and Northern (rail-
way)
BN: Bank Note
Borden Inc. (NYSE)
Burlington Northern (railroad)
BNBG: Bull & Bear Group Inc.
(NAS NMS)
BNC: Regional Financial Shares
Investment Fund Inc.
(NYSE)
BncCtr: Banco Central S.A. (news-
paper)
BncOne: Banc One Corp. (newspa-
per)
bnd: bond
bonded
bndg: bonding
BNDY: Brandywine S&L Assn.
(Pennsylvania) (NAS NMS)
BNE: Bowne & Company Inc. (ASE)
BNF: Braniff International Airways
BNGO: Bingo King Company Inc.
(NAS NMS)
BNHB: BNH Bancshares Inc. (NAS
NMS)
BNHI: Bancorp Hawaii Inc. (NAS
NMS)
BNHN: Benihana National Corp.
(NAS NMS)
BNI: Burlington Northern Inc.
(NYSE)
bnk: bank
BnkAm: BankAmerica Corp. (news-
paper)
BnkBld: Bank Building & Equip-
ment Corporation of
America (newspaper)

BNKF: Bankers First Corp. (NAS NMS)

bnkg: banking

BNKS: United New Mexico Financial Corp. (NAS NMS)

BNL: Beneficial Corp. (NYSE)

BNO: Barrels of New Oil

BNP: Banque National de Paris (France)
Boddie-Noell Restaurant Properties Inc. (ASE)

BNR: Banner Industries Inc. (NYSE)

BNS: Brown & Sharpe Manufacturing Co. (NYSE)

BNTA: George Banta Company Inc. (NAS NMS)

BNY: Bundy Corp. (NYSE)

bo: bonding

B&O: Baltimore and Ohio (railroad)

BO: Back Order
Bad Order
Branch Office
Broker's Order
Buy Order
Buyer's Option

BOAT: Boatmen's Bancshares Inc. (NAS NMS)

BOB: Bureau of the Budget

BOBE: Bob Evans Farms Inc. (NAS NMS)

BOC: Back Office Crunch
Breach of Contract

BOCB: Buffets Inc. (NAS NMS)

BOCI: Business Organization Climate Index

B&O - C&O: Baltimore and Ohio-Chesapeake and Ohio (railroad)

BOD: Bid Opening Date
Board Of Directors

Boddie: Boddie-Noell Restaurant Properties Inc. (newspaper)

BOE: Bank Of England (UK)
Barrels of Oil Equivalent

Boeing: Boeing Co., The (newspaper)

BOF: Bank of San Francisco Holding Co. (ASE)

BOG: Board of Governors

BOGO: Bogert Oil Co. (NAS NMS)

BOHM: Bohemia Inc. (NAS NMS)

BOI: Board of Investments

BoiseC: Boise Cascade Corp. (newspaper)

BOKC: BancOklahoma Corp. (NAS NMS)

BOL: Bausch & Lomb Inc. (NYSE)

BOLT: Bolt Technology Corp. (NAS NMS)

BoltBr: Bolt Beranek & Newman Inc. (newspaper)

BOM: Beginning Of the Month
Bowmar Instrument Corp. (ASE)
Buying On Margin

BOMA: Banks of Mid-America Inc. (NAS NMS)

BOMS: Bancorp. of Mississippi Inc. (NAS NMS)

Bond: Bond International Gold Inc. (newspaper)

bookk: bookkeeping

BOOL: Boole & Babbage Inc. (NAS NMS)

BOON: Boonton Electronics Corp. (NAS NMS)

BOP: Balance Of Payments

BOQ: Beginning of Quarter

bor: borrowings

BordC: Borden Chemicals & Plastics LP (newspaper)

Borden: Borden Inc. (newspaper)

Bormns: Borman's Inc. (newspaper)

BOS: Boston Celtics LP (NYSE)

BOSA: Boston Acoustics Inc. (NAS NMS)

BOST: Boston Digital Corp. (NAS NMS)

BostEd: Boston Edison Co. (newspaper)

bot: bought
BOT: Board Of Trade
Board Of Trustees
BOW: Bowater Inc. (NYSE)
Bowatr: Bowater Inc. (newspaper)
BowlA: Bowl America Inc. (newspaper)
Bowmr: Bowmar Instrument Corp. (newspaper)
Bowne: Bowne & Company Inc. (newspaper)
BowVal: Bow Valley Industries Ltd. (newspaper)
BOY: Beginning of Year
BOYC: Boyne City (railroad)
BP: Bills Payable
Book Profit
Breach of Promise
British Petroleum Company PLC, The (NYSE)
British Pound (currency of United Kingdom)
Burden of Proof
BPAO: Baldwin Piano & Organ Co. (NAS NMS)
B Pay: Bill(s) Payable
BPCD: Barrels Per Calendar Day
BP&CO: Burns, Philip and Company (steamship)
BPCO: Bonneville Pacific Corp. (NAS NMS)
BPD: Barrels Per Day
BPH: Barrels Per Hour
Biopharmaceuticals Inc. (ASE)
BPI: Bamberger Polymers Inc. (ASE)
BPL: Buckeye Partners LP (NYSE)
BPMI: Badger Paper Mills Inc. (NAS NMS)
BPOP: Banco Popular de Puerto Rico (NAS NMS)
BPP: Burnham Pacific Properties Inc. (ASE)
BPQ: Budgetary and Planning Quotations

BQ: Basis Quote
BQC: Qantel Corp. (NYSE)
BQR: Quick & Reilly Group Inc., The (NYSE)
bque: banque (bank) (French)
B/R: Bills Receivable
BR: Bank Rate
Bills Receivable
Blue Ridge (railroad)
Bond Rating
Burlington Resources Inc. (NYSE)
BRA: Bankruptcy Reform Act
BRAE: BRAE Corp. (NAS NMS)
BRAN: Brand Companies Inc. (NAS NMS)
Brazil: Brazil Fund Inc. (newspaper)
BRC: Belt Railway of Chicago
Business Reply Card
BRCO: W. H Brady Co. (NAS NMS)
BRD: Brad Ragan Inc. (ASE)
BRDL: Brendle's Inc. (NAS NMS)
BRDN: Brandon Systems Corp. (NAS NMS)
BRE: BRE Properties Inc. (NYSE) (newspaper)
BREC: Bills Receivable
Bills Recoverable
BREN: Brenco Inc. (NAS NMS)
BRF: Borman's Inc. (NYSE)
BRG: British Gas PLC (NYSE)
BRI: Burlington-Rock Island (railroad)
BRID: Bridgford Foods Corp. (NAS NMS)
BrigSt: Briggs & Stratton Corp. (newspaper)
BRIK: Brinkmann Instruments Inc. (NAS NMS)
BrisMyrSqb: Bristol-Myers Squibb Co. (newspaper)
BristG: Bristol Gaming Corp. (newspaper)
BritAir: British Airways PLC (newspaper)

BritGas: British Gas PLC (newspaper)
BritLnd: British Land of America Inc. (newspaper)
BritPt: British Petroleum Company PLC, The (newspaper)
BritTel: British Telecommunications PLC (newspaper)
BRIX: BRIntec Corp. (NAS NMS)
BRJS: Brajdas Corp. (NAS NMS)
BRL: Barr Laboratories Inc. (ASE)
BRLN: Brooklyn Savings Bank, The (Connecticut) (NAS NMS)
BrlNth: Burlington Northern Inc. (newspaper)
BrlRsc: Burlington Resources Inc. (newspaper)
BRN: Barnwell Industries Inc. (ASE)
BrnFA: Brown-Forman Corp. (newspaper)
BRNO: Bruno's Inc. (NAS NMS)
Brnwk: Brunswick Corp. (newspaper)
Brock: Brock Hotel Corp. (newspaper)
brok: broker
brokerage
BRRS: Barris Industries Inc. (NAS NMS)
BRRY: Berry Petroleum Co. (NAS NMS)
BRS: Brascan Ltd. (ASE)
Brscn: Brascan Ltd. (newspaper)
BrshWl: Brush Wellman Inc. (newspaper)
brt: brought
BR&T: Bowdon Railway and Transportation
BRT: BRT Realty Trust (NYSE) (newspaper)
Brt Fwd: Brought Forward
brupt: bankrupt
bankruptcy
BR&W: Black River and Western (railroad)

BrwnF: Browning-Ferris Industries Inc. (newspaper)
BrwnGp: Brown Group Inc. (newspaper)
BRX: Biotherapeutics Inc. (ASE)
B&S: Bevier and Southern (railroad)
BS: Back Spread
Balance Sheet
Bellweather Stock
Bethlehem Steel Corp. (NYSE)
Bill of Sale
Birmingham Southern (railroad)
Block Sale
Butterfly Spread
BSAF: Bids Solicited As Follows
BSBC: Branford Savings Bank (Connecticut) (NAS NMS)
BSBX: Bell Savings Bank PsSA (Pennsylvania) (NAS NMS)
BSC: Bear Stearns Companies Inc., The (NYSE)
BSD: BSD Bancorp Inc. (ASE) (newspaper)
Buyer has Seven Days to Take Up
B&SE: Birmingham & Southeastern (railroad)
BSE: Boston Edison Co. (NYSE)
Boston Stock Exchange
BSET: Bassett Furniture Industries Inc. (NAS NMS)
BSFF: Buffer Stock Financing Facility
BSH: Bush Industries Inc. (ASE)
BSIA: British Security Industry Association (UK)
BSIM: Burnup & Sims Inc. (NAS NMS)
BS/L: Bills of Lading
BSL: Barber Steamship Lines
Bermuda Star Lines Inc. (ASE)
Bills of Lading
Black Star Line (steamship)

Blue Sea Line (steamship)
Blue Star Line (steamship)
Bull Steamship Lines
BSN: BSN Corp. (ASE) (newspaper)
BSP: Bills Payable
Bt: bought
BT: Bankers Trust New York Corp. (NYSE)
B of T: Board of Trade
BTC: Baltimore Transit Company
Bankers Trust Company
Bethlehem Transportation Corporation (steamship)
BTCI: Brown Transport Company Inc. (NAS NMS)
BTEC: BancTec Inc. (NAS NMS)
BTEK: Baltek Corp. (NAS NMS)
BTFC: BT Financial Corp. (NAS NMS)
BTG: Beating The Gun
BTHL: Bethel Bancorp (Maine) (NAS NMS)
BTI: B.A.T. Industries PLC (ASE)
BTL: Bell Telephone Laboratories
BTLR: Butler Manufacturing Co. (NAS NMS)
BTM: Bulling The Market
BTN: Belton (railroad)
BTRI: BTR Realty Inc. (NAS NMS)
BTRL: Biotech Research Laboratories Inc. (NAS NMS)
BTSB: Braintree Savings Bank, The (Massachusetts) (NAS NMS)
BTU: Pyro Energy Corp. (NYSE)
BTX: BancTEXAS Group Inc. (NYSE)
BTY: British Telecommunications PLC (NYSE)
BU: Brooklyn Union Gas Co., The (NYSE)
BUC: Buffalo, Union-Carolina (railroad)
Buckeye: Buckeye Partners LP (newspaper)
bud: budget

BUD: Anheuser-Busch Companies Inc. (NYSE)
BUE: Buell Industries Inc. (ASE)
Buell: Buell Industries Inc. (newspaper)
Buffton: Buffton Corp. (newspaper)
BUGS: Cooper Development Co. (NAS NMS)
BULL: Bull Run Gold Mines Ltd. (NAS NMS)
BULR: Buehler International Inc. (NAS NMS)
Bundy: Bundy Corp. (newspaper)
BunkrH: Bunker Hill Income Securities Inc. (newspaper)
bur: bureau
BurnAM: Burnham American Properties Inc. (newspaper)
BurnPP: Burnham Pacific Properties Inc. (newspaper)
bus: business
Bush: Bush Industries Inc. (newspaper)
BUSH: Bush Terminal (railroad)
Businld: Businessland Inc. (newspaper)
BUTI: BeutiControl Cosmetics Inc. (NAS NMS)
BUTL: Butler National Corp. (NAS NMS)
BV: BEA Helicopters (airline)
Book Value
BVFS: Bay View Federal S&L Assn. (California) (NAS NMS)
BVI: Bow Valley Industries Ltd. (ASE)
bvr: clearinghouse (banking)
BVS: Bevier & Southern (railroad)
BW: Bendix-Westinghouse
Bid Wanted
Borg-Warner
Brush Wellman Inc. (NYSE)
B&W: Babcock and Wilcox

BWC: Pennsylvania New York Central Transportation Company

BWIN: Baldwin & Lyons Inc. (NAS NMS)

BWL: Bowl America Inc. (ASE)

BwnSh: Brown & Sharpe Manufacturing Co. (newspaper)

BWTF: Bank Wire Transfer of Funds

BX: Bellingham-Seattle (airline)

BY: Budget Year

bypro(s): by-product(s)

BYTE: Compucom Systems Inc. (NAS NMS)

BZ: Bairnco Corp. (NYSE)

BZF: Brazil Fund Inc. (NYSE)

C

c: canceled
carat
cash (stock exchange)
cent
centavo (currency in numerous
 Spanish nations)
centime (currency in France)
chairman
chairperson
chairwoman
collateral
compte (account) (French)
conto (account) (Italian)
controller
cost
coupon
cours (quotation) (price) (French)
currency
C: Chrysler Corp. (NYSE)
Currency component of money
A liquidating dividend in stock
 listings of newspapers
The lowest quality rating for a
 municipal or corporate bond
 (Moody's bond rating)
C 3 Inc.: C3 Inc. (newspaper)
C&A: Classification and Audit
ca: callable (in bond tables and offering sheets)
compagnia (company) (Italian)
compañia (company) (Spanish)
Ca: Speculative-Often in Default
 (Moody's bond rating)
CA: Capital Account
Capital Appreciation
Capital Assets
Carregadores Acoreanos
 (Portuguese-Azorean Cargo
 Carriers)
Cash Account

Chartered Accountant (UK)
Cheque Account (UK)
Chief Accountant
Commercial Agent
Compañia Anónima (Joint
 Stock Company) (Spanish)
Computer Associates Interna-
 tional Inc. (NYSE)
Cost Account
Coupons Attached
Credit Account
Current Account
Current Assets
Custodian Account
Caa: Poor standing (Moody's bond
 rating)
CAA: Central African Airways Cor-
 poration
CAB: CasaBlanca Industries Inc.
 (ASE)
CABA: Charge Account Bankers
 Association
CABEI: Central American Bank for
 Economic Integration
CABK: Colonial American Bank-
 shares Corp. (NAS NMS)
Cablvsn: Cablevision Systems
 Corp. (newspaper)
 Agencies
CAC: CoastAmerica Corp.
 (NYSE)
Cost Account Code
Currency Adjustment Charge
CACC: Colonial Life & Accident
 Insurance Co. (NAS
 NMS)
CACH: Cache Inc. (NAS NMS)
CACHA: Calwestern Automated
 Clearing House Associa-
 tion

CACI: CACI Inc. (NAS NMS)
Chicago Association of Commerce and Industry
CACO: Cato Corp. (NAS NMS)
CAD: Cadiz Railroad
Cash Against Disbursements
Cash Against Documents
CADBY: Cadbury Schweppes PLC (NAS NSM)
CADE: Cade Industries Inc. (NAS NMS)
CADV: Cash Advance
CADX: Cadnetiz Corp. (NAS NMS)
Caesar: Caesars World Inc. (newspaper)
CaesNJ: Caesars New Jersey Inc. (newspaper)
CAF: Cost Adjustment Factor
Cost And Freight
Cost, Assurance, and Freight
Currency Adjustment Factor
Furr's/Bishop's Cafeterias LP (NYSE)
CAFS: Cardinal Federal Savings Bank (Kentucky) (NAS NMS)
CAG: ConAgra Inc. (NYSE)
cage: courtage (brokerage) (French)
CAGE: California Almond Growers Exchange
CagleA: Cagle's Inc. (newspaper)
CAIC: Canadian Association of Investment Clubs
CAII: Capital Associates Inc. (NAS NMS)
CAKE: Charlotte Charles Inc. (NAS NMS)
CAL: CalFed Inc. (NYSE)
China Air Lines
Continental Air Lines
CalEgy: California Energy Co. (newspaper)
CalFed: CalFed Inc. (newspaper)
CalFIP: Cal Fed Income Partners LP (newspaper)

CALI: Calumet Industries Inc. (NAS NMS)
CalJky: California Jockey Club (newspaper)
Callhn: Callahan Mining Corp. (newspaper)
Calmat: CalMat Co. (newspaper)
Calprop: Calprop Cor. (newspaper)
CalRE: California Real Estate Investment Trust (newspaper)
Calton: Calton Inc. (newspaper)
CAMBY: Cambridge Instrument Company, The PLC (NAS NMS)
CAMD: California Micro Devices Corp. (NAS NMS)
CAME: Carme Inc. (NAS NMS)
CAMP: California Amplifier Inc. (NAS NMS)
CAMPS: Cumulative Auction-Market Preferred Stock
CamSp: Campbell Soup Co. (newspaper)
can: cancel
CAN: Cannon Group Inc., The (NYSE)
Cost Account Number
canc: cancel
cancl: canceling
CANNY: Canon Inc. (NAS NMS)
CANO: Canonie Environmental Services Corp. (NAS NMS)
CanonG: Cannon Group Inc., The (newspaper)
CAO: Carolina Freight Corp. (NYSE)
Chief Administrative Officer
cap: capital
capitalization
CAP: Camas Prairie (railroad)
Capital Housing & Mortgage Partners (ASE)
Cost Analysis Plan
CAPB: Capital Bancorporation (NAS NMS)

CapCits: Capital Cities/ABC Inc. (newspaper)
CAPG: Capital Goods
CapHld: Capital Holding Corp. (newspaper)
CapHo: Capital Housing & Mortgage Partners (newspaper)
CAPM: Capital Asset Pricing Model
CAPSR: Cost Account Performance Status Report
CAR: Capital Authorization Request
Carter-Wallace Inc. (NYSE)
Central Australia Railway
CARD: Certificate for Amortizing Revolving Debts
Cardis: Cardis Corp. (newspaper)
CareE: Care Enterprises Inc. (ASE)
CareerC: CareerCom Corp. (newspaper)
CargInd: Carriage Industries Inc. (newspaper)
CARIBANK: Caribbean Development Bank
CARISMA: Computer-Aided Research into Stock Market Applications
CARL: Carl Karcher Enterprises Inc. (NAS NMS)
Carlisle: Carlisle Companies Inc. (newspaper)
Carmel: Carmel Container Systems Ltd. (newspaper)
CARN: Carrington Laboratories Inc. (NAS NMS)
CarnCr: Carnival Cruise Lines Inc. (newspaper)
CaroFt: Carolina Freight Corp. (newspaper)
CarolP: Carolco Pictures Inc. (newspaper)
CarPw: Carolina Power & Light Co. (newspaper)
CARR: Carrollton Railroad
CartBc: Carteret Bancorp Inc. (newspaper)

CarTec: Carpenter Technology Corp. (newspaper)
CartH: Carter Hawley Hale Stores Inc. (newspaper)
CartWl: Carter-Wallace Inc. (newspaper)
CARW: Carolina Western (railroad)
cas: cashier
CAS: A.M. Castle & Co. (ASE)
Cost Accounting Standards
CASB: Cost Accounting Standards Board
Casblan: CasaBlanca Industries (newspaper)
CASC: Cascade Corp. (NAS NMS)
CascNG: Cascade Natural Gas Corp. (newspaper)
CasFd: Castle Convertible Fund Inc. (newspaper)
cash: cashier
CASH: Cash Trade (NYSE)
cashr: cashier
CASO: Canada Southern (railway)
Caspn: Caspen Oil Inc. (newspaper)
CastlA: A.M. Castle & Co. (newspaper)
CastlCk: Castle & Cooke Inc. (newspaper)
CASY: Casey's General Stores Inc. (NAS NMS)
CAT: Caterpillar Inc. (NYSE)
CATA: Capitol Transamerica Corp. (NAS NMS)
CataLt: Catalina Lighting Inc. (newspaper)
Caterp: Caterpillar Inc. (newspaper)
CATS: Certificate of Accrual on Treasury Securities
CATV: Cable TV Industries (NAS NMS)
Catylst: Catalyst Energy Corp. (newspaper)
CAUT: Computer Automation Inc. (NAS NMS)
CavalH: Cavalier Homes Inc. (newspaper)

CAVN: Compania Anonima Venezo-
lana de Navegacion (Ven-
ezuelan Navigation Com-
pany) (steamship)
CAVR: Carver Corp. (NAS NMS)
CAW: Caesars World Inc. (NYSE)
CAYB: Cayuga Savings Bank (New
York) (NAS NMS)
C of B: Confirmation of Balance
CB: Callable Bond
Caribair (airline)
Carte Blanche
Cash Book
Chubb Corp., The (NYSE)
Confidential Bulletin
Corporate Bonds
Coupon Bond
Currency Bond
CBA: Cost-Benefit Analysis
CBAM: Cambrex Corp. (NAS NMS)
CBC: Carbon County (railway)
Carteret Bancorp Inc. (NYSE)
CBCF: Citizens Banking Corp.
(Michigan) (NAS NMS)
CBCT: Cenvest Inc. (NAS NMS)
CBCX: Cambridge BioScience Corp.
(NAS NMS)
CBD: Cash Before Delivery
Central Business District
Certificate of Bank Deposit
Commerce Business Daily
CBE: Cooper Industries Inc.
(NYSE)
CBH: CBI Industries Inc. (NYSE)
CBI: Curtice-Burns Foods Inc.
(ASE)
CBI In: CBI Industries Inc. (newspa-
per)
CBIO: California Biotechnology Inc.
(NAS NMS)
cbk: checkbook
CBKS: Commonwealth Bancshares
Corp. (NAS NMS)
CB/L: Commercial Bill of Lading
CBL: Conemaugh and Black Lick
(railroad)

Corroon & Black Corp.
(NYSE)
CBM: Central Bank Money
Lifecore Biomedical Inc.
(NAS NMS)
CBNEV: Constitution Bancorp of
New England Inc. (NAS
NMS)
CBNH: Community Bankshares
Inc. (New Hampshire)
(NAS NMS)
CBO: Cancel Back Order
Certificate of Beneficial Own-
ership
CBOC: Commercial Bancorp. of
Colorado (NAS NMS)
CBOE: Chicago Board Options Ex-
change
CBOT: Cabot Medical Corp. (NAS
NMS)
CBQ: Chicago, Burlington &
Quincy (railroad)
CBR: Crystal Brands Inc. (NYSE)
CBRL: Cracker Barrel Old Country
Store Inc. (NAS NMS)
CBRY: Northland Cranberries Inc.
(NAS NMS)
CBS: CBS Inc. (NYSE) (newspaper)
Columbia Broadcasting Sys-
tem
Consolidated Balance Sheet
CBSH: Commerce Bancshares Inc.
(Missouri) (NAS NMS)
CBSI: Community Bank System
Inc. (New York) (NAS
NMS)
CBSS: Central Bancshares of the
South Inc. (NAS NMS)
CBT: Cabot Corp. (NYSE)
Chicago Board of Trade
Connecticut Bank and Trust
Company
CBTB: CB & T Bancshares Inc.
(NAS NMS)
CBTF: CB & T Financial Corp.
(NAS NMS)

CBU: Chicago Board of Underwriters
Commodore International Ltd. (NYSE)

CBWA: Central Bancorporation (Washington) (NAS NMS)

C&C: Canton & Carthage (railroad)
Cash and Carry

CC: Aerocosta (airline)
Cancellation Clause
Cancelled Check
Cash Commodity
Cashier's Check
Certified Check
Chamber of Commerce
Chrysler Corporation
Circuit City Stores Inc. (NYSE)
Cumberland Railway and Coal

CCA: Capital Consumption Adjustment (Allowance)
Capital Cost Allowance
Cosmopolitan Care Corp. (ASE)
Current Cost Accounts (London Stock Exchange) (UK)
Customer Cost Analysis

CCAB: Communications & Cable Inc. (NAS NMS)

CCAL: Christensen Canadian African Line (steamship)

CCAM: CCA Industries Inc. (NAS NMS)

CCAX: Corrections Corporation of America (NAS NMS)

CCB: Capital Cities/ABC Inc. (NYSE)

CCBF: CCB Financial Corp. (NAS NMS)

CCBL: C-COR Electronics Inc. (NAS NMS)

CCBT: Cape Cod Bank & Trust Co. (NAS NMS)

CC&C: Cowlitz, Chehalis & Cascade (railroad)

CCC: Commercial Credit Corporation (NYSE)
Commodity Credit Corporation
A quality rating for a municipal or corporate bond

CCCI: 3 CI Inc. (NAS NMS)

CC CO: Commercial Cable Company

CCCS: Consumer Credit Counseling Services

CCCSL: Cleveland, Cincinnati, Chicago & St.Louis (railway)

CCE: Coca-Cola Enterprises Inc. (NYSE)

CCEI: Composite Cost Effectiveness Index

CCEM: CompuChem Corp. (NAS NMS)

CCH: Campbell Resources Inc. (NYSE)
Commercial Clearinghouse

CCI: Citicorp (NYSE)

CCIMF: City Resources Ltd. (NAS NMS)

CCL: Carnival Cruise Lines Inc. (ASE)
Carolina, Clinchfield and Ohio (railway)

CCLR: Commerce Clearing House Inc. (NAS NMS)

CCM: Claremont Capital Corp. (ASE)

CCMC: Commonwealth Mortgage Company Inc. (Massachusetts) (NAS NMS)

CCMS: Commodity Configuration Management System

CCN: Chris-Craft Industries Inc. (NYSE)
Companhia Colonial de Navegacao (Portuguese-Colonial Navigation Company) (steamship)

CCNC: CCNB Corp. (NAS NMS)

CC&O: Carolina, Clinchfield and Ohio (railway)

CCOA: COMCOA Inc. (NAS NMS)

CCON: Circon Corp. (NAS NMS)

CC&ORSC: Carolina, Clinchfield and Ohio Railroad of South Carolina

CCP: Corcap Inc. (ASE)
Credit Card Purchase

CCPA: Consumer Credit Protection Act

CCPT: Concept Inc. (NAS NMS)

CCR: Corinth and Counce Railroad

CCS: Computer Consoles Inc. (ASE)

CCSB: Credit Card Service Bureau

CCT: Central California Traction (railroad)

CCTC: Computer & Communications Technology Corp. (NAS NMS)

CCTVY: Carlton Communications PLC (NAS NMS)

CCU: Clear Channel Communications Inc. (ASE)

CCUR: Concurrent Computer Corp. (NAS NMS)

CCX: CCX Inc. (NYSE) (newspaper)

CCXL: Contel Cellular Inc. (NAS NMS)

C&D: Collection and Delivery

CD: Canadian Dollar (currency of Canada)
Cardinal Airlines
Carried Down
Cash Discount
Certificate of Deposit
Closing Date
Cum Dividend

CDA: Control Data Corp. (NYSE)

CDC: CompuDyne Corp. (ASE)

CDCR: Children's Discovery Center of America Inc. (NAS NMS)

CDE: Coeur d'Alene Mines Corp. (ASE)

CDG: Canandaigua Wine Company Inc. (ASE)

CDGI: Courier Dispatch Group Inc. (NAS NMS)

CDI: CDI Corp. (ASE) (newspaper)

CDIC: Cardinal Distribution Inc. (NAS NMS)

CDIV: Cum Dividend (With Dividend)

CDJI: Dow Jones Index - Commodity

CDL: Citadel Holding Corp. (ASE)

CDM: Cash Dispensing Machine

CDMS: Cadmus Communications Corp. (NAS NMS)

CDNC: Cadence Design Systems Inc. (NAS NMS)

CdnOc: Canadian Occidental Petroleum Ltd. (newspaper)

CdnPac: Canadian Pacific Ltd. (newspaper)

CDO: Comdisco Inc. (NYSE)

CDR: Continental Depositary Receipt

CDS: Canadian Depository for Securities
Cardis Corp. (ASE)
Certificate of Deposit

CDT: Central Daylight Time

CDV: Chambers Development Company Inc. (ASE)

C&E: Commission and Exchange

CE: Capital Expenditure
Cash Earnings
Catalyst Energy Corp. (NYSE)
Caveat Emptor (Let The Buyer Beware)
Certainty Equivalent Coefficient
Chief Executive
Commodity Exchange
Common Era
Cost Effectiveness

CEA: Commodity Exchange Authority
Cost Effectiveness Analysis
Council of Economic Advisors

CEBK: Central Cooperative Bank (Massachusetts) (NAS NMS)

CEC: Cetec Corp. (ASE)
Commodities Exchange Center
Commodity Exchange Commission
Commonwealth Edison Company
Consolidated Edison Company

CECX: Castle Energy Corp. (NAS NMS)

CEDE: Certificate Depository (NYSE)

CedrF: Cedar Fair LP (newspaper)

CEE: C3 Inc. (NYSE)

CEF: Central Fund of Canada Ltd. (ASE)
Closed-End Fund

CEFCO: Cooperative Export Financing Corporation

CEFT: Concor Computing Corp. (NAS NMS)

C&EI: Chicago and Eastern Illinois (railroad)

CEI: Chicago and Eastern Illinois (railroad)
Contract End Item
Cost Effectiveness Index

CEIC: Closed-End Investment Company

CELG: Celgene Corp. (NAS NMS)

CELI: Cel-Sci Corp. (NAS NMS)

CeMPw: Central Maine Power Co. (newspaper)

CEMX: CEM Corp. (NAS NMS)

CenHud: Central Hudson Gas & Electric Corp. (newspaper)

CenSoW: Central & South West Corp. (newspaper)

cent: centavo (currency of Portugal)
centime (currency of France)
centimo (currency of Portugal)
currency of U.S.

CENT: Centuri Inc. (NAS NMS)

Centel: Centel Corp. (newspaper)

CentEn: Centerior Energy Corp. (newspaper)

Centex: Centex Corp. (newspaper)

CentGp: Centennial Group Inc., The (newspaper)

CentrCP: Centronics Data Computer Corp. (newspaper)

Centrst: CenTrust Savings Bank (newspaper)

CentSe: Central Securities Corp. (newspaper)

CenvD: Cenvill Development Corp. (newspaper)

Cenvill: Cenvill Investors Inc. (newspaper)

CEO: Chief Executive Officer

CEP: ConVest Energy Partners Ltd. (ASE)

CEPI: Capital Expenditure Price Index

CEQ: Centennial Group Inc., The (ASE)

CER: CILCORP Inc. (NYSE)
Cost Estimated (Estimating) Report

CERB: CERBCO Inc. (NAS NMS)

CERN: Cerner Corp. (NAS NMS)

cert: certificate
certification
certify

CES: Commonwealth Energy System (NYSE)

CESC: Computer Entry Systems Corp. (NAS NMS)

CET: Central Securities Corp. (ASE)

Cetec: Cetec Corp. (newspaper)

CETH: Catalyst Thermal Energy Corp. (NAS NMS)

CEXX: Circle Express Inc. (NAS NMS)

C&F: Cost and Freight

cf: certificates (in bond listings of newspapers)

CF: Carried Forward
Cash Flow

Collins Foods International Inc.
(NYSE)
Common Fund
Cost and Freight
CFA: Cash Flow Accounting
Chartered Financial Analyst
Component Flow Analysis
Computer Factory, The
(NYSE)
CFB: Citizens First Bancorp
(ASE)
CFBI: Cullen/Frost Bankers Inc.
(NAS NMS)
CFBK: California First Bank (NAS
NMS)
CFBS: Central Fidelity Banks Inc.
(NAS NMS)
CFC: Chartered Financial Consult-
ant
Chrysler Financial Corpora-
tion
Commercial Finance Com-
pany
Consolidated Freight Classifi-
cation
Controlled Foreign Company
CFCda: Central Fund of Canada
Ltd. (newspaper)
CFCN: Commercial Federal Corp.
(NAS NMS)
CFD: Corporate Finance Director
CFED: Charter Federal Savings
Bank (NAS NMS)
CFG: Copelco Financial Services
Group Inc. (ASE)
CFHC: California Financial Hold-
ing Co. (NAS NMS)
CFI: Cal Fed Income Partners LP
(NYSE)
Cost, Freight, and Insurance
CFIB: Consolidated Fibres Inc.
(NAS NMS)
CFIN: Consumers Financial Corp.
(NAS NMS)
CFIP: CF & I Steel Corp. (NAS
NMS)

CFIUS: Committee on Foreign In-
vestment in the United
States
CFIX: Chemfix Technologies Inc.
(NAS NMS)
CFK: Comfed Bancorp Inc. (ASE)
CFMI: Convenient Food Mart Inc.
(NAS NMS)
CFNE: Circle Fine Art Corp. (NAS
NMS)
CFNH: Cheshire Financial Corp.
(NAS NMS)
CFO: Cancel Form Order
Chief Financial Officer
CFP: Certified Financial Planner
CFQ: Quaker Fabric Corp. (ASE)
CFR: Code of Federal Regulations
CFSC: CFS Financial Corp. (NAS
NMS)
CFSF: Coast Federal S&L Assn.
(Florida) (NAS NMS)
CFTC: Commodity Futures Trading
Commission
C&G: Columbus & Greenville (rail-
road)
CG: Capital Gain
Capital Goods
Central of Georgia (railway)
Columbia Gas System Inc., The
(NYSE)
CGAS: Clinton Gas Systems Inc.
(NAS NMS)
CGBR: Central Government Bor-
rowing Requirement
CGC: Cascade Natural Gas Corp.
(NYSE)
CG&E: Cincinnati Gas and Electric
Company
CGE: Carriage Industries Inc.
(NYSE)
Chicago and Eastern Illinois
(railroad)
CGEL&PB: Consolidated Gas, Elec-
tric Light and Power
Company of Baltimore
CGEN: Collagen Corp. (NAS NMS)

CGES: Colonial Gas Co. (NAS NMS)

CGIC: Continental General Insurance Co. (NAS NMS)

CGL: Cagle's Inc. (ASE)

CGN: Cognitronics Corp. (ASE)

CGNE: Calgene Inc. (NAS NMS)

CGO: Chase Medical Group Inc. (ASE)
Contango (London Stock Exchange) (UK)

CGP: Coastal Corp., The (NYSE)

CGPS: Stamford Capital Group Inc. (NAS NMS)

CGR: Chariot Group Inc., The (ASE)

CGS: Consolidated Oil & Gas Inc. (ASE)

CGT: Capital Gains Tax

CGW: Chicago Great Western (railroad)

ch: clearinghouse

C&H: Cheswick and Harmer (railroad)

CH: Champion Products Inc. (ASE)
Chicago Helicopter Airways
Clearing House

chair: chairperson (chairman) (chairwoman)

ChampSp: Champion Spark Plug Co. (newspaper)

CHANF: Chandler Insurance Ltd. (NAS NMS)

CHAP: Champion International Corp. (NYSE)

CHAPS: Clearing House Automated Payments System (London) (UK)

CHAR: Chaparral Resources Inc. (NAS NMS)

Chariot: Chariot Group Inc., The (newspaper)

CHARM: Checking, Accounting and Reporting for Member firms (London Stock Exchange) (UK)

ChartC: Charter Co., The (newspaper)

Chase: Chase Manhattan Corp., The (newspaper)

Chaus: Bernard Chaus Inc. (newspaper)

CHB: Champion Enterprises Inc. (ASE)

CHCO: City Holding Co. (NAS NMS)

CHCR: Chancellor Corp. (NAS NMS)

CHD: Chelsea Industries Inc. (NYSE)

ChDev: Chambers Development Company Inc. (newspaper)

CHE: Chemed Corp. (NYSE)

CHEK: Checkpoint Systems Inc. (NAS NMS)

Chelsea: Chelsea Industries Inc. (newspaper)

Chemed: Chemed Corp. (newspaper)

CHEPSOP: Charitable/Employee Stock Ownership Plan

CHER: Cherry Corp., The (NAS NMS)

Chevrn: Chevron Corp. (newspaper)

CHEY: Cheyenne Software Inc. (NAS NMS)

CHF: Chock Full O'Nuts Corp. (NYSE)

CHFC: Chemical Financial Corp. (NAS NMS)

CHFD: Charter Federal S&L Assn. (Virginia) (NAS NMS)

ChfDv: Chieftain Development Company Ltd. (newspaper)

chg: charge

CHG: Chicago Milwaukee Corp. (NYSE)

CHH: Carter Hawley Hale Stores Inc. (NYSE)

CHHC: C. H. Heist Corp. (NAS NMS)

CHIK: Golden Poultry Company Inc. (NAS NMS)

ChiMlw: Chicago Milwaukee Corp. (newspaper)

CHIPS: Clearing House Interbank Payments Systems (New York)

CHIR: Chiron Corp. (NAS NMS)

ChiRv: Chicago Rivet & Machine Co. (newspaper)

chk: check

CHKE: Cherokee Group, The (NAS NMS)

ChkFull: Chock Full O'Nuts Corp. (newspaper)

CHL: Chemical Banking Corp. (NYSE)

CHLI: Chili's Inc. (NAS NMS)

CHLN: Chalone Inc. (NAS NMS)

chman: chairman

ChmBk: Chemical Banking Corp. (newspaper)

chmn: chairman

ChmpEn: Champion Enterprises Inc. (newspaper)

Chmpln: Champion International Corp. (newspaper)

ChmpPd: Champion Products Inc. (newspaper)

CHMX: Chemex Pharmaceuticals Inc. (NAS NMS)

CHOL: Central Holding Co. (NAS NMS)

CHP: Charter Power Systems Inc. (ASE)

CHPK: Chesapeake Utilities Corp. (NAS NMS)

CHPN: Chapman Energy Inc. (NAS NMS)

CHPS: Chips & Technologies Inc. (NAS NMS)

ChpStl: Chaparral Steel Co. (newspaper)

CHQ: Central Headquarters

CHR: Charter Co., The (NYSE) Chestnut Ridge Railway

ChrisCr: Chris-Craft Industries Inc. (newspaper)

Christn: Christiana Companies Inc., The (newspaper)

CHRS: Charming Shoppes Inc. (NAS NMS)

CHRYS: Chrysler

Chryslr: Chrysler Corp. (newspaper)

CHRZ: Computer Horizons Corp. (NAS NMS)

CHS: Bernard Chaus Inc. (NYSE)

ChsMed: Chase Medical Group Inc. (newspaper)

Chspk: Chesapeake Corp. (newspaper)

CHT: Collection, Holding, and Transfer

CHTB: Cohasset Savings Bank (Massachusetts) (NAS NMS)

ChtMd: Charter Medical Corp. (newspaper)

ChtPwr: Charter Power Systems Inc. (newspaper)

CHTT: Chattem Inc. (NAS NMS) Chicago Heights Terminal Transfer (railroad)

Chubb: Chubb Corp., The (newspaper)

CHV: Chattahoochee Valley (railroad) Chevron Corp. (NYSE)

CHW: Chemical Waste Management Inc. (NYSE) Chesapeake Western (railroad)

ChWst: Chemical Waste Management Inc. (newspaper)

CHX: Pilgrim's Price Corp. (NYSE)

CHY: Chyron Corp. (NYSE)

Chyron: Chyron Corp. (newspaper)

CHZC: Stendig Industries Inc. (NAS NMS)

C&I: Cambria and Indiana (railroad)

CI: Capital Intensive Cash Items

Catalina Island Steamship Line

Certificat d'Investissement (French)

Certificate of Indebtedness

Christmas Island Phosphate Commission

CIGNA Corp. (NYSE)

Compounded Interest

Cost and Insurance

C/I: Certificate of Insurance

Cia: Compagnia (Italian Company)

Companhia (Portuguese Company)

Compañia (Spanish Company)

CIA: Cash In Advance

Certified Internal Auditor

CIC: Cedar Rapids and Iowa City (railway)

Continental Corp., The (NYSE)

CICT: Commission on International Commodity Trade

CID: Chieftain Development Company Ltd. (ASE)

Compound Interest Deposit

CIDN: Computer Identics Corp. (NAS NMS)

CIDs: Civil Investigative Demands

Cie: Compagnie (French company)

CIF: Colonial Intermediate High Income Fund (NYSE)

Corporate Income Fund

Cost, Insurance, and Freight

CIF & C: Cost, Insurance, Freight and Commissions (Charges)

CIFCI: Cost, Insurance, Freight (plus) Commission and Interest

CIFR: Cipher Data Products Inc. (NAS NMS)

CIG: Continental Graphics Corp. (ASE)

CIGNA: CIGNA Corp. (newspaper)

CIGP: Capital Investment Goal Programming

CIH: Continental Illinois Holding Corp. (NYSE)

CII: Collective Investment Institution

CRI Insured Mortgage Investments II Inc. (NYSE)

CI&L: Chicago, Indianapolis & Louisville (railroad)

CIL: Continental Illinois Corp. (NYSE)

Cilcorp: CILCORP Inc. (newspaper)

C&IM: Chicago & Illinois Midland (railroad)

CIM: Capital Investment Model

CIM High Yield Securities (ASE) (newspaper)

CIMC: CIMCO Inc. (NAS NMS)

CIN: Cincinnati Gas & Electric Co., The (NYSE)

CinBel: Cincinnati Bell Inc. (newspaper)

CIND: Central Indiana (railway)

CineOd: Cineplex Odeon Corp. (newspaper)

CINF: Cincinnati Financial Corp. (NAS NMS)

CinGE: Cincinnati Gas & Electric Co., The (newspaper)

CinMil: Cincinnati Milacron Inc. (newspaper)

CINN: Citizens Insurance Company of America (Texas) (NAS NMS)

CIO: Chief Information Officer

Community Investment Officer

CIP: Capital Investment Program

Central Illinois Public Service Co. (NYSE)

CIR: Circus Circuit Enterprises Inc. (NYSE)

Cost Information Report

CircleK: Circle K Corp., The (newspaper)

CirCty: Circuit City Stores Inc. (newspaper)

Circus: Circus Circus Enterprises Inc. (newspaper)

C&IRR: Cambria and Indiana Railroad

CIRR: Chattahoochee Industrial Railroad

CIS: Concord Fabrics Inc. (ASE)

CISA: Citizens Savings Bank FSB (New York) (NAS NMS)

Citadel: Citadel Holding Corp. (newspaper)

CITI: Citipostal Inc. (NAS NMS)

Citicrp: Citicorp (newspaper)

CITIES SERVICE: Cities Service Oil Company

CITN: Citizens Financial Group Inc. (NAS NMS)

CITU: Citizens Utilities Co. (NAS NMS)

CityBcp: Citytrust Bancorp (newspaper)

CitzFst: Citizens First Bancorp (newspaper)

CIV: Columbia Real Estate Investments Inc. (ASE)

CIW: Chicago and Illinois Western (railroad)

CJ: California Jocket Club (ASE)

CJER: Central Jersey Bancorp. (NAS NMS)

CJN: Caesars New Jersey Inc. (ASE)

CJSB: Central Jersey Savings Bank SLA (NAS NMS)

ck: check

CKC: Conchemco Inc. (ASE)

CKCP: CYBERTEK Corp. (NAS NMS)

CKDN: Circadian Inc. (NAS NMS)

CKE: Castle & Cooke Inc. (NYSE)

CKL: Clark Equipment Co. (NYSE)

CKP: Circle K Corp., The (NYSE)

CKR: Check Received

CKSB: CK Federal Savings Bank (North Carolina) (NAS NMS)

CKSO: Condon, Kinzua and Southern (railroad)

CKT: Continental Circuits Corp. (ASE)

cl: clause

CL: Called (NYSE)
Call Loan
Capital Loss
Cash Letter
Ceylon Lines (steamship)
Coast Lines (steamship)
Colgate-Palmolive Co. (NYSE)
Collection Entry
Combined Limit
Contract Law
Conversion Loss
Credit Limit
Current Liabilities

Clabir: Clabir Corp. (newspaper)

ClairSt: Claire's Stores Inc. (newspaper)

ClarkC: Clark Consolidated Industries Inc. (newspaper)

ClarkE: Clark Equipment Co. (newspaper)

Clarmt: Claremont Capital Corp. (newspaper)

CLAUDIUS: Coopers & Lybrand Accounting and Distributive Inventory System

ClayHm: Clayton Homes Inc. (newspaper)

CLBG: Colonial BancGroup Inc. (NAS NMS)

CLC: CLC of America Inc. (NYSE) (newspaper)
Columbia and Cowlitz (railroad)
Cost of Living Council

CLCB: Committee of London Clearing Bankers (UK)

CLCO: Claremont and Concord Railroad

cld: called (in stock listings of newspapers)

cancelled
cleared

CLD: Computerland Corp. (NYSE)

CLDA: Clinical Data Inc. (NAS NMS)

CLDRV: Cliffs Drilling Co. (NAS NMS)

CLE: Claire's Stores Inc. (NYSE)

CLEA: Chemical Leaman Corp. (NAS NMS)

ClearCh: Clear Channel Communications Inc. (newspaper)

CLF: Cleveland-Cliffs Inc. (NYSE)

CLFI: Country Lake Foods Inc. (NAS NMS)

CLG: Clabir Corp. (NYSE)

CLHB: Clean Harbors Inc. (NAS NMS)

CLI: Cost-of-Living Index

CLIC: Clairson International Corp. (NAS NMS)

CLIPPER LINE: Wisconsin and Michigan Steamship Company

CLIX: Compression Labs Inc. (NAS NMS)

CLK: Cadillac and Lake City (railway)
Clark Consolidated Industries Inc. (ASE)

CLM: Clemente Global Growth Fund Inc. (NYSE)

ClmGlb: Clemente Global Growth Fund Inc. (newspaper)

CLO: At The Close
Coleco Industries Inc. (NYSE)

CLOB: Composite Limit Order Book

CLOC: Clean Letter Of Credit

CLODA: Closing Date

Clorox: Clorox Co., The (newspaper)

CLP: Clarendon and Pittsford (railroad)

clr: clear

CLR: Color Systems Technology Inc. (ASE)

CLRI: Computer Language Research Inc. (NAS NMS)

CLRK: Clarcor Inc. (NAS NMS)

CLRR: Camp Lejeune Railroad

CLS: Commercial Loan System

CLSC: Clinical Sciences Inc. (NAS NMS)

clt: client

CLT: Collateral Trust (bond)
Cominco Ltd. (ASE)

CLU: Chartered Life Underwriter

ClubMd: Club Med Inc. (newspaper)

CLV: Ceiling Limit Value

ClvClf: Cleveland-Cliffs Inc. (newspaper)

CLX: Clorox Co., The (NYSE)

CM: Call Money
Call of More
Cheap Money
Compania Maritima (Spanish-Maritime Company)
COPA (Compania Panamena de Aviacion-Panamanian Aviation Company)

CMA: Cash Management Account
Commercial Market Appraisal
Compania Mexicana de Aviacion

CMarc: Canadian Marconi Co. (newspaper)

CMB: Chase Manhattan Corp., The (NYSE)
Compagnie Maritime Belge (French-Belgian Maritime Company) (Royal Belgian Lloyd Steamship)

CMBK: Cumberland Federal Savings Bank, The (Kentucky) (NAS NMS)

CMBS: Conventional Mortgage-Backed Security

CMC: Commercial Metals Co. (NYSE)

CMCA: Comerica Inc. (NAS NMS)
CmcCrd: Commercial Credit Co.
(newspaper)
CmceT: Commerce Total Return
Fund Inc. (newspaper)
CMCL: ChemClear Inc. (NAS NMS)
CMCO: CVN Companies Inc. (NAS
NMS)
CMCS: Comcast Corp. (NAS NMS)
CMD: Charter Medical Corp. (ASE)
CMDL: Comdial Corp. (NAS NMS)
cmdty.: commodity
CME: Chicago Mercantile Ex-
change
CMFB: Chemical Fabrics Corp.
(NAS NMS)
CmFct: Computer Factory Inc., The
(newspaper)
CMH: Clayton Homes Inc. (NYSE)
CMI: Cash Management Institute
Club Med Inc. (NYSE)
CMIC: California Microwave Inc.
(NAS NMS)
CMI Cp: CMI Corp. (newspaper)
CMIK: Carmike Cinemas Inc. (NAS
NMS)
CMIN: Computer Memories Inc.
(NAS NMS)
cml: commercial
CML: CML Group Inc. (NYSE)
(newspaper)
CMLE: Casual Male Corp., The
(NAS NMS)
cmm: commission
CMMP: Commodity Management
Master Plan
Convertible Money Market
Preferred Stock
CmMtl: Commercial Metals Co.
(newspaper)
cmn: commission
CMN: Callahan Mining Corp.
(NYSE)
CMO: CareerCom Corp. (NYSE)
Chicago, St.Paul, Minneapo-
lis and Omaha (railroad)

Collaterized Mortgage Obli-
gation
CMP: Comprehensive Care Corp.
(NYSE)
Cost of Maintaining Product
CmpAs: Computer Associates Inter-
national Inc. (newspaper)
CmpCn: Computer Consoles Inc.
(newspaper)
CmpCre: Comprehensive Care
Corp. (newspaper)
CMPF: Cumulative Preferred
CmpR: Cambell Resources Inc.
(newspaper)
Cmptrc: CompuTrac Inc. (newspa-
per)
CmpTsk: Computer Task Group
Inc. (newspaper)
CMR: Commtron Corp. (ASE)
CMRO: COMARCO Inc. (NAS
NMS)
CMS: Capital Markets Statistics
CMS Energy Corp. (NYSE)
CMS En: CMS Energy Corp. (news-
paper)
CMSNC: China Merchants Steam
Navigation Company
CMSP&P: Chicago, Milwaukee, St.
Paul and Pacific (rail-
road)
CM StP&P: Chicago, Milwaukee,
St. Paul and Pacific
(railroad)
CMT: Cash Management Trust
CMU: Colonial Municipal Income
Trust (NYSE)
CMUC: Comp-U-Check Inc. (NAS
NMS)
CMV: Current Market Value
CMW: Canadian Marconi Co. (ASE)
CmwE: Commonwealth Edison Co.
(newspaper)
CMX: CMI Corp. (ASE)
CMX Cp: CMX Corp. (newspaper)
CMY: Community Psychiatric Cen-
ters (NYSE)

CMZ: Cincinnati Milacron Inc.
(NYSE)
Compagnie Maritime du
Zaiere
cn: consolidated
C&N: Carolina and Northwestern
(railway)
CN: Calton Inc. (NYSE)
Canadian National (railway)
Circular Note
Contract Note
Craft Airlines
Credit Note
CNA: Capital Needs Analysis
CNA Financial Corp. (NYSE)
CNA Fn: CNA Financial Corp.
(newspaper)
CNAI: CNA Income Shares Inc.
(newspaper)
CNBE: CNB Bancshares Inc. (NAS
NMS)
CNBK: Century Bancorp Inc. (NAS
NMS)
CNBT: Community National
Bancorp Inc. (New York)
(NAS NMS)
CNC: China Navigation Company
Conseco Inc. (NYSE)
CNCA: Centel Cable Television Co.
(NAS NMS)
CNCD: Concord Career Colleges
Inc. (NAS NMS)
Cnchm: conchemco Inc. (newspa-
per)
cncl: canceled
CNCL: Commercial National Corp.
(NAS NMS)
cncld: canceled
CNCR: CenCor Inc. (NAS NMS)
CNDN: Chittenden Corp. (NAS
NMS)
CNE: Connecticut Energy Corp.
(NYSE)
CNET: COMNET Corp. (NAS NMS)
CNF: Consolidated Freightways Inc.
(NYSE)

CNG: Consolidated Natural Gas Co.
(NYSE)
CNH: Central Hudson Gas & Elec-
tric Corp. (NYSE)
CNJ: Central of New Jersey (rail-
road)
CNK: Crompton & Knowles Corp.
(NYSE)
CN&L: Columbia, Newberry &
Laurens (railroad)
cnl.: cancel
cancellation
CNL: Central Louisiana Electric
Company Inc. (NYSE)
CnLaEl: Central Louisiana Electric
Company Inc. (newspaper)
CNLF: C N L Financial Corp. (NAS
NMS)
CnllPS: Central Illinois Public Ser-
vice Co. (newspaper)
CNMD: CONMED Corp. (NAS NMS)
CNMW: Cincinnati Microwave Inc.
(NAS NMS)
CNN: CNA Income Shares Inc.
(NYSE)
CNNR: Conner Peripherals Inc.
(NAS NMS)
CNO: Caspen Oil Inc. (ASE)
CNO&TPR: Cincinnati, New Or-
leans and Texas Pa-
cific Railroad
CNP: Compagnie Navigation
Paquet (French-Paquet
Navigation Company)
(steamship)
Crown Central Petroleum
Corp. (ASE)
CnPacC: Central Pacific Corp.
(newspaper)
CNR: Chiriqui National Railroad
(Panama)
CNRD: Canrad Inc. (NAS NMS)
CNS: Canadian National Steamships
Consolidated Stores Corp.
(NYSE)
Continuous Net Settlement

CnsEP: Consolidated Energy Part-
ners LP (newspaper)
CnsFrt: Consolidated Freightways
Inc. (newspaper)
CNSL: Consul Restaurant Corp.
(NAS NMS)
CNSP: Central Sprinkler Corp.
(NAS NMS)
CnStor: Consolidated Stores Corp.
(newspaper)
cnt: count
CNT: Centel Corp. (NYSE)
CntCrd: Countrywide Credit Indus-
tries Inc. (newspaper)
CntlCp: Continental Corp., The
(newspaper)
CntlInfo: Continental Information
Systems Corp. (newspa-
per)
CNTO: Centocor Inc. (NAS NMS)
CNTP: Cincinnati, New Orleans
and Texas Pacific (rail-
road)
CntrMt: Countrywide Mortgage In-
vestments Inc. (newspa-
per)
CntryTl: Century Telephone Enter-
prises Inc. (newspaper)
CNTX: Centex Telemanagement
Inc. (NAS NMS)
CNV: Convertible Holdings Inc.
(NYSE)
CNVX: Convex Computer Corp.
(NAS NMS)
C&NW: Carolina & North Western
(railroad)
Chicago & North Western
(railroad)
CNY: Continental Information Sys-
tems Corp. (NYSE)
C&O: Chesapeake and Ohio (rail-
road)
co: coinsurance
compagnie (company)
(French)
compagno (partner) (Italian)

compañia (company) (Spanish)
company
CO: Call Option
Carried Over
Cash Order
Central Office
Certificate of Origin
Change Order
Charging Order
Chesapeake and Ohio (railway)
Continental Airlines
Cost Of
Covered Option
COA: Change Of Address
Coachmen Industries Inc.
(NYSE)
Current Operating Allow-
ances
Coachm: Coachmen Industries Inc.
(newspaper)
COAS: Columbia First Federal
S&L Assn. (Washington,
D.C.) (NAS NMS)
Coastal: Coastal Corp., The (news-
paper)
CoastR: Coast R.V. Inc. (newspa-
per)
CoastSL: Coast S&L Assn. (Califor-
nia) (newspaper)
COB: Change Order Board
Close Of Business (with date)
Commission des Operations
de Bourse
COBA: Commerce Bancorp Inc.
(New Jersey) (NAS NMS)
COBB: Cobb Resources Corp. (NAS
NMS)
COBE: Cobe Laboratories Inc.
(NAS NMS)
COBK: Co-Operative Bancorp (Mas-
sachusetts) (NAS NMS)
COBY: Current Operating Budget
Year
COC: Comptroller of the Currency
COCA: CoCa Mines Inc. (NAS
NMS)

CocaCl: Coca-Cola Co., The (newspaper)

CocCE: Coca-Cola Enterprises Inc. (newspaper)

COD: Cash On Delivery
Certificate Of Deposit

CODA: Step-Saver Data Systems Inc. (NAS NMS)

CODN: Codenoll Technology Corp. (NAS NMS)

COE: Crude Oil Equivalent
Current Operation Expenditure

COES: Commodore Environmental Services Inc. (NAS NMS)

Coeur: Coeur d'Alene Mines Corp. (newspaper)

COFACTS: Cost Factoring System

COFD: Collective Federal Savings Bank (New Jersey) (NAS NMS)

COFI: Charter One Financial Inc. (NAS NMS)

COGNF: Cognos Inc. (NAS NMS)

Cognitr: Cognitronics Corp. (newspaper)

COGR: Colonial Group Inc., The (NAS NMS)

COH: Cash-On-Hand
Cohu Inc. (ASE)

COHR: Coherent Inc. (NAS NMS)

Cohu: Cohu Inc. (newspaper)

COI: Certificate Of Incorporation
Certificate Of Indebtedness

COKE: Coca-Cola Bottling Company Consolidated (NAS NMS)

COLA: Cost Of Living Adjustment (Allowance)

COLC: Colorado National Bankshares Inc. (NAS NMS)
Cost of Living Council

COLDEMAR: Compania Colombiana de Navegacion Maritima (Colombian Maritime Navigation Company) (steamship)

Coleco: Coleco Industries Inc. (newspaper)

ColFds: Collins Food International Inc. (newspaper)

ColGas: Columbia Gas System Inc., The (newspaper)

ColgPal: Colgate-Palmolive Co. (newspaper)

CollHI: Colonial-Intermediate High Income Fund (newspaper)

Coll: collateral
collection

Collat: collateral

Collins: Collins Industries Inc. (newspaper)

Coll L: Collection Letter

Coll Tr: Collateral Trust (bond)

ColMu: Colonial Municipal Income Trust (newspaper)

ColorSy: Color Systems Technology Inc. (newspaper)

ColPr: Colorado Prime Corp. (newspaper)

ColREI: Columbia Real Estate Investments Inc. (newspaper)

CO LTD: Closed Corporation

ColumS: Columbia S&L Assn. (newspaper)

com: commerce
commercial
commission

COM: Crowley Milner & Co. (ASE)

Com C: Commercial Code

COMD: Command Airways Inc. (NAS NMS)

Comdis: Comdisco Inc. (newspaper)

Comdre: Commodore International Ltd. (newspaper)

ComES: Commonwealth Energy System (newspaper)

COMEX: Commodity Exchange, Inc.

COMFd: Comfed Bancorp Inc. (newspaper)

Cominc: Cominco Ltd. (newspaper)
COMJD: Commodity Journal
coml: commercial
Com'l Ppr: Commercial Paper
comm: commercial
  commission
  committee
COMM: Cellular Communications Inc. (NAS NMS)
commod: commodity
comp: company
  composite
  compound
compa: compañia (company) (Spanish)
Compaq: COMPAQ Computer Corp. (newspaper)
compd: compound
CompD: CompuDyne Corp. (newspaper)
CompSc: Computer Sciences Corp. (newspaper)
compt: comptant (cash) (French)
  comptroller
Comptek: Comptek Research Inc. (newspaper)
compy: company
COMR: Comair Inc. (NAS NMS)
COMS: 3Com Corp. (NAS NMS)
COMSAT: Communications Satellite
  Communications Satellite Corporation (newspaper)
comsn: commission
Comstk: Comstock Partners Strategy Fund Inc. (newspaper)
ComSy: COM Systems Inc. (newspaper)
comt: comptroller
comte: committee
Comtrn: Commtron Corp. (newspaper)
COMW: Commonwealth S&L Assn. FA (Florida) (NAS NMS)

COMX: Comtrex Systems Corp. (NAS NMS)
CON: Connelly Containers Inc. (ASE)
ConAg: ConAgra Inc. (newspaper)
ConcdF: Concord Fabrics Inc. (newspaper)
Con Cr: Contra Credit
Con Ed: Consolidated Edison
CONEX: Container Express
conf: conference
confer: conference
CONH: Continental Homes Holding Corp. (NAS NMS)
ConnE: Connecticut Energy Corp. (newspaper)
Connly: Connelly Containers Inc. (newspaper)
ConnNG: Connecticut Natural Gas Corp. (newspaper)
Conqst: Conquest Exploration Co. (newspaper)
Conrail: Consolidated Rail Corp. (newspaper)
Cons: consolidated
Consec: Conseco Inc. (newspaper)
ConsNG: Consolidated Natural Gas Co. (newspaper)
ConsOG: Consolidated Oil & Gas Inc. (newspaper)
CONSOLS: Consolidated Annuities
Constn: Conston Corp. (newspaper)
Constr: Constar International Inc. (newspaper)
consult: consultant
Cont: contract
  controller
CONT: Continental Airlines
  Continental Medical Systems Inc. (NAS NMS)
Contel: Contel Corp. (newspaper)
ContGr: Continental Graphics Corp. (newspaper)
ContIll: Continental Illinois Corp. (newspaper)

ContMtl: Continental Materials Corp. (newspaper)

Conv: conversion
converted
convertible

ConvHld: Convertible Holdings Inc. (newspaper)

Convsn: Conversion Industries Inc. (newspaper)

Convst: ConVest Energy Partners Ltd. (newspaper)

CONW: Consumers Water Co. (NAS NMS)

COO: Chief Operating Officer
Cooper Companies Inc., The (NYSE)
Cost Of Ownership
Country Of Origin

CoopCo: Cooper Companies Inc., The (newspaper)

Cooper: Cooper Industries Inc. (newspaper)

cop: copyright

COP: City of Prineville (railroad)
Compania Panamena de Aviacion (Panamanian Air Lines)
Copley Properties Inc. (ASE)

COPE: Committee on Paperless Entries (Atlanta)

Copelc: Copelco Financial Services Group Inc. (newspaper)

COPI: Consolidated Products Inc. (NAS NMS)

Copley: Copley Properties Inc. (newspaper)

COPR: Copper Range Railroad

CoprTr: Cooper Tire & Rubber Co. (newspaper)

COPS: Catalytic Optimum Profit-Sharing

COPSI: Council of Profit Sharing Industries (now PSCA)

copt: copyright

Copwld: Copperweld Corp. (newspaper)

copy: copyright

COPY: Copytele Inc. (NAS NMS)

COQ: Cost-Of-Quality

cor: correspondent

COR: Cash On Receipt
Crystal Oil Co. (ASE)

CORBFUS: Copy Of Reply to Be Furnished Us

CorBlk: Corroon & Black Corp. (newspaper)

CORC: Corcom Inc. (NAS NMS)

Corcp: Corcap Inc. (newspaper)

CORD: Cordis Corp. (NAS NMS)

CoreIn: Core Industries Inc. (newspaper)

CornGl: Corning Glass Works (newspaper)

corp: corporate
corporation

cos: companies

COS: Cash On Shipment
Copperweld Corp. (NYSE)

COSA: Chairman of the Office of Savings Association
Cost Of Sales Adjustment

COSF: Cosmetic & Fragrance Concepts Inc. (NAS NMS)

CosmCr: Cosmopolitan Care Corp. (newspaper)

COST: Costco Wholesale Corp. (NAS NMS)

COTG: Cottage Savings Assn. FA (Ohio) (NAS NMS)

COU: Courtaulds PLC (ASE)

coup: coupon
coupon (French)

court: courtage (brokerage) (French)

Courtld: Courtaulds PLC (newspaper)

COUS: Cousins Properties Inc. (NAS NMS)

COVT: Covington Development Group Inc. (NAS NMS)

COW: United Stockyards Corp. (NYSE)

COWPS: Council on Wage and
       Price Stability
coy: company
cp: coupon
C&P: Cumberland & Pennsylvania
       (railroad)
C-P: Colgate-Palmolive
CP: Canadian Pacific Airlines
       Canadian Pacific Ltd. (NYSE)
       Canadian Pacific Railway Co.
       Certificate of Purchase
       Closing Price
       Closing Purchase
       Collar Pricing
       Commercial Paper
       Contract Price
       Corporate Planning
       Cost Price
       Critical Path
C&PA: Coudersport & Port
       Allegany (railroad)
CPA: Canadian Pacific Airways
       Certified Public Accountant
       Chartered Public Accountant
       (UK)
       Chicago Pacific Corp. (NYSE)
       Coudersport and Port
       Allegany (railroad)
       Critical Path Analysis
CPAF: Cost-Plus-Award Fee
CP AIR: Canadian Pacific Airlines
CPAP: Century Papers Inc. (NAS
       NMS)
CPB: Campbell Soup Co. (NYSE)
CPBI: CPB Inc. (NAS NMS)
CPC: CPC International Inc.
       (NYSE)
CPCI: Ciprico Inc. (NAS NMS)
CPCU: Chartered Property & Casu-
       alty Underwriter
CPE: Colorado Prime Corp. (ASE)
CPER: Consolidated Papers Inc.
       (NAS NMS)
CPF: Comstock Partners Strategy
       Fund Inc. (NYSE)
       Cotton Plant-Fargo (railway)

CPFF: Cost Plus Fixed Fee
CPH: Capital Holding Corp.
       (NYSE)
CPI: Commercial Performance In-
       dex
       Consumer Price Index
       Cost Plus Incentive
CPIC: CPI Corp. (NAS NMS)
CPIF: Cost Plus Incentive Fee
CPL: Carolina Power & Light Co.
       (NYSE)
CPLS: Care Plus Inc. (NAS NMS)
CP&LT: Camino, Placerville and
       Lake Tahoe (railroad)
CPN: Commercial Paper Note
       CP National Corp. (NYSE)
CPNF: Cost Plus No Fee
CPO: Commodity Pool Operator
CPP: Calprop Corp. (ASE)
       Current Purchasing Power
CPPC: Cost Plus a Percentage of
       Cost
CPQ: COMPAQ Computer Corp.
       (NYSE)
CPR: Canadian Pacific Railroad
       Cost Performance Report
CP Rail: Canadian Pacific Railroad
CPRD: Computer Products Inc.
       (NAS NMS)
cps: coupons
CPS: Consolidated Energy Partners
       LP (ASE)
       Convertible Preferred Stock
       Cumulative Preferred Stock
CPSA: Central Pennsylvania Fi-
       nancial Corp. (NAS NMS)
CP Ships: Canadian Pacific Steam-
       ships
CPSL: CSC Industries Inc. (NAS
       NMS)
CPST: CPC Rexcel Inc. (NAS
       NMS)
CPsys: Community Psychiatric
       Centers (newspaper)
CPT: Chicago Produce Terminal
CPTC: CPT Corp. (NAS NMS)

CPTD: Computer Data Systems Inc. (NAS NMS)

Cptlnd: Computerland Corp. (newspaper)

CPX: Cineplex Odeon Corp. (NYSE)

CQ: Communications Satellite Corp. (NYSE)

CQX: Conquest Exploration Co. (ASE)

cr: credit
creditor

CR: Cash Reserve
Commodity Rate
Commuter Airlines
Company Risk
Conference Report
Contract Report
Copper Range (railroad)
Cost Reimbursement
Crane Co. (NYSE)
Critical Ratio
Current Rate

CRA: Community Reinvestment Act
Craig Corp.(NYSE)

CRAB: Capt. Crab Inc. (NAS NMS)

Craig: Craig Corp. (newspaper)

CRAN: Crown Anderson Inc. (NAS NMS)

CRANDIC: Cedar Rapids and Iowa City (railway)

Crane: Crane Co. (newspaper)

CRAW: Crawford & Co. (NAS NMS)

CrayRs: Cray Research Inc. (newspaper)

CRB: Commodity Research Bureau

CRBI: Cal Rep Bancorp Inc. (NAS NMS)

CRBN: Calgon Carbon Corp. (NAS NMS)

CRC: Carolco Pictures Inc. (NYSE)

CRCC: Craftmatic/Contour Industries Inc. (NAS NMS)

CRCH: Church & Dwight Company Inc. (NAS NMS)

CrCPB: Crown Central Petroleum Corp. (newspaper)

CRCTC: Crescott Inc. (NAS NMS)

CRD: Central Registration Depository

CRDN: Ceradyne Inc. (NAS NMS)

CRE: Care Enterprises Inc. (ASE)

CREB: Champion Parts Inc. (NAS NMS)

cred: credit
creditor

CREDD: Customer Requested Earlier Due Date

CREF: Commingled Real Estate Funds

CRES: Crestmont Federal S&L Assn. (New Jersey) (NAS NMS)

CRF: Capital Recovery Factor

CRFC: Crestar Financial Corp. (NAS NMS)

CRI: Chicago River and Indiana (railroad)
Core Industries Inc. (NYSE)
CRI Insured Mortgage Investments Inc. (newspaper)

CR&IC: Cedar Rapids and Iowa City (railway)

CRIC: Collaborative Research Inc. (NAS NMS)

CRIIM: CRI Insured Mortgage Investments LP (newspaper)

CRI&P: Chicago, Rock Island & Pacific (railroad)

CR&IR: Chicago River and Indiana Railroad

CRIT: Criterion Group Inc. (NAS NMS)

CRIX: Control Resource Industries Inc. (NAS NMS)

CRL: Customer Requirements List

CRLC: Central Reserve Life Corp. (NAS NMS)

CRLNF: Carolin Mines Ltd. (NAS NMS)

CRM: CRI Insured Mortgage Investments LP (NYSE)

CRMK: Cermetek Microelectronics Inc. (NAS NMS)

CrmpK: Crompton & Knowles Corp. (newspaper)

CRN: Carolina and Northwestern (Southern Railway)

CRNR: Chronar Corp. (NAS NMS)

CRNS: Cronus Industries Inc. (NAS NMS)

CROP: Compliance Registered Options Principal
Crop Genetics International Corp. (NAS NMS)

Crosby: Philip Crosby Associates Inc. (newspaper)

Cross: A.T. Cross Co. (newspaper)

CrowlM: Crowley, Milner & Co. (newspaper)

CRR: Clinchfield Railroad
Consolidated Rail Corp. (NYSE)
Contemporaneous Reserve Requirements

CRRC: Courier Corp. (NAS NMS)

CRRNJ: Central Railroad of New Jersey

CRS: Carpenter Technology Corp. (NYSE)

CRSS: CRS Sirrine Inc. (newspaper)

CRTR: Charter-Crellin Inc. (NAS NMS)

CRU: Collective Reserve Unit

CRUSADER: Crusader Line (steamship)

CRV: Coast R. V. Inc. (ASE)

CRVS: Corvus Systems Inc. (NAS NMS)

CRW: Crown Crafts Inc. (ASE)

CRWN: Crown Books Corp. (NAS NMS)

CrwnCk: Crown Cork & Seal Company Inc. (newspaper)

CrysBd: Crystal Brands Inc. (newspaper)

CrystO: Crystal Oil Co. (newspaper)

CRZY: Crazy Eddie Inc. (NAS NMS)

C&S: Colorado & Southern (railroad)

CS: Capital Stock
Carolina Southern (railroad)
Closing Sale
Common Stock

CSA: Coast S&L Assn. (California) (NYSE)

CSAR: Calstar Inc. (NAS NMS)

CSB: Canada Savings Bond

CSBA: County Savings Bank (California) (NAS NMS)

CSBF: Citizens Savings Bank FSB (Maryland) (NAS NMS)

CSBM: City Savings Bank of Meriden (NAS NMS)

CSC: Clyde Shipping Company
Computer Sciences Corp. (NYSE)

CSCN: CompuScan Inc. (NAS NMS)

CSE: Cincinnati Stock Exchange

CSFCA: Citizens Savings Financial Corp. (Florida) (NAS NMS)

CSFN: CoreStates Financial Corp. (NAS NMS)

CshAm: Cash America Investments Inc. (newspaper)

CSI: Council for the Securities Industry

CSII: Communications Systems Inc. (NAS NMS)

CSIT: Precision Target Marketing Inc. (NAS NMS)

CSK: Chesapeake Corp. (NYSE)

CSL: Canada Steamship Lines
Carlisle Companies Inc. (NYSE)
Chicago Short Line (railway)

csldt: consolidate

CSLH: Cotton States Life & Health Insurance Co. (NAS NMS)
CSM: Chaparral Steel Co. (NYSE)
CSMO: Cosmo Communications Corp. (NAS NMS)
CSN: Cincinnati Bell Inc. (NYSE)
CSO: Cities Service Oil
CSOF: Corporate Software Inc. (NAS NMS)
CSOU: Citizens & Southern Corp. (NAS NMS)
CSP: Combustion Engineering Inc. (NYSE)
Company Standard Practice
CSPI: CSP Inc. (NAS NMS)
CSR: Central & South West Corp. (NYSE)
CSRE: COMSHARE Inc. (NAS NMS)
CSS: Central Certificate Service
Chicago South Shore and South Bend (railroad)
Commodity Stabilization Service
CSS Industries Inc. (ASE) (newspaper)
CSSCO: Cunard Steamship Company
CSS&SBR: Chicago South Shore and South Bend Railroad
CST: Central Standard Time
Christiana Companies Inc., The (NYSE)
Cstam: CoastAmerica Corp. (newspaper)
CSTIF: Challenger International Ltd. (NAS NMS)
CSTK: Comstock Group Inc. (NAS NMS)
CSTL: Constellation Bancorp. (NAS NMS)
CSTN: CornerStone Financial Corp. (NAS NMS)
CSTP: Congress Street Properties Inc. (NAS NMS)

C St.PM&O: Chicago, St.Paul, Minneapolis and Omaha (railroad)
CSTR: Costar Corp. (NAS NMS)
CSV: Cash Surrender Value
Columbia S&L Assn. (NYSE)
CSVLI: Cash Surrender Value of Life Insurance
CSWC: Capital Southwest Corp. (NAS NMS)
CSX: CSX Corp. (NYSE) (newspaper)
ct: cent
certificate
CT: Air Commuter (airlines)
California Real Estate Investment Trust (NYSE)
Cash Trade
Central Time
Certificate (NYSE)
Cleveland Tankers
Collateral Trust (bond)
Credit Transfer
CTA: Central Pacific Corp. (ASE)
Commodity Trading Adviser
CTAS: Cintas Corp. (NAS NMS)
CTB: Collateral Trust Bond
Cooper Tire & Rubber Co. (NYSE)
CTBC: Centerre Bancorporation (NAS NMS)
CTBX: Centerbank (Connecticut) (NAS NMS)
CTC: Contel Corp. (NYSE)
CTCO: Cross & Trecker Corp. (NAS NMS)
CTCQ: Check Technology Corp. (NAS NMS)
CtData: Control Data Corp. (newspaper)
CTEC: Component Technology Corp. (NAS NMS)
CTEK: Commercial Intertech (NAS NMS)
CTEX: C-TEC Corp. (NAS NMS)

CTF: Counsellors Tandem Securities Fund Inc. (NYSE) (newspaper)
Credit Transfer Fee
ctfs: certificates
CTG: Connecticut Natural Gas Corp. (NYSE)
CTH: CRI Insured Mortgage Investments III LP (NYSE)
CTHL: Continental Health Affiliates Inc. (NAS NMS)
CTIA: Communications Transmission Inc. (NAS NMS)
CTK: Comptek Research Inc. (ASE)
CTL: Century Telephone Enterprises Inc. (NYSE)
Coastal Transport Limited (steamship)
CTLC: Consolidated-Tomoka Land Co. (NAS NMS)
CtlCrc: Continental Circuits Corp. (newspaper)
CtlIHld: Continental Illinois Holding Corp. (newspaper)
CTM: COM Systems Inc. (ASE)
CTME: Clothestime Inc., The (NAS NMS)
CTO: Commerce Total Return Fund Inc. (ASE)
CTP: Central Maine Power Co. (NYSE)
CTR: Constar International Inc. (NYSE)
cts: centimes (currency of France) cents
CTS: Communications Technology Satellite
CTS Corp. (NYSE) (newspaper)
CTT: Capital Transfer Tax (UK)
CTUC: Continuum Company Inc., The (NAS NMS)
CTUS: Cetus Corp. (NAS NMS)
CTWL: Chartwell Group Ltd. (NAS NMS)

CTWS: Connecticut Water Service Inc. (NAS NMS)
CTX: Centex Corp. (NYSE)
CTY: Century Communications Corp. (ASE)
CtyCom: Century Communications Corp. (newspaper)
CTYF: CityFed Financial Corp. (NAS NMS)
CTYN: City National Corp. (NAS NMS)
CU: Cours Unique (sole quotation) (French)
CUB: Cubic Corp. (ASE)
Cubic: Cubic Corp. (newspaper)
CUC: Culbro Corp. (NYSE)
CUCD: CUC International Inc. (NAS NMS)
CUE: Quantum Chemical Corp. (NYSE)
Culbro: Culbro Corp. (newspaper)
CULL: Cullum Companies Inc. (NAS NMS)
CULP: Culp Inc. (NAS NMS)
CUM: Cummins Engine Company Inc. (NYSE)
Cum Div: Cum Dividend
CumEn: Cummins Engine Company Inc. (newspaper)
CUNARD: Cunard Steam-Ship Company, Limited
CUO: Continental Materials Corp. (ASE)
Cuplex: Cuplex Inc. (newspaper)
cur: currency
CUR: Current Income Shares Inc. (NYSE)
CurInc: Current Income Shares Inc. (newspaper)
curr: currency
Curtce: Curtice-Burns Foods Inc. (newspaper)
CurtW: Curtiss-Wright Corp. (newspaper)
CURY: Bombay Palace Restaurants Inc. (NAS NMS)

CUS: Customedix Corp. (ASE)

CUSIP: Committee on Uniform Securities Identification Procedures

cust: custodian
custom(s)

Custmd: Customedix Corp. (newspaper)

custr: customer

CUSUM: Cumulative Sum

CUTC: Cincinnati Union Terminal Company

CUV: Current Use Value

CUVA: Cuyahoga Valley (railroad)

cv: convertible

CV: Central Vermont Public Service Corp. (NYSE)
Central Vermont (Railroad)
Collection Voucher
Commercial Value
Convertible (NYSE)

CVBF: CVB Financial Corp. (NAS NMS)

CVC: Cablevision Systems Corp. (ASE)
Convertible Security (in bond and stock listings of newspapers)

CVF: Castle Convertible Fund Inc. (ASE)

CVGT: Convergent Inc. (NAS NMS)

CVI: Cenvill Investors Inc. (NYSE)

CVL: Cenvill Development Corp. (ASE)

CVP: Cost-Volume-Profit

CVR: Chicago Rivet & Machine Co. (ASE)

CVRY: Cuyahoga Valley Railway

CVSNF: Conversion Industries Inc. (NAS NMS)

cvt: convert
convertible

CVT: TCW Convertible Securities Fund Inc. (NYSE)

CVtPS: Central Vermont Public Service Corp. (newspaper)

C&W: Charleston and Western Carolina (railway)
Colorado & Wyoming (railroad)

CW: Channel Airways
Chesapeake Western (railroad)
Curtiss-Wright Corp. (NYSE)

C&WC: Charleston & Western Carolina (railroad)

CWE: Commonwealth Edison Co. (NYSE)

CWI: Chicago and Western Indiana (railroad)

CWine: Canandaigua Wine Company Inc. (newspaper)

CWLD: Child World Inc. (NAS NMS)

CWM: Convertible Wraparound Mortgage
Countrywide Mortgage Investments Inc. (NYSE)

CwnCr: Crown Crafts Inc. (newspaper)

CWO: Cash With Order

CWP: Chicago, West Pullman and Southern (railroad)

CWR: California Western Railroad

CWTR: California Water Service Co. (NAS NMS)

CWTS: Country Wide Transport Services Inc. (NAS NMS)

cx: canceled

CX: Cathay Pacific Airways
Centerior Energy Corp. (NYSE)
Colorado and Southern Railway

CXC: CMX Corp. (ASE)

CXI: Cuplex Inc. (ASE)

CXIM: Criticare Systems Inc. (NAS NMS)

CXR: CXR Telecom Corp. (ASE) (newspaper)

CXV: Cavalier Homes Inc. (ASE)

CXY: Canadian Occidental Petroleum Ltd. (ASE)

cy: currency

CY: Calendar year
   Current Year
   Current Yield
Cycare: CyCare Systems Inc.
   (newspaper)
CYPM: Cyprus Minerals Co. (NAS
   NMS)
CYPR: Cypress Semiconductor
   Corp. (NAS NMS)

CyprFd: Cypress Semiconductor
   Corp. (newspaper)
CYR: Cray Research Inc. (NYSE)
CYS: CyCare Systems Inc.
   (NYSE)
CYTO: Cytogen Corp. (NAS
   NMS)
CYTR: CytRx Corp. (NAS NMS)
CZM: CalMat Co. (NYSE)

D

d: data
debe (debit) (Spanish)
debenture
debit (debit) (French)
default (Standard & Poor's bond
rating)
delivered
delivery
dime
discount
dividend
doit (debit) (French)
dollar
pence
D: Checkable Deposits of depository
institutions
Dominion Resources Inc.
(NYSE)
The price that is the low for the
past year (in stock tables)
DA: CRS Sirrine Inc. (NYSE)
Days after Acceptance
Deductible Average
Demand Assigned
Depletion Allowance
Deposit Account
Discretionary Account
Documents Attached
Documents for (against) Accep-
tance
Dollar Averaging
Dominion Atlantic (railroad)
Dormant Account
DAA: Documents Against Accep-
tance
DAC: Delivery Against Cost
DAD: Documents Against Discre-
tion
DAHL: Dahlberg Inc. (NAS NMS)
DAIO: Data I/O Corp. (NAS NMS)

DAL: Delta Air Lines Inc. (NYSE)
Dallas: Dallas Corp. (newspaper)
DAM: Damson Oil Corp. (ASE)
DamCr: Damon Creations Inc.
(newspaper)
DamE: Damson Energy Company
LP (newspaper)
D'AMICO: D'Amico Line (steam-
ship)
Damson: Damson Oil Corp. (news-
paper)
DAN: Daniel Industries Inc. (NYSE)
Deposit Account Number
DanaCp: Dana Corp. (newspaper)
Danhr: Danaher Corp. (newspaper)
Daniel: Daniel Industries Inc.
(newspaper)
DAP: Do Anything Possible
Documents Against Payment
DAPN: Dauphin Deposit Corp.
(NAS NMS)
DART: Dart Group Corp. (NAS
NMS)
DASW: Data Switch Corp. (NAS
NMS)
DataGn: Data General Corp. (news-
paper)
Datamet: Datametrics Corp. (news-
paper)
DataPd: Dataproducts Corp. (news-
paper)
Datapt: Datapoint Corp. (newspaper)
Datarm: Dataram Corp. (newspa-
per)
D/Atchd: Draft Attached
DATM: Datum Inc. (NAS NMS)
DATX: Data Translation Inc. (NAS
NMS)
DavWtr: Davis Water & Waste In-
dustries Inc. (newspaper)

DAVX: Davox Corp. (NAS NMS)
Daxor: Daxor Corp. (newspaper)
DaytHd: Dayton Hudson Corp. (newspaper)
DAZY: Daisy Systems Corp. (NAS NMS)
db: daybook
debenture
debit
D&B: Dun & Bradstreet, Inc.
DB: Day Book
DBA: Doing Business As
DBAS: DBA Systems Inc. (NAS NMS)
DBCC: District Business Conduct Committee (National Association of Securities Dealers)
DBD: Diebold Inc. (NYSE)
DBF: Drexel Bond-Debenture Trading Fund (NYSE)
DBHI: Dow B. Hickman Inc. (NAS NMS)
DBIO: Damon Biotech Inc. (NAS NMS)
DBRL: Dibrell Brothers Inc. (NAS NMS)
DBRN: Dress Barn Inc., The (NAS NMS)
DB RTS: Debenture Rights
DC: Da Capo (from the beginning)
Datametrics Corp. (ASE)
Debit Collection
Deep Discount Issue (in bond listings of newspapers)
Delray Connecting (railroad)
Double Crown (currency of UK)
DCA: Digital Communications Associates Inc. (NYSE)
DCE: Discounted Cash Equivalent
Domestic Credit Expansion
DCEF: Discounted Cash Equivalent Flow
DCF: Discounted Cash Flow

DCFM: Discounted Cash Flow Method
DCI: Des Moines and Central Iowa (railroad)
Donaldson Company Inc. (NYSE)
DckM: Dickenson Mines Ltd. (newspaper)
DCL: Diners' Club Inc.
Discretionary Credit Limit
DCN: Dana Corp. (NYSE)
Double Crown (currency of UK)
DCNY: DCNY Corp. (newspaper)
DCO: Ducommun Inc. (ASE)
DCOR: Decor Corp. (NAS NMS)
DCPI: dick clark productions inc. (NAS NMS)
DCR: Delray Connecting Railroad
DC&S: Detroit, Caro & Sandusky (railroad)
DCY: DCNY Corp. (NYSE)
D/D: Date of Draft
dated
DD: Command Airways
Day's (Days after) Date
Deadline Data
Declaration Date
De Dato (of this Date)
Deferred Delivery
Delayed Delivery
Demand Draft
Direct Debit
Double Draft
Due Date
E. I. du Pont de Nemours & Co. (NYSE)
DD & A: Depreciation, Depletion, and Amortization
DDA: Demand Deposit Accounts
DDB: Double-Declining-Balance (depreciation method)
DDD: Desired Deposit of Dividends
Direct Deposit of Dividends

DDDI: Downey Designs International Inc. (NAS NMS)

DDIX: DDI Pharmaceuticals Inc. (NAS NMS)

DDL: Data-Design Laboratories Inc. (NYSE)

DDN: Documented Discount Notes

DDP: Direct Deposit of Payroll

DDS: Dillard Department Stores Inc. (ASE)

D&E: De Queen and Eastern (railroad)

de: deve (debit) (Portugueuse)

DE: Deere & Co. (NYSE)
Double Entry

DEAL: Dial REIT Inc. (NAS NMS)

DeanFd: Dean Foods Co. (newspaper)

deb: debenture
debit

DEBS: Deb Shops Inc. (NAS NMS)

dec: decort (deduct) (German)

DEC: Detroit Edison Company
Digital Equipment Corp. (NYSE)

Decorat: Decorator Industries Inc. (newspaper)

deduct: deduction

DEE: Dee Corp. PLC (NYSE)

DeeCp: Dee Corporation PLC (newspaper)

DEER: Deerfield Federal S&L Assn. (Illinois) (NAS NMS)

Deere: Deere & Co. (newspaper)

def: default
deferred
deficit

DEFI: Defiance Precision Products Inc. (NAS NMS)

DEG: De Laurentiis Entertainment Group Inc. (ASE)

DEI: Diversified Energies Inc. (NYSE) (newspaper)

DELACCT: Delinquent Account

DeLau: De Laurentiis Entertainment Group Inc. (newspaper)

DELL: Dell Computer Corp. (NAS NMS)

DelLab: Del Laboratories Inc. (newspaper)

Delmed: Delmed Inc. (newspaper)

DelmP: Delmarva Power & Light Co. (newspaper)

DELTA: Delta Air Lines

DeltaAr: Delta Air Lines Inc. (newspaper)

Deltona: The Deltona Corp. (newspaper)

Deluxe: Deluxe Corp. (newspaper)

DelVal: Del-Val Financial Corp. (newspaper)

delv'd: delivered

dem: demand
demurrage

DEMP: Drug Emporium Inc. (NAS NMS)

demur: demurrage

denom: denomination

DensMf: Dennison Manufacturing Co. (newspaper)

dep: department
deposit
depositary
depositor

DEP: Damson Energy Company LP (ASE)

DEPC: DEP Corp. (NAS NMS)

Dep Ctf: Deposit Certificate

depo: deposit

depr: depreciation

DEPS: Deposit Guaranty Corp. (NAS NMS)

dept: department

DeRose: De Rose Industries Inc. (newspaper)

DESB: Delaware Savings Bank FSB (NAS NMS)

Desgnl: Designcraft Industries Inc. (newspaper)

DeSoto: DeSoto Inc. (newspaper)

DEST: DEST Corp. (NAS NMS)

DETC: Detection Systems Inc. (NAS NMS)

DetEd: Detroit Edison Co., The (newspaper)

DEVC: Devcon International Corp. (NAS NMS)

DEVN: Devon Group Inc. (NAS NMS)

DEW: Delmarva Power & Light Co. (NYSE)

DEWY: Dewey Electronics Corp. (NAS NMS)

DEX: Dexter Corp., The (NYSE)

Dexter: Dexter Corp., The (newspaper)

DF: Dean Foods Co. (NYSE)

DFA: Deposit Fund Account

DFC: Development Finance Company

DFDEL: Deferred Delivery

DFED: Dominion Federal S&L Assn. (Virginia) (NAS NMS)

DFI: Duty Free International Inc. (ASE)

DFL: Degree of Financial Leverage

DFLX: Dataflex Corp. (NAS NMS)

DFP: De Laurentiis Film Partners LP (ASE)

DFT/A: Draft Attached

DFT/C: Clean Draft

DGAS: Delta Natural Gas Company Inc. (NAS NMS)

DGN: Data General Corp. (NYSE)

DGR: Denver and Rio Grande Western (railroad)

DGTC: Digitech Inc. (NAS NMS)

D&H: Delaware and Hudson (railroad)

DH: Dayton Hudson Corp. (NYSE)

DHR: Danaher Corp. (NYSE)

DHTK: DH Technology Inc. (NAS NMS)

DI: Dresser Industries Inc. (NYSE)

DIA: Diasonics Inc. (ASE)
Due In Assets
Dulles International Airport

Diag: Diagnostic/Retrieval Systems Inc. (newspaper)

DiagPr: Diagnostic Products Corp. (newspaper)

DianaCp: Diana Corp., The (newspaper)

DiaSo: Diamond Shamrock Offshore Partners LP (newspaper)

Diasonc: Diasonics Inc. (newspaper)

DIBK: Dime Savings Bank of Wallingford, The (Connecticut) (NAS NMS)

DIC: Demand Increasing Costs

DICN: Diceon Electronics Inc. (NAS NMS)

DIDC: Depository Institutions Deregulation Committee

Diebold: Diebold Inc. (newspaper)

dif: différe (deferred stock) (French)

DIFSD: Diversified Foods Corp. (NAS NMS)

DIG: Di Giorgio Corp. (NYSE)

DIGI: DSC Communications Corp. (NAS NMS)

DiGior: Di Giorgio Corp. (newspaper)

Digital: Digital Equipment Corp. (newspaper)

DigtlCm: Digital Communications Associates Inc. (newspaper)

DII: Decorator Industries Inc. (ASE)

DI IND: DI Industries Inc. (newspaper)

Dillard: Dillard Department Stores Inc. (newspaper)

DILO: Digilog Inc. (NAS NMS)

DimeNY: Dime Savings Bank of New York FSB (newspaper)

din: dinar (currency of Yugoslavia)

DING: Diversified Investment Group Inc. (NAS NMS)
DIO: Diodes Inc. (ASE)
Diodes: Diodes Inc. (newspaper)
DION: Dionics Inc. (NAS NMS)
DIP: Dividend Investment Plan
dir: director
DirActn: Direct Action Marketing Inc. (newspaper)
dis: discount
DIS: Walt Disney Co., The (NYSE)
disb: disburse
disbursement
disbmt: disbursement
disc: discount
DISC: Domestic International Sales Corporation
disct: discount
Disney: Walt Disney Co., The (newspaper)
dist: discount
DIST: Distributed (NYSE)
div: dividend
DIV: PLC Diversifund (ASE)
divd: dividend
DiviHtl: Divi Hotels N.V. (newspaper)
Divrsln: Diversified Industries Inc. (newspaper)
divs: dividends
DIX: Dixieline Products Inc. (ASE)
Dixilne: Dixieline Products Inc. (newspaper)
DixnGp: Dixons Group PLC (newspaper)
DixnTi: Dixon Ticonderoga Co. (newspaper)
diy: Do It Yourself
DJ: Dow-Jones & Company Inc. (NYSE)
D&J: December and June (securities)
D-J: Dow-Jones (average)
DJA: Dow-Jones Averages
DJCO: Daily Journal Co. (NAS NMS)
DJI: Designcraft Industries Inc. (ASE)

Dow-Jones Index
Dow-Jones Industrial (average)
DJIA: Dow-Jones Industrial Average
DJIC: Dow-Jones Index – Composite
DJII: Dow-Jones Index – Industrials
DJIT: Dow-Jones Index – Transport
DJIU: Dow-Jones Index – Utilities
DJNR: Dow-Jones News Retrieval
DJTA: Dow-Jones Transportation Average
DJUA: Dow-Jones Utility Average
DK: Danish Krone (currency of Denmark)
Don't Know
A stock transaction between a broker and another broker in which there is some discrepancy in the records
DKLB: DEKALB Corp. (NAS NMS)
DKS: Doniphan, Kensett and Searcy (railway)
DL: Day Letter
Delta Airlines
Demand Loan
Dominion Shipping (steamship)
DLauF: De Laurentiis Film Partners LP (newspaper)
DLCH: Delchamps Inc. (NAS NMS)
dld: delivered
DLD: Deadline Date
DLI: Del Laboratories Inc. (ASE)
dllrs: dollars
DLOG: Distributed Logic Corp. (NAS NMS)
DLP: CenTrust Savings Bank (ASE)
dlr: dealer
dollar
dls: dollars
DLS: Dallas Corp. (NYSE)
Debt Liquidation Schedule
DLS/SHR: Dollars per Share
DLT: Deltona Corp., The (NYSE)
DLTA: DeltaUS Corp. (NAS NMS)
DLTK: Deltak Corp. (NAS NMS)
DLTX: Daltex Medical Sciences Inc. (NAS NMS)

DL&W: Delaware, Lackawanna & Western (railroad)
DLWD: Delta Woodside Industries Inc. (NAS NMS)
DLX: Deluxe Corp. (NYSE)
D&M: Detroit and Mackinac (railroad)
DM: Debit Memorandum
Deutsche Mark (currency of Germany)
District Manager
DMAR: Datamarine International Inc. (NAS NMS)
DMBK: Dominion Bankshares Corp. (NAS NMS)
DMC: Direct Manufacturing Cost
Diversified Industries Inc. (NYSE)
DMCB: Data Measurement Corp. (NAS NMS)
DMCV: Dairy Mart Convenience Stores Inc. (NAS NMS)
DMD: Delmed Inc. (ASE)
DME: Dime Savings Bank of New York FSB (NYSE)
DMGIF: Dumagami Mines Ltd. (NAS NMS)
DMIC: Digital Microwave Corp. (NAS NMS)
DM&IRR: Duluth, Missabe & Iron Range Railroad
DMJS: December, March, June, September (securities)
DMK: Direct Action Marketing Inc. (ASE)
DML: Dickenson Mines Ltd. (ASE)
DMM: Dansville and Mount Morris (railroad)
DMR: Daily Market Report (Coffee, Sugar and Cocoa Exchange)
DMU: Des Moines Union (railway)
DMWR: Des Moines Western Railway
DN: Debit Note

DNA: Diana Corp., The (NYSE)
Does Not Answer
Does Not Apply
DNAP: DNA Plant Technology Corp. (NAS NMS)
DNB: Dun & Bradstreet Corp., The (NYSE)
DNE: Duluth and Northeastern (railroad)
DNEX: Dionex Corp. (NAS NMS)
DNF: Did Not Finish
DNFC: D&N Financial Corp. (NAS NMS)
DNI: Damon Creations Inc. (ASE)
Distributable Net Income
DNNY: Frances Denney Companies Inc., The (NAS NMS)
DNO: Debit Note Only
DNP: Duff & Phelps Selected Utilities (NYSE)
DNR: Do Not Reduce (order)
Do Not Renew (policy)
DNY: R.R. Donnelley & Sons Co. (NYSE)
do: descuento (discount) (Spanish)
dollar
DO: Day Order
Delivery Order
Disbursing Office (Officer)
District Office
DOA: Date Of Availability
DOB: Date Of Birth
DOC: Direct Operating Costs
Divested Operating Company
DOCO: D. O. C. Optics Corp. (NAS NMS)
DOCP: Delaware Otsego Corp. (NAS NMS)
DOG: Days Of Grace
dol: dollar
DOL: Degree of Operating Leverage
DOLR: Dollar General Corp. (NAS NMS)
Dom Ex: Domestic Exchange
DOMN: Domain Technology Inc. (NAS NMS)

D P I - DiSPoSABle PeRSoNAl ENCoMe

DomRs: Dominion Resources Inc.
(newspaper)
Domtr: Domtar Inc. (newspaper)
DOMZ: Dominguez Water Corp.
(NAS NMS)
DON: Donnelly Corp. (ASE)
Donald: Donaldson Company Inc.
(newspaper)
DONEF: Donegal Resources Ltd.
(NAS NMS)
Donley: R.R. Donnelley & Sons Co.
(newspaper)
DonlyC: Donnelly Corp. (newspaper)
DORR: Delaware Otsego Railroad
DOS: Date Of Shipment
Day Of Sale
DOSK: Doskocil Companies Inc.
(NAS NMS)
DOT: Date Of Trade
Designated Order Turn-
around
DOTX: Dotronix Inc. (NAS NMS)
Double-B: Double-Banked
Double-Bonded
DOUG: Douglas & Lomason Co.
(NAS NMS)
DOV: Dover Corp. (NYSE)
Dover: Dover Corp. (newspaper)
DOW: Dow Chemical Co., The
(NYSE)
Dow-Jones Averages
DowCh: Dow Chemical Co., The
(newspaper)
DowJns: Dow Jones & Company
Inc. (newspaper)
Downey: Downey S&L Assn. (news-
paper)
DP: Deferred Payment
Diagnostic Products Corp.
(NYSE)
Direct Price
Distribution Point
Documents against Payment
Due Process
DPA: Deferred Payment Account
DPB: Deposit PassBook

DPC: Data Processing Center
Dataproducts Corp. (ASE)
DPE: Data Processing Equipment
DPF: Deferred Pay Fund
DPHZ: DATAPHAZ Inc. (NAS NMS)
DPISPS: Department of Primary
Industries Stock Permit
System (Australia)
DP&L: Dallas Power and Light
DPL: DPL Inc. (NYSE) (newspa-
per)
DPO: Dividend Payout Ratio
DPP: Deferred Payment Plan
DPS: Dividends Per Share
dpst: deposit
DPT: Datapoint Corp. (NYSE)
DPX: Duplex Products Inc. (ASE)
DQ: Colony Airlines
DQ&E: Dequeen & Eastern (rail-
road)
DQU: Duquesne Light Co. (NYSE)
dr: debit
debtor
D&R: Dardanelle and Russellville
(railroad)
DR: Daily Report
Data Report
Deposit Receipt
Discount Rate
DRAM: Micron Technology Inc.
(NAS NMS)
DRAN: Dranetz Technologies Inc.
(NAS NMS)
Dravo: Dravo Corp. (newspaper)
DR C: Dernier Cours (Closing Price)
(French)
DRCO: Dynamics Research Corp.
(NAS NMS)
DRE: Duke Realty Investments
(NYSE)
DRES: Dresher Inc. (NAS NMS)
Dresr: Dresser Industries Inc.
(newspaper)
DrexB: Drexel Bond-Debenture
Trading Fund (newspa-
per)

Dreyfus: Dreyfus Corp., The (newspaper)

DRG: Detroit Rubber Group

D&RGW: Denver & Rio Grande Western (railroad)

DRH: Driver-Harris Co. (ASE)

DRI: Davenport, Rock Island and North Western (railway)

De Rose Industries Inc. (ASE)

DrivHar: Driver-Harris Co. (newspaper)

DRKN: Durakon Industries Inc. (NAS NMS)

DRL: DI Industries Inc. (ASE)

DRM: Diamond Shamrock R&M Inc. (NYSE)

Direct Reduction Mortgage

DRMD: Duramed Pharmaceuticals Inc. (NAS NMS)

DRP: Distribution Reinvestment Program

Dividend-Reinvestment Plan

DRR: Discounted Rate of Return

DRS: Diagnostic/Retrieval Systems Inc. (ASE)

DRTK: Duratek Corp. (NAS NMS)

DRV: Dravo Corp. (NYSE)

DRWI: Drew Industries Inc. (NAS NMS)

drx: drachma (currency of Greece)

DRXR: Drexler Technology Corp. (NAS NMS)

DRY: Devco Railway

Dreyfus Corp., The (NYSE)

DRYR: Dreyer's Grand Ice Cream Inc. (NAS NMS)

DryStGn: Dreyfus Strategic Government Income Fund (newspaper)

DryStr: Dreyfus Strategic Municipals Inc. (newspaper)

D&S: Durham & Southern (railroad)

DS: Days after Sight

Debenture Stock

Dominion Shipping (steamship)

DSBC: DS Bancor Inc. (Connecticut) (NAS NMS)

DSC: Detroit Stock Exchange

DSCC: Datasouth Computer Corp. (NAS NMS)

DSCP: Datascope Corp. (NAS NMS)

DSG: Designatronics Inc. (ASE)

Dsgntrn: Designatronics Inc. (newspaper)

DShRM: Diamond Shamrock R&M Inc. (newspaper)

DSI: Dreyfus Strategic Government Income Fund (NYSE)

DSII: Decom Systems Inc. (NAS NMS)

DSL: Downey S&L Assn. (NYSE)

DSMI: Dallas Semiconductor Corp. (NAS NMS)

DSN: Dennison Manufacturing Co. (NYSE)

DSO: Days Sales Outstanding

DeSoto Inc. (NYSE)

DSP: Diamond Shamrock Offshore Partners LP (NYSE)

DSR: Detroit Street Railways

DSRO: Designated Self Regulatory Organization

DSS&A: Duluth, South Shore & Atlantic (railroad)

DST: Daylight Saving Time

dstr: distribution

distributor

DSTS: DST Systems Inc. (NAS NMS)

DT: Detroit Terminal (railroad)

Dow Theory

DtaDsg: Data-Design Laboratories Inc. (newspaper)

DTC: Department of Trade and Commerce (UK)

Depositary Trust Company

Deposit-Taking Company

Domtar Inc. (NYSE)

dtd: dated

DTE: Detroit Edison Co., The (NYSE)

DTF: Daily Transaction File

DT&I: Detroit, Toledo & Ironton (railroad)

DTI: Detroit, Toledo and Ironton (railroad)

DTL: Degree of Total Leverage

DTM: Dataram Corp. (ASE)

DTMD: Dento-Med Industries Inc. (NAS NMS)

DTOM: De Tomaso Industries Inc. (NAS NMS)

DTRX: Detrex Corp. (NAS NMS)

DTSI: Datron Systems, Inc. (NAS NMS)

D&TSL: Detroit & Toledo Shore Line

DtyFr: Duty Free International Inc. (newspaper)

DU: Del Air - Air Cargo (airline)

DUCO: Durham Corp. (NAS NMS)

Ducom: Ducommun Inc. (newspaper)

Du Dat: Due Date

DuffPh: Duff & Phelps Selected Utilities (newspaper)

DUFM: Durr-Fillauer Medical Inc. (NAS NMS)

DUK: Duke Power Co. (NYSE)

DukeP: Duke Power Co. (newspaper)

DukeRln: Duke Realty Investments Inc. (newspaper)

DunBd: Dun & Bradstreet Corp., The (newspaper)

DUNK: Dunkin' Donuts Inc. (NAS NMS)

DUNS: Data Universal Numbering System (Dun's Number)

Duplex: Duplex Products Inc. (newspaper)

duPont: E.I. du Pont de Nemours & Co. (newspaper)

DuqLt: Duquesne Light Co. (newspaper)

DUQN: Duquesne Systems Inc. (NAS NMS)

DURI: Duriron Company Inc., The (NAS NMS)

DVH: Divi Hotels NV (ASE)

DVIS: Datavision Inc. (NAS NMS)

DVL: Del-Val Financial Corp. (NYSE)

DVP: Delivery Versus Payment
Discounted Present Value

DVRS: Diversco Inc. (NAS NMS)

DVS: Delta Valley and Southern (railway)

D&W: Danville & Western (railroad)

DW: Cross Sound Commuter Airlines
Dividend Warranty

DWG: DWG Corp. (ASE) (newspaper)

DWGI: Dean Witter Government Income Trust (newspaper)

DW&P: Duluth, Winnipeg & Pacific (railroad)

DWP: Del E. Webb Investment Properties Inc. (ASE)

DWSN: Dawson Geophysical Co. (NAS NMS)

DWW: Davis Water & Waste Industries Inc. (NYSE)

DXN: Dixons Group PLC (NYSE)

DXR: Daxor Corp. (ASE)

DXT: Dixon Ticonderoga Co. (ASE)

DXTK: Diagnostek Inc. (NAS NMS)

DXYN: Dixie Yarns Inc. (NAS NMS)

DYA: Dynamics Corporation of America (NYSE)

DYAN: Dyansen Corp. (NAS NMS)

DYCO: Dycom Industries Inc. (NAS NMS)

DYN: DynCorp. (NYSE)

DYNA: Dynascan Corp. (NAS NMS)

DynAm: Dynamics Corporation of America (newspaper)

Dyncrp: DynCorp (newspaper)

DYTC: Dynatech Corp. (NAS NMS)

DYTR: Dyatron Corp. (NAS NMS)

e: earnings
escudo (currency of Chile, Portugal)
estimate
E: Declared or Paid in the preceding 12 months (in stock listings of newspapers)
Transco Energy Co. (NYSE)
EA: Eastern Airlines
Electronic Associates Inc. (NYSE) programs (EC)
EAC: EAC Industries Inc. (ASE) (newspaper)
Equity Appreciation Certificate
EACO: EA Engineering Science & Technology Inc. (NAS NMS)
EAFC: Eastland Financial Corp. (NAS NMS)
EAGL: Eagle Financial Corp. (ASE)
EaglCl: Eagle Clothes Inc. (newspaper)
EagleP: Eagle-Picher Industries Inc. (newspaper)
EaglFn: Eagle Financial Corp. (newspaper)
EAN: Expenditure Account Number
EAST: Engineered Support Systems Inc. (NAS NMS)
EastGF: Eastern Gas & Fuel Associates (newspaper)
EastUtl: Eastern Utilities Associates (newspaper)
EATO: Eaton Financial Corp. (NAS NMS)
Eaton: Eaton Corp. (newspaper)
EAVN: Eaton Vance Corp. (NAS NMS)

E&B: Ellerman and Bucknall Steamship Company
EB: Early Bargain (UK)
Ehrlich Bober Financial Corp. (ASE)
Metro-Aire Commuter Airlines
EBCI: Eagle Bancorp Inc. (NAS NMS)
EBF: Ennis Business Forms Inc. (NYSE)
EBIT: Earnings Before Interest and Taxes
EBKC: Eliot Savings Bank (Massachusetts) (NAS NMS)
EBMI: E&B Marine Inc. (NAS NMS)
EBNC: Equitable Báncorporation (Maryland) (NAS NMS)
EBRD: European Bank for Reconstruction and Development
EBS: Edison Brother Stores Inc. (NYSE)
EBSI: Eagle Bancshares Inc. (NAS NMS)
ec: economics
EC: East Carolina (railroad)
Engelhard Corp. (NYSE)
European Community
Ex-Coupon
Extended Coverage
ECC: ECC International Corp. (NYSE) (newspaper)
ECF: Ellsworth Convertible Growth & Income Fund Inc. (ASE)
ECGI: Environmental Control Group Inc. (NAS NMS)
ECH: Echlin Inc. (NYSE)
Echlin: Echlin Inc. (newspaper)

EchoB: Echo Bay Mines Ltd. (newspaper)

ECILF: ECI Telecom Ltd. (NAS NMS)

ECIN: Economic Indicators

ECL: Ecolab Inc. (NYSE)

ECLAY: English China Clays PLC (NAS NMS)

ECN: Ecogen Inc. (ASE)

ECO: Echo Bay Mines Ltd. (ASE)

ECOA: Equal Credit Opportunity Act

Ecogn: Ecogen Inc. (newspaper)

ECOL: American Ecology Corp. (NAS NMS)

Ecolab: Ecolab Inc. (newspaper)

EcolEn: Ecology & Environment Inc. (newspaper)

econ: economics
economist
economy

ECOW: Metropolitan Realty Corp. (ASE)

ECTH: Electro-Catheter Corp. (NAS NMS)

ECTL: Elcotel Inc. (NAS NMS)

ECU: European Currency Unit

ED: Consolidated Edison Company of New York Inc. (NYSE)
Elasticity of Demand
Ex-Dividend
Extra Dividend

EDCO: Edison Control Corp. (NAS NMS)

EDD: End Delivery Date
Estimated Delivery Date
Expected Date of Delivery
Extra Dividend

EDE: Empire District Electric Co., The (NYSE)

EDGC: Edgcomb Corp. (NAS NMS)

EdisBr: Edison Brothers Stores Inc. (newspaper)

EDO: EDO Corp. (NYSE) (newspaper)

EDP: Energy Development Partners Ltd. (ASE)

EDR: European Depositary Receipt

EDSE: Edison Sault Electric Co. (NAS NMS)

EDT: Eastern Daylight Time

EDW: El Dorado and Wesson (railroad)

Edward: A.G. Edwards Inc. (newspaper)

EE: Equity Earnings
Esquire Radio & Electronics Inc. (ASE)

EEC: East Erie Commercial (railroad)
EECO Inc. (ASE)

EECO: EECO Inc. (newspaper)

EEE: Ensource Inc. (NYSE)

EEI: Ecology & Environment Inc. (ASE)

EESI: Eastern Environmental Services Inc. (NAS NMS)

EEZ: Exclusive Economic Zone

EF: Europe Fund, The

EFC: Estimated Final Cost

EFF: Exchange For Futures

effect: effective

EFG: Equitec Financial Group Inc. (NYSE)

EFH: E.F. Hutton Group Inc., The (NYSE)

EFIC: Export Finance & Insurance Corporation

EFL: External Finance Limit

EFP: Exchange For Physicals

EFSB: Elmwood Federal Savings Bank (Pennsylvania) (NAS NMS)

EFT: Electronic Financial Transaction
Electronic Funds Transfer

EFTPOS: Electronic Funds Transfer at Point of Sale

EFTS: Electronic Funds Transfer System

EFU: Eastern Gas & Fuel Associates (NYSE)

EFX: Equifax Inc. (NYSE)

EFY: End of Fiscal Year

EG: GCS Air Service (airline)
EGA: EQK Green Acres LP (NYSE)
EGAS: Energas Co. (NAS NMS)
EGG: EG&G Inc. (NYSE) (newspaper)
EGL: Eagle Clothes Inc. (ASE)
EGLC: Eagle Telephonics Inc. (NAS NMS)
EGN: Energen Corp. (NYSE)
EGP: EastGroup Properties (ASE)
EGPC: English Greenhouse Products Corp. (NAS NMS)
EGX: Engex Inc. (ASE)
EHP: Emerald Homes LP (NYSE)
EhrBbr: Ehrlich Bober Financial Corp. (newspaper)
EI: Earned Income
    Endevco Inc. (ASE)
    Exact Interest
    Ex-Interest
EIB: European Investment Bank
    Export-Import Bank
EIBW: Export-Import Bank of Washington
EILI: E. I. L. Instruments Inc. (NAS NMS)
EIPM: EIP Microwave Inc. (NAS NMS)
EIS: Excelsior Income Shares Inc. (NYSE)
EIV: Effective Initial Value
EJ: Everest & Jennings International Ltd. (ASE)
EJ&E: Elgin, Joliet & Eastern (railway)
EJR: East Jersey Railroad
EK: Eastman Kodak Co. (NYSE)
EKodk: Eastman Kodak Co. (newspaper)
EKR: EQK Realty Investors I (NYSE)
EL: Elevated Railroad
    Erie Lackawanna (railway)
    Even Lots
ELANY: Elan Corporation PLC (NAS NMS)
ELB: Eldorado Bancorp (ASE)

ELBTF: Elbit Computers Ltd. (NAS NMS)
ELC: Europe's Largest Companies
ELCH: El Chico Corp. (NAS NMS)
ELCN: Elco Industries Inc. (NAS NMS)
Elcor: Elcor Corp. (newspaper)
ELD: Eldon Industries Inc. (NYSE)
ELDC: Eldec Corp. (NAS NMS)
Eldon: Eldon Industries Inc. (newspaper)
Eldorad: Eldorado Bancorp (newspaper)
ELE: Empress Nacional de Electricidad S.A. (NYSE)
ElecAs: Electronic Associates Inc. (newspaper)
ElecSd: ElectroSound Group Inc. (newspaper)
ELEX: Elexis Corp. (NAS NMS)
Elgin: Elgin National Industries Inc. (newspaper)
ELK: Elcor Corp. (NYSE)
ELMG: Electromagnetic Sciences Inc. (NAS NMS)
ELPA: El Paso Electric Co. (NAS NMS)
ELRC: Electro Rent Corp. (NAS NMS)
ELRNF: Elron Electronic Industries Ltd. (NAS NMS)
E&LS: Escanaba & Lake Superior (railroad)
ELS: Economic Lot Size
    Elsinore Corp. (ASE)
Elscint: Elscint Ltd. (newspaper)
ELSE: Electro-Sensors Inc. (NAS NMS)
Elsinor: Elsinore Corp. (newspaper)
Elswth: Ellsworth Convertible Growth & Income Fund Inc. (newspaper)
ELSX: ELXSI Corp. (NAS NMS)
ELT: Elscint Ltd. (NYSE)
ELUX: Electrolux AB (NAS NMS)
E&M: Edgmoor and Manetta (railroad)

EM: Electronic Mail
   End-of-Medium (character)
   Entertainment Marketing Inc. (ASE)
EMC: EMC Corp. (NYSE) (newspaper)
   Export Management Company
EmCar: Empire of Carolina Inc. (newspaper)
EMCI: EMC Insurance Group Inc. (NAS NMS)
EMCO: Engineering Measurements Co. (NAS NMS)
EME: Emerson Radio Corp. (NYSE)
EMF: Templeton Emerging Markets Fund Inc. (ASE)
EMI: Encore Marketing International Inc. (ASE)
EML: Eastern Co., The (ASE)
   Estimated Month of Loss
EMLX: Emulex Corp. (NAS NMS)
EMMS: Electronic Mail and Message System
EMP: Empire of Carolina Inc. (ASE)
   End-of-Month Payment
EmpDs: Empire District Electric Co., The (newspaper)
EMPI: EMPI Inc. (NAS NMS)
EmpirA: Empire of America Federal Savings Bank (newspaper)
empl: employee
   employer
   employment
EmpNa: Empress Nacional de Electricidad S.A. (newspaper)
EMPR: Empire Savings Bank SLA (New Jersey) (NAS NMS)
EMQ: Economic Manufacturing Quantity
EMR: Emerson Electric Co. (NYSE)
EmRad: Emerson Radio Corp. (newspaper)

Emrld: Emerald Homes LP (newspaper)
EmrsE: Emerson Electric Co. (newspaper)
EMS: Electronic Mail System
   Electronic Message Service
EMSS: Electronic Message Service System
EMTS: Electronic Money Transfer System
EMU: European Monetary Union
EMUA: European Monetary Unit of Account (EC)
EMV: Expected Monetary Value
EN: Enterra Corp. (NYSE)
ENCC: Encore Computer Corp. (NAS NMS)
encl: enclosure
EncrM: Encore Marketing International Inc. (newspaper)
end: endorsement
End Guar: Endorsement Guaranteed
Endvco: Endevco Inc. (newspaper)
EnDvl: Energy Development Partners Ltd. (newspaper)
ENE: Enron Corp. (NYSE)
ENER: Energy Conversion Devices Inc. (NAS NMS)
Energen: Energen Corp. (newspaper)
ENEX: ENEX Resources Corp. (NAS NMS)
ENG: Enron Oil & Gas Co. (NYSE)
Engex: Engex Inc. (newspaper)
ENGH: Engraph Inc. (NAS NMS)
EnglC: Engelhard Corp. (newspaper)
EnisBu: Ennis Business Forms Inc. (newspaper)
ENNI: EnergyNorth Inc. (NAS NMS)
enq: enquiry
EnrOG: Enron Oil & Gas Co. (newspaper)
Enron: Enron Corp. (newspaper)

ENS: ENSERCH Corp. (NYSE)
ENSCO: Energy Service Company Inc. (newspaper)
EnsExp: Ensearch Exploration Partners Ltd. (newspaper)
ENSR: ENSR Corp. (newspaper)
Ensrce: Ensource Inc. (newspaper)
Ensrch: ENSERCH Corp. (newspaper)
ENTC: Entgronics Corp. (NAS NMS)
Entera: Enterra Corp. (newspaper)
EntMkt: Entertainment Marketing Inc. (newspaper)
ENUC: Electro-Nucleonics Inc. (NAS NMS)
ENV: Enviropact Inc. (ASE)
ENVI: Envirosafe Services Inc. (NAS NMS)
ENVR: Envirodyne Industries Inc. (NAS NMS)
Envrpct: Enviropact Inc. (newspaper)
EnvSys: Environmental Systems Co. (newspaper)
ENVT: Environmental Tectonics Corp. (NAS NMS)
EnvTrt: Environmental Treatment & Technologies Corp. (newspaper)
ENW: Elgin National Industries Inc. (NYSE)
ENX: ENSR Corp. (ASE)
ENZ: Enzo Biochem Inc. (ASE)
ENZN: Enzon Inc. (NAS NMS)
EnzoBi: Enzo Biochem Inc. (newspaper)
EO: Davey Air Services (airline) Executive Order
     Ex Officio (by virtue of the office)
EOA: Effective On (Or) About Empire of America Federal Savings Bank (ASE)
EOB: Expense Operating Budget

EOC: Economic Opportunity Commission
     End Of Contract
EOCY: End Of Calendar Year
EOD: End-Of-Day
EOFY: End Of Fiscal Year
EOM: End Of Month
     European Options Market
     Every Other Month
EOQ: Economical Ordering Quantity
     End Of Quarter
EORR: Empire-Orr Inc. (NAS NMS)
EOY: End Of Year
EP: Earning Power
     Earnings Price
     Effective Par
     Enserch Exploration Partners Ltd. (NYSE)
     Excess Profits
EPAI: El Pollo Asado Inc. (NAS NMS)
EPBX: Electronic Private Branch Exchange
EPI: Eagle-Picher Industries Inc. (NYSE)
EPM: Emigration Portfolio Manager
EPP: Estimated Price Policy
EPR: Earnings-Price Ratio
     Estimated Price Request
EPS: Earnings Per Share
EPSC: EPSCO Inc. (NAS NMS)
EPSI: Earnings Per Share Issued
     Epsilon Data Management Inc. (NAS NMS)
EPT: Excess Profits Tax
EPUB: Entertainment Publications Inc. (NAS NMS)
EQ: Equal (to)
EQIC: Equitable of Iowa Companies (NAS NMS)
EQK: Equimark Corp. (NYSE)
EQK G: EQK Green Acres LP (newspaper)

EQK Rt: EQK Realty Investors I (newspaper)

eql: equal

EQM: Equitable Real Estate Shopping Centers LP (NYSE)

eqpt: equipment

EQT: Equitable Resources Inc. (NYSE)

EqtRes: Equitable Resources Inc. (newspaper)

EqtRl: Equitable Real Estate Shopping Centers LP (newspaper)

EQTX: Equitex Inc. (NAS NMS)

EQTY: Equity Oil Co. (NAS NMS)

equ: equal
equity

EQUI: Equion Corp., The (NAS NMS)

Equifax: Equifax Inc. (newspaper)

Equimk: Equimark Corp. (newspaper)

equip: equipment

Equitec: Equitec Financial Group Inc. (newspaper)

equiv: equivalent

er: error

ER: Earnings Record
Earnings Report
Excess Reserves
Expense Report
Ex-Rights

ERB: Erbamont NV (NYSE)

Erbmnt: Erbamont N.V. (newspaper)

ERC: ERC International Inc. (NYSE) (newspaper)

ERICY: LM Ericsson Telephone Co. (NAS NMS)

ERIE: Erie Railroad

ERISA: Employee Retirement Income Security Act

ERLY: Erly Industries Inc. (NAS NMS)

ERM: Exchange Rate Mechanism

ERO: Ero Industries Inc. (ASE) (newspaper)

ERS: Economic Retention Stock

ERTA: Economic Recovery Tax Act

es: estimated

ES: Earned Surplus
Exempt Securities

ESB: Esselte Business Systems Inc. (NYSE)

ESC: Environmental Systems Co. (NYSE)

ESCA: Escalade Inc. (NAS NMS)

Escagn: Escagenitics Corp. (newspaper)

ESCC: Evans & Sutherland Computer Corp. (NAS NMS)

ESD: Engineered Systems & Development Corp. (ASE) (newspaper)
Estimated Shipping Date
Ex-Stock Dividend

ESE: European Stock Exchange

ESEX: Essex Corp. (NAS NMS)

EsexCh: Essex Chemical Corp. (newspaper)

ESG: ElectroSound Group Inc. (ASE)

ESH: Earl Scheib Inc. (ASE)

ESI: ESI Industries Inc. (ASE) (newspaper)

ESIO: Electro Scientific Industries Inc. (NAS NMS)

ESL: Esterline Corp. (NYSE)

ESLJ: East St. Louis Junction (railroad)

ESN: Escagenitics Corp. (ASE)

ESOP: Employee Stock Ownership Plan

ESOT: Employee Stock Ownership Trust

ESP: Espey Manufacturing & Electronics Corp. (ASE)
Exchange Stock Portfolio

Espey: Espey Manufacturing & Electronics Corp. (newspaper)

Esprit: Esprit Systems Inc. (newspaper)

EsqRd: Esquire Radio & Electronics Inc. (newspaper)
ESR: Electronic Send/Receive
EssBus: Esselte Business Systems Inc. (newspaper)
ESSF: ESSEF Corp. (NAS NMS)
ESSO: Esso Petroleum Company
est: estate
estimated
EST: Earliest Start Time
Eastern Standard Time
Estgp: EastGroup Properties (newspaper)
EstnCo: Eastern Co., The (newspaper)
Estrlne: Esterline Corp. (newspaper)
ESV: Energy Service Company Inc. (ASE)
ESX: Essex Chemical Corp. (NYSE)
ESY: E-Systems Inc. (NYSE)
E Syst: E-Systems Inc. (newspaper)
ET: Eastern Time
Estate Tax
Executive Team
ETA: Energy Tax Act
Estimated Time of Arrival
ETC: Estimated Time of Completion
Export Trading Company
ETCI: Electronic Tele-Communications Inc. (NAS NMS)
ETCO: Earth Technology Corp., The (NAS NMS)
ETEX: Eastex Energy Inc. (NAS NMS)
Ethyl: Ethyl Corp. (newspaper)
ETI: Esprit Systems Inc. (ASE)
ETL: Essex Terminal (railway)
ETLT: Equal To or Less Than
ETN: Eaton Corp. (NYSE)
ETOC: Expected Total Operating Cost
ETOS: Extended Tape Operating System

ETR: Expected Time of Response
ETRC: Entree Corp. (NAS NMS)
ETRE: Entre Computer Centers Inc. (NAS NMS)
ETT: Environmental Treatment & Technologies Corp. (NYSE)
ET&WNC: East Tennessee & Western North Carolina (railroad)
ETZ: Etz Lavud Ltd. (ASE)
EtzLav: Etz Lavud Ltd. (newspaper)
EUA: Eastern Utilities Associates (NYSE)
EUAC: Equivalent Uniform Annual Cost
EUP: Estimated Unit Price
EUR: Unit of Account (EC)
EV: Economic Value
EVAN: Envans Inc. (NAS NMS)
EVER: Evergreen Resources Inc. (NAS NMS)
EVGD: Evergood Products Inc. (NAS NMS)
EvrJ: Everest & Jennings International Ltd. (newspaper)
EVRX: Everex Systems Inc. (NAS NMS)
EVSB: Evansville Federal Savings Bank (NAS NMS)
EW: East Washington (railway)
Ex-Warrants
EWAT: E'town Corp. (NAS NMS)
EWSB: East Weymouth Savings Bank (Massachusetts) (NAS NMS)
EWSC: E. W. Scripps Co. (NAS NMS)
ex: exchange
exchequer
without
EX: Executive Airlines
ExAcct: Expense Account
EXAR: Exar Corp. (NAS NMS)
Ex B/L: Exchange Bill of Lading
exc: exchange
EXC: Excel Industries Inc. (ASE)

Excel: Excel Industries Inc. (newspaper)

Excelsr: Excelsior Income Shares Inc. (newspaper)

EXCG: Exchange Bancorp Inc. (NAS NMS)

exch: exchange
exchequer

Ex Cp: Ex Coupon

Ex D: Ex-Dividend
Without Dividend

Ex Div: Ex-Dividend
Without Dividend

exec: execute
executive

Exec: Executive Officer

execs: executives

exes: expenses

EXIM: Export-Import Bank (United States or Japan)

EXIMBANK: Export-Import Bank (of the United States or Japan)

EXIMBK: Export-Import Bank (United States or Japan)

Ex Int: Ex-Interest (NYSE)

EXLN: Excelan Inc. (NAS NMS)

Ex O: Executive Officer
Executive Order

exp: expense
export
exporter

EXP: Transco Exploration Partners Ltd. (NYSE)

EXPD: Expeditors International of Washington Inc. (NAS NMS)

expend: expenditure

expnd: expenditure

EXPO: Exposaic Industries Inc. (NAS NMS)

exps: expenses

Ex R: Ex-Rights

Ex-Rights: Without the Rights

exs: expenses

EXTRA: Extra Dividend (NYSE)

extve: executive

Ex W: Ex-Warrants

Ex-Warrants: Without Warrants

Exxon: Exxon Corp. (newspaper)

EY: Ethyl Corp. (NYSE)

EZEM: E-Z-Em Inc. (NAS NMS)

f: farthing (currency of UK)
fen (currency of China)
flat (in bond listings in newspapers)
forint (currency of Hungary)
franc (currency of France)
F: Ford Motor Co. (NYSE)
On a ticker tape after a foreign stock symbol showing that the stock has been sold by a foreign owner
F&A: February and August (securities)
Finance and Accounting
FA: Face Amount
February and August (securities)
Fixed Assets
Floating Assets
Florida Airlines
Free Alongside
Frozen Assets
FABC: First Alabama Bancshares Inc. (NAS NMS)
FabCtr: Fabri-Centers of America Inc. (newspaper)
FabInd: Fab Industries Inc. (newspaper)
FABK: First of America Bank Corp. (Michigan) (NAS NMS)
fac: facsimile
factory
FAC: Face-Amount Certificate
FACS: Financial Accounting and Control System
fact: factory
FACT: First Albany Companies Inc. (NAS NMS)
FacTs: Facsimile Transmission
facty: factory

FAHS: Farm & Home Savings Assn. (Missouri) (NAS NMS)
Fairfd: Fairfield Communities Inc. (newspaper)
FAL: Falcon Cable Systems Company LP (ASE)
FalCbl: Falcon Cable Systems Company LP (newspaper)
FALLINE: Federal Atlantic-Lakes Line (steamship)
FAMA: First Amarillo Bancorporation Inc. (NAS NMS)
FAMB: 1st American Bancorp (Massachusetts) (NAS NMS)
FamDlr: Family Dollar Stores Inc. (newspaper)
FAME: Flamemaster Corp. (NAS NMS)
FAMF: First AmFed Corp. (NAS NMS)
FAMR: First American Financial Corp., The (NAS NMS)
FAMS: Famous Restaurants Inc. (NAS NMS)
FANNIE MAE: Federal National Mortgage Association
Fanstel: Fansteel Inc. (newspaper)
FAPS: Financial Application Preprocessor System
FAQ: Free Alongside Quay
Free At Quay
FAR: Financial Accounts Receivable
FARA: Faradyne Electronics Corp. (NAS NMS)
Farah: Farah Manufacturing Company Inc. (newspaper)
FARC: Farr Co. (NAS NMS)

FARF: Fairfield-Noble Corp. (NAS NMS)

FARK: First Federal Savings of Arkansas FA (NAS NMS)

FARM: Farmer Brothers Co. (NAS NMS)

FARR: Farragut Mortgage Co. (NAS NMS)

FarWst: Far West Financial Corp. (newspaper)

FAS: Financial Accounting Standard

Financial Analysis System

Free Alongside Ship

FASB: Financial Accounting Standards Board

First American Savings Bank FSB (Ohio) (NAS NMS)

FASCIA: Fixed Asset System Control Information and Accounting

FAST: Fastenal Co. (NAS NMS)

FAT: Fixed Asset Transfer

FATN: First American Corp. (Tennessee) (NAS NMS)

FAU: Freeport-McMoRan Gold Co. (NYSE)

fax: facsimile

FAX: First Australia Prime Income Fund (ASE)

FAY: Fay's Drug Company Inc. (NYSE)

FB: Fidelity Bond

Foreign Bond

Freight Bill

FBA: Flexible Benefit Account

FBAC: First National Bancorp (Georgia) (NAS NMS)

FBC: First Boston Inc. (NYSE)

FBD: Fibreboard Corp. (ASE)

Full Business Day

FBF: First Boston Income Fund Inc. (NYSE)

FBH: Frank B. Hall & Company Inc. (NYSE)

FBI: First Boston Strategic Income Fund Inc. (NYSE)

FBIC: Firstbank of Illinois Co. (NAS NMS)

FBNC: First Bancorp (North Carolina) (NAS NMS)

FBO: Federal Paper Board Company Inc. (NYSE)

FBOH: First Bancorporation of Ohio (NAS NMS)

FBosIF: First Boston Income Fund Inc. (newspaper)

FBosSt: First Boston Strategic Income Fund Inc. (newspaper)

FBostn: First Boston Inc. (newspaper)

FBRC: Fabricland Inc. (NAS NMS)

FBRX: Fibronics International Inc. (NAS NMS)

FBS: First Bank System Inc. (NYSE)

FBSI: First Banc Securities Inc. (NAS NMS)

FBT: First City Bancorporation of Texas Inc. (NYSE)

FBXC: FBX Corp. (NAS NMS)

FBY: Future Budget Year

F&C: Frankfort & Cincinnati (railroad)

F de C: Ferrocarriles de Cuba (Cuban Railroads)

FC: Finance Charge

Fixed Capital

Fixed Charges

Floating Capital

Ford Motor Company of Canada Ltd. (ASE)

Foreign Currency

Full Charge

Futures Contract

Manufacturers Air Transport Service (airline)

FCA: Fabri-Centers of America Inc. (NYSE)

FCAP: First Capital Corp. (NAS NMS)

FCapHd: First Capitol Financial Corp. (Colorado) (newspaper)

FCB: Foote Cone & Belding Communications Inc. (NYSE)

FCBA: Fair Credit Billing Act

FCBN: Fluorocarbon Co., The (NAS NMS)

FCC: Federal Communications Commission

First Central Financial Corp. (ASE)

FCDA: First Federal S&L Assn. of Coeur D'Alene (NAS NMS)

FCDU: Foreign Currency Deposit Units

FCE: Foreign Currency Exchange

Forest City Enterprises Inc. (ASE)

FCF: Free Cash Flow

FCFI: First Capitol Financial Corp. (Colorado) (NAS NMS)

FC&G: Fernwood, Columbia & Gulf (railroad)

FCH: First Capital Holding Corp. (NYSE)

FCHT: First Federal S&L Assn. of Chattanooga (NAS NMS)

FCI: Fairfield Communities Inc. (NYSE)

FCIA: Foreign Credit Insurance Association

FCIN: Frankfort and Cincinnati (railroad)

FCLR: First Commercial Corp. (Arkansas) (NAS NMS)

FCM: Futures Commission Merchant

FCNC: First Citizens Bancshares Inc. (NAS NMS)

FCO: First Connecticut Small Business Investment Co., The (ASE)

FCOA: Foremost Corporation of America (NAS NMS)

FCOB: First Commercial Bancorp. (California) (NAS NMS)

FCOL: First Colonial Bankshares Corp. (Illinois) (NAS NMS)

FCOM: First Commerce Corp. (Louisiana) (NAS NMS)

FCP: Ferrocarril del Pacifico (Pacific Railroad)

FCPA: Foreign Corrupt Practice Act

FCR: Firstcorp Inc. (ASE)

FCRA: Fair Credit Reporting Act

fcs: franc (currency of France)

FCSC: Foreign Claims Settlement Commission

FCTR: First Charter Corp. (NAS NMS)

fcty: factory

FCU: Federal Credit Union

FCUS: Federal Credit Union System

FCX: Freeport-McMoRan Copper Co. (NYSE)

FCY: First City Industries Inc. (NYSE)

fd: fund

funding

F&D: Freight and Demurrage

FDCPA: Fair Debt Collection Practices Act

FDDM: Fort Dodget, Des Moines and Southern (railway)

fdg: funding

FDI: Foreign Private Direct Investment

FDIC: Federal Deposit Insurance Corporation

FDLN: Food Lion Inc. (NAS NMS)

FdMog: Federal-Mogul Corp. (newspaper)

FDO: Family Dollar Stores Inc. (NYSE)

FDOS: Franklin Computer Corp. (NAS NMS)

FDPC: FDP Corp. (NAS NMS)

FdSgnl: Federal Signal Corp. (newspaper)

FDX: Federal Express Corp. (NYSE)

F&E: Facilities and Equipment

FE: Foreign Exchange Futures Exchange

FEA: Federal Energy Administration

FEBC: First Eastern Corp. (Pennsylvania) (NAS NMS)

FEC: Florida East Coast Railroad

FECDBA: Foreign Exchange and Currency Deposit Brokers Association

FECOM: European Monetary Cooperation Fund

FED: Federal Reserve System FirstFed Financial Corp. (NYSE)

Feders: Fedders Corp. (newspaper)

FedExp: Federal Express Corp. (newspaper)

FEDF: Federated Financial S&L Assn. (Wisconsin) (NAS NMS)

Fed Funds: Federal Funds

FedlPB: Federal Paper Board Company Inc. (newspaper)

FedNM: Federal National Mortgage Assn. (newspaper)

FEDPAC: Federal Pacific Lakes Line (steamship)

FedRlty: Federal Realty Investment Trust (newspaper)

FEDSEA: Federal South East Asia Line (steamship)

FEEDBAC: Foreign Exchange, Eurodollar and Branch Accounting

FEI: Financial Executives Institute Frequency Electronics Inc. (ASE)

FEIA: Foreign Earned Income Act

FELE: Franklin Electric Company Inc. (NAS NMS)

FEmp: First Empire State Corp. (newspaper)

FEOF: Foreign Exchange Operations Fund

FERO: Ferrofluidics Corp. (NAS NMS)

Ferro: Ferro Corp. (newspaper)

FES: First Empire State Corp. (ASE)

FESX: First Essex Bancorp Inc. (NAS NMS)

FET: Federal Excise Tax

FEX: Foreign Exchange

FEXC: First Executive Corp. (NAS NMS)

FF: First Financial Fund Inc. (NYSE)

FFA: FirstFed America Inc. (ASE)

FFAL: First Federal of Alabama FSB (NAS NMS)

FFAM: First Family Group Inc. (NAS NMS)

FFB: Federal Financing Bank First Fidelity Bancorporation (New Jersey) (NYSE) (newspaper)

FFBC: First Financial Bancorp (Ohio) (NAS NMS)

FFBcp: First Federal Bancorp Inc. (Michigan) (newspaper)

FFBK: First Florida Banks Inc. (NAS NMS)

FF&C: Full Faith and Credit

FFC: Fireman's Fund Corp. (NYSE) Full Faith and Credit

FFCA: Carolina Bancorp Inc. (NAS NMS)

FFCH: First Financial Holdings Inc. (West Virginia) (NAS NMS)

FFCS: First Colorado Financial Corp. (NAS NMS)

FFCT: FFB Corp. (NAS NMS)

FFES: First Federal S&L Assn. of East Hartford (NAS NMS)

FFFC: Franklin First Financial Corp. (NAS NMS)

FFHC: First Financial Corp. (Wisconsin) (NAS NMS)

FFHP: First Federal S&L Assn. of Harrisburg (NAS NMS)

FFHS: First Franklin Corp. (NAS NMS)

FFI: Finance For Industry

FFinFd: First Financial Fund Inc. (newspaper)

FFKY: First Federal Savings Bank of Elizabethtown (Kentucky) (NAS NMS)

FFKZ: First Federal S&L of Kalamazoo (NAS NMS)

FFMA: Fidelity Federal Savings Bank (Indiana) (NAS NMS)

FFMC: Federal Farm Mortgage Corporation
First Financial Management Corp. (NAS NMS)

FFMY: First Federal S&L Assn. of Fort Myers (NAS NMS)

FFNS: First Financial Savings Assn. FA (Ohio) (NAS NMS)

FFOD: First Federal Savings Bank (Tennessee) (NAS NMS)

FFOM: First Federal of Michigan (NAS NMS)

FFP: FFP Partners LP (ASE) (newspaper)
Firm Fixed Price

FFPC: Florida First Federal Savings Bank (NAS NMS)

FFPR: First Federal Savings Bank of Puerto Rico (NAS NMS)

FFS: First Federal Bancorp Inc. (Michigan) (ASE)

FFSD: First Federal Savings Bank (Alabama) (NAS NMS)

FFSH: Farm Fresh Inc. (NAS NMS)

FFSL: Fulton Federal S&L Assn. of Atlanta (NAS NMS)

FFSM: First Federal Savings Bank of Montana (NAS NMS)

FFSW: First Federal S&L Assn. of Wooster (Ohio) (NAS NMS)

FFTN: Fidelity Federal S&L Assn. of Tennessee (NAS NMS)

FFWP: First Federal of Western Pennsylvania (NAS NMS)

FFWS: First Farwest Corp. (NAS NMS)

FFWV: First Fidelity Bancorp Inc. (NAS NMS)

FG: USF & G Corp. (NYSE)

FGBC: First Golden Bancorporation (NAS NMS)

FGE: Fitchburg Gas & Electric Light Co. (ASE)

FGI: Foothill Group Inc., The (NYSE)

FGL: Financial General Ledger FMC Gold Co. (NYSE)

fgn: foreign
foreigner

FGN: Flow General Inc. (NYSE)

FGRP: Farmers Group Inc. (NAS NMS)

FGSV: First Georgia Holding Corp. (NAS NMS)

FHB: Federal Home Bank

FHFC: Farm House Foods Corp. (NAS NMS)

FHLBA: Federal Home Loan Bank Administration

FHLBB: Federal Home Loan Bank Board

FHLBS: Federal Home Loan Bank System

FHLMC: Federal Home Loan Mortgage Corporation

FHO: Frederick's of Hollywood Inc. (ASE)

FHR: Fisher Foods Inc. (NYSE)

FHWN: First Hawaiian Inc. (NAS NMS)

FI: Foreign Investment

FIAM: First American Bank & Trust of Palm Beach County (Florida) (NAS NMS)

Fibrbd: Fibreboard Corp. (newspaper)

FIBV: Fédération International des Bourses de Valeurs (International Federation of Stock Exchanges)

FIC: Federal Insurance Contribution
Freight, Insurance, Carriage

FICA: Federal Insurance Contributions Act

FICB: Federal Intermediate Credit Bank

FICI: Fair, Isaac & Company Inc. (NAS NMS)

FICS: Financial Information and Control System
Forecasting and Inventory Control System

fid: fidelity
fiduciary

FID: Fidata Corp. (ASE)

FidlFn: Fidelity National Financial Inc. (newspaper)

FIF: Financial News Composite Fund Inc. (NYSE)

FIGI: Figgie International Holdings Inc. (NAS NMS)

FII: Franked Investment Income

FIIA: First Interstate of Iowa Inc. (NAS NMS)

FILE: FileNet Corp. (NAS NMS)

Filtrk: Filtertek Companies, The (newspaper)

fin: finance
financial

FIN: Financial Corporation of America (NYSE)

FINAR: Financial Analysis and Reporting

FINH: First NH Banks Inc. (NAS NMS)

FINMAN: Financial Management

FinNws: Financial News Composite Fund Inc. (newspaper)

Finstat: Financial Times database of key statistical information

Fintste: First Interstate Bancorp. (newspaper)

Finvst: Finevest Foods Inc. (newspaper)

FINX: Fingermatrix Inc. (NAS NMS)

FIO: For Information Only

FIPS: Foreign Interest Payment Security

FireFd: Fireman's Fund Corp. (newspaper)

FIRF: First Financial Savings Assn. (Pennsylvania) (NAS NMS)

FIRO: First Ohio Bankshares Inc. (NAS NMS)

FIS: Fischbach Corp. (NYSE)

FISB: First Indiana Corp. (NAS NMS)

Fischb: Fischbach Corp. (newspaper)

FischP: Fischer & Porter Co. (newspaper)

FishFd: Fisher Foods Inc. (newspaper)

FISV: FIserv Inc. (NAS NMS)

FIT: Fab Industries Inc. (ASE)
Federal Income Tax
Free In Truck
Free of Income Tax

FITB: Fifth Third Bancorp (Ohio) (NAS NMS)

FITC: Financial Trust Corp. (NAS NMS)

FitcGE: Fitchburg Gas & Electric Light Co. (newspaper)

FITW: Federal Income Tax Withholding

FIWI: First Interstate Corporation of Wisconsin (NAS NMS)

FJ&G: Fonda, Johnstown & Gloversville (railroad)

FJQ: Fedders Corp. (NYSE)

FKL: Franklin Corp., The (ASE)

FKM: John Fluke Manufacturing Company Inc. (ASE)

FLA: Florida East Coast (railway) Florida East Coast Industries Inc. (NYSE)

FlaEC: Florida East Coast Industries Inc. (newspaper)

FLAEF: Florida Employers Insurance Co. (NAS NMS)

FLAG: First Federal S&L Assn. of LaGrange (NAS NMS)

Flanign: Flanigan's Enterprises Inc. (newspaper)

FlaPrg: Florida Progress Corp. (newspaper)

FlaRck: Florida Rock Industries Inc. (newspaper)

FlaStl: Florida Steel Corp. (newspaper)

FLB: Federal Land Bank Federal Loan Bank

FLD: Fieldcrest Cannon Inc. (NYSE)

Fldscrst: Fieldcrest Cannon Inc. (newspaper)

FLE: Fleetwood Enterprises Inc. (NYSE)

FleetEn: Fleetwood Enterprises Inc. (newspaper)

Flemng: Fleming Companies Inc. (newspaper)

FLEX: Flextronics Inc. (NAS NMS)

FLFC: First Liberty Financial Corp. (NAS NMS)

FLFE: Florida Federal S&L Assn. (NAS NMS)

FlghtSf: FlightSafety International Inc. (newspaper)

FLGL: Flagler Bank Corp. (NAS NMS)

FLM: Fleming Companies Inc. (NYSE)

FLO: Flowers Industries Inc. (NYSE)

FloatPt: Floating Point Systems Inc. (newspaper)

FLOG: Falco Oil & Gas Company Inc. (NAS NMS)

FLOW: Flow Systems Inc. (NAS NMS)

Flower: Flowers Industries Inc. (newspaper)

FLP: Floating Point Systems Inc. (NYSE)

FLR: Fixed Loan Rate Fluor Corp. (NYSE)

FLS: Florida Steel Corp. (NYSE)

FLT: Fleet Norstar Financial Corp. (NYSE)

FLTI: Flight International Group Inc., The (NAS NMS)

FltNors: Fleet Norstar Financial Corp. (newspaper)

Fluke: John Fluke Manufacturing Company Inc. (newspaper)

Fluor: Fluor Corp. (newspaper)

FlwGen: Flow General Inc. (newspaper)

FLXS: Flexsteel Industries Inc. (NAS NMS)

FLY: Airlease Ltd. (NYSE)

FM: Financial Management

FMAN: February, May, August, November (securities)

FMBC: First Michigan Bank Corp. (NAS NMS)

FMBI: First Midwest Bancorp Inc. (NAS NMS)

FMC: FMC Corp. (NYSE) (newspaper)

FMCC: Freeport-McMoRan Copper Co. (newspaper)

FMC G: FMC Gold Co. (newspaper)

FMDB: First Maryland Bancorp (NAS NMS)

FMEP: Freeport-McMoRan Energy Partners Ltd. (newspaper)

FMFS: F & M Financial Services Corp. (NAS NMS)

FMGC: Freeport-McMoRan Gold Co. (newspaper)

FMLY: Family Bancorp (NAS NMS)

FMNT: F & M National Corp. (NAS NMS)

FMO: Federal-Mogul Corp. (NYSE)

FMOG: Freeport-McMoRan Oil & Gas Royalty Trust (newspaper)

FMP: Freeport-McMoRan Energy Partners Ltd. (NYSE)

FMR: Freeport-McMoRan Oil & Gas Royalty Trust (NYSE)

FMRP: Freeport-McMoRan Resource Partners LP (newspaper)

FMS: Financial Management System

Fort Meyers Southern (railroad)

FMSB: First Mutual Savings Bank (Washington) (NAS NMS)

FMV: Fair Market Value

FN: First National Corp. (California) (ASE)

St. Louis-San Francisco (railway)

FNAC: First National Cincinnati Corp. (NAS NMS)

FNB: First Chicago Corp. (NYSE)

FNBF: Florida National Banks of Florida Inc. (NAS NMS)

FNBR: F N B Rochester Corp. (NAS NMS)

FNF: Fidelity National Financial Inc. (ASE)

FNGB: First Northern S&L Assn. (Wisconsin) (NAS NMS)

FNL: Fansteel Inc. (NYSE)

FNM: Federal National Mortgage Association (NYSE)

FNMA: Federal National Mortgage Association

FNNG: Finnigan Corp. (NAS NMS)

FNNI: Financial News Network Inc. (NAS NMS)

FNPC: First National Pennsylvania Corp. (NAS NMS)

FnSBar: Financial Corporation of Santa Barbara (newspaper)

FntCal: First National Corp. (California) (newspaper)

FNWB: FNW Bancorp Inc. (NAS NMS)

FO: Firm Offer

Firm Order

FOB: Free On Board

Freight On Board

FOBB: First Oak Brook Bancshares Inc. (NAS NMS)

FOE: Ferro Corp. (NYSE)

FOIA: Freedom of Information Act

FOIL: Forest Oil Corp. (NAS NMS)

FOK: Fill Or Kill

FOMC: Federal Open Market Committee

FONR: FONAR Corp. (NAS NMS)

Foodmk: Foodmaker Inc. (newspaper)

Foodrm: Foodarama Supermarkets Inc. (newspaper)

FOQ: Free On Quay

FOR: Farmer-Owned Reserve

Fore River (railroad)

Free On Rail

FordCn: Ford Motor Company of Canada Ltd. (newspaper)

FordM: Ford Motor Co. (newspaper)

FOREX: Foreign Exchange

FORF: Fortune Financial Group Inc. (NAS NMS)

forg: forgery

ForstC: Forest City Enterprises Inc. (newspaper)

ForstL: Forest Laboratories Inc. (newspaper)

FOS: Free (Freight) On Shipboard (Steamer)

FostWh: Foster Wheeler Corp. (newspaper)

FOT: Free On Truck

FOUR: Forum Group Inc. (NAS NMS)

FOW: Free On Wagon

FOX: Foxboro Co., The (NYSE)

Foxbro: Foxboro Co., The (newspaper)

FP: Fischer & Porter Co. (ASE)
Fixed Price
Floating Point
Fully Paid

FPA: FPA Corp. (newspaper)

FPBT: Fountain Powerboat Industries Inc. (NAS NMS)

FPC: Federal Power Commission
Fixed Price Contract
Florida Progress Corp. (NYSE)

FPD: Full Paid

FPE: Fairport, Painesville and Eastern (railroad)

FP&ER: Fairport, Painesville and Eastern Railway

FPIL: Full Premium If Lost

FPL: FPL Group Inc. (NYSE)

FPL Gp: FPL Group Inc. (newspaper)

FPM: Flexible Payment Mortgage

FPNJ: First Peoples Financial Corp. (NAS NMS)

FPO: Fixed Price Open
FPA Corp. (ASE)

FPR: Federal Procurement Regulations
Fixed Price Redeterminable

FPS: Financial Planning System
First Preferred Stock

FPSI: Florida Payment System, Inc.

FPUT: Florida Public Utilities Co. (NAS NMS)

FQA: Fuqua Industries Inc. (NYSE)

fr: franc

FR: Feather River (railway)
Federal Reserve
Final Report
Freight Release

FRA: Farah Manufacturing Company Inc. (NYSE)
Federal Reserve Act

Franc: France Fund Inc., The (newspaper)

FRB: Federal Reserve Bank (Board)

FRBK: Federal Reserve Bank

FRC: First Republic Bancorp Inc. (California) (ASE)

FRCD: Floating-Rate Certificate of Deposit

FRCS: Federal Reserve Communications System

FRD: Friedman Industries Inc. (ASE)

FrdHly: Frederick's of Hollywood Inc. (newspaper)

FR DIST: Federal Reserve District

FRDN: Ferdinand Railroad

FREDDIE MAC: Federal Home Loan Mortgage Corporation

FREITS: Finite-life Real-Estate Investment Trusts

freq: frequency

FreqEl: Frequency Electronics Inc. (newspaper)

FRFD: First Community Bancorp Inc. (Illinois) (NAS NMS)

frgt: freight

Friedm: Friedman Industries Inc. (newspaper)

FriesEn: Fries Entertainment Inc. (newspaper)

FRISCO: St. Louis-San Francisco (railway)

FRK: Florida Rock Industries Inc. (ASE)

FRKT: Florida Rock & Tank Lines Inc. (NAS NMS)

FRM: First Mississippi Corp. (NYSE)

FRMG: FirstMiss Gold Inc. (NAS NMS)

FRML: Freymiller Trucking Inc. (NAS NMS)

FRMT: Fremont General Corp.
(NAS NMS)

FRN: Floating-Rate Note
France Fund Inc., The
(NYSE)

Frnkln: Franklin Corp., The (newspaper)

FrnkR: Franklin Resources Inc.
(newspaper)

FRP: Freeport-McMoRan Resource
Partners LP (NYSE)

FrptMc: Freeport-McMoRan Inc.
(newspaper)

FRS: Federal Reserve System
Financial Reporting System
Frisch's Restaurants Inc.
(ASE)

FRST: FirsTier Inc. (NAS NMS)

Frstm: Forstmann & Company Inc.
(newspaper)

frt: freight

FRT: Federal Realty Investment
Trust (NYSE)

FRTH: Fourth Financial Corp.
(NAS NMS)

Frt Ppd: Freight Prepaid

FRTR: Frontier Insurance Group
Inc. (NAS NMS)

FruhfB: Fruehauf Corp. (newspaper)

FruitL: Fruit of the Loom Inc.
(newspaper)

FRV: Fur Vault Inc., The (ASE)

FRX: Forest Laboratories Inc. (ASE)

FS: Financial Statement
Futures Spread
Key Airlines

FSA: Farm Security Administration
Flexible Spending Account

FSAM: First American Savings FA
(Pennsylvania) (NAS
NMS)

FSB: Financial Corporation of
Santa Barbara (NYSE)

FSBC: First Savings Bank FSB
(New Mexico) (NAS NMS)

FSBG: First Federal Savings Bank
of Georgia (NAS NMS)

FSBK: First Service Bank for Savings (Massachusetts)
(NAS NMS)

FSBX: Framingham Savings Bank
(Massachusetts) (NAS
NMS)

FSC: Federal Supply Code
Foreign Sales Corporations

FSCB: First Commercial Bancshares
(Alabama) (NAS NMS)

FSCC: First Federal Savings Bank
of Charlotte County (NAS
NMS)

FSCO: First Security Corp. (Utah)
(NAS NMS)

FSCR: Federal Screw Works (NAS
NMS)

FSEB: First Home Federal S&L
Assn. (Florida) (NAS NMS)

FSFC: First Security Financial
Corp. (North Carolina)
(NAS NMS)

FSFI: First State Financial Services
Inc. (NAS NMS)

FSHG: Fisher Scientific Group Inc.
(NAS NMS)

FSI: Flight Safety International Inc.
(NYSE)

FSKY: First Security Corporation of
Kentucky (NAS NMS)

FSLA: Federal Savings and Loan
Association
Franklin S&L Assn. (Michi-
gan) (NAS NMS)

FSLIC: Federal Savings and Loan
Insurance Corporation

FSM: Foodarama Supermarkets Inc.
(ASE)

FSNR: Forschner Group Inc., The
(NAS NMS)

FSPG: First Home Savings Bank
SLA (New Jersey) (NAS
NMS)

FSS: Federal Signal Corp. (NYSE)

FST: Forstmann & Company Inc. (ASE)

Fstcrp: Firstcorp Inc. (newspaper)

FstFd: FirstFed America Inc. (newspaper)

FstFed: FirstFed Financial Corp. (newspaper)

FSTR: L. B. Foster Co. (NAS NMS)

FSVB: Fort Smith and Van Buren (railway)

FT: Financial Times (UK)
Flying Tiger Line (Air Cargo) (airline)

FtAust: First Australia Fund Inc., The (newspaper)

FtBkSy: First Bank System Inc. (newspaper)

FtbTex: First City Bankcorporation of Texas (newspaper)

FTC: Federal Trade Commission
Foreign Trading Company

FtCity: First City Industries Inc. (newspaper)

FtCntrl: First Central Financial Corp. (newspaper)

FtConn: First Connecticut Small Business Investment Co., The (newspaper)

FTD: Fort Dearborn Income Securities Inc. (NYSE)

FTD DM&S: Fort Dodge, Des Moines and Southern (railway)

FtDear: Fort Dearborn Income Securities Inc. (newspaper)

FTEN: First Tennessee National Corp. (NAS NMS)

FthillG: Foothill Group Inc., The (newspaper)

FTI: Financial Times Index (UK)

FtIber: First Iberian Fund (newspaper)

FTIL: First Illinois Corp. (NAS NMS)

FTK: Filtertek Companies, The (NYSE)

FTL: Fruit of the Loom Inc. (ASE)

FtMiss: First Mississippi Corp. (newspaper)

FTNC: First National Corp. (Ohio) (NAS NMS)

FTR: Foreign Trade Reports
Fruehauf Corp. (NYSE)
Funds Transfer

FtRpBc: First Republic Bancorp Inc. (California) (newspaper)

FTSC: First Federal S&L Assn. of South Carolina (NAS NMS)

FTSE: Financial Times Stock Exchange Index (UK)

FTT: Financial Transaction Terminal

FTTR: Fretter Inc. (NAS NMS)

FTU: First Union Corp. (NYSE)

FtVaBk: First Virginia Banks Inc. (newspaper)

FtWach: First Wachovia Corp. (newspaper)

FtWisc: First Wisconsin Corp. (newspaper)

FTX: Freeport-McMoRan Inc. (NYSE)

FTZ: Foreign-Trade Zone

FUDD: Fuddruckers Inc. (NAS NMS)

FULL: H. B. Fuller Co. (NAS NMS)

FULT: Fulton Financial Corp. (Pennsylvania) (NAS NMS)

FUN: Cedar Fair LP (NYSE)

FUND: International Monetary Fund

FUnRI: First Union Real Estate Equity & Mortgage Investments (newspaper)

Fuqua: Fuqua Industries Inc. (newspaper)

FUR: First Union Real Estate Equity & Mortgage Investments (NYSE)

FurrsB: Furr's/Bishop's Cafeterias LP (newspaper)

FURS: Antonovich Inc. (NAS NMS)

FurVlt: Fur Vault Inc., The (newspaper)

FUTC: Fidelity Union Trust Company

FV: Face Value

FVB: First Virginia Banks Inc. (NYSE)

FVIF: Future Value Interest Factor

FW: First Wachovia Corp. (NYSE)
Furness, Withy and Company (steamship)
Wright Airlines

FWB: First Wisconsin Corp. (NYSE)
Fort Worth Belt (railway)

FWC: Foster Wheeler Corp. (NYSE)

FW&D: Fort Worth and Denver (railroad)

fwdr: forwarder

FWES: First Western Financial Corp. (NAS NMS)

FWF: Far West Financial Corp. (NYSE)

FWL: Furness Warren Line (steamship)

FWNC: Fort Wayne National Corp. (NAS NMS)

FWNY: First Women's Bank, The (New York) (NAS NMS)

FWO: First Wyoming Bancorporation (ASE)

FWymB: First Wyoming Bancorporation (newspaper)

FX: Foreign Exchange

FY: Fiscal Year

FYI: For Your Information

FYIG: For Your Information and Guidance

FYO: Fiscal Year Option

FYTQ: Fiscal Year Transition Quarter

G

g: gain
geld (currency of Germany)
gold
G: Dividends and Earnings in Canadian Dollars (stock listings of newspapers)
Greyhound Corp., The (NYSE)
GA: General Account
General Agent
General Automation Inc. (ASE)
General Average
Georgia Railroad
Gross Asset
GAAP: Generally Accepted Accounting Principles
GAAS: Generally Accepted Auditing Standards
GAASS: Government Agency Arbitrage and Swap System
GAB: Gabelli Equity Trust Inc., The (NYSE)
General Arrangements to Borrow
Gabelli: Gabelli Equity Trust Inc., The (newspaper)
GAC: General Acceptance Corporation
General Average Certificate
GACC: Great American Communications Co. (NAS NMS)
GACHA: Georgia Automated Clearing House Association
GACO: Garden America Corp. (NAS NMS)
GAEO: Galileo Electro-Optics Corp. (NAS NMS)
GaGulf: Georgia Gulf Corp. (newspaper)

GAI: Grand Auto Inc. (ASE)
Guaranteed Annual Income
Gainsco: Gainsco Inc. (newspaper)
GAInv: General American Investors Company Inc. (newspaper)
GAL: Lewis Galoob Toys Inc. (NYSE)
GalaxC: Galaxy Carpet Mills Inc. (newspaper)
GALCF: Galactic Resources Ltd. (NAS NMS)
GalHou: Galveston-Houston Co. (newspaper)
Gallagr: Arthur J. Gallagher & Co. (newspaper)
Galoob: Lewis Galoob Toys Inc. (newspaper)
GalxCbl: Galaxy Cablevision LP (newspaper)
GAM: General American Investors Company Inc. (NYSE)
GAMA: Gamma Biologicals Inc.
GAN: Garan Inc. (ASE)
GANDF: Galdalf Technologies Inc. (NAS NMS)
Gannet: Gannett Company Inc. (newspaper)
GANO: Georgia Northern (railway)
GAO: General Accounting Office
Gap: Gap Inc., The (newspaper)
GAP: Great Atlantic & Pacific Tea Company Inc., The (NYSE)
GaPac: Georgia-Pacific Corp. (newspaper)
GAQ: Good Average Quality
Garan: Garan Inc. (newspaper)
GAS: NICOR Inc. (NYSE)
GAS&C: Georgia, Ashburn, Sylvester & Camilla (railroad)

GAT: Greenwich Apparent Time
GATI: Gaming & Technology Inc.
(NAS NMS)
GATS: Gulf Applied Technologies
Inc. (NAS NMS)
GATT: General Agreement on Tar-
iffs and Trade
GATW: Gateway Federal S&L
Assn. (Ohio) (NAS NMS)
GATX: GATX Corp. (newspaper)
GAW: Guaranteed Annual Wage
GaylC: Gaylord Container Corp.
(newspaper)
GB: Gold Bond
Government Bond
Great Britain
Guaranteed Bond
Guardian Bancorp (ASE)
GBAN: Gateway Bancorp Inc. (New
York) (NAS NMS)
GBBS: Great Bay Bankshares Inc.
(NAS NMS)
GBCB: GBC Bancorp (NAS NMS)
GBE: Grubb & Ellis Co. (NYSE)
GBFH: Georgia Bonded Fibers Inc.
(NAS NMS)
GBLD: General Building Products
Corp. (NAS NMS)
GBND: General Binding Corp.
(NAS NMS)
GBS: General Business System
GBTS: General Banking Terminal
System
GB&W: Green Bay & Western (rail-
road)
GC: Gaylord Container (railroad)
General Counsel
Graham County (railroad)
GCA: GCA Corp. (NYSE) (newspa-
per)
GCBK: Great Country Bank (Con-
necticut) (NAS NMS)
GCCC: General Computer Corp.
(NAS NMS)
GCda: Gulf Canada Corp. (newspa-
per)

GCER: General Ceramics Inc. (NAS
NMS)
GCI: Gannett Company Inc.
(NYSE)
General Capital Increase
GCinm: General Cinema Corp.
(newspaper)
GCN: General Cinema Corp.
(NYSE)
GCO: Genesco Inc. (NYSE)
GCOR: Gencor Industries Inc. (NAS
NMS)
GCR: Gaylord Container Corp.
(ASE)
GCRA: Golden Corral Realty Corp.
(NAS NMS)
GCT: Greenwich Civil Time
GCW: Garden City Western (rail-
way)
GD: General Dynamics Corp.
(NYSE)
Good Delivery
Gross Debt
GDC: General DataComm Indus-
tries Inc. (NYSE)
GDMK: GoodMark Foods Inc. (NAS
NMS)
GDP: Gross Domestic Product
Gdrich: B.F. Goodrich Co., The
(newspaper)
GDS: Glenmore Distilleries Co.
(ASE)
GDV: General Development Corp.
(NYSE)
GDW: Golden West Financial Corp.
(NYSE)
GDX: Genovese Drug Stores Inc.
(ASE)
GDYN: Geodynamics Corp. (NAS
NMS)
GE: General Electric Co. (NYSE)
General Expenses
Greater than or Equal to
Gross Earnings
GEB: Gerber Products Co.
(NYSE)

GEC: GEICO Corp. (NYSE)
General Electric Corporation
GECM: Genicom Corp. (NAS NMS)
GED: General Energy Development Ltd. (NYSE)
GEF: Nicholas-Applegate Growth Equity Fund Inc. (NYSE)
GEICO: GEICO Corp. (newspaper)
Government Employees' Insurance Co.
GelmS: Gelman Sciences Inc. (newspaper)
GEM: Graduated Equity Mortgage
Growing Equity Mortgage
GEMC: Geriatric & Medical Centers Inc. (NAS NMS)
Gemco: GEMCO NATIONAL INC. (newspaper)
gen: general
generated
GEN: GenRad Inc. (NYSE)
GenDev: General Development Corp. (newspaper)
GenEl: General Electric Co. (newspaper)
Genetch: Genentech Inc. (newspaper)
GENI: Genetics Institute Inc. (NAS NMS)
Genisco: Genisco Technology Corp. (newspaper)
Gen Led: General Ledger
Gen Mtge: General Mortgage
GenRe: General Re Corp. (newspaper)
Gensco: Genesco Inc. (newspaper)
GenuP: Genuine Parts Co. (newspaper)
GenvD: Genovese Drug Stores Inc. (newspaper)
GENZ: Genzyme Corp. (NAS NMS)
GEO: GEO International Corp. (newspaper)
Geothermal Resources International Inc. (ASE)

GEOD: Geodyne Resources Inc. (NAS NMS)
GeoRes: Geothermal Resources International Inc. (newspaper)
GEOX: Geonex Corp. (NAS NMS)
GER: Germany Fund Inc., The (NYSE)
GerbPd: Gerber Products Co. (newspaper)
GerbSc: Gerber Scientific Inc. (newspaper)
GerFd: Germany Fund Inc., The (newspaper)
GES: Genisco Technology Corp. (ASE)
Gilt-Edged Securities
Gold Exchange Standard
GEST: Guest Supply Inc. (NAS NMS)
Getty: Getty Petroleum Corp. (newspaper)
G&F: Georgia & Florida (railroad)
GF: America First Guaranteed Income Fund (ASE)
Gulf Aviation (airline)
GFB: GF Corp. (NYSE)
GFC: Gibraltar Financial Corp. (NYSE)
GFCF: Gross Fixed Capital Formation
GF Cp: GF Corp. (newspaper)
GFCT: Greenwich Financial Corp. (NAS NMS)
GFD: Gulford Mills Inc. (NYSE)
GFGC: Great Falls Gas Co. (NAS NMS)
GFI: Graham Field Health Products Inc. (ASE)
GFO: Gulf, Mobile & Ohio (railroad)
GFS: Giant Foods Inc. (ASE)
Grand Falls Central (railway)
GG: Golden Pacific Airlines
GGC: Georgia Gulf Corp. (NYSE)

GGF: Global Growth & Income Fund Inc. (NYSE)

GGG: Graco Inc. (NYSE)

GGInc: Global Growth & Income Fund Inc. (newspaper)

GGUY: Good Guys Inc., The (NAS NMS)

GH: General Host Corp. (NYSE)

GH&H: Galveston, Houston and Henderson (railroad)

GHM: Graham Corp. (ASE)

GHO: General Homes Corp. (NYSE)

GHW: General Houseware Corp. (NYSE)

GHX: Galveston-Houston Co. (NYSE)

G&I: Growth and Income

GI: Government Initiated
Gross Inventory
Gross Investment

GIANT: GIANT GROUP LTD. (newspaper)

GiantF: Giant Food Inc. (newspaper)

GibCR: C. R. Gibson Co. (newspaper)

GIBG: Gibson Greetings Inc. (NAS NMS)

GibrFn: Gibraltar Financial Corp. (newspaper)

GIBS: C. R. Gibson Co. (ASE)

GICs: Guaranteed Income Contracts
Guaranteed Investment Contracts

GIGA: Giga-tronics Inc. (NAS NMS)

GII: Greiner Engineering Inc. (ASE)

GIL: Group Investment Linked

GILB: Gilbert Associates Inc. (NAS NMS)

Gillette: Gillette Co., The (newspaper)

GIncPl: Global Income Plus Fund Inc. (newspaper)

GIO: Guaranteed Insurability Option

GIS: General Mills Inc. (NYSE)

GISH: Gish Biomedical Inc. (NAS NMS)

GJ: Greenwich and Johnsonville (railway)

GKSR: G & K Services Inc. (NAS NMS)

GL: General Ledger
General Length
Go Long

GLA: General Ledger Account

Glatflt: P. H. Glatfelter Co. (newspaper)

Glaxo: Glaxo Holdings PLC (newspaper)

GLBC: Great Lakes Bancorp FSB (Michigan) (NAS NMS)

GlbGvt: Global Government Plus Fund Inc., The (newspaper)

GlbM: Global Marine Inc. (newspaper)

GLD: Gould Inc. (NYSE)

GLDC: Golden Enterprises Inc. (NAS NMS)

GldFld: Goldfield Corp., The (newspaper)

GldNug: Golden Nugget Inc. (newspaper)

GldWF: Golden West Financial Corp. (newspaper)

GLE: Gleason Corp. (NYSE)

GleasC: Gleason Corp. (newspaper)

Glenfed: GLENFED Inc. (newspaper)

GlfStUt: Gulf States Utilities Co. (newspaper)

GLGVF: Glamis Gold Ltd. (NAS NMS)

GLI: Global Income Plus Fund Inc. (NYSE)

GLK: Great Lakes Chemical Corp. (NYSE)

GLM: Global Marine Inc. (NYSE)

GLN: GLENFED Inc. (NYSE)

Glnmr: Glenmore Distilleries Co.
(newspaper)
GlobNR: Global Natural Resources
Inc. (newspaper)
GlobYld: Global Yield Fund Inc.,
The (newspaper)
GLP: Gould Investors LP (ASE)
GLT: P. H. Glatfelter Co. (ASE)
GLW: Corning Glass Works (NYSE)
GLX: Glaxo Holdings PLC (NYSE)
GLXIF: Glenex Industries Inc. (NAS
NMS)
GLYT: Genlyte Group Inc. (NAS
NMS)
GM: Gainesville Midland (railroad)
General Manager
General Mortgage
General Motors Corp. (NYSE)
Great Northern Airways
GMAC: General Motors Acceptance
Corp.
GMAT: Greenwich Mean Astronom-
ical Time
GMB: Good Merchandise Brand
GmbH: Gesellschaft mit beschränk-
ter Haftung (Company
with limited liability)
(German)
GMC: General Motors Corporation
Gruen Marketing Corp. (ASE)
GMCC: General Magnaplate Corp.
(NAS NMS)
GME: General Motors Class E Com-
mon Stock (NYSE) (news-
paper)
GMED: GMI Group Inc., The (NAS
NMS)
GMFD: Germania Bank FSB (Illi-
nois) (NAS NMS)
GMGW: Geraghty & Miller Inc.
(NAS NMS)
GMH: General Motors Class H
Common Stock (NYSE)
(newspaper)
GMN: Greenman Brothers Inc.
(ASE)

GM&O: Gulf, Mobile & Ohio (rail-
road)
GMot: General Motors Corp. (news-
paper)
GMP: Green Mountain Power Corp.
(NYSE) (newspaper)
GMRC: Green Mountain Railroad
Corporation
GMROI: Gross Margin Return on
Investment
GMT: GATX Corp. (NYSE)
Greenwich Mean Time
GMV: Guaranteed Minimum Value
GMW: General Microwave Corp.
(ASE)
G&N: Greenville & Northern (rail-
road)
GN: Georgia Northern (railroad)
Great Northern (railway)
GN&A: Graysonia, Nashville &
Ashdown (railroad)
GNA: Gainsco Inc. (ASE)
GnAuto: General Automation Inc.
(newspaper)
GNCrp: GenCorp Inc. (newspaper)
GnData: General DataComm Indus-
tries Inc. (newspaper)
GNDR: Gander Mountain Inc. (NAS
NMS)
GnDyn: General Dynamics Corp.
(newspaper)
GNE: Genentech Inc. (NYSE)
GnEmp: General Employment En-
terprises Inc. (newspa-
per)
GnEngy: General Energy Develop-
ment Ltd. (newspaper)
GNEX: Genex Corp. (NAS NMS)
GNG: Golden Nugget Inc.
(NYSE)
GnHme: General Homes Corp.
(newspaper)
GnHost: General Host Corp. (news-
paper)
GnHous: General Housewares
Corp. (newspaper)

GNI: Great Northern Iron Ore Properties (NYSE)
Gross National Income
GNIC: Guaranty National Corp. (NAS NMS)
GnInst: General Instrument Corp. (newspaper)
GNIrn: Great Northern Iron Ore Properties (newspaper)
GNL: GEMCO NATIONAL Inc. (ASE)
GNMA: Government National Mortgage Association
GnMicr: General Microwave Corp. (newspaper)
GnMills: General Mills Inc. (newspaper)
GNOXF: Golden North Resource Corp. (NAS NMS)
GNP: Gross National Product
GNR: Global Natural Resources Inc. (ASE)
GnRad: GenRad Inc. (newspaper)
GnRefr: General Refractories Co. (newspaper)
GnSignl: General Signal Corp. (newspaper)
GNT: Green Tree Acceptance Inc. (NYSE)
GNTE: Granite Co-Operative Bank (NAS NMS)
GNTX: Gentex Corp. (NAS NMS)
GntYl: Giant Yellowknife Mines Ltd. (newspaper)
GNW: Genessee and Wyoming (railroad)
GO: Collins Industries Inc. (ASE)
General-Obligation (bond)
General Office
General Order
General Organization
Government Obligations
Gulf Oil (steamship)
GOC: Gulf Canada Corp. (ASE)
GOI: Gearhart Industries Inc. (NYSE)

GOOD: Goody Products Inc. (NAS NMS)
Goodyr: Goodyear Tire & Rubber Co., The (newspaper)
GOP: Graham-McCormick Oil & Gas Partnership (ASE)
GorRup: Gorman-Rupp Co., The (newspaper)
GOSH: Oshkosh B'Gosh Inc. (NAS NMS)
GOT: Gottschalks Inc. (NYSE)
Gotchk: Gottschalks Inc. (newspaper)
GOTLF: Gotaas-Larsen Shipping Corp. (NAS NMS)
Gould: Gould Inc. (newspaper)
GOV: Global Government Plus Fund Inc., The (NYSE)
GP: Georgia-Pacific Corp. (NYSE)
Going Public
Gold Points
Grace Periods
Gross Profits
Growth in total Profit
GPAK: Graphic Packaging Corp. (NAS NMS)
GPAM: Graduated-Payment Adjustable Mortgage
GPAR: General Parametrics Corp. (NAS NMS)
GPC: Genuine Parts Co. (NYSE)
GPI: Guardsman Products Inc. (NYSE)
GPL: General Price Level
GPLA: General Price Level Adjusted (Accounting)
GPM: Graduated-Payment Mortgage
GPO: General Post Office
GIANT GROUP LTD. (NYSE)
Government Printing Office
GPPXF: Giant Bay Resources Ltd. (NAS NMS)
GPRL: Gulf Puerto Rico Lines (steamship)
GPRO: Gen-Probe Inc. (NAS NMS)

GPS: Gap Inc., The (NYSE)
GPU: General Public Utilities Corp. (NYSE) (newspaper)
GQ: Golden West Airlines
Grumman Corp. (NYSE)
GR: B. F. Goodrich Co. (NYSE)
General Air (airline)
Gross Receipts
Gross Revenue
GRA: W. R. Grace & Co. (NYSE)
Grace: W. R. Grace & Co. (newspaper)
GRACE: Grace Line (steamship)
Graco: Graco Inc. (newspaper)
Graham: Graham Corp. (newspaper)
GrahMc: Graham-McCormick Oil & Gas Partnership (newspaper)
GRAIN: Bank of Granite Corp. (North Carolina) (NAS NMS)
Graingr: W. W. Grainger Inc. (newspaper)
GRAN FLOTA BLANCA: Great White Fleet (United Fruit Company) (steamship)
Grang: Granges Exploration Ltd. (newspaper)
GRAR: Great American Recreation Inc. (NAS NMS)
GRB: Gerber Scientific Inc. (NYSE)
GRBC: Great Southern Federal Savings Bank (NAS NMS)
GRC: Gorman-Rupp Co., The (ASE)
GRCO: Gradco Systems Inc. (NAS NMS)
GrdnB: Guardian Bancorp. (newspaper)
GrdPrd: Guardsman Products Inc. (newspaper)

GRE: Gulf Resources & Chemical Corp. (NYSE)
Greiner: Greiner Engineering Inc. (newspaper)
Grenm: Greenman Brothers Inc. (newspaper)
GrenTr: Green Tree Acceptance Inc. (newspaper)
GREY: Grey Advertising Inc. (NAS NMS)
Greyh: Greyhound Corp., The (newspaper)
GRGI: Greenery Rehabilitation Group Inc. (NAS NMS)
GrhmFld: Graham Field Health Products Inc. (newspaper)
GRI: G. R. I. Corp. (newspaper)
GRIF: Griffin Technology Inc. (NAS NMS)
GRIT: Grantor Retained Income Trust
Grubb & Ellis Realty Income Trust (NAS NMS)
GRL: General Instrument Corp. (NYSE)
GRN: General Re Corp. (NYSE)
Greenville and Northern Railway
GrndAu: Grand Auto Inc. (newspaper)
GRNR: Grand River Railway
GRO: Grow Group Inc. (NYSE)
GROF: Groff Industries Inc. (NAS NSM)
GROS: Grossman's Inc. (NAS NMS)
GROV: Grove Bank for Savings (NAS NMS)
GrowGp: Grow Group Inc. (newspaper)
GRPH: Graphic Industries Inc. (NAS NMS)
GRPI: Greenwich Pharmaceuticals Inc. (NAS NMS)
GRR: Georgetown Railroad
G. R. I. Corp. (ASE)

GRST: Grist Mill Co. (NAS NMS)

GRT: Graphic Technology Inc. (ASE)
Gross Register(ed) Tonnage

GrTch: Graphic Technology Inc. (newspaper)

GrtLkC: Great Lakes Chemical Corp. (newspaper)

GRTR: Greater New York Savings Bank (NAS NMS)

GrubEl: Grubb & Ellis Co. (newspaper)

Gruen: Gruen Marketing Corp. (newspaper)

Grumn: Grumman Corp. (newspaper)

GRX: General Refractories Co. (NYSE)

GS: Gilette Co., The (NYSE)
Glamour Stock
Government Securities
Gross Sales
Gross Spread
Growth Stock

GSA: General Services Administration
Gulf and South American Steamship Company

GSBI: Granite State Bankshares Inc. (New Hampshire) (NAS NMS)

GSBK: Germantown Savings Bank (Pennsylvania) (NAS NMS)

GSC: Gelman Sciences Inc. (ASE)

GSCC: Graphic Scanning Corp. (NAS NMS)

GSES: Government Sponsored Enterprises

GSF: ACM Government Securities Fund Inc. (NYSE)
Georgia Southern and Florida (railroad)

GSO: Growth Stock Outlook Trust Inc. (NYSE)

GSOF: Group 1 Software Inc. (NAS NMS)

GSP: Generalized Scheme of Preferences
Generalized System of Tariff Preferences

GSR: Global-Shared Resources

GSSC: Grenada Sunburst System Corp. (NAS NMS)

GST: Generation-Skipping Transfer (tax)

GSTP: Generalized System of Tariff Preferences

GSU: Gulf States Utilities Co. (NYSE)

GSW: Great Southwest (railroad)

GSX: General Signal Corp. (NYSE)

GT: Gift Tax
Goodyear Tire & Rubber Co., The (NYSE)
Grand Trunk (railroad)
Gross Tonnage
Gross Tons

GTA: Great American First Savings Bank (NYSE)

GtAFst: Great American First Savings Bank (newspaper)

GTAM: Great American Corp. (NAS NMS)

GtAtPc: Great Atlantic & Pacific Tea Company Inc., The (newspaper)

GTC: Good 'Til Cancelled (Countermanded)

GTCH: GTECH Corp. (NAS NMS)

gtd: guaranteed

GT&E: General Telephone and Electronics Corp.

GTE: GTE Corp. (NYSE) (newspaper)

GthStk: Growth Stock Outlook Trust Inc. (newspaper)

GTI: GTI Corp. (ASE) (newspaper)

GTM: Good-This-Month order

GTOS: Gantos Inc. (NAS NMS)

GTSC: GTS Corp. (NAS NMS)

GTV: Galaxy Cablevision LP (ASE)

GTW: Grand Trunk Western (railroad)

GtWash: Greater Washington Investors Inc. (newspaper)

GtWFn: Great Western Financial Corp. (newspaper)

GTWY: Gateway Bank (Connecticut) (NAS NMS)

GTY: Getty Petroleum Corp. (NYSE)

G&U: Grafton and Upton (railroad)

guar: guarantee

GUC: Good-Until-Canceled order

GULD: Goulds Pumps Inc. (NAS NMS)

GuldLP: Gould Investors LP (newspaper)

GULF: Gulf Oil Corporation (steamship)

Gulfrd: Guilford Mills Inc. (newspaper)

GulfRs: Gulf Resources & Chemical Corp. (newspaper)

GUN: Gundle Environmental Systems Inc. (ASE)

Gundle: Gundle Environmental Systems Inc. (newspaper)

GV: Goldfield Corp., The (ASE) Territory Airlines

GVMF: Golden Valley Microwave Foods Inc. (NAS NMS)

GVMI: GV Medical Inc. (NAS NMS)

GVO: Gross Value of Output

GVT: Dean Witter Government Income Trust (NYSE)

G&W: Genesee and Western (railroad)

GWA: Golden West Airlines

GWAY: Gateway Communications Inc. (NAS NMS)

GWCC: GWC Corp. (NAS NMS)

GWF: Great Western Financial Corp. (NYSE)

GWI: Greater Washington Investors Inc. (ASE)

GWP: Gross World Product

GWR: Great Western Railway

GWSH: George Washington Corp. (NAS NMS)

GWT: GW Utilities Ltd. (ASE)

GWTI: Groundwater Technology Inc. (NAS NMS)

GW Ut: GW Utilities Ltd. (newspaper)

GWW: W. W. Grainger Inc. (NYSE)

GX: GEO International Corp. (NYSE)

Great Lakes Air Service (airline)

GXL: Granges Exploration Ltd. (ASE)

GXY: Galaxy Carpet Mills Inc. (ASE)

GY: GenCorp Inc. (NYSE)

GYK: Giant Yellowknife Mines Ltd. (ASE)

GYSCO: Great Yarmouth Shipping Company

GZT: Greenwich Zone Time

H: Hawaiian Airlines
HelmResources Inc. (ASE)
Declared or paid stock dividend
or split-up (stock listings of
newspapers)
HA: HAL Inc. (ASE)
Home Address
House Account
HABE: Haber Inc. (NAS NMS)
HACH: Hach Co. (NAS NMS)
HAD: Hadson Corp. (NYSE)
Herein After Described
Hadson: Hadson Corp. (newspaper)
HAI: Hampton Industries Inc. (ASE)
HAKO: Hako Minuteman Inc. (NAS
NMS)
HAL: HAL Inc. (newspaper)
Halliburton Co. (NYSE)
(newspaper)
Halifax: Halifax Engineering Inc.
(newspaper)
HALL: Hall Financial Group Inc.
(NAS NMS)
HallFB: Frank B. Hall & Company
Inc. (newspaper)
Halmi: Robert Halmi Inc. (newspa-
per)
Halwod: Hallwood Group Inc., The
(newspaper)
HAML: Hamilton Oil Corp. (NAS
NMS)
HampH: Hampton Healthcare Inc.
(newspaper)
Hamptl: Hampton Industries Inc.
(newspaper)
HAMS: Smithfield Companies Inc.,
The (NAS NMS)
HAN: Hanson Trust PLC (NYSE)
HANA: Hana Biologics Inc. (NAS
NMS)

hand: handling
HandH: Handy & Harman (newspa-
per)
Handlm: Handleman Co. (newspaper)
HanFb: Hancock Fabrics Inc. (news-
paper)
Hanfrd: Hannaford Brothers Co.
(newspaper)
HanJI: John Hancock Investors
Trust (newspaper)
HanJS: John Hancock Income Secu-
rities Trust (newspaper)
Hanna: M. A. Hanna Co. (newspa-
per)
Hanson: Hanson Trust PLC (news-
paper)
HAR: Harman International Indus-
tries Inc. (NYSE)
HarBrJ: Harcourt Brace Jovanovich
Inc. (newspaper)
HARG: Harper Group Inc., The
(NAS NMS)
HARL: Harleysville Savings Assn.
(Pennsylvania) (NAS NMS)
Harley: Harley-Davidson Inc. (news-
paper)
Harlnd: John H. Harland Co., The
(newspaper)
Harman: Harman International In-
dustries Inc. (newspaper)
Harnish: Harnischfeger Industries
Inc. (newspaper)
Harris: Harris Corp. (newspaper)
Harsco: Harsco Corp. (newspaper)
Hartmx: Hartmarx Corp. (newspa-
per)
Harvey: Harvey Group Inc., The
(newspaper)
HARVY: Harvard Securities Group
PLC (NAS NMS)

HAS: Hasbro Inc. (ASE)
Hasbr: Hasbro Inc. (newspaper)
HASR: Hauserman Inc. (NAS NMS)
Hasting: Hastings Manufacturing Co. (newspaper)
HAT: Hatteras Income Securities Inc. (NYSE)
HATH: Hathaway Corp. (NAS NMS)
HattSe: Hatteras Income Securities Inc. (newspaper)
HAVA: Harvard Industries Inc. (NAS NMS)
HAVT: Haverty Furniture Companies Inc. (NAS NMS)
HawEl: Hawaiian Electric Industries Inc. (newspaper)
H&B: Hampton & Branchville (railroad)
HB: Hillenbrand Industries Inc. (NYSE)
HBAN: Huntington Bancshares Inc. (NAS NMS)
HBC: Hudson's Bay Company (steamship)
HBE: Honeybee Inc. (ASE)
HBEN: Home Beneficial Corp. (NAS NMS)
HBJ: Harcourt Brace Jovanovich Inc. (NYSE)
HBLRR: Harbor Belt Line Railroad
HBOC: HBO & Co. (NAS NMS)
HBOL: Hartford Steam Boiler Inspection & Insurance Co. (NAS NMS)
HBS: Hoboken Shore (railroad)
HBSI: Hamptons Bancshares Inc. (NAS NMS)
HBT: Houston Belt and Terminal (railroad)
H&BTM: Huntington & Broad Top Mountain Railroad & Coal Co.
HBW: Howard B. Wolf Inc. (ASE)

HC: Helene Curtis Industries Inc. (NYSE)
Holding Company
HCA: Hospital Care Corporation of America (NYSE) (newspaper)
HCCC: HealthCare COMPARE Corp. (NAS NMS)
HCCI: HCC Industries Inc. (NAS NMS)
HCH: Health-Chem Corp. (ASE)
HCN: Health Care REIT Inc. (ASE)
HCO: HUBCO Inc. (ASE)
HCP: Health Care Property Investors Inc. (NYSE)
HCSB: Home & City Savings Bank (New York) (NAS NMS)
HCSG: Healthcare Services Group Inc. (NAS NMS)
HD: Aero Servicios (airline)
Home Depot Inc., The (NYSE)
HDC: Holder in Due Course
HDCO: HADCO Corp. (NAS NMS)
HDI: Harley-Davidson Inc. (NYSE)
HDL: Handleman Co. (NYSE)
HDR: Heldor Industries Inc. (ASE)
HDRP: HDR Power Systems Inc. (NAS NMS)
HDS: Hills Department Stores Inc. (NYSE)
HDTV: High-Definition Television
HDYN: Healthdyne Inc. (NAS NMS)
HE: Hawaiian Electric Industries Inc.
Hollis and Eastern (railroad)
HECH: Hechinger Co. (NAS NMS)
Hecks: Heck's Inc. (newspaper)
HeclaM: Hecla Mining Co. (newspaper)
HEI: HEICO Corp. (ASE)
HEIC: HEI Corp. (Texas) (NAS NMS)
Heico: HEICO Corp. (newspaper)
HEII: HEI Inc. (Minnesota) (NAS NMS)

Heilig: Heilig-Meyers Co. (newspaper)

HeinWr: Hein-Werner Corp. (newspaper)

Heinz: H. J. Heinz Co. (newspaper)

HEKN: Heekin Can Inc. (NAS NMS)

Heldor: Heldor Industries Inc. (newspaper)

HELE: Helen of Troy Corp. (NAS NMS)

HelmP: Helmerich & Payne Inc. (newspaper)

HelmR: HelmResources Inc. (newspaper)

HelneC: Helene Curtis Industries Inc. (newspaper)

HelthM: Health-Mor Inc. (newspaper)

Helvet: Helvetia Fund Inc., The (newspaper)

HELX: Helix Technology Corp. (NAS NMS)

HEMO: HemoTec Inc. (NAS NMS)

HENG: Henley Group Inc., The (NAS NMS)

Herculs: Hercules Inc. (newspaper)

HeritEn: Heritage Entertainment Inc. (newspaper)

HERS: Heritage Financial Services Inc. (NAS NMS)

HershO: Hershey Oil Corp. (newspaper)

HewlPk: Hewlett-Packard Co. (newspaper)

HEX: Heck's Inc. (NYSE)

Hexcel: Hexcel Corp. (newspaper)

H/F: Held For

HFC: Household Finance Corp.

HFD: Home Federal S&L Assn. (California) (NYSE)

HFED: Heart Federal S&L Assn. (California) (NAS NMS)

HFET: Home Federal S&L Assn. of Upper East Tennessee (NAS NMS)

HFGA: Home Federal Savings Bank of Georgia (NAS NMS)

HFI: Hudson Foods Inc. (ASE)

HFIN: Horizon Financial Services Inc. (NAS NMS)

HFL: Hawaii Freight Lines (steamship)
Homestead Financial Corp. (NYSE)

HFM: Hold For Money

HFMD: Home Federal Corp. (Maryland) (NAS NMS)

HFNO: Home Federal Savings Bank, Northern Ohio (NAS NMS)

HFOX: Home Federal Savings Bank (Ohio) (NAS NMS)

HFR: Hold For Release

HFSF: Home Federal S&L Assn. of San Francisco (NAS NMS)

HGC: Hudson General Corp. (ASE)

HGIC: Harleysville Group Inc. (NAS NMS)

HH: Hetch Hetchy (railroad)
H. Hogarth and Sons (steamship)
Hooper Holmes Inc. (ASE)

HHA: H. H. Anderson Line (steamship)

HHBX: HHB Systems Inc. (NAS NMS)

HHC: Horizon Healthcare Corp. (NYSE)

HHFA: Housing and Home Finance Agency

HHGP: Harris & Harris Group Inc. (NAS NMS)

HHH: Heritage Entertainment Inc. (ASE)

HHI: Hampton Healthcare Inc. (ASE)

HHOT: H & H Oil Tool Company Inc. (NAS NMS)

HI: Holton Inter-Urban (railway)
Hot Issue

Household International Inc. (NYSE)

HIA: Holiday Corp. (NYSE)

HIBC: Hibernia Corp. (NAS NMS)

HIGB: J. Higby's Inc. (NAS NMS)

HIGH: Highland Superstores Inc. (NAS NMS)

HII: Healthcare International Inc. (ASE)

HiInco: High Income Advance Trust (newspaper)

HillDp: Hills Department Stores Inc. (newspaper)

Hillnbd: Hillenbrand Industries Inc. (newspaper)

Hilton: Hilton Hotels Corp. (newspaper)

HIMG: Health Images Inc. (NAS NMS)

Himont: HIMONT Inc. (newspaper)

H In DC: Holder In Due Course

Hindrl: Hinderliter Industries Inc. (newspaper)

HIP: Health Insurance Plan
Hipotronics Inc. (ASE)

HIPT: Hi-Port Industries Inc. (NAS NMS)

Hiptron: Hipotronics Inc. (newspaper)

HiShear: Hi-Shear Industries Inc. (newspaper)

HIT: Hitachi Ltd. (NYSE)

Hitachi: Hitachi Ltd. (newspaper)

HITK: HITK Corp. (NAS NMS)

HIVT: Health Insurance of Vermont Inc. (NAS NMS)

HIWDF: Highwood Resources Ltd. (NAS NMS)

HiYld: High Yield Income Fund Inc., The (newspaper)

HiYldPl: High Yield Plus Fund Inc. (newspaper)

HKF: Hancock Fabrics Inc. (NYSE)

HKIBOR: Hong Kong Inter-Bank Offered Rate

HL: Hecla Mining Co. (NYSE)
Holiday Airlines
Home Lines (steamship)

HLBB: Home Loan Bank Board

HLCO: Healthco International Inc. (NAS NMS)

HLDA: Hold Acknowledge

HII: Healthcare International Inc. (newspaper)

HLME: D. H. Holmes Company Ltd. (NAS NMS)

HLNE: Hillsboro and Northeastern (railroad)

HLT: Highly Leveraged Transaction
Hilton Hotels Corp. (NYSE)

HlthCh: Health-Chem Corp. (newspaper)

HlthCP: Health Care Property Investors Inc. (newspaper)

HlthCr: Health Care REIT Inc. (newspaper)

HlthMn: Health Management Associates Inc. (newspaper)

HltRhB: Health & Rehabilitation Properties Trust (newspaper)

Hltvst: HealthVest (newspaper)

HMA: Health Management Associates Inc. (ASE)

HMC: Honda Motor Company Ltd. (NYSE)

HME: Home Group Inc., The (NYSE)

HmeD: Home Depot Inc., The (newspaper)

HmeGp: Home Group Inc., The (newspaper)

HMF: Hastings Manufacturing Co. (ASE)

HmFB: Homestead Financial Corp. (newspaper)

HmFSD: Home Federal S&L Assn. (California) (newspaper)

HMG: Hedge Mutual Fund
HMG Property Investors Inc. (ASE) (newspaper)

HMI: Health-Mor Inc. (ASE)
HMOA: HMO American Inc. (NAS NMS)
HmpU: Hampton Utilities Trust (newspaper)
HMSB: Home Savings Bank, The (New York) (NAS NMS)
HMSD: Homestead Savings Assn. (Pennsylvania) (NAS NMS)
HMSS: H. M. S. S. Inc. (NAS NMS)
HmstF: Homestead Financial Corp. (newspaper)
Hmstke: Homestake Mining Co. (newspaper)
HMT: HIMONT Inc. (NYSE)
HMY: Heilig-Meyers Co. (NYSE)
HN: Hutchinson and Northern (railroad)
HNBC: Harleysville National Corp. (NAS NMS)
HNCO: Henley Manufacturing Corp. (NAS NMS)
HND: Hinderliter Industries Inc. (ASE)
HNE: Harriman and Northeastern (railroad)
HNH: Handy & Harman (NYSE)
HNIS: Heritage Bancorp Inc. (Massachusetts) (NAS NMS)
HNM: M. A. Hanna Co. (NYSE)
HNW: Hein-Werner Corp. (ASE)
HNZ: H. J. Heinz Co. (NYSE)
HO: Head Office
Home Office
Houston Oil Trust (ASE)
HOBC: Howard Bancorp (NAS NMS)
HOC: Holly Corp. (ASE)
HOF: Hofmann Industries Inc. (ASE)
Hofman: Hofmann Industries Inc. (newspaper)
HOGI: Harken Oil & Gas Inc. (NAS NMS)
HOGN: Hogan Systems Inc. (NAS NMS)
HOI: House Of Issue

HOKEYS: Home Owners' Loan Corporation Bonds
HOL: Holco Mortgage Acceptance Corp. (ASE)
HOLC: Home Owners' Loan Corporation (defunct)
Holco: Holco Mortgage Acceptance Corp. (newspaper)
Holidy: Holiday Corp. (newspaper)
HollyCp: Holly Corp. (newspaper)
HOME: International American Homes Inc. (NAS NMS)
HomeSh: Home Shopping Network Inc. (newspaper)
HOMF: Home Federal Savings Bank (Indiana) (NAS NMS)
HON: Honeywell Inc. (NYSE)
hon'd: honored
Honda: Honda Motor Company Ltd. (newspaper)
HONI: HON INDUSTRIES Inc. (NAS NMS)
Honwell: Honeywell Inc. (newspaper)
Honybe: Honeybee Inc. (newspaper)
HoopHl: Hooper Holmes Inc. (newspaper)
HoprSol: Hopper Soliday Corp. (newspaper)
HOR: Holder Of Record
Horn & Hardart Co., The (ASE)
HO&RC: Humble Oil and Refining Company
Horizon: Horizon Corp. (newspaper)
HORL: Home Office Reference Laboratory Inc. (NAS NMS)
Hormel: George A. Hormel & Co. (newspaper)
HOSP: Hosposable Products Inc. (NAS NMS)
HOT: Hotel Investors Trust/ Corporation (NYSE)
Hotllnv: Hotel Investors Trust/ Corporation (newspaper)
HOU: Houston Industries Inc. (NYSE)

HouFab: House of Fabrics Inc.
(newspaper)
HougM: Houghton Mifflin Co.
(newspaper)
HouInd: Houston Industries Inc.
(newspaper)
HouOR: Houston Oil Royalty Trust
(newspaper)
HouOT: Houston Oil Trust (news-
paper)
HousInt: Household International
Inc. (newspaper)
HOV: Hovnanian Enterprises Inc.
(ASE)
HovnE: Hovnanian Enterprises Inc.
(newspaper)
HOW: Howell Industries Inc. (ASE)
HoweRh: Howe Richardson Inc.
(newspaper)
HowlCp: Howell Corp. (newspaper)
HowlIn: Howell Industries Inc.
(newspaper)
Howtk: Howtek Inc. (newspaper)
HP: Apollo Airways
Helmerich & Payne Inc. (NYSE)
HPBC: Home Port Bancorp Inc.
(NAS NMS)
HPC: Hercules Inc. (NYSE)
HPH: Harnischfeger Industries Inc.
(NYSE)
HPSC: HPSC Inc. (NAS NMS)
HPT&D: High Point, Thomasville &
Denton (railroad)
hq: headquarters
HQ: Valley Airlines
HQH: H & Q Healthcare Investors
(NYSE)
HQ Hlt: H & Q Healthcare Inves-
tors (newspaper)
HR: Pennsylvania Commuter (air-
lines)
HRA: Harvey Group Inc. (ASE)
HRB: H & R Block Inc. (NYSE)
HRCLY: Huntingdon International
Holdings PLC (NAS
NMS)

HRD: Hannaford Brothers Co.
(NYSE)
HRDG: Harding Associates Inc.
(NAS NMS)
HrdRk: Hard Rock Cafe PLC (news-
paper)
HRE: HRE Properties (NYSE)
(newspaper)
HRHC: Hilb Rogal & Hamilton Co.
(NAS NMS)
HRI: Howe Richardson Inc. (ASE)
HRIGV: HRI Group Inc. (NAS NMS)
HRK: Hard Rock Cafe PLC (ASE)
HRL: George A. Hormel & Co. (ASE)
HRLD: Harold's Stores Inc. (NAS
NMS)
HRLN: Harlyn Products Inc. (NAS
NMS)
HRLY: Herley Microwave Systems
Inc. (NAS NMS)
HRMN: Harmon Industries Inc.
(NAS NMS)
HRMR: Hunter-Melnor Inc. (NAS
NMS)
HrnHar: Horn & Hardart Co., The
(newspaper)
HROK: Home Federal S&L Assn. of
the Rockies (NAS NMS)
HRP: Health & Rehabilitation
Properties Trust (NYSE)
HRS: Harris Corp. (NYSE)
Hrshey: Hershey Foods Corp.
(newspaper)
HRT: Harwell Railway
HR-10: Keogh Plan
HRZB: Horizon Bank, A Savings
Bank (Washington) (NAS
NMS)
HrzHlt: Horizon Healthcare Corp.
(newspaper)
HRZN: Horizon Industries Inc.
(NAS NMS)
HS: Hartford and Slocomb (rail-
road)
Hopper Soliday Corp. (NYSE)
Scenic Airlines

HSAI: Healthcare Services of America Inc. (NAS NMS)
HSBK: Hibernia Savings Bank, The (Massachusetts) (NAS NMS)
HSC: Harsco Corp. (NYSE)
HSI: Hi-Shear Industries Inc. (NYSE)
HSLD: Home S&L Assn. Inc. (North Carolina) (NAS NMS)
HSN: Home Shopping Network Inc. (ASE)
HSO: Hershey Oil Corp. (ASE)
HSPA: Home Savings Assn. of Pennsylvania (NAS NMS)
HSRC: HEALTHSOUTH Rehabilitation Corp. (NAS NMS)
HSSI: Hospital Staffing Services Inc. (NAS NMS)
HSW: Helena Southwestern (railroad)
HSY: Hershey Foods Corp. (NYSE)
HTCH: Hutchinson Technology Inc. (NAS NMS)
HTEK: Hytek Microsystems Inc. (NAS NMS)
HTG: Heritage Media Corp. (ASE)
HtgMd: Heritage Media Corp. (newspaper)
HTK: Howtek Inc. (ASE)
HTLD: Heartland Express Inc. (NAS NMS)
HTN: Houghton Mifflin Co. (NYSE)
HT&W: Hoosac Tunnel & Wilmington (railroad)
HU: Cascade Airways Hampton Utilities Trust (ASE)
HUB: Hubbell Inc. (ASE)
HUBCO: HUBCO Inc. (newspaper)
Hubel: Hubbell Inc. (newspaper)
HudFd: Hudson Foods Inc. (newspaper)
HudGn: Hudson General Corp.
HUF: Huffy Corp. (NYSE)
Huffy: Huffy Corp. (newspaper)
HUFK: Huffman Koos Inc. (NAS NMS)

HUG: Hughes Supply Inc. (NYSE)
HughSp: Hughes Supply Inc. (newspaper)
HUHO: Hughes Homes Inc. (NAS NMS)
HUM: Humana Inc. (NYSE)
Human: Humana Inc. (newspaper)
HUN: Hunt Manufacturing Co. (NYSE)
HuntM: Hunt Manufacturing Co. (newspaper)
HURC: Hurco Companies Inc. (NAS NMS)
HUSB: Home Unity S&L Assn. (Pennsylvania) (NAS NMS)
HuttEF: E. F. Hutton Group Inc., The (newspaper)
HVDK: Harvard Knitwear Inc. (NAS NMS)
HVT: HealthVest (ASE)
HWCD: HWC Distribution Corp. (NAS NMS)
HWG: Hallwood Group Inc., The (NYSE)
HWK: Hawkeye Bancorporation (NAS NMS)
HWL: Howell Corp. (NYSE)
HWP: Hewlett-Packard Co. (NYSE)
HWRD: Howard Savings Bank, The (New Jersey) (NAS NMS)
HX: Halifax Engineering Inc. (ASE) Virginia Air Cargo (airline)
HXL: Hexcel Corp. (NYSE)
HY: Houston Metro Airlines
HYDE: Hyde Athletic Industries Inc. (NAS NMS)
Hydral: Hydraulic Co., The (newspaper)
HYI: High Yield Income Fund Inc., The (NYSE)
HYP: High Yield Plus Fund Inc. (NYSE)
HYPX: Hyponex Corp. (NAS NMS)
HY&T: Hooppole, Yorktown & Tampico (railroad)
HZN: Horizon Corp. (NYSE)

i: information
interest (rate of) (symbol)
I: First Interstate Bancorp. (NYSE)
Interest rate (nominal market)
Paid this year, dividend omitted,
deferred, or no action taken at
dividend meeting (stock listings
in newspapers)
IA: Immediately Available
Inactive Account
Income Averaging
Intangible Asset
Interim Audit
IAA: Investment Advisers Act
IAB: Inter-American Bank
IABB: Inter-American Bank Bonds
IACHA: Iowa Automated Clearing
House Association
IACI: Industrial Acoustics Company
Inc. (NAS NMS)
IAD: Inland Steel Industries Inc.
(NYSE)
IADB: Inter-American Development
Bank
IAF: First Australia Fund Inc., The
(ASE)
IAL: International Aluminum Corp.
(NYSE)
IAW: In Accordance With
IB: Income Bond
Insurance Broker
International Bank Bonds
Introducing Broker
Investment Banker
Investment Banking
IBA: Independent Bankers Associa-
tion of America
International Banking Act
Investment Bankers Associa-
tion

IBAA: Independent Bankers Associ-
ation of America
IBAM: Institute of Business Admin-
istration and Management
(Japan)
IBAN: Imperial Bancorp
(NAS NMS)
IBB: International Bank Bonds
IBC: Interstate Bakeries Corp.
(NYSE)
IBCA: International Broadcasting
Corp. (NAS NMS)
IBCP: Independent Bank Corp.
(Michigan) (NAS NMS)
IBEC: International Bank for Eco-
nomic Cooperation
IBELs: Interest-Bearing Eligible
Liabilities
IBES: Institutional Broker's Esti-
mate System
IBF: First Iberian Fund (ASE)
International Banking Facil-
ity
IBFS: International Banking Facili-
ties
IBIS: IBI Security Services Inc.
(NAS NMS)
International Bank Informa-
tion System
IBK: International Banknote Com-
pany Inc. (ASE)
IBL: Iroquois Brands Ltd. (ASE)
IBM: International Business Ma-
chines Corp. (NYSE) (news-
paper)
IBNR: Incurred But Not Reported
IBP: IBP Inc. (NYSE) (newspaper)
IBRD: International Bank for Re-
construction and Develop-
ment

IBS: International Bank for Settlements

IBSI: Independent Bancshares Inc. (Texas) (NAS NMS)

IC: Income Capital
Investment Counselor

I of CA: Institute of Chartered Accountants (UK)

ICA: Imperial Corporation of America (NYSE) (newspaper)
Interstate Commerce Act
Investment Company Act

ICB: InterCapital Income Securities Inc. (NYSE)

IC&C: Invoice Cost and Charges

ICCH: International Commodities Clearing House

ICE: Arctic Alaska Fisheries Corp. (ASE)
International Commercial Exchange

ICEE: ICEE-USA (newspaper)

ICEYF: International Capital Equipment Ltd. (NAS NMS)

ICFC: Industrial and Commercial Finance Corporation

ICG: Inter-City Gas Corp. (ASE)

ICH: I.C.H. Corp. (ASE) (newspaper)

ICI: Imperial Chemical Industries PLC (NYSE)
Investment Company Institute

IC Ind: IC Industries Inc. (newspaper)

ICM: ICM Property Investors Inc. (NYSE) (newspaper)
Institute of Credit Management

ICMA: Institute of Cost and Management Accountants

ICN: ICN Pharmaceuticals Inc. (NYSE)

ICN Bio: ICN Biomedicals Inc. (newspaper)

ICN Ph: ICN Pharmaceuticals Inc. (newspaper)

ICOT: ICOT Corp. (NAS NMS)

ICPYY: Institute of Clinical Pharmacology, The PLC (NAS NMS)

ICS: Issued Capital Stock

ICSI: International Container Systems Inc. (NAS NMS)

ICSID: International Center for the Settlement of Investment Disputes

ICTM: Integrated Circuits Inc. (NAS NMS)

ICX: IC Industries Inc. (NYSE)

ICY: ICEE-USA (ASE)

ID: Immediate Delivery
Import Duty
Income Debenture
Interim Dividend
Interlocking Directors
The discount rate

IDA: Idaho Power Co. (NYSE)

IdahoP: Idaho Power Co. (newspaper)

IDB: Industrial Development Bond
InterAmerican Development Bank

IDBX: IDB Communications Groups Inc. (NAS NMS)

IDEA: Invention Design Engineering Associates Inc. (NAS NMS)

IdealB: Ideal Basic Industries Inc. (newspaper)

IDIS: Interbourse Data Information System (EC)

IDL: Ideal Basic Industries Inc. (NYSE)

IDTI: Integrated Device Technology Inc. (NAS NMS)

I&E: Income and Expense

IEC: PEC Israel Economic Corp. (ASE)

IECE: IEC Electronics Corp. (NAS NMS)

IEHC: Industrial Electronic Hardware Corp. (NAS NMS)

IEI: Indiana Energy Inc. (NYSE)

IE Ind: IE Industries Inc. (newspaper)

IEL: IE Industries Inc. (NYSE)

IES: Income and Expense Statement

IET: Interest Equalization Tax

IEX: Institute of Export

IF: Insufficient Funds

IFA: International Fiscal Association

International Franchise Association

IFAC: International Federation of Accountants

IFB: Invitation For Bid

IFC: International Finance Corporation

IFE: Institute of Financial Education

IFEBS: Integrated Foreign Exchange and Banking System

IFED: InterFederal Savings Bank (Tennessee) (NAS NMS)

IFF: International Flavors & Fragrances Inc. (NYSE)

IFG: Inter-Regional Financial Group Inc. (NYSE)

IFI: Inter-Freight International (steamship)

International Financial Institution

IFII: Indiana Financial Investors Inc. (NAS NMS)

IFL: IMC Fertilizer Group Inc. (NYSE)

IFMS: Integrated Financial Management System

IFMX: Informix Corp. (NAS NMS)

IFPS: Interactive Financial Planning System

IFRS: IFR Systems Inc. (NAS NMS)

IFSB: Independence Federal Savings Banks (Washington, D.C.) (NAS NMS)

IFSI: Interface Inc. (NAS NMS)

IFSL: Indiana Federal S&L Assn. (NAS NMS)

IG: IGI Inc. (ASE)

IGAM: International Game Technology (NAS NMS)

IGAS: Interactive General Accounting System

IGC: Interstate General Company LP (ASE) (newspaper)

IGEI: International Genetic Engineering Inc. (NAS NMS)

IGF: India Growth Fund (NYSE)

IGI: IGI Inc. (newspaper)

IGL: International Minerals & Chemical Corp. (NYSE)

IGLSF: Insituform Group Ltd. (NAS NMS)

IGN: International Great Northern (railroad)

IGSI: Insituform Gulf South Inc. (NAS NMS)

IGU: International Gas Union

IHB: Indiana Harbor Belt (railroad)

IHBI: Indian Head Banks Inc. (New Hampshire) (NAS NMS)

IHEIF: Interhome Energy Inc. (NAS NMS)

IHKSV: Imperial Holly Corp. (NAS NMS)

IHS: IPCO Corp. (NYSE)

II: Institutional Investor

IIA: Institute of Internal Auditors

Insurance Institute of America

IID: Investment In Default

III: Insteel Industries Inc. (ASE)

IINT: Information International Inc. (NAS NMS)

IIP: International Income Property Inc. (ASE) (newspaper)

IIPF: International Institute of Public Finance

IIS: INA Investment Securities Inc. (NYSE)

Investment Income Surcharge

IISLF: I.I.S. Intelligent Information Systems Ltd. (NAS NMS)

IIVI: II-VI Inc. (NAS NMS)

IK: Interlake Corp. (NYSE)
ILC: Irrevocable Letter of Credit
ILCT: ILC Technology Inc. (NAS NMS)
ILFC: International Lease Finance Corp. (NAS NMS)
IllPowr: Illinois Power Co. (newspaper)
ILU: Institute of London Underwriters (UK)
IM: Idle Money
Massachusetts Air Industries (airline)
IMACHA: Intermountain Automated Clearing House Association
IMAT: Imatron Inc. (NAS NMS)
IMC: International Multifoods Corp. (NYSE)
IMC F: IMC Fertilizer Group Inc. (newspaper)
IMD: Imo Delaval Inc. (NYSE)
IMET: Intermetrics Inc. (NAS NMS)
IMF: International Monetary Fund
IMI: Intermark Inc. (ASE)
IMKT: Ingles Markets Inc. (NAS NMS)
imm: immediate
IMM: International Monetary Market
International Money Management
IMMC: International Mobile Machines Corp. (NAS NMS)
IMMU: Immunomedics Inc. (NAS NMS)
IMNX: Immunex Corp. (NAS NMS)
IMO: Imperial Oil Ltd. (ASE)
ImoDv: Imo Delaval Inc. (newspaper)
imp: import
importer
IMP: Industry Market Potential
ImpCh: Imperial Chemical Industries PLC (newspaper)
ImpOil: Imperial Oil Ltd (newspaper)
IMPX: International Microelectronics Products Inc. (NAS NMS)

IMRG: Imreg Inc. (NAS NMS)
in: income
IN: Illinois Northern (railroad)
Income (NYSE)
Installment Note
INAC: Inacomp Computer Centers Inc. (NAS NMS)
INAI: Intellicorp. (NAS NMS)
INAIn: INA Investment Securities Inc. (newspaper)
INAS: Interbank National Authorization System
INAT: Indiana National Corp. (NAS NMS)
INBC: Independence Bancorp Inc. (Pennsylvania) (NAS NMS)
INBS: Iowa National Bancshares Corp. (NAS NMS)
inc: income
incorporate
incorporated
INCL: Intellicall Inc. (NAS NMS)
INCO: Inco Ltd. (newspaper)
INCRF: Inca Resources Inc. (NAS NMS)
Incstar: Incstar Corp. (newspaper)
ind: indicator
industrial
industry
INDB: Independent Bank Corp. (Massachusetts) (NAS NMS)
INDEX: Indiana Exchange Inc.
INDHK: Independent Insurance Group Inc. (NAS NMS)
India: India Growth Fund (newspaper)
IndiEn: Indiana Energy Inc. (newspaper)
Ind Led: Individual Ledger
INDQ: International Dairy Queen Inc. (NAS NMS)
INDR: Industrial Resources Inc. (NAS NMS)
indus: industrial
industry

INDX: Index Technology Corp. (NAS NMS)

INEI: Insituform East Inc. (NAS NMS)

INEL: Intelligent Electronics Inc. (NAS NMS)

INET: Interbank Network Electronic Transfer

INFD: Infodata System Inc. (NAS NMS)

INFN: Infotron Systems Corp. (NAS NMS)

info: inform
information

INFOTEX: Information Via Telex

IngerR: Ingersoll-Rand Co. (newspaper)

INGN: Integrated Genetics Inc. (NAS NMS)

INGR: Intergraph Corp. (NAS NMS)

IngrTec: Ingredient Technology Corp. (newspaper)

inher: inheritance

init: initialize

InldStl: Inland Steel Industries Inc. (newspaper)

INMA: Intermagnetics General Corp. (NAS NMS)

INMC: Inmac Corp. (NAS NMS)

INMT: Intermet Corp. (NAS NMS)

INP: Intelligent Systems Master LP (ASE)

INPH: Interphase Corp. (NAS NMS)

INR: Insilco Corp. (NYSE)

INRD: INRAD Inc. (NAS NMS)

ins: insurance

INS: International Seaway Trading Corp. (ASE)

insce: insurance

INSCO: Intercontinental Shipping Corporation

Insd Val: Insured Value

INSH: International Shipholding Corp. (NAS NMS)

INSI: Information Science Inc. (NAS NMS)

Insilco: Insilco Corp. (newspaper)

INSM: Insituform Mid-America Inc. (NAS NMS)

INSP: InSpeech Inc. (NAS NMS)

InspRs: Inspiration Resources Corp. (newspaper)

inst: installment (instalment)

Insteel: Insteel Industries Inc. (newspaper)

INSTINET: Institutional Networks Corporation

instl: installment (instalment)

InstPw: Interstate Power Co. (newspaper)

Instron: Instron Corp. (newspaper)

InstSy: Instrument Systems Corp. (newspaper)

INSU: Insituform of North America Inc. (NAS NMS)

insur: insurance

INSY: Interim Systems Corp. (NAS NMS)

int: interest
international

INT: International Recovery Corp. (ASE)
Interstate (railroad)

INTABS: International Terminal Accounting and Banking Service

IntAlu: International Aluminum Corp. (newspaper)

IntBknt: International Banknote Company Inc. (newspaper)

IntBkr: Interstate Bakeries Corp. (newspaper)

INTC: Intel Corp. (NAS NMS)

IntCty: Inter-City Gas Corp. (newspaper)

INTE: Intech Inc. (NAS NMS)

INTELSAT: International Telecommunications Satellite Consortium

Interco: INTERCO INCORPORATED (newspaper)

INTF: Interface Systems Inc. (NAS NMS)

IntFlav: International Flavors & Fragrances Inc. (newspaper)
INTG: Intergroup Corp. (NAS NMS)
IntgRsc: Integrated Resources Inc. (newspaper)
intl: international
INTL: Inter-Tel Inc. (NAS NMS)
IntlgSy: Intelligent Systems Master LP (newspaper)
Intlog: Interlogic Trace Inc. (newspaper)
Intmed: Intermedics Inc. (newspaper)
IntMin: International Minerals & Chemical Corp. (newspaper)
IntMult: International Multifoods Corp. (newspaper)
INTO: Initio Inc. (NAS NMS)
IntPap: International Paper Co. (newspaper)
IntpbG: Interpublic Group of Companies Inc., The (newspaper)
IntProt: International Proteins Corp. (newspaper)
IntPwr: International Power Machines Corp. (newspaper)
INTR: INTERMEC Corp. (NAS NMS)
IntRec: International Recovery Corp. (newspaper)
IntRect: International Rectifier Corp. (newspaper)
IntRFn: Inter-Regional Financial Group Inc. (newspaper)
Intrlke: Interlake Corp. (newspaper)
Intrmk: Intermark Inc. (newspaper)
IntSeaw: International Seaway Trading Corp. (newspaper)
IntSec: Interstate Securities Inc. (newspaper)
IntTch: International Telecharge Inc. (newspaper)
IntThr: International Thoroughbred Breeders Inc. (newspaper)

INTX: U. S. Intec Inc. (NAS NMS)
inv: invoice
INVG: INVG Mortgage Securities Corp. (NAS NMS)
INVN: Invitron Corp. (NAS NMS)
INVS: Investors Savings Corp. (Minnesota) (NAS NMS)
INVX: Innovex Inc. (NAS NMS)
IO: Immediate Order
IOC: Immediate-Or-Cancel
    Indirect Operating Costs
IOI: Indication Of Interest
IO LTD: Imperial Oil Ltd. (steamship)
IOMG: Iomega Corp. (NAS NMS)
ION: Ionics Inc. (ASE)
Ionics: Ionics Inc. (newspaper)
IOR: Iowa Resources Inc. (NYSE)
IOT: Iron Ore Transport (steamship)
IOU: I Owe You
IowaRs: Iowa Resources Inc. (newspaper)
Iowllg: Iowa-Illinois Gas & Electric Co. (newspaper)
IP: Incentive Pay
    International Paper Co. (NYSE)
    Issue Price
Ipalco: IPALCO Enterprises Inc. (newspaper)
IPC: Illinois Power Co. (NYSE)
IpcoCp: IPCO Corp. (newspaper)
IPE: Industrial Plant Equipment
IPG: Interpublic Group of Companies Inc., The (NYSE)
IPI: Implicit Price Index
IPL: IPALCO Enterprises Inc. (NYSE)
IPLS: IPL Systems Inc. (NAS NMS)
IPM: IPM Technology Inc. (ASE) (newspaper)
IPO: Initial Public Offering
IPS: American Income Properties LP (ASE)
IPT: IP Timberlands Ltd. (NYSE)
IPTim: IP Timberlands Ltd. (newspaper)

IPW: Interstate Power Co.
(NYSE)
IQ: Import Quota
Information Quick
IR: Ingersoll-Rand Co. (NYSE)
Internal Revenue
Investor Relations
IRA: Individual Retirement Account
Investment-Return Assumption
IRB: Industrial Revenue Bond
IRC: Inspiration Resources Corp.
(NYSE)
Internal Revenue Code
IRD: Income in Respect of a Decedent
IRDV: International Research &
Development Corp. (NAS
NMS)
IRE: Integrated Resources Inc.
(NYSE)
IRF: International Rectifier Corp.
(NYSE)
IRIC: Information Resources Inc.
(NAS NMS)
IRIS: International Remote Imaging
Systems Inc. (NAS NMS)
IRN: Ironton (railroad)
IroqBrd: Iroquois Brands Ltd.
(newspaper)
IRR: Internal Rate of Return
irred: irredeemable
irreg: irregular
IRS: Internal Revenue Service
IRT: IRT Property Co. (NYSE)
(newspaper)
IRT Cp: IRT Corp. (newspaper)
IrvBnk: Irving Bank Corp. (newspaper)
IRWN: Irwin Magnetic Systems Inc.
(NAS NMS)
IS: Income Statement
Income Stocks
Interstate Securities Inc.
(NYSE)

ISBJ: Interchange Financial Services Corp. (New Jersey)
(NAS NMS)
ISCS: ISC Systems Corp. (NAS
NMS)
I-S CURVE: Investment Should Absorb Savings
ISEC: Insituform Southeast Corp.
(NAS NMS)
ISI: ISS-International Service Systems Inc. (ASE)
ISI Sy: ISI Systems Inc. (newspaper)
ISKO: Isco Inc. (NAS NMS)
ISLA: Investors Savings Bank (Virginia)
ISLH: International Holding Capital
Corp. (NAS NMS)
ISMX: Isomedix Inc. (NAS NMS)
ISN: Instron Corp. (ASE)
ISNOT: Is Not Equal To
ISO: Incentive Stock Options
ISPC: Interspec Inc. (NAS NMS)
ISR: Incstar Corp. (ASE)
ISS: INTERCO INCORPORATED
(NYSE)
ISS-International Service System Inc. (newspaper)
ISY: Instrument Systems Corp.
(ASE)
IT: Air Inter (airline)
Income Tax
Interlogic Trace Inc. (NYSE)
International Trade
ITA: Italy Fund Inc., The (NYSE)
Italy: Italy Fund Inc., The (newspaper)
ITAN: InterTAN Inc. (NAS NMS)
ITB: International Thoroughbred
Breeders Inc. (ASE)
Interstate Trade Barriers
Invisible Trade Balance
ITC: Illinois Terminal Company
Income Tax Credit
Ingredient Technology Corp.
(NYSE)
Investment Tax Credit

ITCC: Industrial Training Corp. (NAS NMS)

ITCH: Infotechnology Inc. (NAS NMS)

ITcpSE: InterCapital Income Securities Inc. (newspaper)

IT Crp: International Technology Corp. (newspaper)

ITELO: Itel Corp. (NAS NMS)

ITGN: Integon Corp. (NAS NMS)

ITI: International Telecharge Inc. (ASE)

ITIC: Investors Title Co. (NAS NMS)

ITM: Intermedics Inc. (NYSE)

ITO: International Trade Organization

ITP: Income Tax Plan

ITRC: Iowa Transfer Railway Company

ITRN: Intertrans Corp. (NAS NMS)

ITS: Intermarket Trading System
Iowa Transfer System

ITSI: International Totalizator Systems Inc. (NAS NMS)

ITT: International Telephone and Telegraph Corp.
ITT Corp. (NYSE)

ITT Cp: ITT Corp. (newspaper)

ITW: Illinois Tool Works Inc. (NYSE) (newspaper)

ITX: International Technology Corp. (NYSE)

ITXI: Interactive Technologies Inc. (NAS NMS)

IU: Indiana Union (railway)
IU International Corp. (NYSE) (newspaper)
Midstate Air Commuter (airline)

IUBSSA: International Union of Building Societies and Savings Associations

IUTL: Iowa Southern Utilities Co. (NAS NMS)

IvaxCp: IVAX Corp. (newspaper)

Iverson: Iverson Technology Corp. (newspaper)

IVRC: Invacare Corp. (NAS NMS)

IVT: Iverson Technology Corp. (ASE)

IVX: IVAX Corp. (ASE)

IWG: Iowa-Illinois Gas & Electric Co. (NYSE)

IWRC: IWC Resources Corp. (NAS NMS)

IX: IRT Corp. (ASE)

IY: Swift Airlines

IYCOY: Ito-Yokado Company Ltd. (NAS NMS)

J

JA: Joint Account
JAC: Johnstown American Co. (ASE)
JACK: Jackpot Enterprises Inc. (NYSE)
Jackpot: Jackpot Enterprises Inc. (newspaper)
Jaclyn: Jaclyn Inc. (newspaper)
JACO: Jaco Electronics Inc. (NAS NMS)
Jacobs: Jacobs Engineering Group Inc. (newspaper)
JAGRY: Jaguar PLC (NAS NMS)
JAIL: Adtec Inc. (NAS NMS)
JAJO: January, April, July, October (securities)
JALC: John Adams Life Corp. (NAS NMS)
Jamsw: Jamesway Corp. (newspaper)
JanBel: Jan Bell Marketing Inc. (newspaper)
JASN: Jason Inc. (NAS NMS)
JAYT: Jay Jacobs Inc. (NAS NMS)
JB: Junior Bond
JBAK: J. Baker Inc. (NAS NMS)
JBBB: JB's Restaurants Inc. (NAS NMS)
JBHT: J. B. Hunt Transportation Services Inc. (NAS NMS)
JBM: Jan Bell Marketing Inc. (ASE)
JBNK: Jefferson Bankshares Inc. (Virginia) (NAS NMS)
JC: Jewelcor Inc. (NYSE) Rocky Mountain Airways
JCBS: Jacobson Stores Inc. (NAS NMS)
JCI: Johnson Controls Inc. (NYSE)

JCOR: Jacor Communications Inc. (NAS NMS)
JCP: J. C. Penney Company Inc. (NYSE)
JCT: Johnstown/Consolidated Realty Trust (NYSE)
J&D: June and December (securities)
JD: June and December (securities)
JDI: Joint Declaration of Intent
JE: Jerseyville and Eastern (railroad)
JEC: Jacobs Engineering Group Inc. (ASE)
JeffPl: Jefferson-Pilot Corp. (newspaper)
JEFG: Jefferies Group Inc. (NAS NMS)
JEM: Jewelmasters Inc. (ASE)
JERR: Jerrico Inc. (NAS NMS)
JET: Jetronic Industries Inc. (ASE)
JetCa: Jet Capital Corp. (newspaper)
Jetron: Jetronic Industries Inc. (newspaper)
JETS: Jetborne International Inc. (NAS NMS)
JGIN: JG Industries Inc. (NAS NMS)
JGRP: Jesup Group Inc. (NAS NMS)
JH: Smyer Aircraft John H. Harland Co., The (NYSE)
JHI: John Hancock Investors Trust (NYSE)
JhnCn: Johnson Controls Inc. (newspaper)
JhnCRt: Johnstown/Consolidated Realty Trust (newspaper)

JHS: John Hancock Income Securities Trust (NYSE)

JHSC: Johnstown and Stony Creek (railroad)

JHSL: John Hanson Savings Bank FSB (NAS NMS)

JHSN: Johnson Electronics Inc. (NAS NMS)

JIB: Foodmaker Inc. (NYSE)

JII: Johnston Industries Inc. (NYSE)

JJ: January and July (securities)

JJS: Jumping-Jack Shoes Inc. (ASE)

JJSC: Jefferson Smurfit Corp. (NAS NMS)

JJSF: J & J Snack Foods Corp. (NAS NMS)

JKHY: Jack Henry & Associates Inc. (NAS NMS)

JLGI: JLG Industries Inc. (NAS NMS)

JLN: Jaclyn Inc. (ASE)

JLPT: Japanese Long Term Prime Rate

JLUB: Jiffy Lube International Inc. (NAS NMS)

JMadsn: James Madison Ltd. (newspaper)

JMED: Jones Medical Industries Inc. (NAS NMS)

JML: James Madison Ltd. (ASE)

JMP: J. M. Peters Company Inc. (ASE)

JMY: Jamesway Corp. (NYSE)

JN: Sun Valley Air (airline)

JNBK: Jefferson National Bank (New York) (NAS NMS)

JNJ: Johnson & Johnson (NYSE)

JNT STK: Joint Stock

JO: Joint Ownership

JOB: General Employment Enterprises Inc. (ASE)

JohnAm: Johnstown American Companies (newspaper)

JohnInd: Johnston Industries Inc. (newspaper)

JohnJn: Johnson & Johnson (newspaper)

JohnPd: Johnson Products Company Inc. (newspaper)

JOIN: Jones Intercable Inc. (NAS NMS)

JOJA: July, October, January, April (securities)

JOL: Joule Inc. (ASE)

JOR: Earle M. Jorgensen Co. (NYSE)

Jorgen: Earle M. Jorgensen Co. (newspaper)

JOS: Jostens Inc. (NYSE)

JOSL: Joslyn Corp. (NAS NMS)

Josten: Jostens Inc. (newspaper)

Joule: Joule Inc. (newspaper)

jour: journal

JP: Jefferson-Pilot Corp. (NYSE)

JPC: Johnson Products Company Inc. (ASE)

JPI: J. P. Industries Inc. (NYSE)

JP Ind: J. P. Industries Inc. (newspaper)

JPM: J.P. Morgan & Company Inc. (NYSE)

jr: junior

JR: James River Corporation of Virginia (NYSE)
    Joint Return

JRiver: James River Corporation of Virginia

JRMX: JRM Holdings Inc. (NAS NMS)

JS: Air Champagne Ardennes (airline)

JSBK: Johnstown Savings Bank (Pennsylvania) (NAS NMS)

JSC: Joint Stock Company

JSDM: June, September, December, March (securities)

JSTN: Justin Industries Inc. (NAS NMS)

JT: Joint Tenancy

JTC: Jacksonville Terminal Company (railroad)
    Jet Capital Corp. (ASE)

JUDY: Judy's Inc. (NAS NMS)
JumpJk: Jumping-Jack Shoes Inc. (newspaper)
JUNO: Juno Lighting Inc. (NAS NMS)
JV: Joint Venture
JWAI: Johnson Worldwide Associates Inc. (NAS NMS)

Jwlcr: Jewelcor Inc. (newspaper)
Jwlmst: Jewelmasters Inc. (newspaper)
JW&NW: Jamestown, Westfield & Northwestern (railroad)
JWP: JWP Inc. (NYSE) (newspaper)

K: Declared or paid this year on a cumulative issue with dividends in arrears (stock listings of newspapers)
Kellogg Co. (NYSE)

KAB: Kaneb Services Inc. (NYSE)

KACHA: Kentuckiana Automated Clearing House Association

Kaisrtc: Kaisertech Ltd. (newspaper)

KambEn: Kaneb Energy Partners Ltd. (newspaper)

KAMN: Kaman Corp. (NAS NMS)

KAN: Kansas Power & Light Co., The (NYSE)

Kaneb: Kaneb Services Inc. (newspaper)

KanGE: Kansas Gas & Electric Co. (newspaper)

KanPL: Kansas Power & Light Co., The (newspaper)

Kappa: Kappa Networks Inc.

KASL: Kasler Corp. (NAS NMS)

KATY: Missouri-Kansas-Texas Railroad

Katyln: Katy Industries Inc. (newspaper)

KaukfB: Kaufman & Broad Inc. (newspaper)

KaufBH: Kaufman & Broad Home Corp. (newspaper)

KAY: Kay Corp. (ASE)

KayCp: Kay Corp. (newspaper)

KayJw: Kay Jewelers Inc. (newspaper)

KB: Kaufman & Broad Inc. (NYSE)
Kitsap Aviation (airline)

KBA: Kleinwort Benson Australian Income Fund Inc. (NYSE)

KBAL: Kimball International Inc. (NAS NMS)

KBAukst: Kleinwort Benson Australian Income Fund Inc. (newspaper)

KBH: Kaufman & Broad Home Corp. (NYSE)

KBR: Kankakee Belt Route (railroad)

KC: Key Co., The (ASE)
Kiting Checks

KCBT: Kansas City Board of Trade

KCC: Kansas City Connecting (railroad)

KCH: Ketchum & Company Inc. (ASE)

KCMO: Kansas City, Mexico and Orient (railway)

KCNW: Kelley's Creek and Northwestern (railroad)

KCOP: KenCope Energy Companies (NAS NMS)

KCPSFO: Kansas City Public Service Freight Operation

KCS: Conston Corp. (ASE)
Kansas City Southern (railroad)

KCSG: KCS Group Inc. (NAS NMS)

KCSou: Kansas City Southern Industries Inc. (newspaper)

KCT: Kansas City Terminal (railway)

KCtyPL: Kansas City Power & Light Co. (newspaper)

KD: Knocked Down (price)
Kuwaiti dinar

KDCD: Kuwaiti Dinar Certificate of Deposit

KDI: KDI Corp. (NYSE) (newspaper)

KDNY: Home Intensive Care Inc. (NAS NMS)

KDON: Kaydon Corp. (NAS NMS)

KE: Koger Equity Inc. (ASE)

KEAN: Keane Inc. (NAS NMS)

KearNt: Kearney-National Inc. (newspaper)

KEC: Kent Electronics Corp. (ASE)

KEI: Keithly Instruments Inc. (ASE)

Keithly: Keithly Instruments Inc. (newspaper)

Kellogg: Kellogg Co. (newspaper)

Kellwd: Kellwood Co. (newspaper)

KELY: Kelly Services Inc. (NAS NMS)

KEMC: Kemper Corp. (NAS NMS)

KENC: Kentucky Central Life Insurance Co. (NAS NMS)

Kenmt: Kennametal Inc. (newspaper)

KENS: Kenilworth Systems Corp. (NAS NMS)

KentEl: Kent Electronics Corp. (newspaper)

Kenwin: Kenwin Shops Inc. (newspaper)

KEP: Kaneb Energy Partners Ltd. (NYSE)

KEQU: Kewaunee Scientific Corp. (NAS NMS)

Kerkhf: Kerkhoff Industries Inc. (newspaper)

KerrGl: Kerr Glass Manufacturing Corp. (newspaper)

KerrMcv: Kerr-McGee Corp. (newspaper)

KES: Keystone Consolidated Industries Inc. (NYSE)

Keslr: Kessler Products Ltd. (newspaper)

Ketchm: Ketchum & Company Inc. (newspaper)

KEVN: Kimmins Environmental Service Corp. (NAS NMS)

KEX: Kirby Exploration Company Inc. (ASE)

KEY: KeyCorp. (NYSE)

KEYC: Key Centurion Bancshares Inc. (NAS NMS)

KeyCa: Keystone Camera Products Corp. (newspaper)

KeyCo: Key Co., The

Keycp: KeyCorp (newspaper)

KeyInt: Keystone International Inc. (newspaper)

KeysCo: Keystone Consolidated Industries Inc. (newspaper)

KF: Catskill Airways
Korea Fund Inc., The (NYSE)

KFV: Quest For Value Dual Purpose Fund Inc. (NYSE)

KGB: Kewaunee, Green Bay and Western (railroad)

KGE: Kansas Gas & Electric Co. (NYSE)

KGM: Kerr Glass Manufacturing Corp. (NYSE)

KH: Time Airways

KHGI: Keystone Heritage Group Inc. (NAS NMS)

KHI: Kemper High Income Trust (NYSE)

KHLR: Kahler Corp. (NAS NMS)

KI: Key Industry

KIBOR: Kuwait Interbank Offered Rate

KII: Keystone International Inc. (NYSE)

Kilern: Killearn Properties Inc. (newspaper)

KIMB: Kimbark Oil & Gas Co. (NAS NMS)

KimbC: Kimberly-Clark Corp. (newspaper)

KIN: Kinark Corp. (ASE)

Kinark: Kinark Corp. (newspaper)

KIND: Kinder-Care Learning Centers Inc. (NAS NMS)

Kirby: Kirby Exploration Company Inc. (newspaper)

KISC: Kimmins Corp. (NAS NMS)

KIT: Kentucky and Indiana Terminal (railroad)
Kit Manufacturing Co. (ASE)

Kit Mfg: Kit Manufacturing Co. (newspaper)

KITS: Meridian Diagnostic Inc. (NAS NMS)

KIX: Kerkhoff Industries Inc. (ASE)

KJI: Kay Jewelers Inc. (NYSE)

KK: Kabushiki-Kaisha (Japanese stock company)

KKR: Kohlberg Kravis Roberts

KLAC: KLA Instruments Corp. (NAS NMS)

KleerV: Kleer-Vu Industries Inc. (newspaper)

KLIC: Kulicke & Soffa Industries Inc. (NAS NMS)

KLLM: KLLM Transport Services Inc. (NAS NMS)

KLM: KLM Royal Dutch Airlines (NYSE) (newspaper)

KLT: Kansas City Power & Light Co. (NYSE)

KLU: Kaisertech Ltd. (NYSE)

KLY: Kelley Oil & Gas Partners Ltd. (ASE)

KlyOG: Kelley Oil & Gas Partners Ltd. (newspaper)

K&M: Kansas and Missouri Railway and Terminal Company

KM: K mart Corp. (NYSE)

KMAG: Komag Inc. (NAS NMS)

KMB: Kimberly-Clark Corp. (NYSE)

KMDC: Kirschner Medical Corp. (NAS NMS)

KMG: Kerr-McGee Corp. (NYSE)

KML: Carmel Container Systems Ltd. (ASE)

KmpHi: Kemper High Income Trust (newspaper)

K mrt: K mart Corp. (newspaper)

KMRT: Kansas and Missouri Railway and Terminal Company

KMSI: KMS Industries Inc. (NAS NMS)

KMT: Kennametal Inc. (NYSE)

KMW: KMW Systems Corp. (ASE) (newspaper)

KNAP: Knape & Vogt Manufacturing Co. (NAS NMS)

KNC: Kingcome Navigation Company (steamship)

KNCI: Kinetic Concepts Inc. (NAS NMS)

KNE: KN Energy Inc. (NYSE)

KN Eng: KN Energy Inc. (newspaper)

KnghtR: Knight-Ridder Inc. (newspaper)

KngWld: King World Productions Inc. (newspaper)

KNMC: Knutson Mortgage Corp. (NAS NMS)

KNO: Knogo Corp. (NYSE)

Knogo: Knogo Corp. (newspaper)

KNR: Klamath Northern Railway

KNY: Kearney-National Inc. (ASE)

KO: Coca-Cola Co., The (NYSE)
Kodiak Airways

KO&G: Kansas, Oklahoma & Gulf (railroad)

KOG: Koger Properties Inc. (NYSE)

Koger: Koger Properties Inc. (newspaper)

KogrEq: Koger Equity Inc. (newspaper)

KOL: Kollmorgen Corp. (NYSE)

Kolmor: Kollmorgen Corp. (newspaper)

KOP: Koppers Company Inc. (NYSE)

Kopers: Koppers Company Inc. (newspaper)

Korea: Korea Fund Inc., The (newspaper)
KOSS: Koss Corp. (NAS NMS)
KP: Air Cape (airline)
Keogh Plan
KPA: Kappa Networks Inc. (ASE)
KPI: Killearn Properties Inc. (ASE)
KPRO: Kaypro Corp.(NAS NMS)
KPT: Kenner Parker Toys Inc. (NYSE)
KPTL: Keptel Inc. (NAS NMS)
KPToy: Kenner Parker Toys Inc. (newspaper)
KQ: King Airlines
KR: Kroger Co., The (NYSE)
KRA: Kraft Inc. (NYSE)
Kraft: Kraft Inc. (newspaper)
KREN: Kings Road Entertainment Inc. (NAS NMS)
KRI: Knight-Ridder Inc. (NYSE)
Kroger: Kroger Co., The (newspaper)
KRUE: W. A. Krueger Co. (NAS NMS)
KRUG: KRUG International Corp. (NAS NMS)
KS: Kiting Stocks
KSF: Quaker State Corp. (NYSE)
KSS: Kessler Products Ltd. (ASE)
KSTN: Keystone Financial Inc. (NAS NMS)
KSU: Kansas City Southern Industries Inc. (NYSE)
K&T: Kentucky and Tennessee (railroad)
KT: Katy Industries Inc. (NYSE)

KTCC: Key Tronic Corp. (NAS NMS)
KTCO: Kenan Transport Co. (NAS NMS)
KTII: K-Tron International Inc. (NAS NMS)
KU: Kentucky Utilities Co. (NYSE)
KUB: Kubota Ltd. (NYSE)
Kubota: Kubota Ltd. (newspaper)
KUH: Kuhlman Corp. (NYSE)
Kuhlm: Kuhlman Corp. (newspaper)
KUST: Kustom Electronics Inc. (NAS NMS)
KV: KV Pharmaceutical Co. (ASE)
KVLM: Kevlin Microwave Corp. (NAS NMS)
KV Ph: KV Pharmaceutical Co. (newspaper)
KVU: Kleer-Vu Industries Inc. (ASE)
KW: Dorado Wings (airline)
KWD: Kellwood Co. (NYSE)
KWN: Kenwin Shops Inc. (ASE)
KWP: King World Productions Inc. (NYSE)
KYC: Keystone Camera Products Corp. (ASE)
Know Your Customer
KYO: Kyocera Corp. (NYSE)
Kyocer: Kyocera Corp. (newspaper)
Kysor: Kysor Industrial Corp. (newspaper)
KyUtil: Kentucky Utilities Co. (newspaper)
KZ: Kysor Industrial Corp. (NYSE)

L: Liquid assets of money supply
Listed (securities)

L&A: Louisiana & Arkansas (railroad)

LA: Legal Asset
Letter of Authority
Liquid Assets

LAA: Los Angeles Airways

LAB: Nichols Institute (ASE)

LaBarg: LaBarge Inc. (newspaper)

LABB: Beauty Labs Inc. (NAS NMS)

LABL: Multi-Color Corp. (NAS NMS)

LAC: LAC Minerals Ltd. (NYSE) (newspaper)

LaclGs: Laclede Gas Co. (newspaper)

LADF: LADD Furniture Inc. (NAS NMS)

LAF: Lafarge Corp. (NYSE)

Lafarge: Lafarge Corp. (newspaper)

LAFC: Loan America Financial Corp.

LaGenl: Louisiana General Services Inc. (newspaper)

LAGR: L. A. Gear Inc. (NAS NMS)

LAJ: Los Angeles Junction (railway)

Lajolla: La Jolla Bancorp. (newspaper)

LAKE: Lakeland Industries Inc. (NAS NMS)

LaLand: Louisiana Land & Exploration Co., The (newspaper)

LA&LR: Livonia, Avon and Lakeville Railroad

LAMACHA: Louisiana-Alabama-Mississippi Automated Clearing House Association

LamSes: Lamson & Sessions Co., The (newspaper)

LAN: Lancer Corp. (ASE)

LANC: Lancaster Colony Corp. (NAS NMS)

Lancer: Lancer Corp. (newspaper)

LaPac: Louisiana-Pacific Corp. (newspaper)

LaPnt: La Pointe Industries Inc. (newspaper)

Larizz: Larizza Industries Inc. (newspaper)

LAS: Laser Industries Ltd. (ASE)

Laser: Laser Industries Ltd. (newspaper)

LASR: Laser Precision Corp. (NAS NMS)

LAT: Latshaw Enterprises Inc. (ASE)

Latshw: Latshaw Enterprises Inc. (newspaper)

LAUR: Laurel Entertainment Inc. (NAS NMS)

Lauren: Laurentian Capital Corp. (newspaper)

LAW: Lawter International Inc. (NYSE)

LawrG: Lawrence Insurance Group Inc. (newspaper)

LAWS: Lawson Products Inc. (NAS NMS)

Lawsn: Lawsen Mardon Group Ltd. (newspaper)

Lawtlnt: Lawter International Inc. (newspaper)

LAWV: Lorain and West Virginia (railway)

Laz By: La-Z-Boy Chair Co. (newspaper)

LazKap: Lazare Kaplan International Inc. (newspaper)

LB: LaBarge Inc. (ASE)
Legal Bond
Pound (currency of UK)

LBC: Landbank Bancshares Corp. (NYSE)

LBE: Long Bill of Exchange

LBO: Leveraged BuyOut

LBR: Lowville and Beaver River (railroad)

LbtyAS: Liberty All-Star Equity Fund (newspaper)

L&C: Lancaster & Chester (railroad)

LC: Late Charge
Legal Capital
Letter of Credit
Leverage Contract
Liberty Corp., The (NYSE)
Line of Credit
Listed Company
Loan Capital
Loan Crowd

L/C: Letter of Credit

LCA: Lake Central Airlines

LCBIV: Landmark/Community Bancorp Inc. (NAS NMS)

LCE: London Commodity Exchange (UK)
Lone Star Industries Inc. (NYSE)

LCIC: Leisure Concepts Inc. (NAS NMS)

LCLD: Laclede Steel Co. (NAS NMS)

LCNB: Lincoln Bancorp (NAS NMS)

LCOR: Langly Corp. (NAS NMS)

L/CR: Letter of Credit

LCSI: LCS Industries Inc. (NAS NMS)

LCT: Less than Truckload Lot

L&D: Loans and Discounts

LDBCD: LDB Corp. (NAS NMS)

LDG: Longs Drug Stores Corp. (NYSE)

LDGX: Lodgisix Inc. (NAS NMS)

LDIC: LDI Corp. (NAS NMS)

LDL: Lydall Inc. (ASE)

LDMA: London Discount Market Association (UK)

LDMF: Laidlaw Transportation Ltd. (NAS NMS)

LDMK: Landmark Bank for Savings (Massachusetts) (NAS NMS)

LdmkSv: Landmark Savings Assn. (Pennsylvania) (newspaper)

LE: Lake Geneva Airways
Lands' End Inc. (NYSE)

LEAF: Interleaf Inc. (NAS NMS)

Learnl: LeaRonal Inc. (newspaper)

LearPP: Lear Petroleum Partners LP (newspaper)

LearPt: Lear Petroleum Corp. (newspaper)

led: ledger

LEDA: Lee Data Corp. (NAS NMS)

LEE: Lake Erie and Eastern (railroad)
Lee Enterprises Inc. (NYSE)

LeeEnt: Lee Enterprises Inc. (newspaper)

LeePhr: Lee Pharmaceuticals (newspaper)

LEF: Lake Erie, Franklin and Clarion (railroad)

LE&FW: Lake Erie and Fort Wayne (railroad)

LEG: Leggett & Platt Inc. (NYSE)

LegMas: Legg Mason Inc. (newspaper)

LegPlat: Leggett & Platt Inc. (newspaper)

Lehmn: Lehman Corp., The (newspaper)

Leiner: P. Leiner Nutritional Products Corp. (newspaper)

LeisurT: Leisure & Technology Inc.
(newspaper)
LEIX: Lowrance Electronics Inc.
(NAS NMS)
LEL: Lower Earnings Limit
LEM: Lehman Corp., The (NYSE)
LEN: Lake Erie and Northern (rail-
way)
Lennar Corp. (NYSE)
Lennar: Lennar Corp. (newspaper)
LENS: Concord Camera Corp. (NAS
NMS)
LEO: Dreyfus Strategic Municipals
Inc. (NYSE)
LES: Leslie Fay Companies, The
(NYSE)
LeslFay: Leslie Fay Companies
Inc., The (newspaper)
let: letter
LeucNt: Leucadia National Corp.
(newspaper)
Levitt: Levitt Corp. (newspaper)
LEXB: Lexington Savings Bank
(Massachusetts) (NAS
NMS)
LEXI: Lexicon Corp. (NAS NMS)
LF: Ledger Folio
LFA: Littlefield Adams & Co. (ASE)
LFBR: Longview Fibre Co. (NAS
NMS)
Lfetime: Lifetime Corp. (newspaper)
LFIN: Lincoln FInancial Corp. (NAS
NMS)
LFSA: First Federal S&L Assn. of
Lenawee County (NAS
NMS)
LFT: Lifetime Corp. (ASE)
LG: Laclede Gas Co. (NYSE)
LGL: Lynch Corp. (ASE)
LGN: Logicon Inc. (NYSE)
LGS: Louisiana General Services
Inc. (NYSE)
LH: Legal Holiday
LHC: L & N Housing Corp. (NYSE)
L&HR: Lehigh & Hudson River
(railroad)

li: liabilities
liability
LI: Labor Intensive
Long Island (railroad)
L/I: Letter of Intent
LIBH: Liberty Homes Inc. (NAS
NMS)
LIBO: London Inter-Bank Offered
(rate)
LIBOR: London Inter-Bank Offered
Rate
LibtyCp: Liberty Corp., The (news-
paper)
LIC: Less Industralized Country
LICF: Long Island City Financial
Corp., The (NAS NMS)
LICI: Lilly Industrial Coatings Inc.
(NAS NMS)
LIFE: Lifeline Systems Inc. (NAS
NMS)
LIFFE: London International Finan-
cial Futures Exchange
(UK)
LIG: Liggett Group Inc. (NYSE)
Ligget: Liggett Group Inc. (newspa-
per)
LII: Larizza Industries Inc. (ASE)
LIL: Long Island Lighting Co.
(NYSE)
LILCo: Long Island Lighting Co.
(newspaper)
Lilly: Eli Lilly & Co. (newspaper)
LilVer: Lillian Vernon Corp. (news-
paper)
Limean: The mean of London inter-
bank bid and offer rates
Limited: Limited Inc., The (newspa-
per)
LINB: LIN Broadcasting Corp.
(NAS NMS)
LincNtl: Lincoln National Corp.
(newspaper)
LincPl: Lincoln National Direct
Placement Fund Inc.
(newspaper)
LIND: Lindberg Corp. (NAS NMS)

LINN: Lincoln Foodservice Products Inc. (NAS NMS)

LinPro: Linpro Specific Properties (newspaper)

LIO: Lionel Corp., The (ASE)

Lionel: Lionel Corp., The (newspaper)

LIPO: Liposome Company Inc. (NAS NMS)

LIQB: Liqui-Box Corp. (NAS NMS)

liquid: liquidation

lir: lira (currency of Italy)

LIRC: Low Interest Rate Currency

LIRR: Long Island Railroad

LIT: Life Insurance Trust
Litton Industries Inc. (NYSE)
Local Income Tax

Litfld: Littlefield, Adams & Co. (newspaper)

Litton: Litton Industries Inc. (newspaper)

LIZC: Liz Claiborne Inc. (NAS NMS)

LJC: La Jolla Bancorp. (ASE)

LK: Lockheed Corp. (NYSE)

LKI: Lazare Kaplan International Inc. (ASE)

LK&PRR: Lahaina-Kaanapal and Pacific Railroad (Hawaii)

LL: Limited Liability
Lloyd's of London (UK)

LLB: CompuTrac Inc.

LLEC: Long Lake Energy Corp. (NAS NMS)

LLE Ry: LL & E Royalty Trust (newspaper)

LLOG: Lincoln Logs Ltd. (NAS NMS)

LLOYD'S: Lloyd's Register of Shipping (UK)

LLSI: LSI Logic Corp. (NAS NMS)

LLSL: Lakeland Savings Bank SLA (NAS NMS)

LLTC: Linear Technology Corp. (NAS NMS)

LLX: Louisiana Land & Exploration Co., The (NYSE)

LLY: Eli Lilly & Co. (NYSE)

LM: Legg Mason Inc. (NYSE)
Litchfield and Madison (railway)
Louisiana Midland (railroad)

LMAC: Landmark American Corp. (NAS NMS)

LMAN: Lieberman Enterprises Inc. (NAS NMS)

LMC: Lomas Mortgage Corp. (NYSE)

LME: London Metal Exchange (UK)

LMEC: London Metal Exchange (UK)

LMED: LyphoMed Inc. (NAS NMS)

LMG: Lawsen Mardon Group Ltd. (ASE)

LML: Landmark Land Company Inc. (ASE)

LMS: Lamson & Sessions Co., The (NYSE)

LMT: Local Mean Time

LMV: Long Market Value

L&N: Louisville & Nashville (railroad)

LNAC: Louisville, New Albany and Corydon (railroad)

LNBC: Liberty National Bancorp Inc. (NAS NMS)

LNC: Lincoln National Corp. (NYSE)

LNCE: Lance Inc. (NAS NMS)

LncNC: Lincoln N. C. Realty Fund (newspaper)

LncNtC: Lincoln National Convertible Securities Fund Inc. (newspaper)

LND: Lincoln National Direct Placement Fund Inc. (NYSE)

LndBnc: Landbank Bancshares Corp. (newspaper)

LndEd: Lands' End Inc. (newspaper)

LNDL: Lindal Cedar Homes Inc. (NAS NMS)

Lndmk: Landmark Land Company Inc. (newspaper)

LndPc: Landsing Pacific Fund (newspaper)

L&NE: Lehigh & New England (railroad)

LNF: Lomas & Nettleton Financial Corp. (NYSE)

LN Ho: L & N Housing Corp. (newspaper)

LNP&W: Laramie, North Park & Western (railroad)

L&NR: Ludington and Northern Railway

L&NRY: Laona and Northern Railway

LNSB: Lincoln Savings Bank (Pennsylvania) (NAS NMS)

LnStar: Lone Star Industries Inc. (newspaper)

LNV: Lincoln National Convertible Securities Inc. (NYSE)

L&NW: Louisiana & North West (railroad)

lo: low

LO: Letter of Offer
Limit (limited) Order
Lowest Offer

L/O: Letter of Offer

LOC: Letter Of Credit
Loctite Corp. (NYSE)

Lockhd: Lockheed Corp. (newspaper)

LOCL: Local Federal S&L Assn. (Oklahoma) (NAS NMS)

Loctite: Loctite Corp. (newspaper)

Loews: Loews Corp. (newspaper)

LOG: Rayonier Timberlands LP (NYSE)

Logicon: Logicon Inc. (newspaper)

LOI: Letter Of Instruction

LOLS: Land of Lincoln S&L

LOM: Lomas & Nettleton Mortgage Investors (NYSE)

LomasM: Lomas Mortgage Corp. (newspaper)

LomFn: Lomas & Nettleton Financial Corp. (newspaper)

LOMI: Letter Of Moral Intent

LomMt: Lomas & Nettleton Mortgage Investors (newspaper)

LOND: London House Inc. (NAS NMS)

LongDr: Longs Drug Stores Corp. (newspaper)

LOP&G: Live Oak, Perry & Gulf (railroad)

LOR: Loral Corp. (NYSE)

Loral: Loral Corp. (newspaper)

LoriCp: Lori Corp., The (newspaper)

LOTS: Lotus Development Corp. (NAS NMS)

LOU: Louisville Gas & Electric Co. (NYSE)

LouvGs: Louisville Gas & Electric Co. (newspaper)

LOW: Lowe's Companies Inc. (NYSE)

Lowes: Lowe's Companies Inc. (newspaper)

LOYC: Loyola Capital Corp. (NAS NMS)

LP: Limited Partner
Long Position

LPA: Lease Purchase Agreement

LPAI: La Petite Academy Inc. (NAS NMS)

LPB: Louisiana and Pine Bluff (railway)

LPF: Landsing Pacific Fund (ASE)

LPG: Liquefied Petroleum Gas
Petrolane Partners LP (NYSE)

LPH: Lee Pharmaceuticals (ASE)

LPI: La Pointe Industries Inc. (ASE)

LPLI: LPL Investment Group Inc. (NAS NMS)

LPN: Longview, Portland and Northern (railway)

LPO: Linpro Specific Properties (ASE)

LPP: Lear Petroleum Partners LP (ASE)

LPS: Low-Priced Stock

LPT: Lear Petroleum Corp. (NYSE)

LPX: Louisiana-Pacific Corp. (NYSE)

LQ: Laurentian Capital Corp. (ASE)

LQM: La Quinta Motor Inns Inc. (NYSE)

LQP: La Quinta Motor Inns LP (NYSE)

LQuint: La Quinta Motor Inns Inc. (newspaper)

LQuMt: La Quinta Motor Inns LP (newspaper)

LR: Legal Reserve
Lending Rate
Lloyd's Register (UK)
Loan Rate

LRC: Lori Corp., The (ASE)

LRCX: Lam Research Corp. (NAS NMS)

LRF: Lincoln N.C. Realty Fund (ASE)

LRI: Lawndale Transportation Company
LeaRonal Inc. (NYSE)

LROI: Legal Rate Of Interest

LRS: Laurinburg and Southern Railroad

LRT: LL & E Royalty Trust (NYSE)

L&S: Laurinburg and Southern (railroad)

LS: Letter Stock
Listed Securities (Stock)
Little Stock
Louisiana Southern (railroad)

LSA: Landmark Savings Assn. (Pennsylvania) (ASE)

LSB: LSB Industries Inc. (ASE)

LS&BC: La Salle and Bureau County (railroad)

LSB Ind: LSB Industries Inc. (newspaper)

LSC: Shopco Laurel Centre LP (ASE)

LSCO: LESCO Inc. (NAS NMS)

LSE: London Stock Exchange (UK)

LSER: Laser Corp. (NAS NMS)

Lshld: leasehold

LS&I: Lake Superior and Ishpeming (railroad)

LSNB: Lake Shore Bancorp Inc. (Illinois) (NAS NMS)

LSO: Louisiana Southern (railway)

LSSB: Lake Sunapee Savings Bank FSB (New Hampshire) (NAS NMS)

LSST: Lone Star Technologies Inc. (NAS NMS)

LST&TRC: Lake Superior Terminal and Transfer Railway Company

LT: Lake Terminal (railroad)
Land Tax
Legal Tender
Legal Title
Less Than
Letter of Trust
Long Term
Luxury Tax

LTB: London Transport Board (UK)

LTC: Less Than Carload
Long Term Contract
Long Term Credit

LTCG: Long-Term Capital Gain

LTCL: Long-Term Capital Loss

Ltd: Limited (Company limited in its liability) (Irish) (British) (UK)

LTD: Limited (to any security or purpose)
Limited Inc., The (NYSE)

LTEC: Lincoln Telecommunications Co. (NAS NMS)

LTEK: Life Technologies Inc. (NAS NMS)

LTFV: Less Than Fair Value

LTG: Catalina Lighting Inc. (ASE)
LTIZ: Liposome Technology Inc. (NAS NMS)
LTL: Less-than-Truckload
ltr: letter
LTR: Loews Corp. (NYSE)
LTT: Long-Term Trend
LTV: LTV Corp., The (newspaper)
LTXX: LTX Corp. (NAS NMS)
LUB: Luby's Cafeterias Inc. (NYSE)
LUBE: AutoSpa Corp. (NAS NMS)
Lubrzl: Lubrizol Corp., The (newspaper)
Lubys: Luby's Cafeterias Inc. (newspaper)
LUC: Lukens Inc. (NYSE)
LUCRE: Lower Unit Costs and Related Earnings
LUK: Leucadia National Corp. (NYSE)
Lukens: Lukens Inc. (newspaper)
LUM: Lumex Inc. (ASE)
Lumex: Lumex Inc. (newspaper)
LUND: Lund Enterprises Inc. (NAS NMS)
LUR: L. Luria & Son Inc. (ASE)
Luria: L. Luria & Son Inc. (newspaper)
LUSK: Luskin's Inc. (NAS NMS)

LUV: Southwest Airlines Co. (NYSE)
LUX: Leisure & Technology Inc. (NYSE)
LUXIBOR: Luxembourg Inter-Bank Offered Rate
LV: Lehigh Valley (railroad)
LVC: Lillian Vernon Corp. (ASE)
LVI: LVI Group Inc., The (NYSE)
LVI Gp: LVI Group Inc., The (newspaper)
LVMH: LVMH Moet Hennessy Louis Vuitton (NAS NMS)
LVT: Levitt Corp. (ASE)
L&W: Louisville & Wadley (railroad)
LWR: Lawrence Insurance Group Inc. (ASE)
LWV: Lackawanna & Wyoming Valley (railroad)
LXBK: LSB Bancshares Inc. (North Carolina) (NAS NMS)
LY: Last Year (Year's)
Lydal: Lydall Inc. (newspaper)
LynchC: Lynch Corp. (newspaper)
LYONS: Liquid Yield Option Note
LYTS: LSI Lighting Systems Inc. (NAS NMS)
LZ: Lubrizol Corp., The (NYSE)
LZB: La-Z-Boy Chair Co. (NYSE)

m: matured
M: MCorp. (NYSE)
  The equilibrium nominal Money
    stock
  Matured bonds (in bond listings
    in newspapers)
M&A: Mississippi & Alabama (rail-
    road)
  Missouri and Arkansas (rail-
    road)
MA: Margin Account
  Market Averages
  Moving Average
MABC: Mid-America Bancorp (Ken-
    tucky) (NAS NMS)
MABS: Monoclonal Antibodies Inc.
    (NAS NMS)
MACD: MacDermid Inc. (NAS
    NMS)
MacGrg: MacGregor Sporting
    Goods Inc. (newspa-
    per)
MACHA: Michigan Automated
    Clearing House Associa-
    tion
  MidAmerica Automated
    Clearing House Associa-
    tion
  Mid-Atlantic Automated
    Clearing House Associa-
    tion
  Midwest Automated
    Clearing House Associa-
    tion
MACK: Mack Trucks Inc. (NAS
    NMS)
Macmil: Macmillan Inc. (newspa-
    per)
MacNSc: MacNeal-Schwendler
    Corp., The (newspaper)

MACOM: M/A-Com Inc. (newspa-
    per)
MACR: Minneapolis, Anoka and
    Guyana Range (railroad)
MAGAF: Magna International Inc.
    (NAS NMS)
MAGI: Magna Group Inc. (NAS
    NMS)
MAHI: Monarch Avalon Inc. (NAS
    NMS)
MAI: M/A-Com Inc. (NYSE)
MAIBF: MAI Basic Four Inc. (news-
    paper)
MAIL: Mail Boxes Etc. (NAS
    NMS)
MAIR: Metro Airlines Inc. (NAS
    NMS)
maj: majority
MAJL: Michael Anthony Jewelers
    Inc. (NAS NMS)
MAJR: Major Realty Corp. (NAS
    NMS)
MAJV: Major Video Corp. (NAS
    NMS)
MAKL: Markel Corp. (NAS NMS)
Malart: Malartic Hygrade Gold
    Mines Ltd. (newspaper)
Malaysa: Malaysia Fund Inc., The
    (newspaper)
MALC: Mallard Coach Company
    Inc. (NAS NMS)
MALR: Malrite Communications
    Groups Inc. (NAS NMS)
MAM: Mid-America Industries Inc.
    (ASE)
man: manual
  manufacture
MAN: Manville Corp. (NYSE)
MANA: Manatron Inc. (NAS
    NMS)

manf: manufacture
manufacturer
manufacturing
MANF: May, August, November,
February (securities)
ManfHo: Manufactured Homes Inc.
(newspaper)
ManhNt: Manhattan National Corp.
(newspaper)
ManrCr: Manor Care Inc. (newspaper)
MANT: Manitowoc Company, Inc.,
The (NAS NMS)
manuf: manufacture
manufacturing
Manvl: Manville Corp. (newspaper)
MAO: Marathon Office Supply Inc.
(ASE)
MAP: Maine Public Service Co.
(ASE)
Minimum Annual Premium
MAPCO: MAPCO Inc. (newspaper)
MAPEX: Mid-America Payment Exchange
MAPS: Modern Accounts Payable
System
Monetary and Payments
System
MAR: Marcade Group Inc., The
(NYSE)
Minimum Acceptable Rate of
Return
MARC: M/A/R/C Inc. (NAS NMS)
Marcde: Marcade Group Inc., The
(newspaper)
marg: margin
marginal
MarionMDow: Marion Merrill Dow
Laboratories Inc.
(newspaper)
Maritrn: Maritrans Partners LP
(newspaper)
mark: market
marketing
Marlton: Marlton Technologies Inc.
(newspaper)

MARR: Magma Arizona Railroad
Marriot: Marriott Corp. (newspaper)
MARS: Marsh Supermarkets Inc.
(NAS NMS)
MarsG: Mars Graphic Services Inc.
(newspaper)
MartM: Martin Marietta Corp.
(newspaper)
MAS: Masco Corp. (NYSE)
Monetary Authority of
Singapore
MASB: MASSBANK Corp. (Massachusetts) (NAS NMS)
Masco: Masco Corp. (newspaper)
MasCp: MassMutual Corporate Investors (newspaper)
MasInc: MassMutual Income Investors Inc. (newspaper)
MASX: Masco Industries Inc. (NAS
NMS)
mat: matured (stocks)
maturity
MAT: Mattel Inc. (NYSE)
Matec: MATEC Corp. (newspaper)
Matrix: Matrix Corp. (newspaper)
MatRsh: Materials Research Corp.
(newspaper)
MatSci: Material Sciences Corp.
(newspaper)
Matsu: Matsushita Electric Industrial Company Ltd. (newspaper)
Mattel: Mattel Inc. (newspaper)
MattW: Matthews & Wright Group
Inc. (newspaper)
MauLoa: Mauna Loa Macadamia
Partners LP (newspaper)
MAVR: Maverick Restaurant Corp.
(NAS NMS)
max: maximum
MAX: Matrix Corp. (ASE)
Maxam: MAXXAM Group Inc.
(newspaper)
MAXC: Maxco Inc. (NAS NMS)
MAXE: Max & Erma's Restaurants
Inc. (NAS NMS)

MAXI: Maxicare Health Plans Inc. (NAS NMS)

Maxphrm: MaxPharma Inc. (newspaper)

Maxus: Maxus Energy Corp. (newspaper)

MAYS: J. W. Mays Inc. (NAS NMS)

Maytag: Maytag Co., The (newspaper)

M&B: Marianna & Blountstown (railroad)
Meridian and Bigbee (railroad)

MB: Merchant Bank
Municipal Bond

MBA: Master of Business Administration
Mortgage Bankers Association (of America)

MBC: Mickelberry Corp. (NYSE)

MBD: Million Barrels per Day

MBDOE: Million Barrels per Day Oil Equivalent

MBF: MAI Basic Four Inc. (NYSE)

MBI: Marianna and Blountstown (railroad)
MBIA Inc. (NYSE)

MBIA: MBIA Inc. (newspaper)
Municipal Bond Insurance Association

MBLA: National Mercantile Bancorp (NAS NMS)

MBLE: Mobile Gas Service Corp. (NAS NMS)

MBN: Metrobank NA (California) (ASE)

MBNY: Merchants Bank of New York (NAS NMS)

mbr: member

M&BR: Meridian & Bigbee River (railroad)

MBSX: MBS Textbook Exchange Inc. (NAS NMS)

MBT: Marianna and Blountstown (railroad)

MBVT: Merchants Bancshares Inc. (Vermont) (NAS NMS)

MBY: Middleby Corp. (ASE)

MC: Maine Central (railroad)
Margin Call
Marginal Cost
Matsushita Electric Industrial Company Ltd. (NYSE)
Michigan Central (railroad)
Middle Creek Railroad
Mississippi Central (railroad)
Mortgage Company
Municipal Code

MCA: MCA Inc. (NYSE) (newspaper)

MCAW: McCaw Cellular Communications Inc. (NAS NMS)

MCBK: Merchants Capital Corp. (NAS NMS)

MCC: Mestek Inc. (NYSE)
Mutual Capital Certificate

MCCA: Mobile Communications Corporation of America (NAS NMS)

MCCL: McClain Industries Inc. (NAS NMS)

McCla: McClatchy Newspapers Inc. (newspaper)

MCCRK: McCormick & Company Inc. (NAS NMS)

MCCS: Medco Containment Services Inc. (NAS NMS)

MCD: McDonald's Corp. (NYSE)

McDerI: McDermott International Inc. (newspaper)

McDId: McDonald's Corp. (newspaper)

McDnD: McDonnell Douglas Corp. (newspaper)

McDnI: McDonald & Comany Investments Inc. (newspaper)

MCDY: Microdyne Corp. (NAS NMS)

McFad: McFaddin Ventures Inc. (newspaper)

MCFE: McFarland Energy Inc.
(NAS NMS)

McGrH: McGraw-Hill Inc. (newspaper)

MCH: MedChem Products Inc.
(ASE)

MchER: Michigan Energy Resources Co. (newspaper)

MCHN: Merchants National Corp.
(NAS NMS)

MCI: MassMutual Corporate Investors (NYSE)

MCIC: MCI Communications Corp.
(NAS NMS)

McInt: McIntyre Mines Ltd. (newspaper)

MCK: McKesson Corp. (NYSE)

McKes: McKesson Corp. (newspaper)

MCL: Moore Corporation Ltd.
(NYSE)

McLe: McLean Industries Inc.
(newspaper)

MCM: Monte Carlo Method

MCO: MCO Holdings Inc. (ASE)
Midland Continental (railroad)

MCOA/P: Multi-Company Accounts
Payable

MCO Hd: MCO Holdings Inc.
(newspaper)

MCOM: Midwest Communications
Corp. (NAS NMS)

MCON: EMCON Associates (NAS
NSM)

MCOR: Marine Corp (Illinois) (NAS
NMS)

MCorp: MCorp (newspaper)

MCO Rs: MCO Resources Inc.
(newspaper)

MCP: Marginal-Cost Pricing

MCR: McCloud River (railroad)
MCO Resources Inc. (ASE)

McRae: McRae Industries Inc.
(newspaper)

MCRD: Micro D Inc. (NAS NMS)

MCRO: Micro Mask Inc. (NAS
NMS)

MCRR: Maine Central Road Railroad

MCRS: MICROS Systems Inc. (NAS
NMS)

MCSA: Moscow, Camden and San
Augustine (railroad)

md: Demand for nominal Money

MD: Management Development
Mark Down
Maturity Date
McDonnell Douglas Corp.
(NYSE)
Memorandum of Deposit
Midnight Dumping
Months after Date
Municipal Docks Railway of
the Jacksonville Port Authority

MDA: MAPCO Inc. (NYSE)

MDB: Multilateral Development
Bank

MDC: M.D.C. Holdings Inc. (NYSE)
(newspaper)

MDCA: M.D.C. Asset Investors Inc.
(newspaper)

MDCI: Medical Action Industries
Inc. (NAS NMS)

Mdcore: Medicore Inc. (newspaper)

MDD: McDonald & Company Investments Inc. (NYSE)

MDEX: Medex Inc. (NAS NMS)

MDIN: Medalist Industries Inc.
(NAS NMS)

MDK: Medicore Inc. (ASE)

MdMgt: Medical Management of
America Inc. (newspaper)

MDNT: MNC Financial Inc. (NAS
NMS)

MDO: Monthly Debit Ordinary

MDP: Meredith Corp. (NYSE)

MDR: McDermott International Inc.
(NYSE)
Minimum Daily Requirement

MD&S: Macon, Dublin & Savannah (railroad)
mdse: merchandise
MDSN: Madison Gas & Electric Co. (NAS NMS)
MDST: Medstat Systems Inc. (NAS NMS)
MDT: Medtronic Inc. (NYSE) Mountain Daylight Time
MDTC: MDT Corp. (NAS NMS)
MDU: MDU Resources Group Inc. (NYSE) (newspaper)
MDW: Midway Airlines Inc. (NYSE)
MdwAir: Midway Airlines Inc. (newspaper)
MDXR: Medar Inc. (NAS NMS)
M&E: Morristown and Erie (railroad)
ME: Mercantile Exchange
MEA: Mead Corp., The (NYSE)
Mead: Mead Corp., The (newspaper)
MEC: Maine Central (railroad)
MED: MEDIQ Inc. (ASE)
MEDC: Medical Care International Inc. (NAS NMS)
Medch: MedChem Products Inc. (newspaper)
Media: Media General Inc. (newspaper)
Mediq: MEDIQ Inc. (newspaper)
MedPr: Medical Properties Inc. (newspaper)
Medtrn: Medtronic Inc. (newspaper)
MEG: Media General Inc. (ASE)
MEI: MEI Diversified Inc. (NYSE)
MEL: Mellon Bank Corp. (NYSE)
MELCO: Mitsubishi Electric Corporation (Japan)
Mellon: Mellon Bank Corp. (newspaper)
Melvill: Melville Corp. (newspaper)
mem: memorandum
Mem: MEM Company Inc. (newspaper)
MEM: MEM Company Inc. (ASE)

MENT: Mentor Graphics Corp. (NAS NMS)
MePS: Maine Public Service Co. (newspaper)
MER: Merrill Lynch & Company Inc. (NYSE)
merc: mercantile
Merck: Merck & Company Inc. (newspaper)
MercSL: Mercury S&L Assn. (newspaper)
MercSt: Mercantile Stores Company Inc. (newspaper)
Merdth: Meredith Corp. (newspaper)
MerLyn: Merrill Lynch & Company Inc. (newspaper)
Mermc: Merrimac Industries Inc. (newspaper)
MERY: Merry Land & Investment Company Inc. (NAS NMS)
MES: Melville Corp. (NYSE) Multiple Earning Statement
Mesab: Mesabi Trust (newspaper)
MesaLP: Mesa Limited Partnership (newspaper)
MesaOf: Mesa Offshore Trust (newspaper)
MesaR: Mesa Royalty Trust (newspaper)
MESL: Mesa Airlines Inc. (NAS NMS)
MESOP: Management Enrichment Stock Ownership Plan
Mesrx: Measurex Corp. (newspaper)
Mestek: Mestek Inc. (newspaper)
METB: Metropolitan Bancorp Inc. (NAS NMS)
Metex: Metex Corp. (newspaper)
METH: Methode Electronics Inc. (NAS NMS)
MetPro: Met-Pro Corp. (newspaper)
Metrbkj: Metrobank N.A. (California) (newspaper)

MetrFn: Metropolitan Financial
Corp. (North Dakota)
(newspaper)

MetRlt: Metropolitan Realty Corp.
(newspaper)

METS: Met-Coil Systems Corp.
(NAS NMS)

MEX: Mississippi Export (railroad)

MexFd: Mexico Fund Inc., The
(newspaper)

MEYER: Fred Meyer Inc. (NAS
NMS)

MF: Malaysia Fund Inc., The
(NYSE)
Middle Fork (railroad)
Mutual Fund

MFAC: Market Facts Inc. (NAS
NMS)

MFC: Maritime Fruit Carriers
(steamship)
Metropolitan Financial Corp.
(North Dakota) (NYSE)

MFCO: Microwave Filter Company
Inc. (NAS NMS)

mfd: manufactured

MFD: Munford Inc. (NYSE)

MFED: Maury Federal Savings
Bank (Tennessee) (NAS
NMS)

MFFC: Mayflower Financial Corp.
(NAS NMS)

mfg: manufacturing

MFGC: Midwest Financial Group
Inc. (NAS NMS)

MFGI: Moore FInancial Group Inc.
(NAS NMS)

MFGR: Morsemere Financial Group
Inc. (NAS NMS)

MFLR: Mayflower Co-operative
Bank (Massachusetts)
(NAS NMS)

MFM: MFS Municipal Income Trust
(NYSE) (newspaper)

MFO: MFS Income & Opportunity
Trust (NYSE) (newspaper)

mfr: manufacture
manufactured
manufacturer

MfrHan: Manufacturers Hanover
Corp. (newspaper)

MFSB: MidFed Savings Bank (NAS
NMS)

MFSL: Maryland Federal S&L
Assn. (NAS NMS)

mfst: manifest

MFT: MFS Multimarket Total Return Trust (NYSE) (news-
paper)
Most-Favorable-Terms

MFTN: Metropolitan Federal S&L
Assn. (Tennessee) (NAS
NMS)

M&G: Mobile & Gulf (railroad)

MGC: Morgan Grenfell SMALLCap
Fund Inc. (NYSE)

MGCC: Medical Graphics Corp.
(NAS NMS)

MGCO: Medicare-Glaser Corp.
(NAS NMS)

MGCP: Magma Copper Co. (NAS
NMS)

MGD: Million Gallons per Day

MGI: MGI Properties (NYSE)

MGI Prp: MGI Properties (newspaper)

MGLL: McGill Manufacturing Company Inc. (NAS NMS)

MGM: MGM/UA Communications
Co. (NYSE)

MGMA: Magma Power Co. (NAS
NMS)

mgmt: management

MGMUA: MGM/UA Communications Co. (newspaper)

MGN: Morgan Products Ltd.
(NYSE)

MGNC: MEDIAGENIC (NAS NMS)

MGP: Merchants Group Inc. (ASE)

mgr: manager

MGRC: McGrath RentCorp. (NAS
NMS)

MGRE: Merry-Go-Round Enterprises Inc. (NAS NMS)

MGS: MacGregor Sporting Goods Inc. (ASE)

mgt: management

MGU: Mobile and Gulf (railroad)

MHBK: Mid-Hudson Savings Bank FSB (New York) (NAS NMS)

MHC: Manufacturers Hanover Corp. (NYSE)

MHCIV: Maione-Hirschberg Companies Inc. (NAS NMS)

MHCO: Moore-Handley Inc. (NAS NMS)

MHG: Malartic Hygrade Gold Mines Ltd. (Canada) (ASE)

MHI Gp: MHI Group Inc. (newspaper)

MHM: Mount Hope Mineral (railroad)

M&HMRR: Marquette and Huron Mountain Railroad

MHP: McGraw-Hill Inc. (NYSE)

MHS: Marriott Corp. (NYSE)

MI: Mackey International Air Commuter (airline)
Marshall Industries (NYSE)
Merit Increase
Minority Interest
Miscellaneous Income
Missouri-Illinois (railroad)

MIAM: Mid-Am Inc. (NAS NMS)

MIB: Marketing of Investments Board

MIBOR: Madrid Interbank Offered Rate

MIC: Management Investment Company
Mortgage Insurance Company

MICA: MicroAge Inc. (NAS NMS)

MichStr: Michaels Stores Inc. (newspaper)

Micklby: Mickelberry Corp. (newspaper)

MICO: Midland Continental (railroad)

micron: Micron Products Inc. (newspaper)

MICS: Micom Systems Inc. (NAS NMS)

MID: Midway (railroad)

MidAM: Mid-America Industries Inc. (newspaper)

MIDC: MidConn Bank (Connecticut) (NAS NMS)

MIDL: Midlantic Corp. (NAS NMS)

Midlby: Middleby Corp. (newspaper)

MidInd: Midland Co., The (newspaper)

MidSUt: Middle South Utilities Inc. (newspaper)

MIF: MuniInsured Fund Inc. (ASE)

MIG: Moody's Investment Grade

MIGI: Meridian Insurance Group Inc. (NAS NMS)

MIHO: M/I Schottenstein Homes Inc. (NAS NMS)

MII: McLean Industries Inc. (NYSE)

MIKL: Michael Foods Inc. (NAS NMS)

MIL: Millipore Corp. (NYSE)

MILL: Millicom Inc. (NAS NMS)

Millipre: Millipore Corp. (newspaper)

MILT: Miltope Group Inc. (NAS NMS)

MiltnR: Milton Roy Co. (newspaper)

MILW: Chicago, Milwaukee, St. Paul and Pacific (railroad)
Milwaukee Insurance Group Inc. (NAS NSM)

min: minimum
minority

MIN: MFS Intermediate Income Trust (NYSE) (newspaper)

MIND: Mindscape Inc. (NAS NMS)

MINDD: Minimum Due Date

MINE: Minneapolis Eastern (railway)

MINL: Minnetonka Corp. (NAS NMS)

MinnPl: Minnesota Power & Light Co. (newspaper)

MINTS: Mutual Institutions National Transfer System

MINY: MiniScribe Corp. (NAS NMS)

MIP: Monthly Investment Plan
Mortgage Insurance Premium
Mortgage Investments Plus Inc. (ASE)

MIR: M.D.C. Asset Investors Inc. (NYSE)

MIRAS: Mortgage Interest Relief At Source

MIS: Moody's Investor Service

MissnW: Mission West Properties (newspaper)

MISTI: Multipurpose International Securities Trading Information

MIT: Modern Investment Theory
Municipal Investment Trust

Mitel: Mitel Corp. (newspaper)

MITI: Ministry of International Trade and Industry (Japan)

MITSY: Mitsui & Company Ltd. (NAS NMS)

MIV: MassMutual Income Investors Inc. (NYSE)

MJ: Manufacturers' Junction (railway)

MJSD: March, June, September, December (securities)

mk: marks

MKC: Marion Merrill Dow Laboratories Inc. (NYSE)
McKeesport Connecting (railroad)

MKCO: M. Kamenstein Inc. (NAS NMS)

MKE: Michaels Stores Inc. (ASE)

mkt: market

MKT: Missouri-Kansas-Texas (railroad)

MKTAY: Makita Electric Works Ltd. (NAS NMS)

ML: Martin Marrietta Corp. (NYSE)

MLA: Midland Co., The (ASE)
Mutual Loan Association

MLAB: Monitor Technologies Inc. (NAS NMS)

MLC: Manhattan National Corp. (NYSE)

MLHR: Herman Miller Inc. (NAS NMS)

MLIS: Micropolis Corp. (NAS NMS)

MLL: Macmillan Inc. (NYSE)

MLLE: Martin Lawrence Limited Editions Inc. (NAS NMS)

MLMC: Multi-Local Media Corp. (NAS NMS)

MLP: Master Limited Partnership
Mesa Limited Partnership (NYSE)

M&LS: Manistique & Lake Superior (railroad)

MLT: Mitel Corp. (NYSE)

MLTF: Multibank Financial Corp. (NAS NMS)

MLXX: MLX Corp. (NAS NMS)

MM: Middle Management
Money Market

MMA: Medical Management of America Inc. (ASE)

MMBLF: MacMillan Bloedel Ltd. (NAS NMS)

MMC: Marsh & McLennan Companies Inc. (NYSE)
Money Market Certificate

MMCT: Metro Mobile CTS Inc. (NAS NMS)

MMD: Moore Medical Corp. (ASE)

MMDA: Money Market Deposit Account

MMed: Moore Medical Corp. (newspaper)

MMEDC: Multimedia Inc. (NAS NMS)

MMF: Money Market Fund

MMIM: MMI Medical Inc. (NAS NMS)

MMM: Minnesota Mining & Manufacturing Co. (NYSE) (newspaper)

MMMC: Minimum Monthly Maintenance Charge

MMO: Monarch Machine Tool Co., The (NYSE)

MMPI: Marquest Medical Products Inc. (NAS NMS)

MMRH: MMR Holding Corp. (NAS NMS)

MMSB: Mid Maine Savings Bank FSB (NAS NMS)

MMST: Medmaster Systems Inc. (NAS NMS)

MMT: MFS Multimarket Income Trust (NYSE) (newspaper)

M&N: May and November (securities)

MN: Commercial Airways

MNBC: Miners National Bancorp Inc. (NAS NMS)

MNC: Multinational Corporation

MNCO: Michigan National Corp. (NAS NMS)

MND: Mitchell Energy & Development Corp. (ASE)

M&NE: Manistee & Northeastern (railroad)

MNE: Multi-National Enterprise

MNES: Mine Safety Appliances Co. (NAS NMS)

M&NF: Morehead and North Fork (railroad)

mnfrs: manufacturers

mng: managing

MNH: Manufactured Homes Inc. (ASE)

MNI: McClatchy Newspapers Inc. (ASE)

MNJ: Middletown and New Jersey (railway)

MNPI: Microcom Inc. (NAS NMS)

MNR: Manor Care Inc. (NYSE)

MN&S: Minneapolis, Northfield and Southern (railroad)

MNS: MacNeal-Schwendler Corp., The (ASE)

MNST: Minstar Inc. (NAS NMS)

MNT: Montedison S.p.A. (NYSE)

MNTL: Manufacturers National Corp. (NAS NMS)

MNTR: Mentor Corp. (NAS NMS)

MNTX: Minntech Corp. (NAS NMS)

MNXI: MNX Inc. (NAS NMS)

mo: month

MO: Money Order
Montreal Stock Exchange listings (in newspapers)
Moral Obligation
Philip Morris Companies Inc. (NYSE)

MOAI: Morino Associates Inc. (NAS NMS)

MOB: Mobil Corp. (NYSE)

Mobil: Mobil Corp. (newspaper)

MobIC: Mobile Communications Corporation of America (newspaper)

MOCO: Modern Controls Inc. (NAS NMS)

MODI: Modine Manufacturing Co. (NAS NMS)

MOE: Measure of Effectiveness
Multiple Of Earnings

MOF: Ministry of Finance (Japan)

MOG: Moog Inc. (ASE)

MOGN: Molecular Genetics Inc. (NAS NMS)

MOH: Mohasco Corp. (NYSE)

Mohsc: Mohasco Corp. (newspaper)

MOIL: Maynard Oil Co. (NAS NMS)

MOKG: Morgan Olmstead Kennedy & Gardner Capital Corp. (NAS NMS)

MOLX: Molex Inc. (NAS NMS)

MON: Monarch Capital Corp. (NYSE)
Monon (railroad)

MonCa: Monarch Capital Corp. (newspaper)

MonPw: Montana Power Co., The (newspaper)

Monrch: Monarch Machine Tool Co., The (newspaper)

Monsan: Monsanto Co. (newspaper)

MonSt: Montgomery Street Income Securities Inc. (newspaper)

Monted: Montedison S.p.A. (newspaper)

MONY: Metropolitan Consolidated Industries Inc. (NAS NMS)
MONY Real Estate Investors (newspaper)
Mutual Life Insurance Company of New York

Moog: Moog Inc. (newspaper)

Moore: Moore Corporation Ltd. (newspaper)

MOP: Margin Of Profit
Missouri Pacific (railroad)

MOR: Morgan Keegan Inc. (NYSE)

MORF: Mor-Flo Industries Inc. (NAS NMS)

Morgan: J. P. Morgan & Company Inc. (newspaper)

MorgG: Morgan Grenfell SMALL-Cap Fund Inc. (newspaper)

MorgnF: Morgan's Foods Inc. (newspaper)

MorgnP: Morgan Products Ltd. (newspaper)

MorgSt: Morgan Stanley Group Inc. (newspaper)

MorKeg: Morgan Keegan Inc. (newspaper)

MorKnd: Morrison Knudsen Corp. (newspaper)

MORP: Moore Products Co. (NAS NMS)

MORR: Morrison Inc. (NAS NMS)

Morton: Morton Thiokol Inc. (newspaper)

mos: months

MOS: Mesa Offshore Trust (NYSE)

MOSI: Mosinee Paper Corp. (NAS NMS)

MOT: Motorola Inc. (NYSE)

Motel: Motel 6 LP (newspaper)

Motorla: Motorola Inc. (newspaper)

MOTR: Motor Club of America (NAS NMS)

Motts: Mott's Super Markets Inc. (newspaper)

MOU: Memorandum of Understanding

MOV: Moshassuck Valley (railroad)

MOW: Montana Western (railway)

M&P: Maryland & Pennsylvania (railroad)

MP: Mail Payment
Market Price
McIntyre Mines Ltd. (NYSE)
Missouri Pacific (railroad)

MPA: Maryland and Pennsylvania (railroad)

MPAC: Impact Systems Inc. (NAS NMS)

MPB: Montpelier and Barre (railroad)

MPC: Marginal Propensity to Consume

MPDS: Market Price Display Service (London Stock Exchange) (UK)

MPI: Marginal Propensity to Invest

MPL: Minnesota Power & Light Co. (NYSE)

MPP: Medical Properties Inc. (ASE)

MPPR: Manitous and Pike's Peak Railway

MPR: Met-Pro Corp. (ASE)

MPRO: MicroPro International Corp. (NAS NMS)

MPS: Marginal Propensity to Save

MPSG: MPSI System Inc. (NAS NMS)

MPT: Modern Portfolio Theory

MR: Maintenance Report
Manufacturer's Representative
Marginal Revenue
Market Ratio

McCloud River (railroad)
Memorandum Report
Morgan's Foods Inc. (ASE)
MRA: Malayan Railway Administration
MRBK: Mercantile Bankshares Corp. (Maryland) (NAS NMS)
MRBL: Marble Financial Corp. (NAS NMS)
MRC: Milton Roy Co. (NYSE)
MRCCV: Mark Controls Corp. (NAS NMS)
MrchGp: Merchants Group Inc. (newspaper)
MRCS: Marcus Corp., The (NAS NMS)
MRCY: Mercury General Corp. (NAS NMS)
MRDN: Meridian Bancorp Inc. (NAS NMS)
MRET: Meret Inc. (NAS NMS)
MRGC: Mr. Gasket Co. (NAS NMS)
MRGO: Margo Nursery Farms Inc. (NAS NMS)
MRGX: Margaux Inc. (NAS NMS)
MRI: McRae Industries Inc. (ASE)
MRIS: Marshall & Ilsley Corp. (NAS NMS)
MRK: Merck & Company Inc. (NYSE)
MRL: Malawi Railways Limited
MRLL: Merrill Corp. (NAS NMS)
MRM: Merrimac Industries Inc. (ASE)
MRMK: Merrimack Bancorp Inc. (NAS NMS)
MRN: Morrison Knudsen Corp. (NYSE)
MRP: Mission Resource Partners LP (ASE)
MRS: Manufacturers Railway
Mrshln: Marshall Industries (newspaper)
MrshMc: Marsh & McLennan Companies Inc. (newspaper)

MRT: Mortgage & Realty Trust (NYSE)
MRTA: Marietta Corp. (NAS NMS)
MrthOf: Marathon Office Supply Inc. (newspaper)
MRTN: Marten Transport Ltd. (NAS NMS)
M&S: March and September (securities)
MS: Major Stockholder
Majority Stock (Stockholders)
March and September (securities)
Margin of Safety
Minority Stockholder
Money Supply
Months after Sight
Morgan Stanley Group Inc. (NYSE)
MSA: MSA Realty Corp. (newspaper)
MSACHA: Mid-South Automated Clearing House Association
MSAI: Management Science America Inc. (NAS NMS)
MSAM: Marsam Pharmaceuticals Inc. (NAS NMS)
MSB: Mesabi Trust (NYSE)
Mutual Savings Bank
MSBI: Monclair Savings Bank (New Jersey) (NAS NMS)
MSC: Material Sciences Corp. (ASE)
Mississippi Central (railroad)
MSCA: M. S. Carriers Inc. (NAS NMS)
MSCO: MASSTOR Systems Corp. (NAS NMS)
MSCP: Massachusetts Computer Corp. (NAS NMS)
MSE: Mexican Stock Exchange
Midwest Stock Exchange
Mississippi Export (railroad)
MSEX: Middlesex Water Co. (NAS NMS)
MSFT: Microsoft Corp. (NAS NMS)

MSHK: Megadata Corp. (NAS NMS)

MSHR: Mischer Corp., The (NAS NMS)

MSI: MSI Data Corp. (ASE)

MSI Dt: MSI Data Corp. (newspaper)

MSII: Medicine Shoppe International Inc. (NAS NMS)

MSL: Mercury S&L Assn. (NYSE)
Minneapolis & St. Louis (railroad)

MSLA: Metropolitan Financial S&L Assn. (Texas) (NAS NMS)

MSM: Mott's Super Markets Inc. (ASE)

MsmRs: Mission Resource Partners LP (newspaper)

MSP&SSM: Minneapolis, St. Paul & Sault Ste. Marie (railroad)

MSR: MSR Exploration Ltd. (ASE) (newspaper)

MSRB: Municipal Securities Rulemaking Board

MSRR: MidSouth Corp. (NAS NMS)

MSSC: Microsemi Corp. (NAS NMS)

MSSL: Mid-State Federal S&L Assn. (NAS NMS)

MST: Mercantile Stores Company Inc. (NYSE)
Mountain Standard Time

MSTI: Medical Sterilization Inc. (NAS NMS)

MSTL: Minneapolis-St. Louis (railroad)

MSTR: Massena Terminal Railroad

MSU: Middle South Utilities Inc. (NYSE)

M&SV: Mississippi & Skuna Valley (railroad)

MSW: Mission West Properties (ASE)

MT: Midland Terminal (railroad)
Mountain Time

MTC: Monsanto Co. (NYSE)
Mystic Terminal Company

MtchlE: Mitchell Energy & Development Corp. (newspaper)

MTEC: Machine Technology Inc. (NAS NMS)

MTFR: Minnesota Transfer Railroad

mtg: mortgage

mtgd: mortgaged

mtge: mortgage

mtgee: mortgagee

mtgor: mortgagor

MtgPI: Mortgage Investments Plus Inc. (newspaper)

MtgRty: Mortgage & Realty Trust (newspaper)

MTH: Mount Hood (railway)

mthly: monthly

MTI: Morton Thiokol Inc. (NYSE)

MTIK: Modular Technology Inc. (NAS NMS)

MTIX: Mechanical Technology Inc. (NAS NMS)

MTL: Materials Research Corp. (ASE)

MTLI: Marine Transport Lines Inc. (NAS NMS)

MtMed: Mountain Medical Equipment Inc. (newspaper)

MTN: Mountain Medical Equipment Inc. (ASE)

MTNR: Mountaineer Bankshares of West Virginia Inc. (NAS NMS)

MTOR: Meritor Savings Bank (NAS NMS)

MTP: Montana Power Co., The (NYSE)

MTR: Mesa Royalty Trust (NYSE)

MTRC: Mercantile Bancorporation Inc. (Missouri) (NAS NMS)

MTRM: Moniterm Corp. (NAS NMS)

MTRO: Metro-Tel Corp. (NAS NMS)

MTS: Montgomery Street Income Securities Inc. (NYSE)
Monthly Treasury Statement

MTSC: MTS Systems Corp. (NAS NMS)

MTW: Marinetee, Tomahawk and Western (railroad)
MTWCR: Mt. Washington Cog Railway
MTWN: Mark Twain Bancshares Inc. (NAS NMS)
MTWO: Melamine Chemicals Inc. (NAS NMS)
MTX: Metex Corp. (ASE)
MTY: Marlton Technologies Inc. (ASE)
MUEL: Paul Mueller Co. (NAS NMS)
MUF: Munivest Fund Inc. (ASE)
mun: municipal
MUN: Munsingwear Inc. (NYSE)
Munfrd: Munford Inc. (newspaper)
MUNI: Municipal Bond(s)
Municipal Development Corp. (NAS NMS)
munic: municipal
MunIn: MuniInsured Fund Inc. (newspaper)
Munsng: Munsingwear Inc. (newspaper)
Munvst: Munivest Fund Inc. (newspaper)
MUO: Mutual of Omaha Interest Shares Inc. (NYSE)
MUR: Murphy Oil Corp. (NYSE)
MurpO: Murphy Oil Corp. (newspaper)
MurryO: Murry Ohio Manufacturing Co. (newspaper)
Muscld: Musicland Group Inc., The (newspaper)
MutOm: Mutual of Omaha Interest Shares Inc. (newspaper)
MUTU: Mutual Federal S&L Assn. (North Carolina) (NAS NMS)
MV: Macrobertson Miller Airlines
Market Value
McFaddin Ventures Inc. (ASE)
Midland Valley (railroad)

MW: Matthews & Wright Group Inc. (ASE)
Minimum Wage
Minnesota Western (railroad)
Montana Western (railroad)
Montgomery Ward
MWAY: Microwave Laboratories Inc. (NAS NMS)
MWE: Midwest Energy Co. (NYSE) (newspaper)
MWR: Muncie and Western Railroad
MX: Measurex Corp. (NYSE)
MXC: MATEC Corp. (ASE)
MXF: Mexico Fund Inc., The (NYSE)
MXIM: Maxim Integrated Products Inc. (NAS NMS)
MXM: MAXXAM Group Inc. (NYSE)
MXP: MaxPharma Inc. (ASE)
MXS: Maxus Energy Corp. (NYSE)
MXTR: Maxtor Corp. (NAS NMS)
MXWL: Maxwell Laboratories Inc. (NAS NMS)
MXXX: Mars Stores Inc. (NAS NMS)
MYCO: Mycogen Corp. (NAS NMS)
MYE: Myers Industries Inc. (ASE)
MyerI: Myers Industries Inc. (newspaper)
MyerL: L. E. Meyers Company Group, The (newspaper)
MYFR: Mayfair Super Markets (NAS NMS)
MYG: Maytag Co., The (NYSE)
MYL: Mylan Laboratories Inc. (NYSE)
Mylan: Mylan Laboratories Inc. (newspaper)
Mylex: Mylex Corp. (newspaper)
MYM: MONY Real Estate Investors (NYSE)
MYO: Murry Ohio Manufacturing Co. (NYSE)
MYR: L. E. Myers Company Group, The (NYSE)
M-ZONE: Manufacturing Zone

N: Inco Ltd. (NYSE)
New issue (stock listings of
newspaper)
NA: National Airlines
Net Assets
No Account
No Approval required
Nostro Account
Not Applicable
Not Appropriated
Not Authorized
Not Available
NAB: National Australia Bank Ltd.
(NYSE)
NACCO: NACCO Industries Inc.
(newspaper)
NACHA: National Automated
Clearing House Associa-
tion
NAF: NAFCO Financial Group Inc.
(NYSE)
Nonappropriated Funds
NAFC: Nash-Finch Co. (NAS NMS)
NAFCO: NAFCO Financial Group
Inc. (newspaper)
NAFI: Northern Air Freight Inc.
(NAS NMS)
NA&G: North Atlantic and Gulf
Steamship Company
NAG: Net Annual Gain
NAHL: North American Holding
Corp. (NAS NMS)
NAIC: National Association of In-
vestment Clubs
NAIG: National Insurance Group
(NAS NMS)
NAJ: Napierville Junction (railway)
Nalco: Nalco Chemical Co. (news-
paper)
NAMSB: National Association of
Mutual Savings Banks

NANC: North American National
Corp. (NAS NMS)
NAN: Nantucket Industries Inc.
(ASE)
NANO: Nanometrics Inc. (NAS
NMS)
Nantck: Nantucket Industries Inc.
(newspaper)
NAP: Narragansett Pier (railroad)
NAPE: National Properties Corp.
(NAS NMS)
NAPF: National Association of Pen-
sion Funds
NAS: Nasta International Inc.
(ASE)
Non-Assessable Stock
NASA: National Association of Se-
curities Administrators
NASD: National Association of Se-
curities Dealers
NASDAQ: National Association of
Securities Dealers' Au-
tomated Quotations
NASDIM: National Association of
Security Dealers and
Investment Managers
Nashua: Nashua Corp. (newspaper)
NASS: National Association of
Steel Stockholders
Nasta: Nasta International Inc.
(newspaper)
nat: national
NatEdu: National Education Corp.
(newspaper)
NatFG: National Fuel Gas Co.
(newspaper)
NATG: National Guardian Corp.,
The (NAS NMS)
NATIONAL: National Airlines
NATL: North Atlantic Industries
Inc. (NAS NMS)

NAV: Navistar International Corp.
(NYSE)
Net Asset Value
NAVG: Navigators Group Inc. (NAS
NMS)
NAVI: North American Ventures
Inc. (NAS NMS)
Navistr: Navistar International
Corp. (newspaper)
NB: National Bank
Newport Air Park (airline)
NBA: National Bankers Association
National Banking Association
National Bankruptcy Act
NBAK: National Bancorp of Alaska
Inc. (NAS NMS)
NBB: New Bedford Institutions for
Savings (NYSE)
NBBS: National Better Business
Bureau
NB&C: Norfolk, Baltimore and
Carolina Line (steamship)
NBC: National Broadcasting Com-
pany
NBCC: National Banc of Commerce
Co. (West Virginia) (NAS
NMS)
NBCT: National Bancshares Corpo-
ration of Texas (NAS
NMS)
NBD: NBD Bancorp Inc. (NYSE)
(newspaper)
NBI: National BankAmericard In-
corporated
NBI Inc. (NYSE) (newspaper)
NBIC: Northeast Bancorp Inc. (NAS
NMS)
NBIO: North American Biologicals
Inc. (NAS NMS)
NBL: Noble Affiliates Inc. (NYSE)
NBR: Net Borrowing Requirement
Nonborrowed Reserve
NBSC: New Brunswick Scientific
Co. (NAS NMS)
NBSIF: National Business Systems
Inc. (NAS NMS)

NBSS: National Bank Surveillance
System
NBTY: Nature's Bounty Inc. (NAS
NMS)
nc: noncallable
NC: NACCO Industries Inc.
(NYSE)
Narrow Coverage
Net Capital
Net Cost
No Charge
North Central Airlines
NCA: Nuveen California Municipal
Value Fund Inc. (NYSE)
NCB: NCNB Corp. (NYSE)
Noncallable Bond
NCBC: National Commerce Bancor-
poration (NAS NMS)
NCBM: National City Bancorpora-
tion (Minnesota) (NAS
NMS)
NCBR: National Community Bank
of New Jersey (NAS NMS)
NCCB: National Consumer Cooper-
ative Bank
NCCO: Enseco Inc. (NAS NMS)
NCD: No Claims Discount
Non-Cumulative Dividend
North Canadian Oils Ltd.
(ASE)
NCdO: North Canadian Oils Ltd.
(newspaper)
NCEF: National Commission on
Electronic Funds Transfer
NCF: NCF Financial Corp. (news-
paper)
Net Cash Flow
NCH: NCH Corp. (NYSE) (newspa-
per)
N CHG: Normal Charge
NCL: S. E. Nichols Inc. (ASE)
NCM: Nuveen California Municipal
Income Fund (NYSE)
NCNB: NCNB Corp. (newspaper)
NCNG: North Carolina Natural Gas
Corp. (NAS NMS)

NCR: National Cash Register
   NCR Corp. (NYSE) (newspaper)
NCS: National Convenience Stores Inc. (NYSE)
   Non-Callable Securities
NC&SL: Nashville, Chattanooga & St. Louis (railroad)
NCT: Non-Competitive Tenders
NCTY: National City Corp. (NAS NMS)
NCV: No Commercial Value
ND: National Debt
   Net Debt
   Next Day (newspaper)
   No Date
   Not Dated
NDCO: Noble Drilling Corp. (NAS NMS)
NDI: Nuclear Data Inc. (ASE)
NDSN: Nordson Corp. (NAS NMS)
NDTA: National Data Corp. (NAS NMS)
NE: Net Earnings
   Northeast Airlines
NEA: Northeast Airlines
NEACH: New England Automated Clearing House Association
NEB: Bank of New England Corp. (NYSE)
NEBS: New England Business Service Inc. (NAS NMS)
NEC: National Education Corp. (NYSE)
NECC: New England Critical Care Inc. (NAS NMS)
NECO: NECO Enterprises Inc. (newspaper)
NEE: New England Express (steamship)
NEEC: NEECO Inc. (NAS NMS)
negb: negotiable
Neg Inst: Negotiable Instrument
NEGTAX: Negative (income) Tax

NEI: National Enterprises Inc. (NYSE)
NeimM: Nieman-Marcus Group Inc., The (newspaper)
NELL: Nellcor Inc. (NAS NMS)
NelsnH: Nelson Holdings International Ltd. (newspaper)
NEM: Newmont Mining Corp. (NYSE)
NEMS: National Exchange Market System
NeMtge: NorthEastern Mortgage Company Inc. (newspaper)
NENB: Nevada National Bancorporation (NAS NMS)
NEngEl: New England Electric System (newspaper)
NER: NERCO Inc. (NYSE)
Nergo: NERCO Inc. (newspaper)
NERX: NeoRx Corp. (NAS NMS)
NES: New England Electric System (NYSE)
NESB: NESB Corp. (NAS NMS)
NEST: Nestor Inc. (NAS NMS)
NestSv: Northeast Savings F.A. (newspaper)
NET: North European Oil Royalty Trust (NYSE)
NETX: Network Equipment Technologies Inc. (NAS NMS)
NEurO: North European Oil Royalty Trust (newspaper)
NevPw: Nevada Power Co. (newspaper)
NEW: Newcor Inc. (ASE)
Newcor: Newcor Inc. (newspaper)
NEWE: Newport Electronics Inc. (NAS NMS)
Newell: Newell Co. (newspaper)
Newhll: Newhall Land & Farming Co., The (newspaper)
NewLew: Newmark & Lewis Inc. (newspaper)
NewLine: New Line Cinema Corp. (newspaper)

NEWP: Newport Corp. (NAS NMS)

NewsCp: News Corporation Ltd., The (newspaper)

NEXCO: National Association of Export Management Companies

NF: No Funds
Non-Fundable

NFA: National Futures Association

NFBC: North Fork Bancorporation (NAS NMS)

NFC: National Freight Corporation
NCF Financial Corp. (ASE)
Not Favorably Considered

NFD: Norfolk, Franklin and Danville (railway)

NFG: National Fuel Gas Co. (NYSE)

NFK: Norfolk and Western (railway)

NflkSo: Norfolk Southern Corp. (newspaper)

NFS: Not For Sale

NFSF: NFS Financial Corp. (NAS NMS)

NFSL: Newman Federal S&L Assn. (Georgia) (NAS NMS)

NG: No (Not) Good (checks)

NGC: Newmont Gold Co. (NYSE)

NGE: New York State Electric & Gas Corp. (NYSE)

NGFCF: Nevada Goldfields Corp. (NAS NMS)

NGNA: Neutrogena Corp. (NAS NMS)

NGS: Niagara Share Corp. (NYSE)

NGX: Northgate Exploration Ltd. (NYSE)

NH: New High
New York, New Haven and Hartford (railroad)
Not Held

NHCI: National Healthcare Inc. (NAS NMS)

NHDI: NHD Stores Inc. (NAS NMS)

NHI: Nelson Holdings International Ltd. (ASE)

NHIC: Nichols-Homeshield Inc. (NAS NMS)

NHIR: New Hope and Ivyland Railroad

NHL: Newhall Land & Farming Co., The (NYSE)

NHLI: National Health Laboratories Inc. (NAS NMS)

NHMO: National HMO Corp. (NAS NMS)

NHR: National Heritage Inc. (NYSE)

NHSB: New Hampshire Savings Bank Corp. (NAS NMS)

NHY: Norsk Hydro A.S. (NYSE)

NI: National Income
Negotiable Instrument
Net Income
Net Interest
NIPSCO Industries Inc. (NYSE)

NiagSh: Niagara Share Corp. (newspaper)

NiaMP: Niagara Mohawk Power Corp. (newspaper)

NIBOR: New York Interbank Official Rate

NIC: Nicolet Instrument Corp. (NYSE)

NichApl: Nichols-Applegate Growth Equity Fund Inc. (newspaper)

NichIn: Nichols Institute (newspaper)

Nichols: S.E. Nichols Inc. (newspaper)

NICLF: Ni-Cal Developments Ltd. (NAS NMS)

Nicolet: Nicolet Instrument Corp. (newspaper)

NICOR: NICOR Inc. (newspaper)

NICs: Newly Industrializing Countries

NIEX: Niagara Exchange Corp. (NAS NMS)

NII: National Intergroup Inc. (NYSE)

National Intergroup Inc. (news-
paper)
NIKE: NIKE Inc. (NAS NMS)
NINOW: Non-Interest bearing NOW
account
NIP: Newhall Investment Proper-
ties (NYSE)
Normal Investment Practice
NIPNY: NEC Corp. (NAS NMS)
NIPSCO: NIPSCO Industries Inc.
(newspaper)
NIT: Negative Income Tax
New Investment Technology
NJ: Air South (airline)
Niagara Junction (railway)
NJI&I: New Jersey, Indiana and
Illinois (railroad)
NJ&NY: New Jersey & New York
(railroad)
NJR: New Jersey Resources Corp.
(NYSE)
NJRsc: New Jersey Resources
Corp. (newspaper)
NJSB: New Jersey Savings Bank
(NAS NMS)
NJST: New Jersey Steel Corp.
(NAS NMS)
NL: Net Loss
Night Letter
NL Industries Inc. (NYSE)
No-Load (funds)
NLBK: National Loan Bank (Texas)
(NAS NMS)
NLC: Nalco Chemical Co. (NYSE)
New Orleans and Lower
Coast (railroad)
NLCS: National Computer Systems
Inc. (NAS NMS)
NLF: No-Load Funds
NLG: National Gas & Oil Co.
(ASE)
North Louisiana and Gulf
(railroad)
NLI: Newmark & Lewis Inc. (ASE)
NL Ind: NL Industries Inc. (newspa-
per)

NLN: New Line Cinema Corp.
(ASE)
NLO: No-Limit Order
NLP: National Realty LP (ASE)
NLT: Not Later Than
Not Less Than
N&M: November and May (securi-
ties)
NM: Mt. Cook Airlines
Narrow Market
NorthEastern Mortgage Com-
pany Inc. (ASE)
NMBC: Merchants Bancorp Inc.,
The (Connecticut) (NAS
NMS)
NMC: Numac Oil & Gas Ltd. (ASE)
NMDY: Normandy Oil & Gas Co.
(NAS NMS)
NME: National Medical Enterprises
Inc. (NYSE)
NMedE: National Medical Enter-
prises Inc. (newspaper)
NMF: Non-Member Firm
NMG: Neiman-Marcus Group Inc.,
The (NYSE)
NMI: Nuveen Municipal Income
Fund (NYSE)
NMIC: National Micronetics Inc.
(NAS NMS)
NMineS: National Mine Service Co.
(newspaper)
NMK: Niagara Mohawk Power
Corp. (NYSE)
NMRC: American Health Services
Corp. (NAS NMS)
NMS: National Market System
National Mines Service Co.
(NYSE)
NMSB: NewMil Bancorp Inc. (NAS
NMS)
NMTX: Novametrix Medical Sys-
tems Inc. (NAS NMS)
NMxAr: New Mexico & Arizona
Land Co. (newspaper)
NN: Nevada Northern (railroad)
NNI: Net-Net Income

NNM: Nuveen N.Y. Municipal Income Fund (ASE)

NNP: Net National Product
New National Product

NNSL: Newport News Savings Bank (Virginia) (NAS NMS)

NNX: Northern Central Railway Company

NNY: Nuveen New York Municipal Value Fund Inc. (NYSE)

N/O: Name Of (registered in)

NOA: Nullification Of Agreement

No AC: No Account

No Adv: No Advice

NOAX: NEOAX Inc. (NAS NMS)

NOB: Northwest Corp. (NYSE)

NOBE: Nordstrom Inc. (NAS NMS)

NoblAf: Noble Affiliates Inc. (newspaper)

NOBLF: Nobel Insurance Ltd. (NAS NMS)

NOC: Northrop Cor. (NYSE)

NOE: Net Operating Earnings

Noellnd: Noel Industries Inc. (newspaper)

NoestUt: Northeast Utilities (newspaper)

NOHL: North Hills Electronics Inc. (NAS NMS)

NOK: Next Of Kin

NOL: Net Operating Loss
Noel Industries Inc. (ASE)
Norse Oriental Lines

NO&LC: New Orleans & Lower Coast (railroad)

NOLD: Noland Co. (NAS NMS)

non-can: noncancellable

non-cum: noncumulative

NONE: New Orleans and Northeastern (railroad)

non-par: nonparticipating

NORCACHA: North Carolina Automated Clearing House Association

NordRs: Nord Resources Corp. (newspaper)

NORKZ: Norsk-Data A. S. (NAS NMS)

Norsk: Norsk Hydro a.s. (newspaper)

Nortek: Nortek Inc. (newspaper)

NorTel: Northern Telecom Ltd. (newspaper)

NORTHWEST: Northwest Orient Airlines

Norton: Norton Co. (newspaper)

Nortrp: Northrop Corp. (newspaper)

Norwst: Northwest Corp. (newspaper)

NOS: Notice Of Sale
Not Otherwise Specified

NoStPw: Northern States Power Co. (newspaper)

NOT: New Orleans Terminal (railroad)

Nova: Nova Corp. (newspaper)

NOVL: Novell Inc. (NAS NMS)

Novo: Novo Industri A/S (newspaper)

NOVO: Novo Corp. (NAS NMS)

NOVR: Novar Electronics Corp. (NAS NMS)

NOVX: Nova Pharmaceutical Corp. (NAS NMS)

NOW: Negotiable Order of Withdrawal

NOWT: North-West Telecommunications Inc. (NAS NMS)

NOXL: Noxell Corp. (NAS NMS)

NOZ: New Process Co. (ASE)

NP: Narragansett Pier (railroad)
Net Position
Net Price
Net Proceeds
Net Profit
Normal Profit
Northern Pacific Railway Comany
Notary Public
Note(s) Payable

N&PB: Norfolk and Portsmouth Belt Line (railroad)

NPBC: National Penn Bancshares Inc. (NAS NMS)
NPC: Non-Profit Corporation
NPCL: North Pacific Coast Line (steamship)
NPCO: Napco International Inc. (NAS NMS)
NPD: National Patent Development Corp. (ASE)
NPI: Nuveen Premium Income Municipal Fund Inc. (NYSE)
NPK: National Presto Industries Inc. (NYSE)
NPlnRl: New Plan Realty Trust (newspaper)
NPR: New Plan Realty Trust (NYSE)
NProc: New Process Co. (newspaper)
NPS: Noncumulative Preferred Stock
No-Par Stock
NPT: NECO Enterprises Inc. ASE)
NPV: Net Present Value
No Par Value
NPVS: No-Par-Value Stock
NQA: Net Quick Assets
NQB: National Quotation Bureau
No Qualified Bidders
NR: Newhall Resources (NYSE)
Northward Aviation Limited
Not Rated
Not Responsible for
Note(s) Receivable
NRD: Nord Resources Corp. (NYSE)
NREC: NAC Re Corp. (NAS NMS)
NRES: Nichols Research Corp. (NAS NMS)
NRG: California Energy Co. (ASE)
NRM: NRM Energy Company LP (ASE) (newspaper)
NRO: Non-Resident-Owned (funds)
NRPC: National Railroad Passenger Corporation (Amtrak)
NRRD: Norstan Inc. (NAS NMS)
NRT: Norton Co. (NYSE)

NRTN: Norton Enterprises Inc. (NAS NMS)
NS: Net Sales
Net Surplus
New Series
Noncumulative Stock
Norfolk Southern (railroad)
Northeast Airlines
Not Specified
Not Sufficient
NSB: Northeast Savings FA (NYSE)
NSBA: National Savings Bank of Albany (NAS NMS)
NSBK: North Side Savings Bank (New York) (NAS NMS)
NSC: Norfolk Southern Corp. (NYSE)
Normal Standard Cost
NSCB: NBSC Corp. (NAS NMS)
NSCC: National Securities Clearing Corporation
NSCO: Network Systems Corp. (NAS NMS)
NSD: National-Standard Co. (NYSE)
N&SE: Nacogdoches & Southeastern (railroad)
NSE: National Stock Exchange
NSF: (Non) Not Sufficient Funds
NS Gp: NS Group Inc. (newspaper)
NSH: Nashua Corp. (NYSE)
NSI: National Service Industries Inc. (NYSE)
National Stock Exchange
NSIC: National Security Insurance Co. (NAS NMS)
N&SL: Norwood & St. Lawrence (railroad)
NSM: National Semiconductor Corp. (NYSE)
NSP: Northern States Power Co. (NYSE)
NSPF: Not Specifically Provided For
NSR: Norfolk Southern Railway

NSRU: North Star Universal Inc. (NAS NMS)

NSS: Newburgh and South Shore (railway)
NS Group Inc. (ASE)

NSSB: Norwich Financial Corp. (NAS NMS)

NSSI: Nuclear Support Services Inc. (NAS NMS)

NSSX: National Sanitary Supply Co. (NAS NMS)

NSTA: National Securities Trade Association

NStand: National-Standard Co. (newspaper)

NSTC: Not Subject To Call

NSTS: National Securities Trading System

NSW: Northwestern Steel & Wire Co. (NYSE)

NT: Northern Telecom Ltd. (NYSE)
Nuisance Tax

N/T: Net Tonnage

NTAust: National Australia Bank Ltd. (newspaper)

NTE: Not To Exceed

NtEnt: National Enterprises Inc. (newspaper)

NtGsO: National Gas & Oil Co. (newspaper)

NtHert: National Heritage Inc. (newspaper)

Nthgat: Northgate Exploration Ltd. (newspaper)

NTK: Nortek Inc. (NYSE)

NTLB: National Lumber & Supply Inc. (NAS NMS)

NtlCnv: National Convenience Stores Inc. (newspaper)

NtPatnt: National Patent Development Corp. (newspaper)

NtPrest: National Presto Industries Inc. (newspaper)

NTRS: Northern Trust Corp. (NAS NMS)

NtRty: National Realty LP (newspaper)

NT&SA: National Trust & Savings Association

NTSC: National Technical Systems (NAS NMS)

NtSemi: National Semiconductor Corp. (newspaper)

NtSvIn: National Service Industries Inc. (newspaper)

NTU: Normal Trading Unit

NtWst: National Westminster Bank PLC (newspaper)

NU: Northeast Utilities (NYSE)
Southwest Airlines

NuclDt: Nuclear Data Inc. (newspaper)

NUCM: Nuclear Metals Inc. (NAS NMS)

NUCO: Nucorp Energy Inc. (NAS NMS)

Nucor: Nucor Corp. (newspaper)

NUCP: New Visions Entertainment Corp. (NAS NMS)

NUE: Nucor Corp. (NYSE)

NUH: Nu Horizons Electronics Corp. (ASE)

NuHrz: Nu Horizons Electronics Corp. (newspaper)

NUI: NUI Corp. (NYSE) (newspaper)

NUL: No Upper Limit

Numac: Numac Oil & Gas Ltd. (newspaper)

NUME: Numerica Financial Corp. (NAS NMS)

NUMR: Numerex Corp. (NAS NMS)

NUMS: Nu-Med Inc. (NAS NMS)

NUR: Natchez, Urania and Ruston (railway)

NUT: Mauna Loa Macadamia Partners LP (NYSE)

NUTM: Nutmeg Industries Inc. (NAS NMS)

NUV: Nuveen Municipal Value Fund Inc. (NYSE)

NuvCal: Nuveen California Municipal Value Fund Inc. (newspaper)

NUVI: NuVision Inc. (NAS NMS)

NuvMu: Nuveen Municipal Value Fund Inc. (newspaper)

NuvNY: Nuveen New York Municipal Value Fund Inc. (newspaper)

NuvPI: Nuveen Premium Income Municipal Fund Inc. (newspaper)

NV: Naamloze vennootscap (Company with limited liability) (Dutch) Non-Voting

NVA: Nova Corp. (NYSE)

NVBC: Napa Valley Bancorp (NAS NMS)

NvCMI: Nuveen California Municipal Income Fund (newspaper)

NVCO: Nodaway Valley Co. (NAS NMS)

NVIS: National Video Inc. (NAS NMS)

NVLS: Novellus Systems Inc. (NAS NMS)

NvMuI: Nuveen Municipal Income Fund (newspaper)

NvNYM: Nuveen N.Y. Municipal Income Fund (newspaper)

NVO: Novo Industri A/S (NYSE)

NVP: Nevada Power Co. (NYSE)

NVR: NVRyan LP (ASE)

NVRyn: NV Ryan LP (newspaper)

NVS: Non-Voting Stock

N&W: Norfolk & Western (railway)

NW: National Westminister Bank PLC (NYSE)
Net Worth
Norfolk and Western (railroad)
Northwest Orient Airlines

NWA: Northwest Airlines

NWACHA: Northwest Automated Clearing House Association

NwAM: New American High Income Fund (newspaper)

NwASh: New American Shoe Corp. (newspaper)

NwBedf: New Bedford Institution for Savings (newspaper)

NWC: Net Working Capital

NWE: New World Entertainment Ltd. (ASE)

NWEN: Northwest Engineering Co. (NAS NMS)

NWGI: N-W Group Inc. (NAS NMS)

Nwhall: Newhall Investment Properties (newspaper)

NwhlRs: Newhall Resources (newspaper)

NWIB: Northwest Illinois Bancorp Inc. (NAS NMS)

NWL: Newell Co. (NYSE)

NWldE: New World Entertainment Ltd. (newspaper)

NWLI: National Western Life Insurance Co. (NAS NMS)

NwmtGd: Newmont Gold Co. (newspaper)

NWNG: Northwest Natural Gas Co. (NAS NMS)

NWNL: Northwestern National Life Insurance Co. (NAS NSM)

NWOR: Neworld Bancorp Inc. (Massachusetts) (NAS NMS)

NWP: Northwestern Pacific (railroad)

NWPH: Newport Pharmaceuticals International Inc. (NAS NMS)

NWPS: Northwestern Public Service Co. (NAS NMS)

NWRK: Network Electronics Corp. (NAS NMS)

NWS: News Corporation Ltd., The (NYSE)

NwStW: Northwestern Steel & Wire Co. (newspaper)

NWTL: Northwest Teleproductions Inc. (NAS NMS)

NwtM: Newmont Mining Corp. (newspaper)

NX: Quanex Corp. (NYSE)

NY: Net Yield
New York Airways

NYB: New American High Income Fund (NYSE)

NYBC: New York Bancorp Inc. (NAS NMS)

Nybor: New York Inter-Bank Offered Rate

NYC: New York Central (railroad)

NYCE: New York Curb Exchange

NYCHA: New York Clearing House Association

NYCO: NYCOR Inc. (NAS NMS)

NYCSCE: New York Coffee, Sugar and Cocoa Exchange

NYC&SL: New York, Chicago and St. Louis (railroad)

NYCTNCA: New York Cotton Exchange, Citrus Associates

NYD: New York Dock (railway)

NYFE: New York Futures Exchange

NY&LB: New York and Long Branch (railroad)

NYME: New York Mercantile Exchange

NYMEX: New York Mercantile Exchange

NYMG: New York Marine & General Insurance Co. (NAS NMS)

NYN: NYNEX Corp. (NYSE)

Nynex: NYNEX Corp. (newspaper)

NYNH&H: New York, New Haven & Hartford (railroad)

NYO&W: New York, Ontario and Western (railroad)

NYSE: New York Stock Exchange

NYSEG: New York State Electric & Gas Corp. (newspaper)

NYS&W: New York, Susquehanna & Western (railroad)

NYT: New York Times Co., The (ASE)

NyTEI: New York Tax-Exempt Income Fund Inc., The (newspaper)

NY Time: New York Times Co., The (newspaper)

NZ: New Mexico & Arizona Land Co. (ASE)

NZSG: Non-Zero-Sum Game

o: old (in options listings of newspapers)
   output
O: Odetics Inc. (ASE)
O&A: October and April (securities)
OA: On Account
   On or About
   Open Account
OAC: On Approved Credit
OACHA: Oregon Automated Clearing House Association
OAK: Oak Industries Inc. (NYSE)
OakInd: Oak Industries Inc. (newspaper)
OakiteP: Oakite Products Inc. (newspaper)
Oakwd: Oakwood Homes Corp. (newspaper)
OAPEC: Organization of Arab Petroleum Exporting Countries
OAR: Ohio Art Co., The (ASE)
   Ordering As Required
OAT: Quaker Oats Co., The (NYSE)
OB: Obligation Bond
   Opening of Books
   Operating Budget
   Or Better
   Ordered Back
OB/L: Ocean Bill of Lading
oblg: obligate
   obligation
OBrien: O'Brien Energy Systems Inc. (newspaper)
OBS: O'Brien Energy Systems Inc. (ASE)
OBU: Offshore Banking Unit
o/c: overcharge
OC: Operating Company
   Operating Cost

Opportunity Cost
Orion Capital Corp. (NYSE)
Over-the-Counter
OCAA: Oklahoma City-Ada-Atoka (railroad)
OCAS: Ohio Casualty Corp. (NAS NMS)
OCB: Over-the-Counter Batch
OCC: Options Clearing Corporation
OcciPet: Occidental Petroleum Corp. (newspaper)
OC&E: Oregon, California & Eastern (railroad)
OCER: Oceaneering International Inc. (NAS NMS)
OCF: Owens-Corning Fiberglass Corp. (NYSE)
OCGT: OCG Technology Inc. (NAS NMS)
OCIL: Ocilla Industries Inc. (NAS NMS)
OCLI: Optical Coating Laboratory Inc. (NAS NMS)
OCOM: Outlet Communications Inc. (NAS NMS)
OCQ: Oneida Ltd. (NYSE)
OCR: Omnicare Inc. (NYSE)
OCU: Over-the-Counter Control Unit
od: overdraft
   overdraw
   overdue
OD: On Demand
   Outstanding Debt
ODECO: Ocean Drilling & Exploration Co. (newspaper)
Odet: Odetics Inc. (newspaper)
ODR: Ocean Drilling & Exploration Co. (NYSE)

ODSI: Old Dominion Systems Inc.
(NAS NMS)
OE: North-Air (airline)
Operating Expenses
Oregon Electric (railway)
OEA: OEA Inc. (ASE) (newspaper)
OEC: Ohio Edison Co. (NYSE)
Open-End Company
Open-End Credit
OEH: Orient Express Hotels Inc.
(NYSE)
OEIC: Open-End Investment Com-
pany
OEIT: Open-End Investment Trust
OEN: Oxford Energy Co., The
(ASE)
OEO: Office of Economic Opportu-
nity
of: overflow
OF: Offshore Funds
ofc: office
ofd: offered (stocks)
OFD: Offered (NYSE)
OFDI: Office of Foreign Direct In-
vestment
OFFI: Old Fashion Foods Inc. (NAS
NMS)
ofl: overflow
OFSB: Orient Federal Savings
Bank (Puerto Rico) (NAS
NMS)
OG: Chalk's Flying Service (airline)
Gross and Sons Ltd. (steam-
ship)
Ogden Corp. (NYSE)
Ogden: Ogden Corp. (newspaper)
OGE: Oklahoma Gas & Electric Co.
(NYSE)
OGIL: Ogilvy Group Inc., The (NAS
NMS)
OGLE: Oglebay Norton Co. (NAS
NMS)
oh: overhead
OH: Oakwood Homes Corp. (NYSE)
San Francisco and Oakland -
Helicopter (airline)

OhArt: Ohio Art Co., The (newspa-
per)
OHBC: Ohio Bancorp (NAS NMS)
OHC: Oriole Homes Corp. (ASE)
OhioEd: Ohio Edison Co. (newspa-
per)
OHSC: Oak Hill Sportswear Corp.
(NAS NMS)
OI: Operating Income
Ordinary Interest
OID: Original Issue Discount (bond)
OIL: Triton Energy Corp. (NYSE)
OILC: Oil-Dri Corporation of Amer-
ica (NAS NMS)
OIT: Office of International Trade
OJ: Orange-co Inc. (NYSE)
Stol Commuters (airline)
OJAJ: October, January, April,
July (securities)
ok: correct
OKE: ONEOK Inc. (NYSE)
OKEN: Old Kent Financial Corp.
(NAS NMS)
OklaGE: Oklahoma Gas & Electric
Co. (newspaper)
OKP: O'okiep Copper Company Ltd.
(ASE)
OKT: Oakite Products Inc. (NYSE)
Oakland Terminal (railway)
OL: Odd Lot
Operating Losses
OLB: Odd-Lot Broker
OL&BR: Omaha, Lincoln and
Beatrice Railway
OLDR: Old Republic International
Corp. (NAS NMS)
OLGR: Oilgear Co. (NAS NMS)
Olin: Olin Corp. (newspaper)
OLN: Olin Corp. (NYSE)
OLOGP: Offshore Logistics Inc.
(NAS NMS)
OLP: One Liberty Properties Inc.
(ASE)
OLS: Olsten Corp., The (ASE)
OLSN: Olson Industries Inc. (NAS
NMS)

Olsten: Olsten Corp., The (newspaper)

OM: Office Manager
On Margin
On Market
Open Market
Outboard Marine Corp. (NYSE)

OMB: Office of Management and Budget

OMCM: Omnicom Group Inc. (NAS NMS)

OMD: Ormand Industries Inc. (ASE)

OMET: Orthomet Inc. (NAS NMS)

OMI: Owens & Minor Inc. (NYSE)

OMIC: OMI Corp. (NAS NMS)

Omncre: Omnicare Inc. (newspaper)

OMS: Oppenheimer Multi-Sector Income Trust (NYSE)

O&N: Oregon & Northwestern (railroad)

ON: North American Airlines

ONA: Oneita Industries Inc. (ASE)
Overseas National Airlines

ONCS: Oncogene Science Inc. (NAS NMS)

ONE: Banc One Corp. (NYSE)

Oneida: Oneida Ltd. (newspaper)

Oneita: Oneita Industries Inc. (newspaper)

OneLibt: One Liberty Properties Inc. (newspaper)

ONEOK: ONEOK Inc. (newspaper)

OnLne: On-Line Software International Inc. (newspaper)

ONPR: One Price Clothing Stores Inc. (NAS NMS)

ONRY: Ogdensburg and Norwood Railway

O&NW: Oregon and Northwestern (railroad)

O&O: Owned and Operated
Owner and Operator

OO: Open Order

OOkiep: O'okiep Copper Company Ltd. (newspaper)

OOP: Out-Of-Pocket

OP: Offering Price
Open Position
Opening Price
Opening Purchase
Operating Profit

OPC: Orion Pictures Corp. (NYSE)

opd: opened (stocks)

OPD: Delayed Opening (stocks)
Opened (NYSE)

OP&E: Oregon, Pacific & Eastern (railroad)

OPEC: Organization of Petroleum Exporting Countries

oper: operational

OPIC: Overseas Private Investment Corporation

OPM: Options Pricing Model
Other People's Money

OpnMI: Oppenheimer Multi-Sector Income Trust (newspaper)

OPP: Oppenheimer Industries Inc. (ASE)

Oppenh: Oppenheimer Industries Inc. (newspaper)

OPRA: Options Price Reporting Authority

ops: operations

opt: option

OPTO: Opto Mechanik Inc. (NAS NMS)

OPTX: Optek Technology Inc. (NAS NMS)

OR: Operating Reserves
Operational Requirement
Over Run
Owner's Risk

OrangRk: Orange & Rockland Utilities Inc. (newspaper)

ORBT: Orbit Instrument Corp. (NAS NMS)

ORCL: Oracle Systems Corp. (NAS NMS)

ORCO: Optical Radiation Corp.
(NAS NMS)

ord: order

OregSt: Oregon Steel Mills Inc.
(newspaper)

OREM: Oregon Metallurgical Corp.
(NAS NMS)

ORFA: ORFA Corporation of America (NAS NMS)

org: organization

ORG: Organogensis Inc. (ASE)

ORG CHART: Organizational Chart

orgl: organizational

orgn: organization

Orgngn: Organogensis Inc. (newspaper)

Orient: Orient Express Hotels Inc.
(newspaper)

OriolH: Oriole Homes Corp. (newspaper)

OrionC: Orion Capital Corp. (newspaper)

OrionP: Orion Pictures Corp. (newspaper)

ORIR: Orion Research Inc.
(NAS NMS)

Ormand: Ormand Industries Inc.
(newspaper)

OrngCo: Orange-co Inc. (newspaper)

ORU: Orange & Rockland Utilities Inc. (NYSE)

O&S: Over and Short (account)

OS: Office System
Old Series
Opening Sale
Optimum Size
Option Spreading
Oregon Steel Mills Inc. (ASE)
Out of Stock

OSA: Office of Savings Associations

OSB: One-Statement Banking

OS&D: Over, Short, and Damaged

OSG: Overseas Shipholding Group Inc. (NYSE)

OSHM: Oshman's Sporting Goods Inc. (NAS NMS)

OSI: On-Line Software International Inc. (NYSE)

OSIC: Osicom Technologies Inc.
(NAS NMS)

OSIX: Optical Specialties Inc.
(NAS NMS)

OSL: Oregon Short Line (railroad)
O'Sullivan Corp. (ASE)

OSMO: Osmonics Inc. (NAS NMS)

OSTN: Old Stone Corp. (NAS NMS)

OSulvn: O'Sullivan Corp. (newspaper)

OSWI: Old Spaghetti Warehouse Inc. (NAS NMS)

OT: Office of Telecommunications (U.S.)
Oregon Trunk (railroad)

OTB: Off-The-Board
Open To Buy

OTC: Over-The-Counter

OTRK: Oshkosh Truck Corp.
(NAS NMS)

OTS: Office of Thrift Supervision

OTTR: Otter Tail Power Co.
(NAS NMS)

OUCH: Occupational-Urgent Care Health Systems Inc.
(NAS NMS)

OUR&D: Ogden Union Railway and Depot

OutbdM: Outboard Marine Corp.
(newspaper)

outstg: outstanding

ovhd: overhead

ovpd: overpaid

OvShip: Overseas Shipholding Group Inc. (newspaper)

OVWV: One Valley Bancorp of West Virginia Inc.
(NAS NMS)

O&W: Oneida & Western (railroad)

OW: Offer Wanted

OWC: Owner Will Carry

OwenC: Owens-Corning Fiberglass Corp. (newspaper)

OwenM: Owens & Minor Inc.
(newspaper)

OX: American Courier (airline)
OxfEgy: Oxford Energy Co., The
     (newspaper)
Oxford: Oxford Industries Inc.
     (newspaper)
OXID: Oxidyne Group Inc., The
     (NAS NMS)

OXM: Oxfore Industries Inc.
     (NYSE)
OXY: Occidental Petroleum Corp.
     (NYSE)
OY: Air North (airline)
OZ: Ozark Airlines
OZA: Ozark Airlines

p: parity
partnership
payee
peso (currency of Spanish-speaking nations)
purchaser
P: Paid this year (in stock listings of newspapers)
Phillips Petroleum Co. (NYSE)
Put (in options listings of newspapers)
P-A: Pan-Atlantic Steamship Corporation
P&A: Pennsylvania & Atlantic (railroad)
Price and Availability
PA: Pan American World Airways
Per Annum
Power of Attorney
Primerica Corp. (NYSE)
Private Account
Private Trust
PAA: Pan American World Airways
Pennsylvania and Atlantic (railroad)
PAC: Pacific Telesis Group (NYSE)
PacAS: Pacific American Income Shares Inc. (newspaper)
PACC: Pacific Coast (railroad)
Provident Life & Accident Insurance Co. (NAS NMS)
PacEnt: Pacific Enterprises Ltd. (newspaper)
PacGE: Pacific Gas & Electric Co. (newspaper)
Pacifcp: PacifiCorp (newspaper)
PACN: Pacific Nuclear Systems Inc. (NAS NMS)
PacSci: Pacific Scientific Co. (newspaper)

PacTel: Pacific Telesis Group (newspaper)
PAE: Pioneer Systems Inc. (ASE)
PAHC: Pioneer American Holding Co. (NAS NMS)
PAI: Pacific American Income Shares Inc. (NYSE)
PainWb: PaineWebber Group Inc. (newspaper)
PAL: Preapproved Loan
PallCp: Pall Corp. (newspaper)
PALM: PALFED Inc. (NAS NMS)
PA&M: Pittsburgh, Allegheny and McKees Rocks (railroad)
PAMC: Provident American Corp. (NAS NMS)
PAMX: Pancho's Mexican Buffet Inc. (NAS NMS)
PANAGRA: Pan-American Grace Airways
PanAm: Pan Am Corp. (newspaper)
PAN AM: Pan American World Airways
PanEC: Panhandle Eastern Corp. (newspaper)
Panill: Pannill Knitting Company Inc. (newspaper)
Pansph: Pansophic Systems Inc. (newspaper)
PANT: Pantera's Corp. (NAS NMS)
Pantast: Pantasote Inc. (newspaper)
PAP: Prearranged Payments
PaPL: Pennsylvania Power & Light Co. (newspaper)
P&AR: Pacific and Arctic Railway
PAR: Precision Aerotech Inc. (ASE)
Price-Adjusted Rate preferred (stock)
PARC: Park Communications Inc. (NAS NMS)

ParCom: Paramount Communications Inc. (newspaper)

ParkDrl: Parker Drilling Co. (newspaper)

ParkEl: Park Electrochemical Corp. (newspaper)

ParkHn: Parker Hannifin Corp. (newspaper)

ParPh: Par Pharmaceutical Inc. (newspaper)

part: participating
participation

ParTch: PAR Technology Corp. (newspaper)

PASB: Perpetual Savings Bank FSB (Virginia) (NAS NMS)

PASI: Pacific Silver Corp. (NAS NMS)

pat: patent

PAT: Patten Corp. (NYSE)
Prearranged Transfers

patd: patented

PATH: Port Authority Trans-Hudson Corporation (railway)

PATK: Patrick Industries Inc. (NAS NMS)

PatPtr: Patrick Petroleum Co. (newspaper)

PatTch: Patient Technology Inc. (newspaper)

Patten: Patten Corp. (newspaper)

paty: payment

PaulPt: Pauley Petroleum Inc. (newspaper)

PAW: Port Angeles Western (railroad)

PAX: Private Automatic Exchange

Paxar: PAXAR Corp. (newspaper)

PAXT: Frank Paxton Co. (NAS NMS)

PAYC: Payco American Corp. (NAS NMS)

PayCsh: Payless Cashways Inc. (newspaper)

PAYE: Pay As You Earn

PayFon: Pay-Fone Systems Inc. (newspaper)

PAYN: Pay'n Save Inc. (NAS NMS)

PAYSOP: Payroll-based Stock Ownership Plan

payt: payment

PAYX: Paychex Inc. (NAS NMS)

PB: Par Bond
Paris Bourse
Pass Book
Permit Bond
Preference Bond

PBCT: People's Bank (Connecticut) (NAS NMS)

PBEN: Puritan-Bennett Corp. (NAS NMS)

PBFI: Paris Business Forms Inc. (NAS NMS)

PBGC: Pension Benefit Guaranty Corporation

PBGI: Piedmont Bankgroup Inc. (NAS NMS)

PBI: Pitney Bowes Inc. (NYSE)

PBKB: People's Savings Bank of Brockton (Massachusetts) (NAS NMS)

PBKC: Premier Bancshares Corp. (NAS NMS)

PBKS: Provident Bankshares Corp. (NAS NMS)

PBNB: Peoples Savings Bank of New Britain, The (Connecticut) (NAS NMS)

PBNC: Peoples Bancorporation (North Carolina) (NAS NMS)

PBNE: Philadelphia, Bethlehem and New England (railroad)

PBR: Patapsco and Back Rivers (railroad)

PBS: Pilgrim Regional Bank Shares Inc. (NYSE)

PBT: Permian Basin Royalty Trust (NYSE)

PBWSE: Philadelphia-Baltimore-Washington Stock Exchange

PBY: Pep Boys-Manny, Moe & Jack, The (NYSE)

pc: paycheck
percent

P&C: Puts and Calls

PC: Penn Central Corp., The (NYSE) (railroad)
Petty Cash
Prime Cost
Profit Center

PCAI: PCA International Inc. (NAS NMS)

PCAR: PACCAR Inc. (NAS NMS)

PCB: Petty Cash Book

PCC: Production Credit Corporation

PCE Personal Consumption Expenditures

PCE: Professional Care Inc. (ASE)

PCEP: Perception Technology Corp. (NAS NMS)

PCF: Putnam High Income Convertible & Bond Fund (NYSE)

PCG: Pacific Gas & Electric Co. (NYSE)

PCH: Potlatch Corp. (NYSE)

PCI: Paramount Communications Inc. (NYSE)
Per Capita Income

PCL: PCL Diversifund (newspaper)

PCLB: Price Co., The (NAS NMS)

PCN: Point Comfort and Northern (railroad)

PCO: Pittston Co., The (NYSE)
Put and Call Option

PCOR: PSICOR Inc. (NAS NMS)

PCR: Perini Corp. (ASE)

PCS: Preferred Capital Stock

PCSE: Pacific Coast Stock Exchange

PCSI: PCS Inc. (NAS NMS)

PCST: Precision Castparts Corp. (NAS NMS)

pct: percent

PCT: Property Capital Trust (ASE)

PCY: Pittsburgh, Chartiers and Youghiogheny (railway)

pd: paid

PD: Past Due
Payroll Deduction
Per Diem (by the day)
Phelps Dodge Corp. (NYSE)

PDA: Personal Deposit Account
Princeton Diagnostic Laboratories of America (ASE)

PDAS: PDA Engineering (NAS NMS)

PDC: Public Dividend Capital

PDG: Placer Dome Inc. (NYSE)

PDL: Presidential Realty Corp. (ASE)

PDLPY: Pacific Dunlop Ltd. (NAS NMS)

PDM: Pitt-DesMoines Inc. (ASE)

pdn: production

PDP: Payroll Deduction Plan

PD&PL: Property Damage and Public Liability (insurance)

PDQ: Prime Motor Inns Inc. (NYSE)

PDS: Perry Drug Stores Inc. (NYSE)

PDT: Pacific Daylight Time

P&E: Peoria and Eastern (railway)

P/E: Price-Earnings ratio

PE: Pacific Electric (railway)
Philadelphia Electric Co. (NYSE)
Prepaid Expense
Price-Earnings ratio (stock listings of newspapers)

PEBW: Peoples Bancorp of Worcester Inc. (Massachusetts) (NAS NMS)

PEC Isr: PEC Israel Economic Corp. (newspaper)

PECN: Publishers Equipment Corp. (NAS NMS)

PeerTu: Peerless Tube Co. (newspaper)

PEFCO: Private Export Funding
    Corporation
PEG: Public Service Enterprise
    Group Inc. (NYSE)
PegGld: Pegasus Gold Ltd. (news-
    paper)
PEI: Pennsylvania Real Estate In-
    vestment Trust (ASE)
PEL: Panhandle Eastern Corp.
    (NYSE)
PEN: Pentron Industries Inc. (ASE)
PenCn: Penn Central Corp., The
    (newspaper)
PenEM: Penn Engineering & Man-
    ufacturing Corp. (news-
    paper)
Penney: J.C. Penney Company Inc.
    (newspaper)
Pennsol: Pennzoil Co. (newspaper)
Penob: Penobscot Shoe Co. (news-
    paper)
PenRE: Pennsylvania Real Estate
    Investment Trust (news-
    paper)
Penril: Penril Corp. (newspaper)
PENT: Pennsylvania Enterprises
    Inc. (NAS NMS)
PenTr: Penn Traffic Co. (newspa-
    per)
Pentron: Pentron Industries Inc.
    (newspaper)
PENW: PENWEST LTD.
    (NAS NMS)
PEO: Petroleum & Resources Corp.
    (NYSE)
PeopEn: Peoples Energy Corp.
    (newspaper)
PEP: PepsiCo Inc. (NYSE)
PepBy: Pep Boys-Manny, Moe &
    Jack, The (newspaper)
PepsiCo: PepsiCo Inc. (newspaper)
PER: Per Exchange Rate
    Pope, Evans & Robbins Inc.
    (ASE)
    Pre-Emptive Right
    Price-Earnings Ratio

perc: perquisite
PERC: Perceptronics Inc. (NAS
    NMS)
Per Cap: Per Capita (by the indi-
    vidual)
perf: performance
Perigo: Perrigo Co. (newspaper)
Perinil: Perini Investment Proper-
    ties Inc. (newspaper)
PerkEl: Perkin-Elmer Corp., The
    (newspaper)
PerkF: Perkins Family Restaurants
    L.P. (newspaper)
perks: perquisites
PeryDr: Perry Drug Stores Inc.
    (newspaper)
PET: Pacific Enterprises Ltd.
    (NYSE)
    Paperless Entry Transfer Sys-
    tem (Oregon)
PETD: Petroleum Development
    Corp. (NAS NMS)
Peters: J.M. Peters Company Inc.
    (newspaper)
Petrie: Petrie Stores Corp. (newspa-
    per)
PetRs: Petroleum & Resources
    Corp. (newspaper)
pf: preferred
P&F: Pioneer and Fayette (railroad)
PF: Pension Fund
PFBS: Ponce Federal Bank PSB
    (Puerto Rico)
PFC: Personal Finance Company
    Privately Financed Consump-
    tion
pfd: preferred (stock)
PfdHlt: Preferred Health Care Ltd.
    (newspaper)
PFDR: Preferred Risk Life Insur-
    ance Co. (NAS NMS)
PFE: Pfizer Inc. (NYSE)
PFFS: Pacific First Financial Corp.
    (NAS NMS)
PFIN: P&F Industries Inc.
    (NAS NMS)

Pfizer: Pfizer Inc. (newspaper)
PFLY: Polifly Financial Corp.
(NAS NMS)
PFNC: Progress Financial Corp.
(NAS NMS)
PFP: Prime Financial Partners LP
(ASE)
PFR: Perkins Family Restaurants
LP (NYSE)
PFSB: Piedmont Federal Savings
Bank (Virginia)
(NAS NMS)
PFSI: Pioneer Financial Services
Inc. (Illinois) (NAS NMS)
PFSL: Prudential Financial Ser-
vices Corp. (NAS NMS)
PFT: Pittsburgh, Fort Wayne and
Chicago Railway Company
PFTS: Profit Systems Inc.
(NAS NMS)
P-G: Prudential Grace Lines
(steamship)
P&G: Procter and Gamble Com-
pany
PG: Paper Gain
Procter & Gamble Co., The
(NYSE)
PGA: Punta Gorda Isles Inc. (ASE)
PGE: Pacific Great Eastern (rail-
way)
PGEN: Plant Genetics Inc.
(NAS NMS)
PGI: Ply*Gem Industries Inc. (ASE)
PGL: Peoples Energy Corp. (NYSE)
pgm: program
PGN: Portland General Corp.
(NYSE)
PGR: Progressive Corp., The (Ohio)
(NYSE)
PGU: Pegasus Gold Ltd. (ASE)
PGY: Global Yield Fund Inc., The
(NYSE)
P&H: Postage and Handling
PH: Parker Hannifin Corp. (NYSE)
PHA: Public Housing Administra-
tion (Authority)

PHABY: Pharmacia AB
(NAS NMS)
PHAR: PharmaControl Corp.
(NAS NMS)
PHC: Pratt Hotel Corp. (ASE)
PH&D: Port Huron and Detroit
(railroad)
PhelpD: Phelps Dodge Corp. (news-
paper)
PHG: Philips NV (NYSE)
PHH: PHH Group Inc. (NYSE)
(newspaper)
PHI: Philadelphia Long Distance
Telephone Co. (ASE)
PhilaEl: Philadelphia Electric Co.
(newspaper)
PhilGl: Philips N.V. (newspaper)
PhilMr: Philip Morris Companies
Inc. (newspaper)
PhilPet: Phillips Petroleum Co.
(newspaper)
PhilpIn: Philips Industries Inc.
(newspaper)
PhilSub: Philadelphia Suburban
Corp. (newspaper)
PHL: Philips Industries Inc. (NYSE)
Phlcrp: PHLCORP Inc. (newspaper)
PhILD: Philadelphia Long Distance
Telephone Co. (newspa-
per)
PhIVH: Phillips-Van Heusen Corp.
(newspaper)
PHM: PHM Corp. (NYSE) (newspa-
per)
PHMT: Phone-Mate Inc.
(NAS NMS)
PHNX: Phoenix Medical Technology
Inc. (NAS NMS)
PhnxR: Pheonix Realty Investors
Inc. (newspaper)
PHOC: Photo Control Corp.
(NAS NMS)
PHP: Petroleum Heat & Power
Company Inc. (ASE)
PHPH: PHP Healthcare Corp.
(NAS NMS)

PHR: Phoenix Realty Investors Inc. (ASE)

PHRS: Paul Harris Stores Inc. (NAS NMS)

PHSY: PacifiCare Health Systems Inc. (NAS NMS)

PHX: PHLCORP Inc. (NYSE)

PHXA: Phoenix American Inc. (NAS NMS)

PHYB: Pioneer Hi-Bred International Inc. (NAS NMS)

PHYP: Physicians Pharmaceutical Services Inc. (NAS NMS)

P&I: Paducah and Illinois (railroad) Principal and Interest

PI: Performance Index
Perpetual Inventory
Personal Income
Prime Interest (rate)
Productivity Index
Public Interest

PIC: Paid-In Capital
Pickens (railroad)

PICC: Piccadilly Cafeterias Inc. (NAS NMS)

PICI: Polymer International Corp. (NAS NMS)

PICN: Pic 'N' Save Corp. (NAS NMS)

PICO: Physicians Insurance Company of Ohio (NAS NMS)

PicoPd: Pico Products Inc. (newspaper)

PIDS: Public Investment Data System

PiedNG: Piedmont Natural Gas Company Inc. (newspaper)

Pier 1: Pier 1 Imports Inc. (newspaper)

PIF: Prudential Intermediate Income Fund Inc. (NYSE)

PII: Pueblo International Inc. (NYSE)

PIIBK: Peoples Heritage Financial Group Inc. (Maine) (NAS NMS)

PIK: Payment-In-Kind

PIL: Petroleum Investments Ltd. (NYSE)

PilgPr: Pilgrim's Pride Corp. (newspaper)

PilgRg: Pilgrim Regional Bank Shares Inc. (newspaper)

PIM: Putnam Master Intermediate Income Trust (NYSE)

PIN: PSI Holdings Inc. (NYSE)

PinWst: Pinnacle West Capital Corp. (newspaper)

PIO: Pioneer Electronic Corp. (NYSE)

PIOG: Pioneer Group Inc., The (NAS NMS)

PION: Pioneer Financial Corp. (Virginia) (NAS NMS)

PionrEl: Pioneer Electronic Corp. (newspaper)

PionrSy: Pioneer Systems Inc. (newspaper)

PIOS: Pioneer-Standard Electronics Inc. (NAS NMS)

PIP: Postal Instant Press (ASE)

PIPR: Piper Jaffray Inc. (NAS NMS)

PIR: Pier 1 Imports Inc. (NYSE)

PISC: Pacific International Services Corp. (NAS NMS)

PitDsm: Pitt-DesMoines Inc. (newspaper)

PITI: Principal, Interest, Taxes, Insurance

PitnyB: Pitney Bowes Inc. (newspaper)

Pittstn: Pittston Co., The (newspaper)

Pittway: Pittway Corp. (newspaper)

PitWVa: Pittsburgh & West Virginia Railroad (newspaper)

PIX: School Pictures Inc. (ASE)

PIZA: National Pizza Co. (NAS NMS)

PKC: Pannill Knitting Company Inc. (NYSE)

PKD: Parker Drilling Co. (NYSE)
PKE: Park Electrochemical Corp. (NYSE)
PKLB: PharmaKinetics Laboratories Inc. (NAS NMS)
PKN: Perkin-Elmer Co., The (NYSE)
PKOH: Park-Ohio Industries Inc. (NAS NMS)
PKPS: Poughkeepsie Savings Bank FSB (NAS NMS)
PKWY: Parkway Co. (NAS NMS)
P&L: Profit and Loss
pl: place (stock)
PL: Paper Loss
Port Line (steamship)
Price Level
Price List
Prince Line (steamship)
Private Loan
Profit and Loss
PLA: Playboy Enterprises Inc. (NYSE)
PLAB: Photronic Labs Inc. (NAS NMS)
PlainsP: Plains Petroleum Co. (newspaper)
PLAM: Price-Level Adjusted Mortgage
Plantrn: Plantronics Inc. (newspaper)
Playboy: Playboy Enterprises Inc. (newspaper)
PLB: Prior-Lien Bond
PLC: Public Limited Company (British)
PlcrD: Placer Dome Inc. (newspaper)
plcy: policy
P&LE: Pittsburgh & Lake Erie (railroad)
PLEN: Plenum Publishing Corp. (NAS NMS)
Plesey: Plessey Company PLC., The (newspaper)
PLFC: Pulaski Furniture Corp. (NAS NMS)

PLFE: Presidential Life Corp. (NAS NMS)
PLI: P. Leiner Nutritional Products Corp. (ASE)
PLIT: Petrolite Corp. (NAS NMS)
PLL: Pall Corp. (ASE)
Play the Market
Prince Line Limited (steamship)
PLNS: Plains Resources Inc. (NAS NMS)
PLP: Plains Petroleum Co. (NYSE)
PL&PD: Public Liability and Property Damage (insurance)
PLR: Plymouth Rubber Company Inc. (ASE)
PLS: Peerless Tube Co. (ASE)
PLTZC: Pulitzer Publishing Co. (NAS NMS)
PLUS: Plus System - EFT Network (Rocky Mountain Bank Card System)
PLX: Plantronics Inc. (NYSE)
PLXS: Plexus Corp. (NAS NMS)
PLY: Plessey Company PLC, The (NYSE)
PlyGem: Ply*Gem Industries Inc. (newspaper)
PlyR: Plymouth Rubber Company Inc. (newspaper)
PLZA: Plaza Commerce Bancorp (NAS NMS)
pm: paymaster
PM: Pilgrim Airlines
Pratt & Lambert Inc. (ASE)
Premium Money
Primary Market
Project Manager (Management)
Purchase Money
Push Money
PMAN: Piedmont Management Company Inc. (NAS NMS)

PMBK: PRIMEBANK FSB (Michigan) (NAS NMS)
PMC: Prod-Med Capital Inc. (ASE)
PMFG: Peerless Manufacturing Co. (NAS NMS)
PMI: Premark International Inc. (NYSE)
PMK: Primark Corp. (NYSE)
PML: Probable Maximum Loss
PMM: Purchase-Money Mortgage
PMN: Pullman Co. (NYSE)
PMP: Prime Motor Inns LP (NYSE)
    Profit-Maximizing Price
PMR: Micron Products Inc. (ASE)
PMSC: Policy Management Systems Corp. (NAS NMS)
PMSI: Prime Medical Services Inc. (NAS NMS)
PMT: Putnam Master Income Trust (NYSE)
PMWI: PACE Membership Warehouse Inc. (NAS NMS)
P&N: Piedmont and Northern (railway)
PN: Pan Am Corp. (NYSE)
    Pan American World Airways
    Please Note
    Promissory Note
P/N: Promissory Note
PNBA: Pennbancorp (NAS NMS)
PNBT: Planters Corp., The (NAS NMS)
PNC: PNC Financial Corp. (NYSE) (newspaper)
PNET: ProNet Inc. (NAS NMS)
PneuSc: Pneumatic Scale Corp. (newspaper)
PNF: Penn Traffic Co. (ASE)
PNI: Participate but do Not Initiate
PNL: Penril Corp. (ASE)
PNM: Public Service Company of New Mexico (NYSE)
PNN: Penn Engineering & Manufacturing Corp. (ASE)

PNRE: Pan Atlantic Re Inc. (NAS NSM)
PNS: Pansophic Systems Inc. (NYSE)
PNT: Pantasote Inc. (ASE)
PNTA: Pentair Inc. (NAS NMS)
PNTC: Panatech Research and Development Corp. (NAS NMS)
PNU: Pneumatic Scale Corp. (ASE)
PNV: Perini Investment Properties Inc. (ASE)
P&NW: Prescott & Northwestern (railroad)
PNW: Pinnacle West Capital Corp. (NYSE)
PNY: Piedmont Natural Gas Company Inc. (NYSE)
PNYA: Port of New York Authority
P&O: Peninsular & Oriental Steam Navigation Company
PO: Patent Office
    Preauthorization Order
    Public Offering
    Purchase Order
POA: Power Of Attorney
POB: Point Of Business
POBS: Portsmouth Bank Shares Inc. (NAS NMS)
POC: Preservation Of Capital
POCI: Ports of Call Inc. (NAS NMS)
POD: Pay On Delivery
    Port Of Departure
POE: Port Of Entry
PogoPd: Pogo Producing Co. (newspaper)
pol: policy
Polard: Polaroid Corp. (newspaper)
POLK: Polk Audio Inc. (NAS NMS)
Polrin: Polaris Industries Partners L.P. (newspaper)
POLY: Poly-Tech Inc. (NAS NMS)
POM: Potomec Electric Power Co. (NYSE)

POOL: Poseidon Pools of America Inc. (NAS NMS)

POP: Point-Of-Purchase
Pope & Talbot Inc. (NYSE)

PopeEv: Pope, Evans & Robbins Inc. (newspaper)

PopTal: Pope & Talbot Inc. (newspaper)

POR: Payable-On-Receipt
Pay-On-Receipt
Pay On Return
Portec Inc. (NYSE)

Portage: Portage Industries Corp. (newspaper)

Portec: Portec Inc. (newspaper)

PortGC: Portland General Corp. (newspaper)

PortSys: Porta Systems Corp. (newspaper)

pos: position

POS: Point-Of-Sale

POSS: Possis Corp. (NAS NMS)

PostlPr: Postal Instant Press (newspaper)

Potltch: Potlatch Corp. (newspaper)

PotmE: Potomec Electric Power Co. (newspaper)

P&OV: Pittsburgh and Ohio Valley (railroad)

POW: Pay Order of Withdrawal
Power of attorney
PSE Inc. (ASE)

POWL: Powell Industries Inc. (NAS NMS)

POWR: Environmental Power Corp. (NAS NMS)

POY: Prairie Oil Royalties Company Ltd. (ASE)

pp: postpaid
prepaid
prepay

PP: Paper Profit
Parity Price
Partial Payment
Pauley Petroleum Inc. (ASE)
Pension Plan

Phillips Michigan City Flying Service (airline)
Private Property
Purchase Price

PPC: Patrick Petroleum Co. (NYSE)

ppd: postpaid

PPD: Pre-Paid Legal Services Inc. (ASE)
Purchasing Power of the Dollar

PPG: PPG Industries Inc. (NYSE)

PPI: Pico Products Inc. (ASE)
Producer Price Index

PPL: Pennsylvania Power & Light Co. (NYSE)

PPP: Pogo Producing Co. (NYSE)
Prior-Participating Preferred (stock)
Purchasing Power Parity theory

PPS: Participating Preferred Stock
Prior-Preferred Stock

PPSA: Prospect Park Financial Corp. (New Jersey) (NAS NMS)

PPT: Personal Property Tax
Putnam Premier Income Trust (NYSE)

P&PU: Peoria and Pekin union (railroad)

PPW: PacifiCorp. (NYSE)

PQ: Puerto Rico International Airlines

PQB: Quebecor Inc. (ASE)

pr: payroll
preferred (stock)
principal

PR: Parity Ratio
Physical Record
Preliminary Report
Price Communications Corp. (ASE)
Price Rate
Progress Report

Project Report
Pro Rata
P-R: Pennsylvania-Reading Seashore Lines (railroad)
PraireO: Prairie Oil Royalties Company Ltd. (newspaper)
PratHt: Pratt Hotel Corp. (newspaper)
PratLm: Pratt & Lambert Inc. (newspaper)
PRBC: Premier Bancorp Inc. (Louisiana) (NAS NMS)
PrcCm: Price Communications Corp. (newspaper)
PR Cem: Puerto Rican Cement Company Inc. (newspaper)
PRD: Pay Roll Deduction
Polaroid Corp. (NYSE)
pre: prefix
PRE: Premier Industrial Corp. (NYSE)
prec: precedent
precomp: precomputed (loan)
PrecsA: Precision Aerotech Inc. (newspaper)
pref: preference (stock)
prem: premium
Premr: Premier Industrial Corp. (newspaper)
Premrk: Premark International Inc. (newspaper)
pres: president
Presd: Presidio Oil Co. (newspaper)
PresR: Presidential Realty Corp. (newspaper)
PREV: Revere Fund Inc. (NAS NMS)
PRFT: Proffitt's Inc. (NAS NMS)
PrgInc: Progressive Income Equity Fund Inc. (newspaper)
PRGR: ProGroup Inc. (NAS NMS)
pri: priority
PRIA: Priam Corp (NAS NMS)
Primca: Primerica Corp. (newspaper)

PrimeM: Prime Motor Inns Inc. (newspaper)
Primrk: Primark Corp. (newspaper)
prin: principal
Prism: Prism Entertainment Corp. (newspaper)
Pr Ln: Prior Lien
PRLX: Parlex Corp. (NAS NMS)
PRME: Prime Capital Corp. (NAS NMS)
PrmFn: Prime Financial Partners L.P. (newspaper)
Prmian: Permian Basin Royalty Trust (newspaper)
PrMLt: Prime Motor Inns L. P. (newspaper)
PRN: Puerto Rican Cement Company Inc. (NYSE)
PrnDia: Princeton Diagnostic Laboratories of America (newspaper)
pro: procurement
PRO: International Proteins Corp. (ASE)
ProctG: Procter & Gamble Co., The (newspaper)
prod: product
production
PROF: Professional Investors Insurance Group Inc. (NAS NMS)
ProfCre: Professional Care Inc. (newspaper)
ProgCp: Progressive Corp., The (Ohio) (newspaper)
PROI: Project Return On Investment
proj: project
Proler: Proler International Corp. (newspaper)
ProMed: Pro-Med Capital Inc. (newspaper)
prop: property
PROP: Production Operators Corp. (NAS NMS)
Profit Rating of Projects

PropCT: Property Capital Trust (newspaper)

PRO RATA: According to the Rate (Latin)

PROSZ: Prospect Group Inc., The (NAS NMS)

PROT: Protective Life Corp. (NAS NMS)

ProvEn: Providence Energy Corp. (newspaper)

PrpdLg: Pre-Paid Legal Services Inc. (newspaper)

PRR: Pennsylvania Railroad (Penn Central)
Perrigo Co. (ASE)

PRS: Pennsylvania Reading Seashore (railroad)
Presidio Oil Co. (ASE)

PRSL: Pennsylvania Reading Shore Line

PRTD: Portland Railroad and Terminal Division

prty: priority

PruInt: Prudential Intermediate Income Fund Inc. (newspaper)

PruStr: Prudential Strategic Income Fund (newspaper)

PRV: Pearl River Valley (railroad)

PRX: Par Pharmaceutical Inc. (NYSE)

PRXS: Praxis Biologics Inc. (NAS NMS)

PRY: Pittway Corp. (ASE)

PRZ: Prism Entertainment Corp. (ASE)

P&S: Pittsburgh & Shawmut (railroad)
Purchase and Sale (Statement)

PS: Par Selling
Penny Stock
Personal Savings
Pink Sheet
Pittsburgh and Shawmut (railroad)

Preferred Stock
Price Spread
Prime Rate
Profit Sharing
Proler International Corp. (NYSE)
Public Sale

PSA: Pacific Southwest Airlines
Preliminary Sales Agreement
Public Securities Association

PSBF: Pioneer Savings Bank (Florida) (NAS NMS)

PSBK: Progressive Bank Inc. (New York) (NAS NMS)

PSBN: Pioneer Savings Bank Inc. (North Carolina) (NAS NMS)

PSBX: Peoples Savings Bank FSB (Michigan) (NAS NMS)

PSC: Philadelphia Suburban Corp. (NYSE)
Point Shipping Company (steamship)

PSD: Puget Sound Power & Light Co. (NYSE)

PSE: Pacific Stock Exchange
PSE Inc. (newspaper)

PSEG: Public Service Enterprise Group Inc. (newspaper)

PSF: Prudential Strategic Income Fund (NYSE)

PSFL: Puget Sound Freight Lines (steamship)

PSG: PS Group Inc. (NYSE)

PS Grp: PS Group Inc. (newspaper)

PSI: Porta Systems Corp. (ASE)
PSI Holdings Inc. (newspaper)

PSLA: Preferred Savings Bank Inc. (North Carolina) (NAS NMS)

PSNB: Puget Sound Bancorp (NAS NMS)

PSNC: Pacific Steam Navigation Company
Public Service Company of

North Carolina Inc. (NAS NMS)

PSO: Penobscot Shoe Co. (ASE)

PSP: Profit Sharing Plan

PSPA: Pennview Savings Assn. (Pennsylvania) (NAS NMS)

PSR: Public Service Company of Colorado

PSSP: Price/Stern/Sloan Publishers Inc. (NAS NMS)

PST: Pacific Standard time
Petrie Stores Corp. (NYSE)
Profit-Sharing Trust

P-STAR: Federal Reserve predictor of long-term inflation rate

PsvCol: Public Service Company of Colorado (newspaper)

PsvNM: Public Service Company of New Mexico (newspaper)

PSX: Pacific Scientific Co. (NYSE)

PSYS: Programming & Systems Inc. (NAS NMS)

pt: point

PT: Paper Title
Passing Title
Perfect Title
Pope and Talbot (steamship)
Profit Taking
Progressive Tax
Property Tax
Provincetown-Boston Airline and Naples Airline Division

PTAC: Penn Treaty American Corp. (NAS NMS)

ptas: peseta

PTC: PAR Technology Corp. (NYSE)
Peoria Terminal Company (railroad)
Philadelphia Transportation Company
Propensity To Consume

PT CL: Part Called (NYSE)

PTCM: Pacific Telecom Inc. (NAS NMS)

PTCO: Petroleum Equipment Tools Co. (NAS NMS)

PTE: Pretax Earning

PTG: Portage Industries Corp. (ASE)

PtHeat: Petroleum Heat & Power Company Inc. (newspaper)

PTI: Patient Technology Inc. (ASE)

PTLX: Patlex Corp (NAS NMS)

PTM: Portland Terminal Company (railroad)

PTNX: Printronix Inc. (NAS NMS)

PTP: Promise To Pay

PtPar: Petrolane Partners L.P. (newspaper)

Pt Pd: Part Paid (stock)

PTR: Parr Terminal Railroad

P TR: Private Trust

PT RD: Part Redeemed (stock)

PtrInv: Petroleum Investments Ltd. (newspaper)

PTRK: Preston Corp. (NAS NMS)

PTRL: Petrol Industries Inc. (NAS NMS)

PTRO: Petrominerals Corp. (NAS NMS)

PTS: Port Townsend (railroad)
Public Telephone Service

PTSI: P.A.M. Transportation Services Inc. (NAS NMS)

PTT: Cleveland and Pittsburgh Railroad Company

PU: Public Utility

Publick: Publicker Industries Inc. (newspaper)

PUBO: Pubco Corp. (NAS NMS)

PUD: Public Utility District (bonds)

Pueblo: Pueblo International Inc. (newspaper)

PugetP: Puget Sound Power & Light Co. (newspaper)

PUHCA: Public Utility Holding Company Act

PUL: Publicker Industries Inc. (NYSE)

Pullmn: Pullman Co., The (newspaper)

PULS: Pulawksi S&L Assn. (New Jersey) (NAS NMS)

PuntaG: Punta Gorda Isles Inc. (newspaper)

PUPU: Purchasing Power (accounting method)

pur: purchase
purchaser
purchasing

purch: purchasing

PURE: Pure Oil Company (steamship)

PUT: Put option

PutMas: Putnam Master Income Trust (newspaper)

PutMI: Putnam Master Intermediate Income Trust (newspaper)

PutnHi: Putnam High Income Convertible & Bond Fund (newspaper)

PutPr: Putnam Premier Income Trust (newspaper)

PV: Eastern Provincial Airways
Par Value
Present Value

PVDC: Princeville Corp. (NAS NMS)

PVH: Phillips-Van Heusen Corp. (NYSE)

PVIR: Penn Virginia Corp. (NAS NMS)

PVNA: Provena Foods Inc. (NAS NMS)

PVR: Profit/Volume Ratio

PVS: Pecos Valley Southern (railroad)

PVSA: Parkvale Savings Assn. (Pennsylvania) (NAS NMS)

PVY: Providence Energy Corp. (ASE)

PW: Pacific Western Airlines
Pittsburgh and West Virginia Railroad (ASE)
Present Worth
Prevailing Wage

P&WA: Pratt and Whitney Aircraft

PWA: Pacific Western Airlines Corp. (NAS NMS)

PWF: Present Worth Factor

PWJ: PaineWebber Group Inc. (NYSE)

PWN: Cash America Investments Inc. (ASE)

PWR: International Power Machines Corp. (ASE)

PWSB: Peoples Westchester Savings Bank (New York) (NAS NMS)

P&WV: Pittsburgh & West Virginia (railroad)

PX: Aspen Airlines
Price on an offering sheet or on other releases dealing with securities

PXR: PAXAR Corp. (ASE)

PXRE: Phoenix Re Corp. (NAS NMS)

PY: Preferred Health Care Ltd. (ASE)

PY: Prior Year

PYA: Pittsburgh, Youngstown & Ashland Railway Company

PYE: Progressive Income Equity Fund Inc. (NYSE)

PYF: Pay-Fone System Inc. (ASE)

pymt: payment

PYRD: Pyramid Technology Corp. (NAS NMS)

Pyro: Pyro Energy Corp. (newspaper)

PZC: Point of Zero Charge

PZL: Pennzoil Co. (NYSE)

q: quarterly

Q: In receivership or bankruptcy proceedings (NYSE)

Q&A: Questions and Answers

QA: Dixie Airlines
Quick Asset

Qantel: Qantel Corp. (newspaper)

QA&P: Quanah, Acme & Pacific (railroad)

QB: Qualified Buyers

QBDL: Flanigan's Enterprises Inc. (ASE)

QC: Quality Control
Quasi Contract
Quasi Corporation

QCHM: Quaker Chemical Corp. (NAS NMS)

QEDX: QED Exploration Inc. (NAS NMS)

QEKG: Q-MED Inc. (NAS NMS)

QFCI: Quality Food Centers Inc. (NAS NMS)

QH: St. Thomas Tax-Air (airline)

QI: Quarterly Index

QK: Aroostook Airways

QkReily: Quick & Reily Group Inc., The (newspaper)

QMAX: QMax Technology Group Inc. (NAS NMS)

QMED: Quest Medical Inc. (NAS NMS)

QMH: MHI Group Inc. (NYSE)

QMS: QMS Inc. (newspaper)

qn: quotation

QNS: Quantity Not Sufficient

QNTL: Arizona Instrument Corp. (NAS NMS)

QNTM: Quantum Corp. (NAS NMS)

QO: Bar Harbor Airlines

QP: Quoted Price

QPC: Quasi-Public Company

QPON: Seven Oaks International Inc. (NAS NMS)

QR: Quotation Request

Q-RATIO: Ratio of total market value of physical assets

QRXL: Quarex Industries Inc. (NAS NMS)

QS: Air Michigan (airline)
Quality Stock

QSII: Quality Systems Inc. (NAS NMS)

QstVl: Quest for Value Dual Purpose Fund Inc. (newspaper)

QT: Questioned Trade
Quotation Ticker

QTEC: QuesTech Inc. (NAS NMS)

Q-TIP: Qualified Terminable Interest Property (trust)

qtly: quarterly

qtr: quarter

QU: Mississippi Valley Airways

QUAD: Quadrex Corp. (NAS NMS)

QuakFb: Quaker Fabric Corp. (newspaper)

QuakO: Quaker Oats Co., The (newspaper)

QuakSC: Quaker State Corp. (newspaper)

qual: quality

QUAN: Quantronix Corp. (NAS NMS)

Quanex: Quanex Corp. (newspaper)

Quantm: Quantum Chemical Corp. (newspaper)

quar: quarter

Quebc: Quebecor Inc. (newspaper)

Questar: Questar Corp. (newspaper)

QUI: Quincy (railroad)

QUID PRO QUO: Something for Something

QUIK: Quicksilver Inc. (NAS NMS)

QUIP: Quipp Inc. (NAS NMS)

QUIX: Quixote Corp. (NAS NMS)

QUME: Qume Corp. (NAS NMS)

quote: quotation

QUO WARRANTO: By What Authority

QV: Monarch Airline
Quode Vide (Reference to related sources of information)

QVCN: QVC Network Inc. (NAS NMS)

QZMGF: Quartz Mountain Gold Corp. (NAS NMS)

r: recommendation
register
regulation
report
request
research
reset
resistor
right (stocks)
R: L.F. Rothschild Unterberg
Towbin Holdings Inc. (NYSE)
Option not traded (in option list-
ings in newspapers)
RA: Restricted Account
RABT: Rabbit Software Corp. (NAS
NMS)
RAC: RAC Mortgage Investment
Corp. (newspaper)
RAI Research Corp. (ASE)
RAD: Rite Aid Corp. (NYSE)
Radice: Radice Corp. (newspaper)
RADS: Radiation Systems Inc.
(NAS NMS)
RADX: Radionics Inc. (NAS NMS)
Ragan: Brad Ragan Inc. (newspa-
per)
RAGN: Ragen Corp. (NAS NMS)
RAGS: Coated Sales Inc. (NAS NMS)
RAI: RAI Research Corp. (newspa-
per)
rail: railroad
railway
RAL: Ralston Purina Co. (NYSE)
RalsPur: Ralston Purina Co. (news-
paper)
RAM: Ramada Inc. (NYSE)
Reverse Annuity Mortgage
Ramad: Ramada Inc. (newspaper)
RAND: Research And Development
RANG: Rangaire Corp. (NAS NMS)

RangrO: Ranger Oil Ltd. (newspa-
per)
Ransbg: Ransburg Corp. (newspa-
per)
RARB: Raritan Bancorp Inc. (NAS
NMS)
RATNY: Ratners Group PLC (NAS
NMS)
RAUT: Republic Automotive Parts
Inc. (NAS NMS)
RAV: Raven Industries Inc. (ASE)
Raven: Raven Industries Inc.
(newspaper)
RAWC: Republic American Corp.
(NAS NMS)
RAXR: Rax Restaurants Inc. (NAS
NMS)
RAY: Raytech Corp. (NYSE)
Raycom: Raycomm Transworld In-
dustries Inc. (newspa-
per)
RAYM: Raymond Corp., The (NAS
NMS)
Rayonr: Rayonier Timberlands L.P.
(newspaper)
Raytch: Raytech Corp. (newspaper)
Raythn: Raytheon Co. (newspaper)
RB: Railroad Bonds
Reading & Bates Corp. (NYSE)
Redeemable Bond
Reserve Bank
Revenue Bond
RBC: Regal-Beloit Corp. (ASE)
RBCO: Ryan Beck & Co. (NAS
NMS)
RBD: Rubbermaid Inc. (NYSE)
RBG: Ransburg Corp. (ASE)
RBI: RB Industries Inc. (NYSE)
RBInd: RB Industries Inc. (newspa-
per)

RBK: Reebok International Ltd. (NYSE)

RBNH: Rockingham Bancorp (New Hampshire) (NAS NMS)

RBOCs: Regional Bell Operating Companies

RBSN: Robeson Industries Corp. (NAS NMS)

RBW: RB & W Corp. (ASE) (newspaper)

RC: Recurring Charges
Registered Check
Reserve Capital
Restrictive Covenant
Risk Capital

RCA: Radio Corporation of America

RCBI: Robert C. Brown & Company Inc. (NAS NMS)

RCC: Re Capital Corp. (ASE)

rcd: received (stocks)
record

RCDC: Ross Cosmetics Distribution Centers Inc. (NAS NMS)

RCE: Reece Corp., The (NYSE)

RCHF: Richfood Holdings Inc. (NAS NMS)

RckCtr: Rockefeller Center Properties Inc. (newspaper)

Rckwy: Rockaway Corp. (newspaper)

RCM: ARCO Chemical Co. (NYSE)

RCOA: Retailing Corporation of America (NAS NMS)

RCOT: Recoton Corp. (NAS NMS)

RCP: Rockefeller Center Properties Inc. (NYSE)

RCPC: Regional Check Processing Center

rcpt: receipt

RCSB: Rochester Community Savings Bank, The (NAS NMS)

rct: receipt (stocks)

RCT: Real Estate Investment Trust of California (NYSE)

rcv: receive

R&D: Research and Development

rd: redeemable (stocks)

RD: Research and Development
Royal Dutch Petroleum Co. (NYSE)
Rural Delivery

RDC: Rowan Companies Inc. (NYSE)

RDG: Reading Company (railroad)

RDGC: Reading Co. (NAS NMS)

RDK: Ruddick Corp. (ASE)

RDKN: Redken Laboratories Inc. (NAS NMS)

RDL: Redlaw Industries Inc. (ASE)

RDR: Ryder System Inc. (NYSE)

RDWI: Roadway Motor Plazas Inc. (NAS NMS)

rdy: ready

RE: Rate of Exchange
Real Estate
Redman Industries Inc. (NYSE)

R/E: Rate of Exchange

REA: Railway Express Agency
Reader (railroad)

ReadBt: Reading & Bates Corp. (newspaper)

REAL: Reliability Inc. (NAS NMS)

Rebok: Reebok International Ltd. (newspaper)

rec: receipt
record

REC: Recognition Equipment Inc. (NYSE)

ReCap: Re Capital Corp. (newspaper)

recd: received

RecnEq: Recognition Equipment Inc. (newspaper)

Reco: RECO International Inc. (newspaper)

recpt: receipt

rect: receipt

RED: Red Lion Inns LP (ASE)

REDI: Readicare Inc. (NAS NMS)

redisc: rediscount

RedLn: Red Lion Inns L. P. (newspaper)

Redlw: Redlaw Industries Inc. (newspaper)

Redmn: Redman Industries Inc.
(newspaper)
Reece: Reece Corp., The (newspaper)
REED: Reeds Jewelers Inc. (NAS
NMS)
ref: referee
reference
refunding (stocks)
REFC: REFAC Technology Devel-
opment Corp. (NAS NMS)
reg: register
registered (stocks)
REG: Registered (NYSE)
Regal: Regal International Inc.
(newspaper)
RegalB: Regal-Beloit Corp. (news-
paper)
REGB: Regional Bancorp Inc.
(NAS NMS)
REGI: Regina Company Inc. (NAS
NMS)
RegIFn: Regional Financial Shares
Investment Fund Inc.
(newspaper)
regs: regulations
REI: Real Estate Investment Trust
of America
REIC: Research Industries Corp.
(NAS NMS)
ReichT: Reich & Tang L. P. (news-
paper)
reimb: reimburse
reimbursement
REIT: Real Estate Investment Trust
Real Estate Investment Trust
of California (newspaper)
rel: release
relocatable
REL: Reliance Group Holdings Inc.
(NYSE)
RelGrp: Reliance Group Holdings
Inc. (newspaper)
RELL: Richardson Electronics Ltd.
(NAS NMS)
RELY: Relational Technology Inc.
(NAS NMS)
rem: remittance

REMIC: Real Estate Mortgage In-
vestment
remitt: remittance
REN: Rollins Environmental Ser-
vices Inc. (NYSE)
REO: Real Estate Owned
REOP: Reopening (after a halt in
trading)
rep: representative
REPEX: Regional Payments Ex-
change (Dayton, Ohio)
RepGyp: Republic Gypsum Co.
(newspaper)
RepNY: Republic New York Corp.
(newspaper)
REPO: Repurchase Agreement
REPOS: Repurchase Agreements
req: request
res: reserve
RES: RPC Energy Services Inc.
(NYSE)
RESC: Roanoke Electric Steel Corp.
(NAS NMS)
RESec: Real Estate Securities In-
come Fund Inc. (newspa-
per)
RESM: Restaurant Management
Services Inc. (NAS NMS)
RESP: Respironics Inc. (NAS NMS)
RESPA: Real Estate Settlement
Procedures Act
RESR: Research Inc. (NAS NMS)
ResRs: Residential Resources Mort-
gages Investments Corp.
(newspaper)
Resrt: Resorts International Inc.
(newspaper)
RestMg: Residential Mortgage In-
vestments Inc. (newspa-
per)
Rexhm: Rexham Corp. (newspaper)
RET: Real-Estate Tax
REUT: Reuter Inc. (NAS NMS)
REXI: Resource Exploration Inc.
(NAS NMS)
REXN: Rexon Inc. (NAS NMS)
REXW: Rexworks Inc. (NAS NMS)

ReyMt: Reynolds Metals Co. (newspaper)

REYNA: Reynolds & Reynolds Co., The (NAS NMS)

RF: Revolving Fund

RFB: Request For Bid

RFBC: River Forest Bancorp. (NAS NMS)

RFBK: Raleigh Federal Savings Bank (North Carolina) (NAS NMS)

RFC: Reconstruction Finance Corporation (defunct)

RFED: Roosevelt bank FSB (Missouri)

rfg: refunding

RF&P: Richmond, Fredericksburg & Potomac (railroad)

RFQ: Request For Quotation (Quote)

RFSB: Reistertown Federal Savings Bank (Maryland) (NAS NMS)

RFTN: Reflectone Inc. (NAS NMS)

RGB: R. G. Barry Corp. (ASE)

RGC: Republic Gypsum Co. (NYSE)

RGCY: Regency Electronics Inc. (NAS NMS)

RGEN: Repligen Corp. (NAS NMS)

RGEQ: Regency Equities Corp. (NAS NMS)

RGIS: Regis Corp. (NAS NMS)

RGL: Regal International Inc. (NYSE)

RGLD: Royal Gold Inc. (NAS NMS)

RGO: Ranger Oil Ltd. (NYSE)

RGS: Rio Grande Southern (railroad)

Rochester Gas & Electric Corp. (NYSE)

RH: Red Herring

RHD: Rhodes Inc. (NYSE)

RHEM: Rheometrics Inc. (NAS NMS)

RHH: H. H. Robertson Co. (NYSE)

RHI: Robert Halmi Inc. (ASE)

RHII: Robert Half Inc. (NAS NMS)

Rhodes: Rhodes Inc. (newspaper)

RHPOY: Rhone-Poulenc SA (NAS NMS)

RHR: Rohr Industries Inc. (NYSE)

RI: Chicago, Rock Island and Pacific Railroad Company

Radice Corp. (NYSE)

Real Income

Tricon International Airlines

RIBI: Ribi ImmunoChem Research Inc. (NAS NMS)

RICH: Richmond Hills Savings Bank (NAS NMS)

RIE: Riedel Environmental Technologies Inc. (ASE)

Riedel: Riedel Environmental Technologies Inc. (newspaper)

RIF: Real Estate Securities Income Fund Inc. (ASE)

RIGS: Riggs National Corp. (NAS NMS)

RIHL: Richton International Corp. (NAS NMS)

RIO: Royal International Optical Corp. (NYSE)

RioAl: Rio Algom Ltd. (newspaper)

RIR: Request Immediate Reply

RIS: Rock Island Southern (railroad)

Riser: Riser Foods Inc. (newspaper)

RIT: Reverse Income Tax

RiteAid: Rite Aid Corp. (newspaper)

RITZ: G. D. Ritzy's Inc. (NAS NMS)

RIV: Riverbend International Corp. (ASE)

Rivbnd: Riverbend International Corp. (newspaper)

RJamFn: Raymond James Financial Inc. (newspaper)

RJF: Raymond James Financial Inc. (NYSE)

RK: Ark Restaurants Corp. (ASE)

RKG: Rockingham (railroad)

RKWD: Rockwood Holding Co. (NAS NMS)

RKY: Rockaway Corp. (NYSE)
RL: Regent's Line (steamship)
　　Round Lot
RLC: RLC Corp. (NYSE) (newspaper)
RLI: RLI Corp. (NYSE)
RLI Cp: RLI Corp. (newspaper)
RLM: Reynolds Metal Co. (NYSE)
RLO: Round Lot Orders
RLT: Living Trust
RltRef: Realty ReFund Trust (newspaper)
RltSou: Realty South Investors Inc. (newspaper)
RM: Registered Mail
RMACHA: Rocky Mountain Automated Clearing House Association
RMC: American Restaurant Partners LP (ASE)
RMCI: Right Management Consultants Inc. (NAS NMS)
RMD: Ready Money Down
RMI: Residential Mortgage Investments Inc. (ASE)
RMK: Robert - Mark Inc. (ASE)
RML: Russell Corp. (NYSE)
RMPO: Ramapo Financial Corp. (NAS NMS)
RMR: RAC Mortgage Investment Corp. (ASE)
RMS: Real Market Share
　　RMS International Inc. (ASE)
RMS Int: RMS International Inc. (newspaper)
RMUC: Rocky Mount Undergarment Company Inc. (NAS NMS)
RNB: Received - Not Billed
　　Republic New York Corp. (NYSE)
RNIC: Robinson Nugent Inc. (NAS NMS)
RNRC: Riverside National Bank (California) (NAS NMS)

RNT: RECO International Inc. (ASE)
RO: Receive Only
　　Regional Office
ROA: Return On Assets
ROAD: Roadway Services Inc. (NAS NMS)
ROAM: Return On Assets Managed
ROB: Run On Bank
RobMk: Robert-Mark Inc. (newspaper)
ROBN: Robbins & Myers Inc. (NAS NMS)
Robtsn: H. H. Robertson Co. (newspaper)
ROBV: Robotic Vision Systems Inc. (NAS NMS)
ROC: Reevaluation Of Capital
ROCE: Return On Capital Employed
RochG: Rochester Gas & Electric Corp. (newspaper)
RochTl: Rochester Telephone Corp. (newspaper)
Rockwl: Rockwell International Corp. (newspaper)
RodRen: Rodman & Renshaw Capital Group Inc. (newspaper)
ROE: Rate Of Exchange
　　Return-On-Equity
　　Roebling Property Investors Inc. (ASE)
Roeblg: Roebling Property Investors Inc. (newspaper)
ROG: Receipt-Of-Goods
　　Rogers Corp. (ASE)
Rogers: Rogers Corp. (newspaper)
ROH: Rohm & Haas Co. (NYSE)
RoHaas: Rohm & Haas Co. (newspaper)
Rohr: Rohr Industries Inc. (newspaper)
ROI: Rate Of Interest
　　Return On Invested capital
　　Return On Investment

River Oaks Industries Inc.
(NYSE)
ROK: Rockwell International Corp.
(NYSE)
ROL: Rollins Inc. (NYSE)
RolinE: Rollins Environmental Ser-
vices Inc. (newspaper)
Rollins: Rollins Inc. (newspaper)
ROM: Rio Algom Ltd. (ASE)
ROMV: Return On Market Value
RONC: Ronson Corp. (NAS NMS)
ROOI: Return On Original Invest-
ment
ROP: Registered Options Principal
Right Of Possession
ROPK: Ropak Corp. (NAS NMS)
ROR: Rate Of Return
Right Of Rescission
Rorer Group Inc. (NYSE)
Rorer: Rorer Group Inc. (newspa-
per)
ROS: Return On Sales
Rights Of Stockholders
(Shareholders)
ROST: Ross Stores Inc. (NAS
NMS)
ROTC: RoTech Medical Corp. (NAS
NMS)
Rothch: L. F. Rothschild Unterberg
Towbin Holdings Inc.
(newspaper)
ROTO: Roto-Rooter Inc. (NAS
NMS)
ROUS: Rouse Co., The (NAS NMS)
Rowan: Rowan Companies Inc.
(newspaper)
ROWE: Rowe Furniture Corp.
(NAS NMS)
Royce: Royce Value Trust Inc.
(newspaper)
ROYG: Royal Business Group Inc.
(NAS NMS)
RoyInt: Royal International Optical
Corp. (newspaper)
ROYL: Royalpar Industries Inc.
(NAS NMS)

RoylBu: Royal Business Group Inc.
(newspaper)
RoylD: Royal Dutch Petroleum Co.
(newspaper)
RP: Real Property
RPAL: Royal Palm Savings Assn.
(Florida) (NAS NMS)
RPAPF: Repap Enterprises Corp.
Inc. (NAS NMS)
RPC: RPC Energy Services Inc.
(newspaper)
RPCH: Rospatch Corp. (NAS NMS)
RPCO: Repco Inc. (NAS NMS)
RPIC: Republic Pictures Corp.
(NAS NMS)
RPOW: RPM Inc. (NAS NMS)
RPQ: Request for Price Quotation
rr: railroad
RR: Raritan River (railroad)
Rate of Return
Rediscount Rate
Register to Register
Registered Representative
Reserve Requirement
Return Rate
Rodman & Renshaw Capital
Group Inc. (NYSE)
RRF: Realty ReFund Trust (NYSE)
RRM: Renegotiable-Rate Mortgage
RRP: Reverse Repurchase (agree-
ment)
RRR: Raritan River Railroad
Residential Resources Mort-
gages Investments Corp.
(ASE)
RS: Redeemable Stock
Registered Securities
Revenue Sharing
RSDL: Resdel Industries (NAS
NMS)
RSE: Richmond Stock Exchange
RSFC: Republic Savings Financial
Corp. (Florida) (NAS
NMS)
RSGI: Riverside Group Inc. (NAS
NMS)

RSI: Realty South Investors Inc.
(ASE)
RSIC: RSI Corp. (NAS NMS)
RSLA: Republic Capital Group Inc.
(NAS NMS)
RSP: Roscoe, Snyder and Pacific
(railroad)
RSR: Riser Foods Inc. (ASE)
RSS: Rockdale, Sandow and South-
ern (railroad)
RSTO: Rose's Stores Inc. (NAS
NMS)
rt: right
RT: Regressive Tax
Resorts International Inc.
(ASE)
Restraint of Trade
River Terminal (railway)
RTC: Resolution Trust Corporation
Rochester Telephone Corp.
(NYSE)
RTE: RTE Corp. (NYSE) (newspa-
per)
RTH: Houston Oil Royalty Trust
(NYSE)
RTII: RTI Inc. (NAS NMS)
RTM: Railway Transfer Company of
Minneapolis
Registered Trade Mark
RTN: Raytheon Co. (NYSE)
RTP: Reich & Tang LP (NYSE)
RTRSY: Reuters Holdings PLC
(NAS NMS)
rts: rights
RTS: Russ Togs Inc. (NYSE)
RU: Rousseau Aviation (airline)
Rubmd: Rubbermaid Inc. (newspa-
per)
Rudick: Ruddick Corp. (newspaper)
RUDY: Rudy's Restaurant Group
Inc. (NAS NMS)
RUF: Revolving Underwriting Fa-
cility
RULE: Rule Industries Inc. (NAS
NMS)

RUS: Russ Berrie & Company Inc.
(NYSE)
RussBr: Russ Berrie & Company
Inc. (newspaper)
Russell: Russell Corp. (newspa-
per)
RusTg: Russ Togs Inc. (newspa-
per)
RV: Rahway Valley (railway)
RVCC: Reeves Communications
Corp. (NAS NMS)
RVR: American Land Cruisers Inc.
(ASE)
RvrOak: River Oaks Industries Inc.
(newspaper)
RVT: Royce Value Trust Inc.
(NYSE)
RWPI: Ridgewood Properties Inc.
(NAS NMS)
rwy: railway
rx: receive
RX: Capitol Air Services (airline)
Rxene: Rexene Corp. (newspaper)
RXH: Rexham Corp. (NYSE)
RXN: Rexene Corp. (NYSE)
ry: railway
RYAN: Ryan's Family Steak Houses
Inc. (NAS NMS)
RYC: Raychem Corp. (NYSE)
Ryder: Ryder System Inc. (newspa-
per)
RYFL: Family Steak Houses of
Florida Inc. (NAS NMS)
RYK: Rykoff-Sexton Inc. (NYSE)
Rykoff: Rykoff-Sexton Inc. (newspa-
per)
RYL: Ryland Group Inc., The
(NYSE)
Ryland: Ryland Group Inc., The
(newspaper)
Rymer: Rymer Co., The (newspa-
per)
RYR: Rymer Company, The
(NYSE)
RZ: Aero Mech (airline)

S

s: schilling (currency of Austria)
seasonal
second
seller
silversmith
sold
stockbroker

S: No option offered (option listings of newspapers)
Sears Roebuck & Co. (NYSE)
Signed (before signature on typed copy of document)
Split or Stock dividend (stock listings of newspapers)

sa: semiannual(ly)

S/A: Survivorship Agreement (banking)

S&A: Savannah & Atlanta (railroad)

SA: Salary Administration
Savings Account
Security Analyst
Sociedad Añonima (Spanish corporation)
Société Anonyme (Belgium and French corporation)
Special Assessment
Stage II Apparel Corp. (ASE)
Subject to Approval

SAA: Saatchi & Saatchi Company PLC (NYSE)
Special Arbitrage Account

Saatchi: Saatchi & Saatchi Company PLC (newspaper)

SAB: Sabine Corp. (NYSE)
Special Assessment Bond

Sabine: Sabine Corp. (newspaper)

SabnR: Sabine Royalty Trust (newspaper)

SAF: Scudder New Asia Fund Inc. (NYSE)

SAFC: SAFECO Corp. (NAS NMS)

SAFE: Security American Financial Enterprises Inc. (NAS NMS)
Settlement and Accelerated Funds Exchange (Chicago)
SWIFT and Foreign Exchange

SAFM: Sanderson Farms Inc. (NAS NMS)

SaftKln: Safety-Kleen Corp. (newspaper)

SAG: Sage Energy Co. (ASE)

Sage: Sage Energy Co. (newspaper)

SAH: Sahara Casino Partners LP (NYSE)

SahCas: Sahara Casino Partners L.P. (newspaper)

SAI: Allstar Inns LP (ASE)

SAJ: St. Joseph Light & Power Co. (NYSE)

sal: salary

SAL: Sale And Leaseback
Savings and Loan Association
Seaboard Air Line (railroad)

Salant: Salant Corp. (newspaper)

Salem: Salem Corp. (newspaper)

SallieM: Student Loan Marketing Assn. (newspaper)

SALN: Sahlen & Associates Inc. (NAS NMS)

Salomn: Salomon Inc. (newspaper)

SAM: Samson Energy Company LP (ASE)
Shared-Appreciation Mortgage

Samson: Samson Energy Company L.P. (newspaper)

185

SAN: San Carlos Milling Company
    Inc. (ASE)
    Sandersville (railroad)
Sandy: Sandy Corp. (newspaper)
SANF: Sanford Corp. (NAS NMS)
SAnitRt: Santa Anita Realty Enter-
    prises Inc. (newspaper)
Sanmrk: Sanmark-Stardust Inc.
    (newspaper)
SANR: Subject to Approval-No Risks
SAP: Soon As Possible
SAR: Santa Anita Realty Enter-
    prises Inc. (NYSE)
    Semiannual Report
    Stock-Appreciation Relief
    (UK)
    Stock-Appreciation Rights
SaraLee: Sara Lee Corp. (newspa-
    per)
SAS: Statement of Auditing Stan-
    dards
    Statistical Analysis System
SAT: Schafer Value Trust Inc.
    (NYSE)
SATA: Sherman Anti-Trust Act
SATIATER: Statistical Approach to
    Investment Appraisal
    to Evaluate Risk
SaulRE: B. F. Saul Real Estate In-
    vestment Trust (newspa-
    per)
sav: save
    savings
SAV: Stock At Valuation
Savin: Savin Corp. (newspaper)
SAX: Saxon Oil Development Part-
    ners LP (ASE)
SaxnO: Saxon Oil Development
    Partners L.P. (newspa-
    per)
SAXO: Saxon Oil Co. (NAS NMS)
SAYI: S.A.Y. Industries Inc. (NAS
    NMS)
sb: stockbroker
SB: Salomon Inc. (NYSE)
    Samurai Bond (Japan)

Savings Bank
Savings Bond
Seaboard World Airways
Senior Bond
Short Bill
Small Business
South Buffalo (railway)
Surety Bond
SBA: Sbarro Inc. (ASE)
    Small Business Administra-
    tion
    Strategic Business Area
Sbarro: Sbarro Inc. (newspaper)
SBC: Southwestern Bell Corp.
    (NYSE)
SBCC: Senate Bonding and Cur-
    rency Committee
SBCF: Seacoast Banking Corpora-
    tion of Florida (NAS NMS)
SBCL: Special Buyer Credit Limit
SBD: Savings Bond Division
    Seaboard Coast Line (rail-
    road)
SBDC: Small Business Develop-
    ment Center
SbdCp: Seaboard Corp. (newspaper)
SBF: Supplementary Fringe Bene-
    fits
SBI: Savings Bank Insurance
    Share of Beneficial Interest
SBIC: Small Business Investment
    Company
SBIG: Seibels Bruce Group Inc.,
    The (NAS NMS)
SBIO: Synbiotics Corp. (NAS NMS)
SBIR: Small Business Innovation
    Research
SBK: Signet Banking Corp. (NYSE)
SBL: Symbol Technologies Inc.
    (NYSE)
SBLI: Savings Bank Life Insurance
SBM: Speed-O-Print Business Ma-
    chines Corp. (ASE)
SBN: Sunbelt Nursery Group Inc.
    (ASE)
SBO: Showboat Inc. (NYSE)

SBOS: Boston Bancorp. (NAS NMS)

SBP: Standard Brands Paint Co. (NYSE)

SBR: Sabine Royalty Trust (NYSE)

SBRU: Subaru of America Inc. (NAS NMS)

SBS: Salem Corp. (ASE)

SBTC: SBT Corp. (NAS NMS)

SBU: Strategic Business Unit

S&C: Shipper and Carrier
Sized and Calendered
Star and Crescent (steamship)
Sumter & Choctaw (railroad)

SC: Safe Custody
Safety Clause
Service Charge
Seul Cours (Sole Quotation) (French)
Sharp Cash
Shell Transport & Trading Company PLC, The (NYSE)
Shopping Center
Silver Certificates
Special Committee
Stock Certificate
Subsidiary Company
Sumter and Choctaw (railway)
Sweetheart Contract (Clause)
Sylvania Central (railroad)

SCA: Servo Corporation of America (ASE)
Shareholder Credit Accounting

SCAF: Surgical Care Affiliates Inc. (NAS NMS)

SCalEd: Southern California Edison Co. (newspaper)

SCAN: Stockmarket Computer Answering Network (UK)

SCANA: SCANA Corp. (newspaper)

ScandF: Scandinavia Fund Inc., The (newspaper)

SCAPY: Svenska Cellulosa AB (NAS NMS)

SCarlo: San Carlos Milling Company Inc. (newspaper)

SCC: Security Capital Corp. (ASE)
Shipping and Coal Company (steamship)
Stock Clearing Corporation

SCCS: Standard Commodity Classification System

ScdNA: Scudder New Asia Fund Inc. (newspaper)

SCE: Southern California Edison Co. (NYSE)

Sceptre: Sceptre Resources Ltd. (newspaper)

SCF: Scandinavia Fund Inc., The (ASE)

SCFB: South Carolina Federal Corp. (NAS NMS)

SCFM: Scanforms Inc. (NAS NMS)

SCG: SCANA Corp. (NYSE)

sch: schedule

SCH: Charles Schwab Corp., The (NYSE)

SCHC: R. P. Scherer Corp. (NAS NMS)

Scheib: Earl Scheib Inc. (newspaper)

Schfr: Schafer Value Trust Inc. (newspaper)

Schlmb: Schlumberger Ltd. (newspaper)

SchoolP: School Pictures Inc. (newspaper)

SchrPlg: Schering-Plough Corp. (newspaper)

Schwab: Schwab Safe Company Inc. (newspaper)

Schwb: Charles Schwab Corp., The (newspaper)

SCI: Sea Containers Incorporated (steamship)

SciAtl: Scientific-Atlanta Inc. (newspaper)

SCIE: Scicom Data Services Ltd. (NAS NMS)

SciLsg: Scientific Leasing Inc. (newspaper)

SciMgt: Science Management Corp. (newspaper)

SCIS: SCI Systems Inc. (NAS NMS)

SCIXF: Scitex Corporation Ltd. (NAS NMS)

SCL: Seaboard Coast Line (railroad)
Stepan Co. (ASE)

SC&MR: Strouds Creek and Muddlety Railroad

SCNC: South Carolina National Corp. (NAS NMS)

SCOM: SCS/Compute Inc. (NAS NMS)

Scope: Scope Industries (newspaper)

SCOR: Syncor International Corp. (NAS NMS)

SCORE: Service Corps Of Retired Executives
Special Claim On Residual Equity

SCOR U: SCOR U.S. Corp. (newspaper)

SCOT: Scott & Stringfellow Financial Inc. (NAS NMS)

ScottP: Scott Paper Co. (newspaper)

Scottys: Scotty's Inc. (newspaper)

SCP: Scope Industries (ASE)

SCR: Sea Containers Ltd. (NYSE)

SCREAM: Society for the Registration of Estate Agents and Mortgage Brokers

SCRP: Scripps Howard Broadcasting Co. (NAS NMS)

SCT: Sioux City Terminal (railway)

SCTC: Systems & Computer Technology Corp. (NAS NMS)

ScurRn: Scurry-Rainbow Oil Ltd. (newspaper)

SCX: L. S. Starrett Co., The (NYSE)

sd: stamped (stocks)

S&D: Sealed and Delivered
Supply and Demand

SD: Sales Department
Sales Director
Same Day
Scrip Department
Secondary Distribution
Service Department
Settlement Date
Sight Draft
Single Density
Stamped (NYSE)
Stock Dividend
Supply Department

SD&AE: San Diego & Arizona Eastern (railroad)

SDB: Special District Bond

SDBL: Sight Draft Bill of Lading

SD CO: Safe Deposit Company

SDMJ: September, December, March, June (securities)

SDNB: SDNB Financial Corp. (NAS NMS)

SDP: Sun Distributors LP (NYSE)

SDW: Southdown Inc. (NYSE)

SDY: Sandy Corp. (ASE)

SDYN: Staodynamics Inc. (NAS NMS)

SE: Shareholder's Equity
Stock Exchange
Sun Electric Corp. (NYSE)

SEAB: Seaboard S&L Assn. (Virginia) (NAS NMS)

SEABOARD: Seaboard World Airways

SeaCnt: Sea Containers Ltd. (newspaper)

SEAG: Sea Galley Stores Inc. (NAS NMS)

Seagrm: Seagram Company Ltd., The (newspaper)

Seagul: Seagull Energy Corp. (newspaper)

SealAir: Sealed Air Corp. (newspaper)

Seamn: Seamen's Corp. (newspaper)

Seaport: Seaport Corp. (newspaper)

SEAQ: Stock Exchange Automated Quotation System (UK)

Sears: Sears Roebuck & Co. (newspaper)

SEATS: Stock Exchange Automated Trading System (Australia)

SEB: Seaboard Corp. (ASE)

sec: second

SEC: Securities and Exchange Commission
Sterling Electronics Corp. (ASE)

SECB: Security Bancorp Inc. (NAS NMS)

SecCap: Security Capital Corp. (newspaper)

SECMA: Stock Exchange Computer Managers Association

SECO: Securities and Exchange Commission Organization

SecPac: Security Pacific Corp. (newspaper)

SEE: Sealed Air Corp. (NYSE)

SEEQ: Seeq Technology Inc. (NAS NMS)

SEI: Self-Employed Income

SEIC: SEI Corp. (NAS NMS)

Selas: Selas Corporation of America (newspaper)

SeligAs: Seligman & Associates Inc. (newspaper)

SELLER: Seller's Option (NYSE)

SEM: Shared Equity Mortgage
Systems Engineering & Manufacturing Corp. (ASE)

Semtch: Semtech Corp. (newspaper)

SEND: Securities and Exchange Commission News Digest

SENE: Seneca Foods Corp. (NAS NMS)

SEO: Seaport Corp. (ASE)

SEQ: Storage Equities Inc. (NYSE)

SEQP: Supreme Equipment & Systems Corp. (NAS NMS)

Sequa: Sequa Corp. (newspaper)

ser: serial
series

SER: Sierracin Corp. (ASE)

SERA: Sierra Railroad

SERF: Service Fracturing Co. (NAS NMS)

Servo: Servo Corporation of America (newspaper)

Servotr: Servotronics Inc. (newspaper)

SES: Stock Exchange of Singapore

SESDAQ: Stock Exchange of Singapore Dealing and Automated Quotation System

SESL: Southeastern S&L Co. (North Carolina) (NAS NSM)

SETC: Sierra Real Estate Equity Trust '84 (NAS NMS)

SETD: Sierra Capital Realty Trust IV Co. (NAS NMS)

S&EV: Saratoga & Encampment Valley (railroad)

SEWY: Seaway Food Town Inc. (NAS NMS)

SF: Scale Factor
Seasonal Fluctuation
Sinking Fund
Stifel Financial Corp. (NYSE)
Stock Fund

S&FA: Shipping and Forwarding Agent

SFA: Scientific-Atlanta Inc. (NYSE)

SFAS: Statements of Financial Accounting Standards

SFB: Standard Federal Bank (NYSE)

SFBM: Security Federal Savings Bank (Montana) (NAS NMS)

SFBRR: San Francisco Belt Railroad

SFC: Sales Finance Companies
S-bank Frequency Converter

SFCD: SafeCard Services Inc. (NAS NMS)

SFDS: Smithfield Foods Inc. (NAS NMS)

SFeEP: Santa Fe Energy Partners L.P. (newspaper)

SFEM: Second-Tiered Foreign Exchange Market
SFE Technologies (NAS NMS)

SFeSP: Santa Fe Southern Pacific Corp. (newspaper)

SFFD: SFFeD Corp. (California) (NAS NMS)

SFGD: Safeguard Health Enterprises Inc. (NAS NMS)

SfgdSc: Safeguard Scientifics Inc. (newspaper)

SFGI: Security Financial Group Inc. (Minnesota) (NAS NMS)

SFIN: Southland Financial Corp. (NAS NMS)

SFM: SFM Corp. (ASE) (newspaper)

SFMR: San Francisco Municipal Railway

SFNS: Spear Financial Services Inc. (NAS NMS)

SFOK: Sooner Federal S&L Assn. (NAS NMS)

SFP: Santa Fe Energy Partners LP (NYSE)
Straight Fixed Price

SFR: Sinking Fund Return

SFS: Super Food Services Inc. (ASE)

SFSE: San Francisco Stock Exchange

SFSI: Sunwest Financial Services Inc. (NAS NMS)

SFT: Special Financial Transactions

SFX: Santa Fe Southern Pacific Corp. (NYSE)

SFY: Swift Energy Co. (ASE)

SG: Scientific Leasing Inc. (ASE)
South Georgia (railroad)

SGAT: Seagate Technology (NAS NMS)

SGC: Superior Surgical Manufacturing Company Inc. (ASE)

SGHB: Sag Harbour Savings Bank (New York) (NAS NMS)

SGI: Slattery Group Inc. (NYSE)

SGIC: Silicon Graphics Inc. (NAS NMS)

SgnlApl: Signal Apparel Company Inc. (newspaper)

SGO: Seagull Energy Corp. (NYSE)

SGP: Schering-Plough Corp. (NYSE)

SGSI: Sage Software Inc. (NAS NMS)

sh: shareholder
stockholder

SH: Spartech Corp. (ASE)
Steelton and Highspire (railroad)

SHA: Smith-Hughes Act

ShaerS: Shaer Shoe Corp. (newspaper)

ShawIn: Shaw Industries Inc. (newspaper)

SHB: Scotty's Inc. (NYSE)

SHCI: Salick Health Care Inc. (NAS NMS)

SHCO: Schult Homes Corp. (NAS NMS)

SHD: Sherwood Group Inc., The (ASE)

SHE: Shearson Lehman Brothers Holdings Inc. (NYSE)

SHEF: Sandwich Chef Inc. (NAS NMS)

SHEL: Sheldahl Inc. (NAS NMS)

Shelby: Shelby Williams Industries Inc. (newspaper)

SHELL: Shell Oil Company

ShellT: Shell Transport & Trading Company PLC., The (newspaper)

SHEX: Sundays and Holidays Excepted

ship: ship
shipment
shipping

SHIP: Regency Cruises Inc. (NAS NMS)

shipmt: shipment

SHKIF: SHL Systemhouse Inc. (NAS NMS)

SHLB: Shelby Federal Savings Bank (Indiana) (NAS NMS)

ShLeh: Shearson Lehman Brothers Holdings Inc. (newspaper)

SHLM: A. Schulman Inc. (NAS NMS)

ShltCm: Shelter Components Corp. (newspaper)

SHNA: Shawmut National Corp. (NAS NMS)

SHO: Starrett Housing Corp. (ASE)

SHON: Shoney's Inc. (NAS NMS)

SHOP: Shopsmith Inc. (NAS NMS)

Shopco: Shopco Laurel Centre L. P. (newspaper)

SHOR: Shorewood Packaging Corp. (NAS NMS)

SHP: Securities Shipped as Instructed

shr: share (stock)

SHRE: Sahara Resorts Inc. (NAS NMS)

SHREAD: Share Registration and Dividend Warrants

SHRP: Sharper Image Corp. (NAS NMS)

shrs: shares (stocks)

Shrwin: Sherwin-Williams Co., The (newspaper)

shs: shares

SHS: Shaer Shoe Corp. (ASE)

SHV: Standard Havens Inc. (ASE)

SHW: Sherwin-Williams Co., The (NYSE)

Shwbt: Showboat Inc. (newspaper)

ShwdG: Sherwood Group Inc., The (newspaper)

SHX: Shaw Industries Inc. (NYSE)

S&I: Stocked and Issued

SI: ACM Government Spectrum Fund (NYSE)
Seasonal Industry
Short Interest
Simple Interest
Sound Investment
Spokane International (railroad)

SIA: Securities Industry Association
Signal Apparel Company Inc. (NYSE)
Society of Industrial Accountants (Canada)
Special Investor Account

SIAC: Securities Industry Automation Corporation

SIAL: Sigma-Aldfrich Corp. (NAS NMS)

SIB: Securities and Investments Board (UK)

SIB-MIBOC: Securities and Investments Board and the Marketing of Investments Board Organization Commission (UK)

SIBOR: Singapore Interbank Offered Rate

SIBR: Sybra Inc. (NAS NMS)

SIC: Split Investment Company

SICAV: Societes d'Investissement a Capital Variable

SICOM: Securities Industry Communications

SIDX: Science Dynamics Corp. (NAS NMS)

SIE: Sierra Health Service Inc. (ASE)

SierCap: Sierra Capital Realty Trust IV (newspaper)

SierCa7: Sierra Capital Realty Trust VII (newspaper)
Siercn: Sierracin Corp. (newspaper)
SierHS: Sierra Health Services Inc. (newspaper)
SierPac: Sierra Pacific Resources (newspaper)
SierSpg: Sierra Spring Water Co. (newspaper)
SIF: SIFCO Industries Inc. (ASE)
Sifco: SIFCO Industries Inc. (newspaper)
SIFF: Stock Index Futures Fund
sig: signature
SIG: Southern Indiana Gas & Electric Co. (NYSE)
Sig CD: Signature Card
SIGI: Selective Insurance Group Inc. (NAS NMS)
SIGM: Sigma Designs Inc. (NAS NMS)
Sig Mis: Signature Missing
SIGN: Plasti-Line Inc. (NAS NMS)
Signet: Signet Banking Corp. (newspaper)
Sig Unk: Signature Unknown
SII: Smith International Inc. (NYSE)
   Strategic Impediments Initiative
   Structural Impediments Initiative
Sikes: Sikes Corp. (newspaper)
SILI: Siliconix Inc. (NAS NMS)
SILN: Silicon General Inc. (NAS NMS)
SILV: Silver King Mines Inc. (NAS NMS)
Silvrcst: Silvercrest Corp. (newspaper)
SIN: System Integrators Inc. (NYSE)
SIP: Securities Investor Protection Corporation
   Sharebuilder Investment Plan
SIPA: Securities Investor Protection Act

SIPC: Securities Investor Protection Corporation
SIR: Society of Industrial Realtors
   Staten Island Rapid Transit (railway)
SIRRI: Southern Industrial Railroad Incorporated
SIRT: Staten Island Rapid Transit
SISB: Sis Corp. (NAS NMS)
SISC: Stewart Information Services Corp. (NAS NMS)
SIVB: Silicon Valley Bancshares (California) (NAS NMS)
SIX: Motel 6 LP (NYSE)
SIZ: Sizeler Property Investors Inc. (NYSE)
Sizeler: Sizeler Property Investors Inc. (newspaper)
SIZZ: Sizzler Restaurants International Inc. (NAS NMS)
SJ: St. Johnsbury and Lamoille County (railroad)
SJerIn: South Jersey Industries Inc. (newspaper)
SJI: South Jersey Industries Inc. (NYSE)
SJ&LC: St. Johnsbury & Lake Champlain (railroad)
SJM: J. M. Smucker Co., The (NYSE)
SJR: San Juan Racing Assn. Inc. (NYSE)
SJS: Sunshine-Jr. Stores Inc. (ASE)
SJT: San Juan Basin Royalty Trust (NYSE)
SJTR: St. Joseph Terminal Railroad
SJuanB: San Juan Basin Royalty Trust (newspaper)
SJuanR: San Juan Racing Association Inc. (newspaper)
SJW: SJW Corp. (ASE) (newspaper)
sk: safekeeping
SK: Safety-Kleen Corp. (NYSE)
   Sikes Corp. (ASE)
SKAN: Skaneateles Savings Bank (New York) (NAS NMS)

SKB: SmithKline Beecham Corp.
(NYSE)
SKFB: S&K Famous Brands Inc.
(NAS NMS)
SKFRY: SKF AB (NAS NMS)
skg: safekeeping
SKII: S-K-I Ltd. (NAS NMS)
SKIP: Skippers Inc. (NAS NMS)
SKN: Skolnicks Inc. (ASE)
Skolnk: Skolniks Inc. (newspaper)
SKSL: Skaneateles Short Line (rail-
road)
SKY: Skyline Corp. (NYSE)
Skyline: Skyline Corp. (newspaper)
SKYW: SkyWest Inc. (NAS NMS)
S&L: Sale and Leaseback
Savings and Loan (Associa-
tion)
Sydney and Louisburg (rail-
road)
sl: sold (stocks)
SL: Savings and Loan (Association)
Skilled Labor
SL Industries Inc. (NYSE)
Southeast Airlines
Southern Lines (steamship)
SLA: Sales and Loan Association
State Liquor Authority
Slattery: Slattery Group Inc. (news-
paper)
S&LB: Sale and Lease-Back
SLB: Schlumberger Ltd (NYSE)
SLC: San Luis Central (railroad)
SLCR: Salem Carpet Mills Inc.
(NAS NMS)
sld: sold (stocks)
SLD: Sold (NYSE)
Straight Line Depreciation
SLE: Sara Lee Corp. (NYSE)
SLG: Seligman & Associates Inc.
(ASE)
SLGW: Salt Lake, Garfield and
Western (railway)
SLHC: Southlife Holding Co. (NAS
NMS)
SLIC: Savings and Loan Insurance
Corporation

SLIM: Stock Line Inventory Man-
agement
Store Labor and Inventory
Management
SL Ind: SL Industries Inc. (newspa-
per)
SLM: Student Loan Marketing
Assn. (NYSE)
SLMA: Student Loan Marketing
Association
SLMAJ: Student Loan Marketing
Association (Voting)
(NAS NMS)
SLO: Stop-Limit Order
Stop-Loss Order
SLP: Sun Energy Partners LP
(NYSE)
SLS: Sea-Land Service (steamship)
Selas Corporation of America
(ASE)
SLSF: St. Louis-San Francisco (rail-
road)
slsman: salesman
slsmen: salesmen
slsmgr: salesmanager
SLSW: St. Louis Southwestern
(railroad)
SLT: Salant Corp. (NYSE)
SLTG: Sterner Lighting Systems
Inc. (NAS NMS)
SLTM: SelecTerm Inc. (NAS NMS)
SLTX: Sales Tax
SLV: Silvercrest Corp. (ASE)
SLVS: San Luis Valley Southern
(railroad)
S&M: September and March (secu-
rities)
SM: Sales Manager
Second Mortgage
Secondary Market
Seller's Market
Smoky Mountain (railroad)
Southmark Corp. (NYSE)
Special Memorandum
St. Mary's (railroad)
SMA: San Manuel Arizona (rail-
road)

Special Miscellaneous Account

SMBX: Symbolics Inc. (NAS NMS)

SMC: A.O. Smith Corp. (ASE)

SMCH: Service Merchandise Company Inc. (NAS NMS)

SMCR: Summcorp (NAS NMS)

SMED: Shared Medical Systems Corp. (NAS NMS)

SMG: Science Management Corp. (ASE)

SMGS: Southeastern Michigan Gas Enterprises Inc. (NAS NMS)

SMH: Semtech Corp. (ASE)

SMI: Springs Industries Inc. (NYSE)

SMIN: Southern Mineral Corp. (NAS NMS)

SmithIn: Smith International Inc. (newspaper)

SmithKBeech: SmithKline Beecham Inc. (newspaper)

SMK: Sanmark-Stardust Inc. (ASE)

SML: States Marine Lines (steamship)

SMLB: Smith Laboratories Inc. (NAS NMS)

SMLS: SciMed Life Systems Inc. (NAS NMS)

SMMT: Summit Savings Assn. (Washington) (NAS NMS)

SMN: Seamen's Corp. (ASE)

SMNA: Samna Corp. (NAS NMS)

SMNI: Satellite Music Network Inc. (NAS NMS)

SMP: Standard Motor Products Inc. (NYSE)

SMPS: Simpson Industries Inc. (NAS NMS)

SMS: State Mutual Securities Trust (NYSE)

SMSC: Standard Microsystems Corp. (NAS NMS)

SMSI: Scientific Micro Systems Inc. (NAS NMS)

Smth: A.O. Smith Corp. (ASE)

Smuckr: J. M. Smucker Co., The (newspaper)

SMV: Santa Maria Valley (railroad)

SN: Sacramento Northern (railway)

SNA: Snap-on Tools Corp. (NYSE)

SnapOn: Snap-on Tools Corp. (newspaper)

SNAT: Southern National Corp. (NAS NMS)

SNCO: Sensor Control Corp. (NAS NMS)

SNDS: Sands Regent, The (NAS NMS)

SNDT: SunGard Data Systems Inc. (NAS NMS)

SNE: Sony Corp. (NYSE)

SNEL: Snelling & Snelling Inc. (NAS NMS)

SNETI: Southern New England Telecommunications Corp. (newspaper)

SNF: Spain Fund Inc. (NYSE)

SNFS: Second National Federal Savings Bank (Maryland) (NAS NMS)

SNG: Southern New England Telecommunications Corp. (NYSE)

SNI: Sun City Industries Inc. (ASE)

SNLF: S. N. L. Financial Corp. (NAS NMS)

SNLT: Sunlite Inc. (NAS NMS)

SNMD: Sunrise Medical Inc. (NAS NMS)

SNO: Polaris Industries Partners LP (ASE)

SNRU: Sunair Electronics Inc. (NAS NMS)

SNS: Sundstrand Corp. (NYSE)

SNSR: Sensormatic Electronics Corp. (NAS NMS)

SNST: Sonesta International Hotels Corp. (NAS NMS)

SNT: Sonat Inc. (NYSE)
SNY: Southern New York (railway)
Snyder: Snyder Oil Partners L. P.
    (newspaper)
SO: Sales Office
    Seller's Option
    Southern Airways
    Southern Co., The (NYSE)
    Special Order
    Standing Order
    Stock Option
SOBK: Southern Bankshares Inc.
    (NAS NMS)
SOCACHA: South Carolina Auto-
        mated Clearing
        House Association
SOCI: Society Corp. (NAS NMS)
SOCO: Standard Oil Company of
    California
SOCONY: Standard Oil Corporation
    of New York
SOCR: Scan-Optics Inc. (NAS NSM)
SOCS: Society for Savings Bancorp
    Inc., The (Connecticut)
    (NAS NMS)
SOD: Solitron Devices Inc. (NYSE)
SODA: A & W Brands Inc. (NAS
    NMS)
SOE: Short Of Exchange
SoestBk: Southeast Banking Corp.
    (newspaper)
SOFT: SofTech Inc. (NAS NMS)
SOH: Standard Oil Company (Ohio)
SOHIO: Standard Oil Company
    (Ohio)
SOI: Snyder Oil Partners LP
    (NYSE)
    Southern Indiana (railway)
SoIndGs: Southern Indiana Gas &
        Electric Co. (newspa-
        per)
SOL: Standard Of Living
    Statute Of Limitations
SOLI: Solitec Inc. (NAS NMS)
Solitron: Solitron Devices Inc.
    (newspaper)

SOLR: Applied Solar Energy Corp.
    (NAS NSM)
SOMB: Somerset Bancorp Inc.
    (NAS NSM)
SOME: State-O-Maine Inc. (NAS
    NMS)
SOMR: Somerset Group Inc., The
    (NAS NMS)
Sonat: Sonat Inc. (newspaper)
SONNF: Sonora Gold Corp. (NAS
    NMS)
SONO: Sonoco Products Co. (NAS
    NMS)
SonyCp: Sony Corp. (newspaper)
SOO: Soo Line Corp. (NYSE)
SooLin: Soo Line Corp. (newspaper)
SOON: Sooner Defense of Florida
    Inc. (NAS NMS)
SOP: Standard Operating Proce-
    dure
    Statement Of Policy
SOR: Source Capital Inc. (NYSE)
    Specific Operational (Operat-
    ing) Requirement
    Stockholder Of Record
SorgInc: Sorg Inc. (newspaper)
SOSA: Somerset Savings Bank
    (Massachusetts) (NAS
    NMS)
SOT: South Omaha Terminal (rail-
    way)
Sothby: Sotheby's Holdings Inc.
    (newspaper)
SOTR: SouthTrust Corp. (NAS NSM)
Soudwn: Southdown Inc. (newspa-
    per)
Soumrk: Southmark Corp. (newspa-
    per)
SoUnCo: Southern Union Co.
    (newspaper)
SourcC: Source Capital Inc. (news-
    paper)
SOUT: SouthernNet Inc. (NAS
    NSM)
SouthCo: Southern Co., The (news-
    paper)

SOV: Sovran Financial Corp. (NYSE)

Sovran: Sovran Financial Corp. (newspaper)

SOYD: Sum Of the Years' Digits (depreciation)

sp: special (stocks)

S&P: Standard and Poor's Corporation

SP: Aaron Spelling Productions Inc. (ASE)
Selling Price
Short Position
Signal Processor
Sine Prole (without issue)
Sole Proprietor
Spot Price
Stop Payment

SpA: Società per Azioni (joint stock company) (Italian)

SPA: Sparton Corp. (NYSE)

SPAI: Strategic Planning Associates Inc. (NAS NMS)

Spain: Spain Fund Inc. (newspaper)

SPAN: Span-America Medical Systems Inc. (NAS NMS)

SPAR: Spartan Motors Inc. (NAS NMS)

Spartc: Spartech Corp. (newspaper)

Sparton: Sparton Corp. (newspaper)

SPBC: St. Paul Bancorp Inc. (NAS NMS)

SPBD: Springboard Software Inc. (NAS NMS)

SPC: Security Pacific Corp. (NYSE)
Standard and Poor's Corporation

SPCC: Southern Pacific Communications Company

SpcEq: Specialty Equipment Companies Inc. (newspaper)

SPCM: Specialty Composite Corp. (NAS NMS)

SPCO: Software Publishing Corp. (NAS NMS)

SPD: Standard Products Co., The (NYSE)

SPDA: Single-Premium Deferred Annuity

SPE: Specialty Equipment Companies Inc. (NYSE)

SPEC: Spectrum Control Inc. (NAS NMS)

SpedOP: Speed-O-Print Business Machines Corp. (newspaper)

SPEK: Spec's Music Inc. (NAS NMS)

Spellng: Aaron Spelling Productions Inc. (newspaper)

SPF: Standard-Pacific Corp. (NYSE)

SPG: Sprague Technologies Inc. (NYSE)

SPGL: Spiegel Inc. (NAS NSM)

SPGT: Springfield Terminal (railroad)

SPI: SPI Pharmaceuticals Inc.

SPILF: S.P.I.-Suspension & Parts Industries Ltd. (NAS NMS)

SPI Ph: SPI Pharmaceuticals Inc. (newspaper)

SPIR: Spire Corp. (NAS NMS)

SPLI: Single-Premium Life Insurance

SPLK: Jones Spacelink Ltd. (NAS NMS)

SP OFF: Special Offering (stocks)

SPP: Scott Paper Co. (NYSE)
Stock Purchase Plan

SPQR: Small Profits, Quick Returns

SPR: Sterling Capital Corp. (ASE)

Sprage: Sprague Technologies Inc. (newspaper)

SPRH: Spearhead Industries Inc. (NAS NMS)

Spring: Springs Industries Inc. (newspaper)

SPRL: Societé de Personnes a Responsabilite Limitee (Belgian corporation)

SP&S: Spokane, Portland & Seattle (railroad)

SPS: Second Preferred Stock
Southwestern Public Service
Co. (NYSE)
SPSTec: SPS Technologies Inc.
(newspaper)
SPTR: SpecTran Corp. (NAS NMS)
SPW: SPX Corp. (NYSE)
Stock Purchase Warrant
SPX Cp: SPX Corp. (newspaper)
SQ: Norcanair (airline)
SQA: Sequa Corp. (NYSE)
SQAI: Square Industries Inc. (NAS
NMS)
SQD: Square D Co. (NYSE)
SQNT: Sequent Computer Systems
Inc. (NAS NMS)
SquarD: Square D Co. (newspaper)
sr: senior (stocks)
S&R: Safety and Reliability
SR: Sierra Railroad
Skagit River (railroad)
Southern Railway
Special Register
Summary Report
Surtax Rate
SRB: Scurry-Rainbow Oil Ltd.
(ASE)
SRC: Service Resources Corp.
(NYSE)
SRCE: 1st Source Corp. (NAS
NMS)
SRCO: Sealright Company Inc.
(NAS NMS)
SRDS: Standard Rate and Data
Service, Inc.
SRE: Stoneridge Resources Inc.
(NYSE)
SREA: Society of Real Estate Ap-
praisers
SREG: Standard Register Co., The
(NAS NMS)
SRFI: Super Rite Foods Inc. (NAS
NMS)
SRG: Sorg Inc. (ASE)
SRL: Sceptre Resources Ltd. (ASE)
SRN: Sabine River and Northern
(railroad)

SRP: Sierra Pacific Resources
(NYSE)
SRR: Stride Rite Corp., The
(NYSE)
SRRC: Sierra Railroad Company
Strasburg Rail Road Com-
pany
SRRCO: Sandersville Railroad
Company
SRSL: Sunrise Federal S&L Assn.
(Kentucky) (NAS NMS)
SRT: Spousal Remainder Trust
SRV: Service Corporation Interna-
tional (NYSE)
SRVI: Servico Inc. (NAS NMS)
S&S: Saratoga & Schuylerville
(railroad)
SS: Schwab Safe Company Inc.
(ASE)
Selling Short
Senior Securities
Seven Sisters (oil companies)
Short Sale
Shrinking Stocks
Social Security
Stock Split
Stopped Stock
SSAL: Shelton Savings Bank (Con-
necticut) (NAS NMS)
SSAX: Systems Software Associates
Inc. (NAS NMS)
SSBA: Seacoast Savings Bank
(New Hampshire) (NAS
NMS)
SSBB: Southington Savings Bank
(Connecticut) (NAS NMS)
SSC: Sunshine Mining Holding Co.
(NYSE)
SSDK: Savannah State Docks (rail-
road)
SSFT: Scientific Software-Inter-
comp Inc. (NAS NMS)
SSI: Supplemental Security Income
SSIA: Stockholder Systems Inc.
(NAS NMS)
SSLN: Security Savings Bank SLA
(New Jersey) (NAS NMS)

SSLVRR: Southern San Luis Valley Railroad
SSOA: Software Services of America Inc. (NAS NMS)
SSRY: Sand Springs Railway
SSS: MSA Realty Corp. (ASE)
SSSL: Sun State S&L Assn. (Arizona) (NAS NMS)
SSSS: Stewart & Stevenson Services Inc. (NAS NMS)
SST: Shelter Components Corp. (ASE)
SSW: St. Louis Southwestern (railway)
Sterling Software Inc. (ASE)
st: stamped (stocks)
stopped (stocks)
ST: Chicago, Milwaukee, St. Paul and Pacific Railroad Company
Sales Tax
SPS Technologies Inc. (NYSE)
Stock Transfer
STAAR: STAAR Surgical Co. (NAS NMS)
STAF: Staff Builders Inc. (NAS NMS)
STAG: Security Tag Systems Inc. (NAS NMS)
Stage: Stage II Apparel Corp. (newspaper)
StaMSe: State Mutual Securities Trust (newspaper)
stan: standard
standardization
Standex: Standex International Corp. (newspaper)
Stanhm: Stanhome Inc. (newspaper)
StanlWk: Stanley Works, The (newspaper)
STANVAC: Standard-Vacuum Oil Company (steamship)
STANY: Security Traders' Association of New York
STAQ: Security Trader's Automated Quotations

STAR: Stars To Go Inc. (NAS NMS)
Starrett: L. S. Starrett Co., The (newspaper)
StarrtH: Starrett Housing Corp. (newspaper)
stat: statistics
status
STB: Southeast Banking Corp. (NYSE)
Special Tax Bond
STBK: State Street Boston Corp. (NAS NMS)
StBPnt: Standard Brands Paint Co. (newspaper)
STBY: Stansbury Mining Corp. (NAS NMS)
STC: Short-Term Credit
Subject To Call
STCG: Short-Term Capital Gain
STCL: Short-Term Capital Loss
std: standard
STD: Banco Santander (NYSE)
Short-Term Debt
StdCom: Standard Commercial Corp. (newspaper)
StdPac: Standard-Pacific Corp. (newspaper)
StdPrd: Standard Products Co., The (newspaper)
StdShr: Standard Shares Inc. (newspaper)
ST&E: Stockton, Terminal & Eastern (railroad)
Steego: Steego Corp. (newspaper)
Stepan: Stepan Co. (newspaper)
SterlEl: Sterling Electronics Corp. (newspaper)
SterlSft: Sterling Software Inc. (newspaper)
StevnJ: J. P. Stevens & Company Inc. (newspaper)
stf: staff
StFBk: Standard Federal Bank (newspaper)
stg: sterling
STG: Steego Corp. (NYSE)

STGA: Saratoga Standardbreds Inc.
(NAS NMS)
STGM: Status Game Corp. (NAS
NMS)
STH: Stanhome Inc. (NYSE)
StHavn: Standard Havens Inc.
(newspaper)
STHF: Stanley Interiors Corp. (NAS
NMS)
STI: SunTrust Banks Inc. (NYSE)
Stifel: Stifel Financial Corp. (news-
paper)
STII: Stanford Telecommunications
Inc. (NAS NMS)
STJM: St. Jude Medical Inc. (NAS
NMS)
StJoLP: St. Joseph Light & Power
Co. (newspaper)
stk: stock
STK: Storage Technology Corp.
(NYSE)
Stk Ex: Stock Exchange
STKR: Stockekr & Yale Inc. (NAS
NMS)
STKY: Stokely USA Inc. (NAS NMS)
STL: Seatrain Lines (steamship)
Short-Term Loan
Sterling Bancorp (NYSE)
STLTF: Stolt Tankers & Terminals
SA (NAS NMS)
STM: Straddle The Market
Strategic Mortgage Invest-
ments Inc. (NYSE)
StMotr: Standard Motor Products
Inc. (newspaper)
stmt: statement
STN: J. P. Stevens & Company Inc.
(NYSE)
STO: Stone Container Corp.
(NYSE)
StoneC: Stone Container Corp.
(newspaper)
StoneW: Stone & Webster Inc.
(newspaper)
StonRs: Stoneridge Resources Inc.
(newspaper)

STOP: Stopped Bonds (NYSE)
StorEq: Storage Equities Inc.
(newspaper)
StorTch: Storage Technology Corp.
(newspaper)
STOT: Stotler Group Inc. (NAS
NMS)
stpd: stamped
stopped (stocks)
STPL: St. Paul Companies Inc., The
(NAS NMS)
STPT: Starpointe Savings Bank
(New Jersey) (NAS
NMS)
STR: Questar Corp. (NYSE)
STRA: Stratus Computer Inc. (NAS
NMS)
StratMt: Strategic Mortgage In-
vestments Inc. (news-
paper)
STRB: Strober Organization Inc.
(NAS NMS)
StridRt: Stride Rite Corp., The
(newspaper)
STRIP: Strip Bond
StrlBcp: Sterling Bancorp (newspa-
per)
StrlCap: Sterling Capital Corp.
(newspaper)
STRM: Strum Ruger & Company
Inc. (NAS NMS)
STRN: Sutron Corp. (NAS NMS)
STROP: Stock Ratio Optimizing
STRR: Star Technologies Inc. (NAS
NMS)
STRS: Sprouse-Reitz Stores Inc.
(NAS NMS)
STRT: Stewartstown (railroad)
StrutW: Struthers Wells Corp.
(newspaper)
STRW: Strawbridge & Clothier
(NAS NMS)
STRX: Syntrex Inc. (NAS NMS)
STRY: Stryker Corp. (NAS NMS)
STTG: Statesman Group Inc., The
(NAS NMS)

STTX: Steel Technologies Inc. (NAS NMS)

STUH: Stuart Hall Company Inc. (NAS NMS)

STUS: Stuarts Department Stores Inc. (NAS NMS)

StvGph: Stevens Graphics Corp. (newspaper)

STVI: STV Engineers Inc. (NAS NMS)

STW: Standard Commercial Corp. (NYSE)

STWB: Statewide Bancorp (NAS NMS)

SU: Seasonal Unemployment Secular Unemployment Structural Unemployed

SUA: Shipped Unassembled Summit Tax Exempt Bond Fund LP (ASE)

SuavSh: Suave Shoe Corp. (newspaper)

sub: subordination (stocks)

SUBB: Suburban Bancorp Inc. (NAS NMS)

SUBK: Suffolk Bancorp (NAS NMS)

SUBN: Summit Bancorporation, The (NAS NMS)

suby: subsidiary

SUC: Start-Up Costs

SUDS: Sudbury Holding Corp. (NAS NMS)

SUG: Southern Union Co. (NYSE)

SUHC: Summit Holding Corp. (NAS NMS)

SUMA: Summa Medical Corp. (NAS NMS)

SUMH: Summit Health Ltd. (NAS NMS)

SUMI: Sumitomo Bank of California (NAS NMS)

SumtTx: Summit Tax Exempt Bond Fund L.P. (newspaper)

SUN: Sun Company Inc. (NYSE)

SunbNu: Sunbelt Nursery Group Inc. (newspaper)

SunCo: Sun Company Inc. (newspaper)

SunCty: Sun City Industries Inc. (newspaper)

SUND: Sound Advice Inc. (NAS NMS)

SunDis: Sun Distributors L.P. (newspaper)

Sundstr: Sundstrand Corp. (newspaper)

SunEl: Sun Electric Corp. (newspaper)

SunEng: Sun Energy Partners L.P. (newspaper)

SUNF: Sunstar Foods Inc. (NAS NMS)

SUNI: Sun Coast Plastics Inc. (NAS NMS)

SunJr: Sunshine-Jr. Stores Inc. (newspaper)

SunMn: Sunshine Mining Holding Co. (newspaper)

SUNOCO: Sun Oil Company

SunTr: SunTrust Banks Inc. (newspaper)

SUNW: Sun Microsystems Inc. (NAS NMS)

SUP: Superior Industries International Inc. (ASE)

SUPE: Superior Electric Co., The (NAS NMS)

SupInd: Superior Industries International Inc. (newspaper)

SuprFd: Super Food Services Inc. (newspaper)

SuprSr: Superior Surgical Mfg. Co. Inc. (newspaper)

supv: supervisor

SupValu: Super Value Stores Inc. (newspaper)

supvr: supervisor

supvry: supervisory

SUPX: Supertex Inc. (NAS NMS)

sur: surplus

SUR: Saturn Airways
SCOR US Corp. (NYSE)
SURV: Survival Technology Inc.
(NAS NMS)
susp: suspended (stocks)
SUSQ: Susquehanna Bancshares
Inc. (NAS NMS)
SUW: Struthers Wells Corp. (ASE)
SVAN: Savannah Foods & Indus-
tries Inc. (NAS NMS)
SVB: Savin Corp. (NYSE)
SvcCp: Service Corporation Inter-
national (newspaper)
Svcmst: ServiceMaster L.P. (news-
paper)
SvcRes: Service Resources Corp.
(newspaper)
SVG: Stevens Graphics Corp. (ASE)
SVGI: Silicon Valley Group Inc.
(NAS NSM)
SVM: ServiceMaster LP (NYSE)
SVRL: Silvar-Lisco (NAS NMS)
SVRN: Sovereign Bancorp Inc.
(NAS NMS)
SVT: Servotronics Inc. (ASE)
SVU: Super Value Stores Inc.
(NYSE)
SW: Stone & Webster Inc. (NYSE)
SWA: Seaboard World Airlines
SWACHA: Southwestern Auto-
mated Clearing House
Association
SwAirl: Southwest Airlines Co.
(newspaper)
SWAR: Schwartz Brothers Inc.
(NAS NMS)
SWB: Southwest Bancorp (Califor-
nia) (ASE)
SwBcp: Southwest Bancorp (Cali-
fornia) (newspaper)
SwBell: Southwestern Bell Corp.
(newspaper)
SWCB: Sandwich Co-operative
Bank, The (Massachu-
setts) (NAS NMS)
SWD: Standard Shares Inc. (ASE)

SWEL: Southwestern Electric Ser-
vice Co. (NAS NMS)
SwEnr: Southwestern Energy Co.
(newspaper)
SwftEng: Swift Energy Co. (news-
paper)
SWHI: Sound Warehouse Inc. (NAS
NMS)
SWIFT: Society for Worldwide Inter-
bank Financial Telecom-
munications
SWIS: St. Ives Laboratories Corp.
(NAS NMS)
SWK: Stanley Works, The (NYSE)
SWL: Southwest Realty Ltd. (ASE)
SWMC: Stan West Mining Corp.
(NAS NMS)
SWN: Southwestern Energy Co.
(NYSE)
SWPA: Southwest National Corp.
(NAS NMS)
SwstRlt: Southwest Realty Ltd.
(newspaper)
SwtGas: Southwest Gas Corp.
(newspaper)
SwtPS: Southwestern Public Ser-
vice Co. (newspaper)
SWTR: Southern California Water
Co. (NAS NMS)
SWTX: Southwall Technologies Inc.
(NAS NMS)
SWV: Suave Shoe Corp. (NYSE)
SWVA: Steel of West Virginia Inc.
(NAS NMS)
SWWC: Southwest Water Co. (NAS
NMS)
SWX: Southwest Gas Corp. (NYSE)
SWZ: Helvetia Fund Inc., The
(NYSE)
SX: Skyways Coach (airline)
SXI: Standex International Corp.
(NYSE)
SY: Shelby Williams Industries Inc.
(NYSE)
SyblTc: Symbol Technologies Inc.
(newspaper)

SYGN: Synergen Inc. (NAS NMS)
sym: symbol
SYM: Syms Corp. (NYSE)
SYMB: Symbion Inc. (NAS NMS)
SYMK: Sym-Tek Systems Inc. (NAS NMS)
SymsCp: Syms Corp. (newspaper)
SYN: Syntex Corp. (NYSE)
Synaloy: Synalloy Corp. (newspaper)
SYNEP: Syntech International Inc. (NAS NMS)
SYNR: Synercom Technology Inc. (NAS NMS)
SYNT: Syntro Corp. (NAS NMS)
Syntex: Syntex Corp. (newspaper)
SYO: Synalloy Corp. (ASE)
SYRA: Syracuse Supply Co. (NAS NMS)

sys: system
SYS: ISI Systems Inc. (ASE)
Sysco: Sysco Corp. (newspaper)
SYSM: System Industries Inc. (NAS NMS)
syst: system
SYST: Systematics Inc. (NAS NMS)
SystEn: Systems Engineering & Manufacturing Corp. (newspaper)
SystInt: System Integrators Inc. (newspaper)
SYX: Bayou Steel Corporation of La Place (ASE)
SYY: Sysco Corp. (NYSE)
SZF: Sierra Capital Realty Trust VI (ASE)
SZG: Sierra Capital Realty Trust VII (ASE)

t: transaction
T: American Telephone and Telegraph Co. (NYSE)
Toronto Stock Exchange (in newspaper statements)
Treasury (as in T-bill, T-bond)
T&A: Taken and Accepted
TA: Tangible Asset
Tax Abatement
Tax Amortization
Texas Air Corporation (airline)
Transamerica Corp. (NYSE)
TAB: Tandy Brands Inc. (ASE)
Tax Anticipation Bill
TabPrd: Tab Products Co. (newspaper)
TABS: Total Automatic Banking System
TAC: Tandycrafts Inc. (NYSE)
Texas Air Corporation (airline)
TacBt: Tacoma Boatbuilding Co. (newspaper)
TACHA: Tennessee Automated Clearing House Association
TA&G: Tennessee, Alabama, and Georgia (railroad)
TAG: Transfer Agent
TAI: Transamerica Income Shares Inc. (NYSE)
Taiwan: Taiwan Fund Inc., The (newspaper)
TAL: Talley Industries Inc. (NYSE)
TALISMAN: Transfer Accounting and Lodgement for Investors, Stock Management for Jobbers (London Stock Exchange) (UK)

Talley: Talley Industries Inc. (newspaper)
Tambd: Tambrands Inc. (newspaper)
TAN: Tandy Corp. (NYSE)
Tax-Anticipation Note
TandB: Tandy Brands Inc. (newspaper)
Tandm: Tandem Computers Inc. (newspaper)
Tandy: Tandy Corp. (newspaper)
TANT: Tennant Co. (NAS NMS)
TASD: Terminal Railway Alabama State Docks
Tasty: Tasty Baking Co. (newspaper)
TAT: Transatlantic Telephone Cable
TATE: Ashton-Tate (NAS NMS)
TAVI: Thorn Apple Valley Inc. (NAS NMS)
TA&W: Toledo, Angola & Western (railroad)
tax: taxation
taxes
TB: Treasury Bonds (U.S.)
Twin Branch (railroad)
TBC: Tasty Baking Co. (ASE)
TBCC: TBC Corp. (NAS NMS)
T-BILL: Treasury Bill
TBL: Timberland Co., The (ASE)
TBO: Tacoma Boatbuilding Co. (NYSE)
T-BOND: Treasury Bond
TBP: Tab Products Co. (ASE)
TBR: Treasury Bill Rate
TBS: Turner Broadcasting System Inc. (ASE)
TC: Tax Certificate
Tax Court

Telex Corp., The (NYSE)
Tennessee Central (railroad)
Treasury Certificate
Trust Company
TCA: Trans-Canada Airlines
Trans-Caribbean Airways
TCAT: TCA Cable TV Inc. (NAS NMS)
TCBC: Trustcompany Bancorporation, The (New Jersey) (NAS NMS)
TCBY: TCBY Enterprises Inc. (NAS NMS)
TCC: TeleConcepts Corp. (ASE)
TCCO: Technical Communications Corp. (NAS NMS)
TCFC: TCF Financial Corp. (Minnesota) (NAS NMS)
TC&GB: Tucson, Cornella & Gila Bend (railroad)
TCGN: Tecogen Inc. (NAS NMS)
TchOpL: Tech/Ops Landauer Inc. (newspaper)
TchOpS: Tech-Ops Sevcon Inc. (newspaper)
TchSym: Tech-Sym Corp. (newspaper)
TCII: Technology for Communications International Inc. (NAS NMS)
TCIS: TELEX Computer Inquiry Service
TCK: TEC Inc. (ASE)
TCL: Transatlantic Carriers Limited (steamship)
Transcon Inc. (NYSE)
TCOM: Tele-Communications Inc. (NAS NMS)
TCOR: Tandon Corp. (NAS NMS)
TCR: Texas City Refining (steamship)
Trammell Crow Real Estate Investors (NYSE)
TCRD: Telecredit Inc. (NAS NMS)
TCSFY: Thomson-CSF (NAS NMS)

TCT: Texas City Terminal (railway)
Tricentrol PLC (NYSE)
TCTC: Tompkins County Trust Co. (New York) (NAS NMS)
TCW: TCW Convertible Securities Fund Inc. (newspaper)
TD: Time Deposit
Total Debt
Trade Deficit
Treasury Department
Trust Deed
T/D: Time Deposit
TDA: Tax Deferred Annuity
Tax Deposit Account
TDAT: Teradata Corp. (NAS NMS)
TDD: Three D Departments Inc. (ASE)
TDI: Twin Disc Inc. (NYSE)
TDK: TDK Corp. (NYSE) (newspaper)
TDM: Tandem Computers Inc. (NYSE)
TDOA: Time Deposit Open Account
TDRLF: Tudor Corporation Ltd. (NAS NMS)
TDS: Telephone & Data Systems Inc. (ASE)
TDW: Tidewater Inc. (NYSE)
TDY: Teledyne Inc. (NYSE)
TE: Tax Exemption
TECO Energy Inc. (NYSE)
Total Earnings
Team: Team Inc. (newspaper)
TEB: Tax-Exempt Bond
TEC: TEC Inc. (newspaper)
TECD: Tech Data Corp. (NAS NMS)
Technd: Technodyne Inc. (newspaper)
TECH REPT: Technical Report
TechTp: Technical Tape Inc. (newspaper)
Techtrl: Technitrol Inc. (newspaper)
TECN: Technalysis Corp. (NAS NMS)

TECO: TECO Energy Inc. (newspaper)

TECU: Tecumseh Products Co. (NAS NMS)

TED: Tax-Exempt Dividend Tenders Electronic Daily

TEE: Trans-Europe-Express

TEF: Companie Telefonica Nacional de Espana SA (NYSE)

TEFRA: Tax Equity and Fiscal Responsibility Act

TejnR: Tejon Ranch Co. (newspaper)

TEK: Tektronix Inc. (NYSE)

Tektrnx: Tektronix Inc. (newspaper)

TEL: TeleCom. Corp. (NYSE)

TELC: Telco Systems Inc. (NAS NMS)

Telcom: TeleCom Corp. (newspaper)

TelDta: Telephone & Data Systems Inc. (newspaper)

Teldyn: Teledyne Inc. (newspaper)

TELE: TPI Enterprises Inc. (NAS NMS)

Telecon: TeleConcepts Corp. (newspaper)

Telef: Companie Telefonica Nacional de Espana S.A. (newspaper)

Teleflex: Teleflex Inc. (newspaper)

Telesph: Telesphere International Inc. (newspaper)

Telex: Telex Corp., The (newspaper)

TELNET: Telecommunications Network

TELQ: TeleQuest Inc. (NAS NMS)

Telrte: Telerate Inc. (newspaper)

TELV: TeleVideo Systems Inc. (NAS NMS)

TEMC: Temco Home Health Care Products Inc. (NAS NMS)

Temp Ctfs: Temporary Certificates

Templ: Temple-Inland Inc. (newspaper)

TEMPO: TEMPO Enterprises Inc. (newspaper)

TENN: Tennessee Railroad

Tennco: Tenneco Inc. (newspaper)

Tenney: Tenney Engineering Inc. (newspaper)

TEP: Tucson Electric Power Co. (NYSE)

TEQ: Turner Equity Investors Inc. (ASE)

TER: Teradyne Inc. (NYSE)

Terdyn: Teradyne Inc. (newspaper)

TERM: Terminal Data Corp. (NAS NMS)

Tesoro: Tesoro Petroleum Corp. (newspaper)

TEV: Thermo Environmental Corp. (ASE)

TEVIY: Teva Pharmaceutical Industries Inc. (NAS NMS)

tex: telex

TEX: Texas Air Corp. (ASE)

Texaco: Texaco Inc. (newspaper)

TEXACO: Texas Company, The (steamship)

TexAir: Texas Air Corp. (newspaper)

TEXARKANA: Texas, Arkansas, Louisiana (railroad)

TEXAS AIR: Texas Air Corporation (airline)

TEXC: Texas Central (railroad)

TexCd: Texaco Canada Inc. (newspaper)

Texfi: Texfi Industries Inc. (newspaper)

TexInd: Texas Industries Inc. (newspaper)

Textrn: Textron Inc. (newspaper)

TexUtil: Texas Utilities Co. (newspaper)

TF: Tallulah Falls (railroad)

TFC: TransCapital Financial Corp. (NYSE)

TFLX: Termiflex Corp. (NAS NMS)

TFSB: Federal Savings Bank, The (Connecticut) (NAS NMS)

TFTY: Thrifty Rent-A-Car System Inc. (NAS NMS)

TFX: Teleflex Inc. (ASE)

tg: telegraph

TG: Tangible Goods

TGCO: Transidyne General Corp. (NAS NMS)

TGI: TGI Friday's Inc. (NYSE)

TGIF: TGI Friday's Inc. (newspaper)

TGL: Triton Group Ltd. (NYSE)

TGT: Tenneco Inc. (NYSE)

TH: Tax Haven
   Thorvald Hansen (steamship)

Thack: Thackey Corp. (newspaper)

Thai: Thai Fund (newspaper)

TH&B: Toronto, Hamilton and Buffalo (railroad)

THC: Hydraulic Co., The (NYSE)

THCO: Hammond Co. (NAS NMS)

THFI: Plymouth Five Cents Savings Bank (Massachusetts) (NAS NMS)

THFR: Thetford Corp. (NAS NMS)

THI: Thermo Instrument Systems Inc. (ASE)

THK: Thackey Corp. (NYSE)

ThmBet: Thomas & Betts Corp. (newspaper)

ThmMed: Thompson Medical Company Inc. (newspaper)

THO: Thor Industries Inc. (NYSE)

ThomIn: Thomas Industries Inc. (newspaper)

ThorEn: Thor Energy Resources Inc. (newspaper)

ThorInd: Thor Industries Inc. (newspaper)

Thortec: Thortec International Inc. (newspaper)

THP: Take-Home Pay
   Triangle Home Products Inc. (ASE)

THPR: Thermal Profiles Inc. (NAS NMS)

THR: Thor Energy Resources Inc. (ASE)

ThrD: Three D Departments Inc. (newspaper)

ThrIns: Thermo Instrument Systems Inc. (newspaper)

Thrmd: Thermedics Inc. (newspaper)

ThrmE: Thermo Environmental Corp. (newspaper)

ThrmEl: Thermo Electron Corp. (newspaper)

ThrmP: Thermo Process Systems Inc. (newspaper)

THT: Thortec International Inc. (ASE)

TI: Taxable Income

TIA: Tax Institute of America
   Trans-International Airlines

TIC: Travelers Corp., The (NYSE)

Tidwtr: Tidewater Inc. (newspaper)

TIE: TIE/communications Inc. (newspaper)

TIER: Tierco Group Inc., The (NAS NMS)

TIF: Tiffany & Co. (NYSE)

Tiffny: Tiffany & Co. (newspaper)

TIFR: Total Investment For Return

TIGER: Treasury Investment Growth Receipt

TIGR: Treasury Investment Growth Receipt

TII: Thomas Industries Inc. (NYSE)
   TII Industries Inc. (newspaper)

TILA: Truth-In-Lending Act

TIM: Templeton Global Income Fund (NYSE)

TimeWarner: Time Warner Inc. (newspaper)

Timken: Timken Co., The (newspaper)

TIMS: Trust for Investments in Mortgages

TIN: Taxpayer Identification Number
   Temple-Inland Inc. (NYSE)

TIP: Tax-based Income Policy
TIS: TIS Mortgage Investment Co. (NYSE) (newspaper)
Titan: Titan Corp. (newspaper)
TJCO: Trus Joist Corp. (NAS NMS)
TJX: TJX Companies Inc., The (NYSE) (newspaper)
TKA: Tonka Corp. (NYSE)
TKAI: Teknowledge Inc. (NAS NMS)
TKIOY: Tokio Marine & Fire Insurance Company Ltd. (NAS NMS)
TKLC: Tekelec (NAS NMS)
TKR: Timken Co., The (NYSE)
T&L: Thrift and Loan
TL: Term Loan
Time Loan
Total Loss
Trade Last
Trade List
Trading Limit
TLA: Truth-In-Lending Act
TLAB: Tellabs Inc. (NAS NMS)
TLAM: Tony Lama Company Inc. (NAS NMS)
TLCR: Telecrafter Corp. (NAS NMS)
TLHT: Total Health Systems Inc. (NAS NMS)
TLI: Term Life Insurance
Transferable Loan Instrument
TLII: Trans Leasing International Inc. (NAS NMS)
TLMD: Telemundo Group Inc. (NAS NMS)
TLMN: Talman Home Federal S&L Assn. of Illinois (NAS NMS)
TLO: Total Loss Only
TLOS: Telos Corp. (NAS NMS)
TLR: Telerate Inc. (NYSE)
TLX: Trans-Lux Corp. (ASE)
TLXN: Telxon Corp. (NAS NMS)
tm: trademark
TM: Texas Mexican (railroad)
Third Market

Third Mortgage
Thompson Medical Company Inc. (NYSE)
Tight Money
Top Management
TMA: Thomson McKinnon Asset Management LP (NYSE)
TMAM: Thomson McKinnon Asset Management L.P. (newspaper)
TMAX: Telematrics International Inc. (NAS NMS)
TMB: Tambrands Inc. (NYSE)
TmbCo: Timberland Co., The (newspaper)
TMBR: Tom Brown Inc. (NAS NMS)
TMBS: Timberline Software Corp. (NAS NMS)
TMC: Times Mirror Co., The (NYSE)
Total Manufacturing Cost
TMCI: TIM Communications Inc. (NAS NMS)
TMD: Thermedics Inc. (ASE)
TMED: Trimedyne Inc. (NAS NMS)
TMG: Musicland Group Inc., The (NYSE)
TMI: Team Inc. (ASE)
TMK: Torchmark Corp. (NYSE)
TmMir: Times Mirror Co., The (newspaper)
TMO: Thermo Electron Corp. (NYSE)
TmpGI: Templeton Global Income Fund (newspaper)
TmplE: Templeton Emerging Markets Fund Inc. (newspaper)
TMRA: Technical and Miscellaneous Revenue Act
TMS: Treasury Market Securities
TMTX: Temtex Industries Inc. (NAS NMS)
TN: Texas and Northern (railway)
Transferable Notice
Treasury Notes (U.S.)

TNB: Thomas & Betts Corp. (NYSE)

T&NC: Tennessee & North Carolina (railroad)

TNC: Town & Country Jewelry Manufacturing Corp. (ASE)

TND: Technodyne Inc. (ASE)

TNDS: TS Industries Inc. (NAS NMS)

Tndycft: Tandycrafts Inc. (newspaper)

TNEL: Nelson Thomas Inc. (NAS NMS)

TNI: Transico Industries Inc. (ASE)

TNII: Telecommunications Network Inc. (NAS NMS)

TNL: Technitrol Inc. (ASE)

TNLS: Trans-National Leasing Inc. (NAS NMS)

TNM: Texas-New Mexico (railroad)

T&NO: Texas and New Orleans (railroad)

T-NOTE: Treasury Note

TNP: TNP Enterprises Inc. (NYSE) (newspaper)

TNV: Trinova Corp. (NYSE)

TNY: Tenney Engineering Inc. (ASE)

TNZ: Tranzonic Companies, The (ASE)

to: turnover

TO: Telephone Order
Treasury Obligations

TOBK: Tolland Bank FSB (Connecticut) (NAS NMS)

TOC: Pennsylvania New York Central Transportation Company
Tech-Ops Sevcon Inc. (ASE)

TOD: Time Of Delivery
Todd Shipyards Corp. (NYSE)

TODD: Todd-AO Corp. (NAS NMS)

TodSh: Todd Shipyards Corp. (newspaper)

TO&E: Texas, Oklahoma & Eastern (railroad)

TOE: Tons of Oil Equivalent

TOF: Tofutti Brands Inc. (ASE)

Tofutti: Tofutti Brands Inc. (newspaper)

TOK: Tokheim Corp. (NYSE)

Tokhem: Tokheim Corp. (newspaper)

TOL: Toll Brothers Inc. (NYSE)

TollBr: Toll Brothers Inc. (newspaper)

TONE: One Bancorp, The (NAS NMS)

Tonka: Tonka Corp. (newspaper)

tonn: tonnage

TOOL: Easco Hand Tools Inc. (NAS NMS)

TOOT: 202 Data System Inc. (NAS NMS)

TootRl: Tootsie Roll Industries Inc. (newspaper)

TOPP: Topps Company Inc. (NAS NMS)

Toro: Toro Co., The (newspaper)

Tortel: Torotel Inc. (newspaper)

TOS: Tosco Corp. (NYSE)

Tosco: Tosco Corp. (newspaper)

TOT: Terms Of Trade

TOTE: United Tote Inc. (NAS NMS)

TotlPt: Total Petroleum (North America) Ltd. (newspaper)

TOV: Tech/Ops Landauer Inc. (ASE)
Tooele Valley (railway)

TOY: Toys "R" Us Inc. (NYSE)

ToyRU: Toys "R" Us Inc. (newspaper)

T&P: Texas and Pacific (railroad)

TP: Tangible Property

TPA Am: TPA of America Inc. (newspaper)

TPD: Tons Per Day

TPH: Tons Per Hour

TPI: Tax and Prices Index
Thermo Process Systems Inc. (ASE)

TPL: Texas Pacific Land Trust (NYSE)

TPMP: Texas-Pacific-Missiouri Pacific Terminal Railroad of New Orleans

TPN: Total Petroleum (North America) Ltd. (ASE)

TPO: TEMPO Enterprises Inc. (ASE)

TPS: TPA of America Inc. (ASE)
Trigger-Price System

TPT: Third-Party Transaction
Trenton-Princeton Traction Company (railroad)

TP&W: Toledo, Peoria & Western (railroad)

TQ: Trans Central Airlines

tr: trust

TR: Tax Rate
Tax Roll
Technical Report
Tons Registered
Tootsie Roll Industries Inc. (NYSE)
Trade Representative
Treasury Receipt
Trust Receipt

tra: transfer

TRA: Tax Reform Act

TRACE: Total Risk Assessing Cost Estimate

TRAD: Traditional Industries Inc. (NAS NMS)

Tramel: Trammell Crow Real Estate Investors (newspaper)

tran: transaction

TranEx: Transco Exploration Partners Ltd. (newspaper)

TranInc: Transamerica Income Shares Inc. (newspaper)

Transcn: Transcon Inc. (newspaper)

Transco: Transco Energy Co. (newspaper)

Transm: Transamerica Corp. (newspaper)

TRASOP: Tax Reduction Act Stock Ownership Plan

Travler: Travelers Corp., The (newspaper)

TRB: Tribune Co. (NYSE)

TRC: Tejon Ranch Co. (ASE)
TRC Companies Inc. (newspaper)
Trona Railway Company

Trchmk: Torchmark Corp. (newspaper)

Tr Co: Trust Company

TRCO: Trico Products Corp. (NAS NMS)

trdg: trading

treas: treasurer
treasury

TREN: Trenwick Group Inc. (NAS NMS)

TREX: Intrex Financial Services Inc. (NAS NMS)

trf: transfer

TRFI: Trans Financial Bancorp Inc. (NAS NMS)

TRG: Triangle Corp., The (ASE)

TRGL: Toreador Royalty Corp. (NAS NMS)

TRIA: Triangle Industries Inc. (NAS NMS)

TriaCp: Triangle Corp., The (newspaper)

Tribun: Tribune Co. (newspaper)

Tricntr: Tricentrol PLC (newspaper)

TriCom: Tri-Continental Corp. (newspaper)

Tridex: Tridex Corp. (newspaper)

TriHme: Triangle Home Products Inc. (newspaper)

TRIN: Trading Index (short term)
Trans-Industries Inc. (NAS NMS)

Trinov: Trinova Corp. (newspaper)

Trinty: Trinity Industries Inc. (newspaper)

TRI-SACH: Tri-State Automated Clearing House Association

TriSM: Tri-State Motor Transit Company of Delaware (newspaper)

TritEng: Triton Energy Corp. (newspaper)

TritnG: Triton Group Ltd. (newspaper)

TRKA: Trak Auto Corp. (NAS NMS)

TRLS: Thousand Trails Inc. (NAS NMS)

TRN: Trinity Industries Inc. (NYSE)

TrnCda: TransCanada PipeLines Ltd. (newspaper)

TrnEq: Turner Equity Investors Inc. (newspaper)

TRNS: Transmation Inc. (NAS NMS)

Trnscap: TransCapital Financial Corp. (newspaper)

Trnsco: Transico Industries Inc. (newspaper)

TrnsLx: Trans-Lux Corp. (newspaper)

TrnsTec: TransTechnology Corp. (newspaper)

TRNT: TransNet Corp. (NAS NMS)

Trnzn: Tranzonic Companies, The (newspaper)

TRON: Trion Inc. (NAS NMS)

TROW: T. Rowe Price Associates Inc. (NAS NMS)

TRP: TransCanada PipeLines Ltd. (NYSE)

TRR: Trade Regulation Rule
TRC Companies Inc. (ASE)

TRRA: Terminal Railroad Association of St. Louis

TRS: Trust America Service Corp. (ASE)

TRSA: Tax Reduction and Simplification Act

TRSC: Triad Systems Corp. (NAS NMS)

TRST: Trustco Bank Corp. (New York) (NAS NMS)

TRTI: Transtech Industries Inc. (NAS NMS)

TRUK: Builders Transport Inc. (NAS NMS)

TRUMP: Trump Airlines

TRVMF: TRV Minerals Corp. (NAS NMS)

TRW: TRW Inc. (NYSE) (newspaper)

trx: transaction

TS: Alhoa Airlines
Tasmanian Steamers (steamship)
Tax Shelter
Tax Straddle
Tidewater Southern (railroad)
Treasury Stock
Trumann Southern (railroad)

TSA: Tax Sheltered Annuity

TS-E: Texas South-Eastern (railroad)

TSE: Tokyo Stock Exchange
Toronto Stock Exchange

TSIC: Transducer Systems Inc. (NAS NMS)

TSII: TSI Inc. (NAS NMS)

tsk: task

TSK: Computer Task Group Inc. (NYSE)

TSM: Tri-State Motor Transit Company of Delaware (ASE)

TSO: Technical Standards Orders
Tesoro Petroleum Corp. (NYSE)

TSP: Telesphere International Inc. (ASE)

TSQ: T2 Medical Inc. (ASE)

TSR: Technical Summary Report

TSRI: TSR Inc. (NAS NMS)

TSS: Trade Support System

TstAm: Trust America Service Corp. (newspaper)

TSY: Tech-Sym Corp. (NYSE)

TSYS: Total System Services Inc. (NAS NMS)

tt: teletype

TT: Teller Terminal
Terms of Trade
Texas International Airlines
Toledo Terminal (railroad)
TransTechnology Corp. (NYSE)

TTA: Total Tangible Assets
Trans-Texas Airways

TTC: Toro Co., The (NYSE)

TTCO: Trustcorp Inc. (NAS NMS)

TTE: Total Tax Expenditures

ttees: trustees

TTF: Thai Fund (NYSE)

TTI: Technical Tape Inc. (ASE)

TT & L: Treasury Tax & Loan account

TTL: Torotel Inc. (ASE)

TTN: Titan Corp. (NYSE)

TTOI: TEMPEST Technologies Inc. (NAS NMS)

TTOR: Transtector Systems Inc. (NAS NMS)

TTOY: Tyco Toys Inc. (NAS NMS)

TTP: Total Taxable Pay

TTSL: Treasury Tax and Loan Account

TTT: Transamerica Trailer Transport (steamship)

ttw: teletypewriter

T2 Md: T2 Medical Inc. (newspaper)

TTX: Tultex Corp. (NYSE)

tty: teletype
teletypewriter

TTY: Telephone-Teletypewriter

TU: Trading Unit

TubMex: Tubos de Acero de Mexico S.A. (newspaper)

TUC: Transportation, Utilities, Communications industries

TUCK: Tucker Drilling Co. (NAS NMS)

TUES: Tuesday Morning Inc. (NAS NMS)

TUG: Maritrans Partners LP (NYSE)

TUHC: Tucker Holding Co. (NAS NMS)

Tultex: Tultex Corp. (newspaper)

TUR: Turner Corp., The (ASE)

TurnB: Turner Broadcasting System Inc. (newspaper)

TurnrC: Turner Corp., The (newspaper)

TUSC: Tuscarora Plastics Inc. (NAS NMS)

tv: television

TV: Trans International Airlines

TVA: Tax on Value Added
Tennessee Valley Authority

TVG: Tavares and Gulf (railroad)

TVIV: Taco Viva Inc. (NAS NMS)

TVLA: Taco Villa Inc. (NAS NMS)

TVRY: Tooele Valley Railway

TVXG: TVX Broadcast Group Inc. (NAS NMS)

TW: Tax Writeoff
TWA (Trans World Airlines)

TWA: Trans World Airlines Inc. (NYSE) (newspaper)

TWBC: Transworld Bancorp (NAS NMS)

TwCty: Town & Country Jewelry Mfg. Corp. (newspaper)

TWEN: 20th Century Industries Inc. (NAS NMS)

TWIMC: To Whom It May Concern

TwinDs: Twin Disc Inc. (newspaper)

TWMC: Trans World Music Corp. (NAS NMS)

TWN: Taiwan Fund Inc., The (ASE)

TWP: Two Pesos Inc. (ASE)

TwPeso: Two Pesos Inc. (newspaper)

TWST: Twistee Treat Corp. (NAS NMS)

TWX: Time Warner Inc. (NYSE)

TX: Texaco Inc. (NYSE)

TXA: Texas American Bancshares Inc. (NYSE)

TxABc: Texas American Bancshares Inc. (newspaper)

TXC: Texaco Canada Inc. (ASE)

TXF: Texfi Industries Inc. (NYSE)

TXI: Texas Industries Inc. (NYSE)

TxInst: Texas Instruments Inc. (newspaper)

TXN: Texas Instruments Inc. (NYSE)

TxPac: Texas Pacific Land Trust (newspaper)

TXT: Textron Inc. (NYSE)

TXU: Texas Utilities Co. (NYSE)

TY: Tri-Continental Corp. (NYSE)

TYC: Tyco Laboratories Inc. (NYSE)

TycoL: Tyco Laboratories Inc. (newspaper)

TYGR: Tigera Group Inc. (NAS NMS)

TYL: Tyler Corp. (NYSE)

Tyler: Tyler Corp. (newspaper)

TYLN: Tylan Corp. (NAS NMS)

typ: type
    typical
    typically

TYSN: Tyson Foods Inc. (NAS NMS)

TZ: Transair Limited (airline)

u: unit
update
U: The intraday high is a new high for the last 52 weeks (in newspaper reports of transations)
USAir Group Inc. (NYSE)
UA: Underwriting Account
UA: United Airlines
Units of Account
UAC: Unicorp American Corp. (ASE)
UACI: United Artists Communications Inc. (NAS NMS)
UAL: UAL Corp. (NYSE)
UAL Cp: UAL Corp. (newspaper)
UAM: United Asset Management Corp. (NYSE) (newspaper)
UB: United Brands Co. (NYSE)
Unpaid Balance
UBCP: Unibancorp Inc. (NAS NMS)
UBIT: Unrelated Business Income Tax
UBKR: United Bankers Inc. (NAS NMS)
UBKS: United Banks of Colorado Inc. (NAS NMS)
UBM: Unit Bill of Material
UBMT: United Savings Bank FA (Montana) (NAS NMS)
UBN: University Bank NA (ASE)
UBOT: Unfavorable Balance Of Trade
UBSC: United Building Services Corporation of Delaware (NAS NMS)
UBSI: United Bankshares Inc. (Virginia) (NAS NMS)

UC: Under Construction
Unfair Competition
Unit Cost
UCAR: United Carolina Bancshares Corp. (NAS NMS)
UCarb: Union Carbide Corp. (newspaper)
UCC: Uniform Commercial Code
Union Camp Corp. (NYSE)
UCCC: Uniform Consumer Credit Code
UCIT: United Cities Gas Co. (NAS NMS)
UCITS: Collective Instrument in Transferable Securities (EC)
UCL: Unocal Corp. (NYSE)
UCmp: Union Camp Corp. (newspaper)
UCO: Union Corp., The (NYSE)
UCOA: United Coasts Corp. (NAS NMS)
UCOP: Unit Cost Of Production
UCR: Utah Coal Route (railway)
UCU: UtiliCorp United Inc. (NYSE)
UCV: Unimproved Capital Value
UD: Brower Flight Service (airline)
Unsecured Debt
UDC: UDC-Universal Development LP (NYSE) (newspaper)
UDP: Uniform Delivered Price
UDRT: United Dominion Realty Trust Inc. (NAS NMS)
UE: Trans Magic Airlines
Utility Expenditures
UEL: Upper Earnings Limit
UEP: Union Electric Co. (NYSE)
UESS: United Education & Software (NAS NMS)

UFC: Uniform Freight Classification
United Fruit Company (railroad)
Universal Foods Corp. (NYSE)

UFCS: United Fire & Casualty Co. (NAS NMS)

UFD: United Foods Inc. (ASE)

UFF: UnionFed Financial Corp. (NYSE)

UFGI: United Financial Group Inc. (NAS NMS)

UFN: UniCARE Financial Corp. (ASE)

UFood: United Foods Inc. (newspaper)

UFS: Universal Financial System

UFSB: University Savings Bank (Washington) (NAS NMS)

UFST: Unifast Industries Inc. (NAS NMS)

UFURF: Universal Furniture Ltd. (NAS NMS)

UGI: UGI Corp. (NYSE) (newspaper)

UGMA: Uniform Gift to Minors Act

UH: U. S. Home Corp. (NYSE)

UHC: Ultimate Holding Company

UHCO: Universal Holding Corp. (NAS NMS)

UHLI: United Home Life Insurance Co. (NAS NSM)

UHSI: Universal Health Services Inc. (NAS NMS)

UHT: Universal Health Realty Income Trust (NYSE)

UI: Star Airlines
Unearned Income
United Inns Inc. (NYSE)

UIC: United Industrial Corp. (NYSE)

UICI: United Insurance Companies Inc. (NAS NMS)

UIF: USLIFE Income Fund Inc. (NYSE)

UIL: United Illuminating Co., The (NYSE)

UIllum: United Illuminating Co., The (newspaper)

UIO: Units In Operation

UIS: Unisys Corp. (NYSE)

UIT: Unified Income Tax
Unit Investment Trust

UJB: United Jersey Banks (NYSE)

UJerBk: United Jersey Banks (newspaper)

UJF: Unsatisfied Judgment Fund

UK: United Carbide Corp. (NYSE)
United Kingdom

UKing: United Kingdom Fund Inc., The (newspaper)

UKM: United Kingdom Fund Inc., The (NYSE)

UL: Underwriters Laboratories, Inc.
Unilever PLC (NYSE)
Upper Limit

ULCC: Ultra-Large Crude Carrier

ULI: Underwriters Laboratories, Inc.

ULS: Unsecured Loan Stock

ULSI: Ultra Large-Scale Integration

ULT: Ultimate Corp., The (NYSE)

ULTB: Ultra Bancorporation (NAS NMS)

Ultmte: Ultimate Corp., The (newspaper)

UM: Morris Air Transport (airline)
United Medical Corp. (ASE)

UMACHA: Upper Midwest Automated Clearing House Association

UMatch: Universal Matchbox Group Ltd. (newspaper)

UMB: Universal Medical Buildings LP (NYSE)

UMED: Unimed Inc. (NAS NMS)

UMG: Universal Matchbox Group Ltd. (NYSE)

UMM: United Merchants and Manufacturers Inc. (NYSE)

UMP: Upper Merion and Plymouth (railroad)

UMR: Unimar Co. (ASE)

UMSB: United Missouri Bancshares Inc. (NAS NMS)

UN: Unilever NV (NYSE)

UNAM: Unico American Corp. (NAS NMS)

UNBC: Union National Corp. (NAS NMS)

UnBrnd: United Brands Co. (newspaper)

UNC: UNC Inc. (NYSE)

UNCF: United Companies Financial Corp. (NAS NMS)

UNCInc: UNC Inc. (newspaper)

UnElec: Union Electric Co. (newspaper)

UNEWY: United Newspapers Public Limited Co. (NAS NMS)

UnExp: Union Exploration Partners Ltd. (newspaper)

UNF: UniFirst Corp. (NYSE) Union Freight (railroad)

UnfedF: UnionFed Financial Corp. (newspaper)

UNFI: Unifi Inc. (NAS NMS)

UNFR: Uniforce Temporary Personnel Inc. (NAS NMS)

UNI: Undistributed Net Income Unity (railways)

Unicorp: Uniocorp American Corp. (newspaper)

UniCre: UniCARE Financial Corp. (newspaper)

UniFrst: UniFirst Corp. (newspaper)

UNIH: United HealthCare Corp. (NAS NMS)

Unilvr: Unilever PLC (newspaper)

Unimar: Unimar Co. (newspaper)

UnionC: Union Corp., The (newspaper)

UNIR: United-Guardian Inc. (NAS NMS)

Unisys: Unisys Corp. (newspaper)

Unit: Unit Corp. (newspaper)

UNITED: United Airlines

UniTel: United Telecommunications Inc. (newspaper)

UnitelV: Unitel Video Inc. (newspaper)

Unitil: UNITIL Corp. (newspaper)

UnitInd: United Industrial Corp. (newspaper)

UnitInn: United Inns Inc. (newspaper)

Unitrde: Unitrode Corp. (newspaper)

Univar: Univar Corp. (newspaper)

UNM: UNUM Corp. (NYSE)

UNMA: Uni-Marts Inc. (NAS NMS)

UNNB: University National Bank & Trust Co. (NAS NMS)

UnNV: Unilever N.V. (newspaper)

UNO: UNO Restaurant Corp. (ASE)

Unocal: Unocal Corp. (newspaper)

UnoRt: UNO Restaurant Corp. (newspaper)

UNP: Union Pacific Corp. (NYSE)

UnPAc: Union Pacific Corp. (newspaper)

unpad: unpaid

unpd: unpaid

unqual: unqualified

UNSA: United Financial Corporation of South Carolina Inc. (NAS NMS)

UNSI: United Service Source Inc. (NAS NMS)

UnStck: United Stockyards Corp. (newspaper)

UNSVA: United Savings Assn. (Florida) (NAS NMS)

UNT: Unit Corp. (NYSE)

UNTD: First United Bancshares Inc. (Arkansas) (NAS NMS)

UnTech: United Technologies Corp. (newspaper)

UnTex: Union Texas Petroleum Holdings Inc. (newspaper)

UNUM: UNUM Corp. (newspaper)

UNV: Unitel Video Inc. (ASE)
UnValy: Union Valley Corp. (newspaper)
UnvBk: University Bank N.A. (newspaper)
UnvFds: Universal Foods Corp. (newspaper)
UnvHR: Universal Health Realty Income Trust (newspaper)
UnvlCp: Universal Corp. (newspaper)
UnvMed: Universal Medical Buildings L.P. (newspaper)
UnvPat: University Patents Inc. (newspaper)
UO: Union Railroad-Oregon
UOA: Units Of Account
UOG: Unit Of Grading
UOP: Unit Of Production
UOT: Unit Of Trading
UOV: Unit Of Value
UP: Uncovered Position
Unearned Premium
Union Pacific (railroad)
Unit Price
Unrealized Profits
Upset Price
UPA: Uniform Partnership Act
Unique Product Advantage
UPC: Uniform Practice Code
Universal Product Code
USPCI Inc. (NYSE)
UPCM: Union Planters Corp. (NAS NMS)
UPCO: United Presidential Corp. (NAS NMS)
upd: unpaid
UPEN: Upper Peninsula Power Co. (NAS NMS)
UPJ: Upjohn Co., The (NYSE)
Upjohn: Upjohn Co., The (newspaper)
UPK: United Park City Mines Co. (NYSE)

UPkMn: United Park City Mines Co. (newspaper)
UPT: Undistributed Profits Tax
University Patents Inc. (ASE)
UQ: Suburban Airlines
UR: Under Rule (stocks)
URR: Union Railroad-Pittsburgh
URT: USP Real Estate Investment Trust (ASE)
US: Underlying Stock (Security)
United States (of America)
Unlisted Security
Unregistered Stock
USA: Liberty All-Star Equity Fund (NYSE)
United States of America
USAB: USA Bancorp Inc. (NAS NMS)
USAC: United States Antimony Corp. (NAS NMS)
USACaf: USACafes L.P. (newspaper)
USAIR: US Airlines
UsairG: USAir Group Inc. (newspaper)
USBA: United Savings Bank (Oregon) (NAS NMS)
USBC: U. S. Bancorp (NAS NMS)
USBI: United Saver's Bancorp Inc. (NAS NMS)
USBK: United Savings Bank (Virginia) (NAS NMS)
USBP: USBANCORP (Pennsylvania) (NAS NMS)
USC: United States Code
USLICO Corp. (NYSE)
USCC: United States Chamber of Commerce
US Cel: United States Cellular Corp. (newspaper)
U-Schatze: Unverzinsliche Schatzanweisunger
USEC: Universal Security Instruments Inc. (NAS NMS)

USEG: U.S. Energy Corp.
(NAS NMS)
USF: USACafes LP (NYSE)
USFG: USF&G Corp. (newspaper)
USG: United States Government
USG Corp. (NYSE) (news-
paper)
USGL: U. S. Gold Corp. (NAS NMS)
USH: USLIFE Corp. (NYSE)
USHC: U. S. Healthcare Inc.
(NAS NMS)
USHI: U. S. Health Inc. (NAS NMS)
USHom: U. S. Home Corp. (newspa-
per)
USIT: Unit Share Investment Trust
USL: United States Lines Company
UslfeF: USLIFE Income Fund Inc.
(newspaper)
USLICO: USLICO Corp. (newspa-
per)
USLIFE: USLIFE Corp. (newspaper)
USM: United States Cellular Corp.
(ASE)
United States Mint
Unlisted Securities Market
USMX: US Minerals Exploration
Co. (NAS NMS)
USPCI: USPCI Inc. (newspaper)
USPMF: U. S. Precious Metals Inc.
(NAS NMS)
USPRI: USP Real Estate Invest-
ment Trust (newspaper)
USR: United States Shoe Corp.,
The (NYSE)
USRE: US Facilities Corp.
(NAS NMS)
USS: United States Surgical Corp.
(NYSE)
USShoe: United States Shoe Corp.,
The (newspaper)
USSS: United States Steamship
U.S. Shelter Corp.
(NAS NMS)
US Surg: United States Surgical
Corp. (newspaper)

UST: UST Inc. (NYSE) (newspaper)
USTB: UST Corp. (NAS NMS)
USTC: U. S. Trust Corp. (NAS NMS)
USTR: United Stationers Inc.
(NAS NMS)
USW: U S West Inc. (NYSE)
USWest: U S West Inc. (newspaper)
USWN: U S WEST New Vector
Group Inc. (NAS NMS)
USX: USX Corp. (newspaper)
U/T: Under Trust
UT: Union Terminal (railway)
United Telecommunications
Inc. (NYSE)
Universal Time
UTA: Unit Trust Association
UTAH: Utah Railway
UTDMK: United Investors Manage-
ment Co. (NAS NMS)
UtdMM: United Merchants & Manu-
facturers Inc. (newspaper)
UTH: Union Texas Petroleum Hold-
ings Inc. (NYSE)
UtiliCo: UtiliCorp United Inc.
(newspaper)
UTL: UNITIL Corp. (ASE)
UTLC: UTL Corp. (NAS NMS)
UtMed: United Medical Corp.
(newspaper)
UTR: Union Transportation Com-
pany (railroad)
Unitrode Corp. (NYSE)
UTRX: Unitronix Corp. (NAS NMS)
UTVI: United Television Inc.
(NAS NMS)
UTX: United Technologies Corp.
(NYSE)
UV: Unadilla Valley (railroad)
UVC: Union Valley Corp. (ASE)
UVOL: Universal Voltronics Corp.
(NAS NMS)
UVTB: United Vermont Bancor-
poration (NAS NMS)
UVV: Universal Corp. (NYSE)
UVX: Univar Corp. (NYSE)

uw: underwriter
underwritten
UW: Midwest Airlines
UWR: United Water Resources Inc.
(NYSE) (newspaper)

UX: Air Illinois (airline)
UXP: Union Exploration Partners
Ltd. (NYSE)
UY: Buckeye Air Service
(airline)

V: Irving Bank Corp. (NYSE)
VABF: Virginia Beach Savings Bank (NAS NMS)
VABM: Value Added By Manufacturer
Vermont American Corp. (ASE)
VACHA: Virginia's Automated Clearing House Association
Vader: Vader Group Inc. (newspaper)
VAGO: Vanderbilt Gold Corp. (NAS NMS)
val: value
VAL: Valspar Corp., The (ASE)
VALDEFD: Value Defined
Valero: Valero Energy Corp. (newspaper)
Valeyln: Valley Industries Inc. (newspaper)
ValFrg: Valley Forge Corp. (newspaper)
Valhi: Valhi Inc. (newspaper)
VALM: Vallen Corp. (NAS NMS)
ValNG: Velero Natural Gas Partners L.P. (newspaper)
Valspr: Valspar Corp., The (newspaper)
VALU: Value Line Inc. (NAS NMS)
ValyRs: Valley Resources Inc. (newspaper)
VanDrn: Van Dorn Co. (newspaper)
VANZ: Vanzetti Systems Inc. (NAS NMS)
VAR: Varian Associates Inc. (NYSE)
Varco: Varco International Inc. (newspaper)

Varian: Varian Associates Inc. (newspaper)
Varity: Varity Corp. (newspaper)
Varo: Varo Inc. (newspaper)
VAT: Value-Added Tax
Varity Corp. (NYSE)
VB: Voluntary Bankruptcy
VBAN: V-Band Systems Inc. (NAS NMS)
VBND: VeloBind Inc. (NAS NMS)
VBR: Virginia Blue Ridge (railway)
VC: Variable Costs
Venture Capital
Victoria Carriers (steamship)
Virginia Central (railway)
Vista Chemical Co. (NYSE)
VCCN: Valley Capital Corp. (NAS NMS)
VCEL: Vanguard Cellular-Systems Inc. (NAS NMS)
VCF: Venture Capital Fund
VCRE: Vari-Care Inc. (NAS NMS)
V&CS: Virginia & Carolina Southern (railroad)
VCY: Ventura County (railway)
VD: Port Augusta Air Services (airline)
Various Dates
Volume Discount
VDC: Van Dorn Co. (NYSE)
VDEF: Vie de France Corp. (NAS NMS)
VDR: Vader Group Inc. (ASE)
VEN: Vendo Co., The (NYSE)
Vendo: Vendo Co., The (newspaper)
VENT: Venturian Corp. (NAS NMS)
VEOXF: Veronex Resources Ltd. (NAS NMS)

ver: verify
VER: Verit Industries (ASE)
Verit: Verit Industries (newspaper)
Versar: Versar Inc. (newspaper)
Vertple: Vertipile Inc. (newspaper)
VES: Vestaur Securities Inc.
(NYSE)
Vestrn: Vestron Inc. (newspaper)
VestSe: Vestaur Securities Inc.
(newspaper)
VETS: Animed Inc. (NAS NMS)
VF: Valley Forge Corp. (ASE)
VFBK: Eastern Bancorp Inc.
(NAS NMS)
VFC: V. F. Corp. (NYSE)
VF Cp: V. F. Corp. (newspaper)
VFED: Valley Federal S&L Assn.
(NAS NMS)
VFM: Value For Money
VFOX: Uicon Fiber Optics Corp.
(NAS NMS)
VFSB: Virginia First Savings Bank
FSB (NAS NMS)
VFSC: Vermont Financial Services
Corp. (NAS NMS)
VGC: Visual Graphics Corp. (ASE)
VGINY: Virgin Group PLC
(NAS NMS)
VGN: Virginian Railway
VHI: Valhi Inc. (NYSE)
VHT: VMS Hotel Investment Fund
(ASE) (newspaper)
VI: Valley Industries Inc. (NYSE)
Vested Interest
VIA: Viacom Inc. (ASE)
Viacm: Viacom Inc. (newspaper)
Viatch: Viatech Inc. (newspaper)
Vicon: Vicon Industries Inc. (news-
paper)
VICT: Victoria Bankshares Inc.
(NAS NMS)
VIDE: Video Display Corp.
(NAS NMS)
VII: Vicon Industries Inc. (ASE)
VIKG: Viking Freight Inc.
(NAS NMS)

VIN: Vintage Enterprises Inc. (ASE)
Vintge: Vintage Enterprises Inc.
(newspaper)
VIPLF: Vulcan Packaging Inc.
(NAS NMS)
VIR: Virco Manufacturing Corp.
(ASE)
VIRA: Viratek Inc. (NAS NMS)
Virco: Virco Manufacturing Corp.
(newspaper)
VISA: Vista Organization Ltd.
(NAS NMS)
VISC: Visual Industries Inc.
(NAS NMS)
Vishay: Vishay Intertechnology Inc.
(newspaper)
VisIG: Visual Graphics Corp. (news-
paper)
VistaC: Vista Chemical Co. (news-
paper)
VITA: Vitalink Communications
Corp. (NAS NMS)
VITC: Victoria Creations Inc.
(NAS NMS)
VITX: Vitronics Corp. (NAS NMS)
VIVI: Vivigen Inc. (NAS NMS)
VJ: Allen Aviation (airline)
VK: Trans Michigan Airlines
VKmp: Van Kampen Merritt Mu-
nicipal Income Trust
(newspaper)
VKSI: Vikonics Inc. (NAS NMS)
VL: Value Line Investment Survey
VLAB: JVipont Laboratories Inc.
(NAS NMS)
VLC: Valley Line Company (steam-
ship)
VLCM: ValCom Inc. (NAS NMS)
VLGE: Village Super Market Inc.
(NAS NMS)
VLID: Valid Logic Systems Inc.
(NAS NMS)
VLO: Valero Energy Corp. (NYSE)
VLP: Valero Natural Gas Partners
LP (NYSE)
VLR: Variable Loan Rate

VLSI: Very Large Scale Integration
VLSI Technology Inc.
(NAS NMS)
VLU: Worldwide Value Fund Inc.
(NYSE)
VM: Monmouth Airlines
Vertical Merger
VMC: Vulcan Materials Co.
(NYSE)
VMIG: View-Master Ideal Group
Inc. (NAS NMS)
VMLI: Veterans Mortgage Life In-
surance
VMS: Vertical Market Structure
VMSI: VM Software Inc.
(NAS NMS)
VMT: Van Kampen Merritt Munici-
pal Income Trust (NYSE)
VMXI: VMX Inc. (NAS NMS)
VNBP: Valley National Bancorp
(New Jersey) (NAS NMS)
VNCP: Valley National Corp.
(NAS NMS)
VNO: Vornado Inc. (NYSE)
VO: Seagram Company Ltd., The
(NYSE)
vol: volume
VOLT: Volt Information Sciences
Inc. (NAS NMS)
VOLVY: Volvo AB (NAS NMS)
VON: Vons Companies Inc., The
(NYSE)
Vons: Vons Companies Inc., The
(newspaper)
VOP: Value Of Product
Voplex: Voplex Corp. (newspaper)
Vornad: Vornado Inc. (newspaper)
VOS: Value Of Stock
VOT: Voplex Corp. (ASE)
vou: voucher
VOX: Audiovox Corp. (ASE)
V&P: Vendor and Purchaser
VP: Vice President
VPA: Volume Purchase Agreement
VPP: Vested Pension Plan
VQA: Vendor Quality Assurance

VQC: Vendor Quality Certification
VQD: Vendor Quality Defect
VQZD: Vendor Quality Zero Defects
VR: Valley Resources Inc. (ASE)
Vested Rights
VRA: Value Received Analysis
VRC: Varco International Inc.
(NYSE)
VRE: Vermont Research Corp.
(ASE)
VRES: VICORP Restaurants Inc.
(NAS NMS)
VRLN: Varlen Corp. (NAS NMS)
VRM: Variable-Rate Mortgage
VRO: Varo Inc. (NYSE)
VRSA: Versa Technologies Inc.
(NAS NMS)
VRSY: Varitronic Systems Inc.
(NAS NMS)
VRT: Vertipile Inc. (ASE)
V&S: Valley & Siletz (railroad)
VS: Voting Stock
VSEC: VSE Corp. (NAS NMS)
VSH: Vishay Intertechnology Inc.
(NYSE)
VSL: Valley and Siletz (railroad)
VSO: Valdosta Southern (railroad)
VSR: Versar Inc. (ASE)
VSTR: Vestar Inc. (NAS NMS)
VT: Voting Trust
VtAmC: Vermont American Corp.
(newspaper)
VTC: Voting Trust Certificate
VTEX: Vertex Communications
Corp. (NAS NMS)
vtg: voting (stock)
VTK: Viatech Inc. (ASE)
VTR: Vermont Railway
VtRsh: Vermont Research Corp.
(newspaper)
VTRX: Ventrex Laboratories Inc.
(NAS NMS)
VTX: VTX Electronics Corp. (ASE)
(newspaper)
VUL: Vulcan Corp. (ASE)
VulcCp: Vulcan Corp. (newspaper)

VulcM: Vulcan Materials Co. (newspaper)

VV: Vestron Inc. (NYSE)

VW: Civil Flying Services (airline)
Volkswagen

VWRX: VWR Corp. (NAS NMS)

VY: Vyquest Inc. (ASE)

VYBN: Valley Bancorporation (Wisconsin) (NAS NMS)

Vyqust: Vyquest Inc. (newspaper)

W: Western Airlines
  Westvaco Corp. (NYSE)
W&A: Wiel and Amundsen (steamship)
W of A: Western Railway of Alabama
WA: Wabash (railroad)
  WAL (Western Airlines)
  Western Allegheny (railroad)
  With Average
WAB: Wabash (railroad)
  WESTAMERICA BANCORPORATION (ASE)
WAC: Wells American Corp. (ASE)
WACCC: Worldwide Air Cargo Commodity Classification
WACH: West African Clearing House
WACHA: Wisconsin Automated Clearing House Association
Wackht: Wackenhut Corp., The (newspaper)
WADB: West African Development Bank
WAE: Wilfred American Educational Corp. (NYSE)
WAG: Walgreen Co. (NYSE)
  Wellsville, Addison and Galeton (railroad)
Wainoc: Wainoco Oil Corp. (newspaper)
WAK: Wackenhut Corp., The (NYSE)
WAL: Western Air Lines
WALB: Walbro Corp. (NAS NMS)
WalCSv: Wallace Computer Services Inc. (newspaper)
Walgrn: Walgreen Co. (newspaper)

WalMt: Wal-Mart Stores Inc. (newspaper)
WALS: Walshire Assurance Co. (NAS NMS)
WamB: WESTAMERICA BANCORPORATION (newspaper)
WAMU: Washington Mutual Savings Bank (NAS NMS)
WAN: Wang Laboratories Inc. (ASE)
Wang: Wang Laboratories Inc. (newspaper)
WarnrL: Warner-Lambert Co. (newspaper)
warr: warrant (stocks)
WASC: Western Auto Supply Co. (NAS NMS)
WashGs: Washington Gas Light Co. (newspaper)
Waste: Waste Management Inc. (newspaper)
WATC: Washington Terminal Company (railroad)
WATFY: Waterford Glass Group PLC (NAS NMS)
WatkJn: Watkins-Johnson Co. (newspaper)
Watsc: Watsco Inc. (newspaper)
WATT: Watts Industries Inc. (NAS NMS)
WAVR: Waverly Inc. (NAS NMS)
WAW: Waynesburg and Washington (railroad)
WAXM: Waxman Industries Inc. (NAS NMS)
wb: waybill
WB: Shawnee Airlines
  Warehouse Book
  World Bank (for Reconstruction and Development)

WBAT: Westport Bancorp Inc.
    (NAS NMS)
WBB: Del E. Webb Corp. (NYSE)
    World Bank Bonds
WBC: Westbridge Capital Corp.
    (ASE)
WBCRR: Wilkes-Barre Connecting
    Railroad
WBED: Classic Corp. (NAS NMS)
WBNC: Washington Bancorp Inc.
    (New Jersey) (NAS NMS)
WBST: Webster Financial Corp.
    (NAS NMS)
WBT&SRC: Waco, Beaumont, Trin-
    ity and Sabine Rail-
    way Company
WC: Sien Consolidated Airlines
    Watered Capital
    Weiman Company Inc. (ASE)
    Without Charge
    Working Capital
WCA: Working-Capital Account
WCAT: WICAT Systems Inc.
    (NAS NMS)
WCBK: Workingmens Corp. (Mas-
    sachusetts) (NAS NMS)
WCCC: Western Commercial Inc.
    (NAS NMS)
WCLB: Warehouse Club Inc.
    (NAS NMS)
WCNA: Western Company of North
    America, The (newspa-
    per)
WCP: Warner Computer Systems
    Inc. (NYSE)
WCRP: Westcorp. (ASE)
WCRSY: WCRS Group PLC, The
    (NAS NMS)
WCS: Wallace Computer Services
    Inc. (NYSE)
WCYS: Bank Worcester Corp.
    (NAS NMS)
wd: withdrawal
    withdrawn
WD: Warranty Deed
    When Distributed (NYSE)

WDB: With Due Bills (stocks)
WDC: Western Digital Corp. (ASE)
WDFC: WD-40 Co. (NAS NMS)
WDG: Wedgestone Financial Trust
    (NYSE)
WDH: Winchell's Donut Houses LP
    (NYSE)
WDHD: Woodhead Industries Inc.
    (NAS NMS)
WDigitl: Western Digital Corp.
    (newspaper)
WDMR: Windmere Corp.
    (NAS NMS)
WDSI: Worlco Data Systems Inc.
    (NAS NMS)
Wdstrm: Woodstream Corp. (news-
    paper)
WE: Westcoast Energy Inc. (NYSE)
    Western Electric Company
WeanU: Wean Inc. (newspaper)
WebbD: Del E. Webb Corp. (news-
    paper)
WebInv: Del E. Webb Investment
    Properties Inc. (newspa-
    per)
WEBS: Webster Clothes Inc.
    (NAS NMS)
WEC: Wisconsin Energy Corp.
    (NYSE)
WECA: Western Capital Invest-
    ment Corp. (NAS NMS)
WECO: Washington Energy Co.
    (NAS NMS)
WED: Wedco Technology Inc. (ASE)
Wedco: Wedco Technology Inc.
    (newspaper)
Wedgtn: Wedgestone Financial
    Trust (newspaper)
Weiman: Weiman Company Inc.
    (newspaper)
WeingR: Weingarten Realty Inc.
    (newspaper)
WEIS: Weisfield's Inc. (NAS NMS)
WeisM: Weis Markets Inc. (newspa-
    per)
WELB: Welbilt Corp. (NAS NMS)

Weldtrn: Weldotron Corp. (newspaper)

WelFM: Wells Fargo Mortgage & Equity Trust (newspaper)

WelGrd: Wells-Gardner Electronics Corp. (newspaper)

WellAm: Wells American Corp. (newspaper)

Wellco: Wellco Enterprises Inc. (newspaper)

Wellmn: Wellman Inc. (newspaper)

WellsF: Wells Fargo & Co. (newspaper)

WEN: Wendy's International Inc. (NYSE)

Wendys: Wendy's International Inc. (newspaper)

WERN: Werner Enterprises Inc. (NAS NMS)

Wesco: Wesco Financial Corp. (newspaper)

Wespcp: Wespercorp. (newspaper)

West: West Company Inc., The (newspaper)

Westcp: Westcorp (newspaper)

WETT: Wetterau Inc. (NAS NMS)

WEXC: Wolverine Exploration Co. (NAS NMS)

Weyerh: Weyerhaeuser Co. (newspaper)

WEYS: Weyenberg Shoe Manufacturing Co. (NAS NMS)

WF: West Feliciana (railroad) Winston Furniture Company Inc. (ASE)

WFC: Wanted For Cash Wells Fargo & Co. (NYSE)

WFCS: Warren Five Cents Savings Bank (Massachusetts) (NAS NMS)

WFM: Wells Fargo Mortgage & Equity Trust (NYSE)

WFOR: Washington Federal Savings Bank (Oregon) (NAS NMS)

WFPR: Western Federal Savings Bank (Puerto Rico) (NAS NMS)

WF&S: Wichita Falls & Southern (railroad)

WFSA: Western Federal S&L Assn. (California) (NAS NMS)

WFSB: Washington Federal Savings Bank (Washington D.C.) (NAS NMS)

WFSL: Washington Federal S&L Assn. of Seattle (NAS NMS)

WG: Willcox & Gibbs Inc. (NYSE)

WGA: Wells-Gardner Electronics Corp. (ASE)

WGHT: Weigh-Tronix Inc. (NAS NMS)

WGL: Washington Gas Light Co. (NYSE)

WGO: Winnebago Industries Inc. (NYSE)

WhelLE: Wheeling & Lake Erie Railway Co., The (newspaper)

Whitehl: Whitehall Corp. (newspaper)

Whittak: Whittaker Corp. (newspaper)

WHLS: Wholesale Club Inc., The (NAS NMS)

WHMV & NSSA: Woods Hole, Martha's Vineyard and Nantucket Steamship Authority

whl: wholesale

whol: wholesale wholesaler

WHOO: Waterhouse Investor Services Inc. (NAS NMS)

whous: warehouse

WHP: Western Health Plans Inc. (ASE)

WhPit: Wheeling-Pittsburgh Steel Corp. (newspaper)

WHR: Whirlpool Corp. (NYSE)

WHRG: Waters Instruments Inc. (NAS NMS)

Whrlpl: Whirlpool Corp. (newspaper)

whse: warehouse

whsl: wholesale

WHT: Whitehall Corp. (NYSE)

WHTI: Wheelabrator Technologies Inc. (NAS NMS)

WHX: Wheeling-Pittsburgh Steel Corp. (NYSE)

WI: When, as, and if Issued (stocks) When Issued (NYSE)

WIB: When-Issued Basis (stocks)

WIC: WICOR Inc. (NYSE)

WichRv: Wichita River Corp. (newspaper)

WICOR: WICOR Inc. (newspaper)

WID: Wean Inc. (NYSE)

Wiener: Wiener Enterprises Inc. (newspaper)

WII: Weatherford International Inc. (ASE)

WIL: Wilson Sporting Goods Co. (ASE)

WILCO: Will Comply

WILF: Wilson Foods Corp. (NAS NMS)

Wilfred: Wilfred American Educational Corp. (newspaper)

WILL: John Wiley & Sons Inc. (NAS NMS)

WillcG: Willcox & Gibbs Inc. (newspaper)

William: Williams Companies Inc., The (newspaper)

WILM: Wilmington Trust Co. (NAS NMS)

WilshrO: Wilshire Oil Company of Texas (newspaper)

WI&M: Washington, Idaho & Montana (railroad)

WIMI: Warwick Insurance Managers Inc. (NAS NMS)

WIN: Winn-Dixie Stores Inc. (NYSE)

Winchl: Winchell's Donut Houses L.P. (newspaper)

WinDix: Winn-Dixie Stores Inc. (newspaper)

WinFur: Winston Furniture Company Inc. (newspaper)

Winjak: Winjak Inc. (newspaper)

Winnbg: Winnebago Industries Inc. (newspaper)

Winner: Winners Corp. (newspaper)

WinRs: Winston Resources Inc. (newspaper)

Wintln: Winthrop Insured Mortgage Investors II (newspaper)

WIR: Western Investment Real Estate Trust (ASE)

WIRET: Western Investment Real Estate Trust (newspaper)

WISC: Wisconsin Southern Gas Company Inc. (NAS NMS)

WISE: Wiser Oil Co., The (NAS NMS)

WisEn: Wisconsin Energy Corp. (newspaper)

WisPS: Wisconsin Southern Gas Company Inc. (newspaper)

WIT: Witco Corp. (NYSE)

Witco: Witco Corp. (newspaper)

WJ: Jet Air (airline) Watkins-Johnson Co. (NYSE)

WJI: Winjak Inc. (NYSE)

WJR: Cypress Fund Inc. (ASE)

WK: Western Alaska (airline) White Knight

WKR: Whittaker Corp. (NYSE)

W&L: Westcott and Laurance Line (steamship)

WL: Lao Airlines

WLA: Warner-Lambert Co. (NYSE)

WLBK: Waltham Corp. (NAS NMS)

WLC: Wellco Enterprises Inc. (ASE)

WLD: Weldotron Corp. (ASE)

WldInc: World Income Fund Inc. (newspaper)

W&LE: Wheeling and Lake Erie Railway Company

WLE: Wheeling & Lake Erie Railway Co., The (NYSE)

WLHN: Wolohan Lumber Co. (NAS NMS)

WLM: Wellman Inc. (NYSE)

WLO: Waterloo (railroad)

WlsnSp: Wilson Sporting Goods Co. (newspaper)

WLTN: Wilton Enterprises Inc. (NAS NMS)

Wlwth: F. W. Woolworth Co. (newspaper)

WM: Western Maryland (railroad)

WMB: Williams Companies Inc., The (NYSE)

WMBS: West Massachusetts Bankshares Inc. (NAS NMS)

WMD: Mars Graphic Services Inc. (ASE)

WMI: Winthrop Insured Mortgage Investors II (ASE)

WMIC: Western Microwave Inc. (NAS NMS)

WMK: Weis Markets Inc. (NYSE)

WMOR: Westmoreland Coal Co. (NAS NMS)

WMR: Wasatch Mountain Railway

WMRK: Westmark International Inc. (NAS NMS)

WMS: WMS Industries Inc. (NYSE) (newspaper)

WMSI: Williams Industries Inc. (NAS NMS)

W&M SS CO: Wisconsin and Michigan Steamship Company

WMT: Wal-Mart Stores Inc. (NYSE)

WMTA: Washington Metropolitan Transit Authority

WMTT: Willimette Industries Inc. (NAS NMS)

WMWN: Weatherford, Mineral Wells and Northwestern (railway)

WMX: Waste Management Inc. (NYSE)

W&N: Wharton & Northern (railroad)

WN: Wynn's International Inc. (NYSE)

WNDP: With No Down Payment

WNDT: Wendt-Bristol Co. (NAS NMS)

WNF: Winfield (railroad)

W&NO: Wharton and Northern (railroad)

WNP: Wire Non-Payment

WNR: Winners Corp. (NYSE)

WNSB: West Newton Savings Bank (Massachusetts) (NAS NMS)

WNSI: WNS Inc. (NAS NMS)

WNT: Washington National Corp. (NYSE)

wo: without (stocks)

WO: Wait Order

WOA: World Airways, Incorporated WorldCorp Inc. (NYSE)

WOBS: First Woburn Bancorp Inc. (NAS NMS)

WOC: Wilshire Oil Company of Texas (NYSE)

W&OD: Washington & Old Dominion (railroad)

WOD: Woodstream Corp. (ASE)

WOI: World Income Fund Inc. (ASE)

WOL: Wainoco Oil COrp. (NYSE)

WolfHB: Howard B. Wolf Inc. (newspaper)

WolvrW: Wolverine World Wide Inc. (newspaper)

WolvTc: Wolverine Technologies Inc. (newspaper)

WON: Waiver Of Notice

WONE: Westwood One Inc. (NAS NMS)

WOP: Waiver Of Premium

WOR: Worthen Banking Corp. (ASE)

Worthn: Worthen Banking Corp. (newspaper)

WOS: Wholly-Owned Subsidiary

W&OV: Warren & Ouchita Valley (railroad)
WOV: Wolverine Technologies Inc. (NYSE)
WOW: Written Order of Withdrawal
WP: Waiting Period
Wespercorp (ASE)
Western Pacific (railroad)
Windfall Profit
Wire Payment
WPA: With Particular Average
WPB: Wiener Enterprises Inc. (ASE)
WPER: West Pittston-Execter Railroad
WPGI: Western Publishing Group Inc. (NAS NMS)
WPI: Wholesale Price Index
WPL: WPL Holdings Inc. (NYSE)
WPL Hld: WPL Holdings Inc. (newspaper)
WPO: Washington Post Co., The (ASE)
WPPGY: WPP Group PLC (NAS NMS)
WPS: Wisconsin Public Service Corp. (NYSE)
WPT: Windfall Profits Tax
WP3: Working Party Three
WP&Y: White Pass and Yukon (railway)
WQ: Georgia Air (airline)
W&R: Wholesale & Retail
WR: Altus Airlines
Warehouse Receipt
WRA: Western Railroad Association
Western Railway of Alabama
WRE: Washington Real Estate Investment Trust (ASE)
WRFAF: Wharf Resources Ltd. (NAS NMS)
WRI: Weingarten Realty Inc. (NYSE)
Wrigly: William Wrigley Jr. Co. (newspaper)

WRIT: Washington Real Estate Investment Trust (newspaper)
WrldCp: WorldCorp Inc. (newspaper)
WrldVl: Worldwide Value Fund Inc. (newspaper)
WrnCpt: Warner Computer Systems Inc. (newspaper)
WRNT: Warrenton (railroad)
WRO: Wichita River Corp. (ASE)
WRS: Western Pacific Railroad Company
Winston Resources Inc. (ASE)
WRTC: Writer Corp., The (NAS NMS)
WRWK: Warwick (railway)
ws: warrants (stocks)
WS: Northern Wings-Limited (airline)
Wadley Southern (railroad)
Wall Street
Ware Shoals (railroad)
Wash Sale
Watered Stock
White Squire
WSAU: Wausau Paper Mills Co. (NAS NMS)
WSBC: Wesbanco Inc. (NAS NMS)
WSBK: Western Bank (Oregon) (NAS NMS)
WSBXV: Washington Savings Bank (NAS NMS)
WSC: Wesco Financial Corp. (ASE)
WSCI: Washington Scientific Industries Inc. (NAS NMS)
WSFS: Washington State Ferry System
Wilmington Savings Fund Society FSB (NAS NMS)
WSGC: Williams-Sonoma Inc. (NAS NMS)
WshNat: Washington National Corp. (newspaper)
WshPst: Washington Post Co., The (newspaper)

WshWt: Washington Water Power Co., The (newspaper)
WSJ: Wall Street Journal
WSL: Western S&L Assn. (NYSE)
WSM: World Solar Markets
WSMC: WestMarc Communications Inc. (NAS NMS)
WSMP: WSMP Inc. (NAS NMS)
WSN: Western Company of North America, The (NYSE)
WSO: Watsco Inc. (ASE)
WSPG: Wall Street Planning Group
W&SR: Warren & Saline River (railroad)
WSS: Winston-Salem Southbound (railroad)
WSSX: Wessex Corp. (NAS NMS)
WST: West Company Inc., The (NYSE)
WstBrC: Westbridge Capital Corp. (newspaper)
WstctE: Westcoast Energy Inc. (newspaper)
WSTF: Western Financial Corp. (NAS NMS)
WstgE: Westinghouse Electric Corp. (newspaper)
WstHlth: Western Health Plans Inc. (newspaper)
WSTM: Western Micro Technology Inc. (NAS NMS)
WSTN: Roy F. Weston Inc. (NAS NMS)
WstnSL: Western S&L Assn. (newspaper)
Wstvc: Westvaco Corp. (newspaper)
WSVS: Wiland Services Inc. (NAS NMS)
WSYP: White Sulphur Springs and Yellowstone Park (railway)
wt: warrant (stocks)
weight
W&T: Wrightsville & Tennille (railroad)

WT: Waiting Time
Wire Transfer
Withholding Tax
W/TAX: Withholding Tax
WTBK: Westerbeke Corp. (NAS NMS)
WTC: Western Transportation Company
World Trade Center
WTD: World Trade Directory
WTDI: WTD Industries Inc. (NAS NMS)
WTEL: Walker Telecommunications Corp. (NAS NMS)
Wthfrd: Weatherford International Inc. (newspaper)
WTHG: Worthington Industries Inc. (NAS NMS)
WTOY: Wisconsin Toy Co. (NAS NMS)
WTR: Sierra Spring Water Co. (ASE)
Wrightsville and Tennille Railroad
WTWS: Wall to Wall Sound & Video Inc. (NAS NMS)
WU: Avna (airline)
Western Union Corp. (NYSE)
WUC: Western Union Corp.
WUI: Western Union International
WUnion: Western Union Corp. (newspaper)
WUR: WurlTech Industries Inc. (NYSE)
Wurltch: WurlTech Industries Inc. (newspaper)
WV: Weight in Volume
West Pacific Airlines
WVN: West Virginia Northern (railroad)
WVTK: Wavetek Corp. (NAS NMS)
WW: Warehouse Warrant
Weight in Weight
Winchester and Western (railroad)
With Warrants (NYSE)

WWBC: Washington Bancorporation (Washington DC) (NAS NMS)

WWC: World Wide Companies

WWGPY: Ward White Group PLC (NAS NMS)

WWIN: Western Waste Industries (NAS NMS)

WWP: Washington Water Power Co., The (NYSE)

WWW: Wolverine World Wide Inc. (NYSE)

WWWM: W. W. Williams Co. (NAS NMS)

WWY: William Wrigley Jr. Co. (NYSE)

WX: Westinghouse Electric Corp. (NYSE)

WY: Aztec Airways Weyerhaeuser Co. (NYSE)

WYL: Wyle Laboratories (NYSE)

WyleLb: Wyle Laboratories (newspaper)

WYMN: Wyman-Gordon Co. (NAS NMS)

WYNB: Wyoming National Bancorporation (NAS NMS)

Wynns: Wynn's International Inc. (newspaper)

WYS: Wyandotte Southern (railroad) Wyse Technology (NYSE)

WYT: Wyandotte Terminal (railroad)

X

x: express
transport

X: Ex-Dividend (newspaper listings of stock trading)
Ex-Interest (newspaper listing of bond trading)
No Protest
USX Corp. (NYSE)

XC: Ex (Without) Coupon (stocks)

XCEL: Excel Bancorp Inc. (NAS NMS)

xch: exchange

XCL: Excess Current Liabilities
Exclearing House

XCOL: Exploration Company of Louisiana Inc., The (NAS NMS)

XCP: Ex-Coupon

XD: Ex (Without) Dividend (in newspaper listings)

X DIS: Ex (Without) Distribution (NYSE)

XDIV: Without Dividend (stocks)

XD XE: Hub Airlines

XEBC: Xebec (NAS NMS)

xec: execute

xeq: execute

Xerox: Xerox Corp. (newspaper)

XF: Murchison Air Services (airline)

xge: exchange

XI: Ex-Interest (stocks)

XICO: Xicor Inc. (NAS NMS)

XIN: Ex (Without) Interest (stocks)

XK: Air California (Airline)

XLDC: XL/Datacomp Inc. (NAS NMS)

XLGX: Xylogics Inc. (NAS NMS)

XM: Windward Islands Airways

XO: Executive Officer

XOMA: XOMA Corp. (NAS NMS)

XON: Exxon Corp. (NYSE)

XOVR: Exovir Inc. (NAS NMS)

XPLR: Xplor Corp. (NAS NMS)

XPR: Ex (Without) Privileges (stocks)

XQ: Air New England (airline)

XR: Ex (Without) Rights (stocks)

XRAY: GENDEX Corp. (NAS NMS)

XRIT: X-Rite Inc. (NAS NMS)

XRT: Ex (Without) Rights (stocks)

XRX: Xerox Corp. (NYSE)

XSCR: Xscribe Corp. (NAS NMS)

XT: Southern Airlines

XTEN: Xerox Telecommunications Network

XTGX: TGX Corp. (NAS NMS)

XTON: Executone Information Systems Inc. (NAS NMS)

XTR: XTRA Corp. (NYSE)

XTRA: XTRA Corp. (newspaper)

XTX: New York Tax-Exempt Income Fund Inc., The (ASE)

XU: Trans Mo Airlines

XV: Ambassador Airlines

XW: Ex (Without) Warrants (NYSE)

XWARR: Ex (Warrants) (stocks)

XX: Chicago and Southern Airlines Without Securities or Warrants (stocks)

XY: Downeast Airlines

XYVI: Xyvision Inc. (NAS NMS)

Y: Alleghany Corp. (NYSE)
Ex-Dividend and Sales in full (in
stock listings of newspapers)
Nominal Gross National Product

YankCo: Yankee Companies Inc.,
The (newspaper)

YCSL: Yorkridge-Calvert S&L
Assn. (Maryland)
(NAS NMS)

YED: Year-End Dividend

YELL: Yellow Freight System Inc.
of Delaware (NAS NMS)

YFED: York Financial Corp.
(NAS NMS)

YG: Yield Grade

YH: Amistad Airlines

YLD: High Income Advantage Trust
(NYSE)
Yield (in stock listings of
newspapers)

Y&N: Youngstown and Northern
(railroad)

YNK: Yankee Companies Inc., The
(ASE)

YORK: York Research Corp.
(NAS NMS)

YorkIn: York International Corp.
(newspaper)

YP: Yield Point

yr: year

YRK: York International Corp.
(NYSE)

Y&S: Youngstown & Southern (railroad)

YS: Yield Spread
Yield Strength
Youngstown and Southern
(railway)

YTB: Yield To Broker

YTC: Yield To Call

YTD: Year To Date

YTM: Yield To Maturity

YVT: Yakima Valley Transportation Company

YW: Yreka Western (railroad)

YYS: Yo-Yo Stocks

Z

Z: F. W. Woolworth Co. (NYSE)
In report of closing Mutual Fund
Prices in newspapers should
fund not supply the bid-offer
price by publication
In stock tables indicating total
Volume that should not be
multiplied by 100

Zapata: Zapata Corp. (newspaper)

ZAPSV: Cooper Life Sciences Inc.
(NAS NMS)

ZB: Midwest Commuter Airways

ZBB: Zero-Base Budgeting

ZCAD: Zycad Corp. (NAS NMS)

ZDC: Philip Crosby Associates Inc.
(ASE)

ZE: Zenith Electronics Corp.
(NYSE)

ZEBRA: Zero Coupon Eurosterling
Bearer or Registered Ac-
cruing securities

ZEGL: Ziegler Company Inc., The
(NAS NMS)

Zemex: Zemex Corp. (newspaper)

ZEN: Zenith Laboratories Inc.
(NYSE)

ZenIn: Zenith Income Fund (newspaper)

ZenithE: Zenith Electronics Corp.
(newspaper)

ZenLab: Zenith Laboratories Inc.
(newspaper)

ZenNtl: Zenith National Insurance
Corp. (newspaper)

ZENT: Zentec Corp. (NAS NMS)

Zero: Zero Corp. (newspaper)

Zeus: Zeus Components Inc.
(NAS NMS)

ZF: Village Airways
Zweig Fund Inc., The (NYSE)

ZH: Royal Hawaiian Airways

ZIF: Zenith Income Fund (NYSE)

ZIGO: Zygo Corp. (NAS NMS)

ZIM: Zimmer Corp. (ASE)

Zimer: Zimmer Corp. (newspaper)

ZION: Zions Bancorporation (Utah)
(NAS NMS)

ZITL: Zitel Corp. (NAS NMS)

ZK: Davis Airlines

ZM: Winnipesaukee Aviation (airline)

ZMOS: ZyMOS Corp. (NAS NMS)

ZMX: Zemex Corp. (NYSE)

ZN: Cherokee Airways

ZNT: Zenith National Insurance
Corp. (NYSE)

ZOND: Zondervan Corp., The
(NAS NMS)

ZOS: Zapata Corp. (NYSE)

ZR: Zero-Coupon security (in bond
listings of newspapers)

ZRN: Zurn Industries Inc. (NYSE)

ZRO: Zero Corp. (NYSE)

ZS: Sizer Airways

ZSC: Zeeland Steamship Company

ZSEV: Z-Seven Fund Inc.
(NAS NMS)

ZurnIn: Zurn Industries Inc. (newspaper)

ZV: Air Midwest (airline)

ZW: Air Wisconsin (airline)

Zweig: Zweig Fund Inc., The (newspaper)

ZY: Skyway Aviation (airline)